the watercolor artist's guide to exceptional color

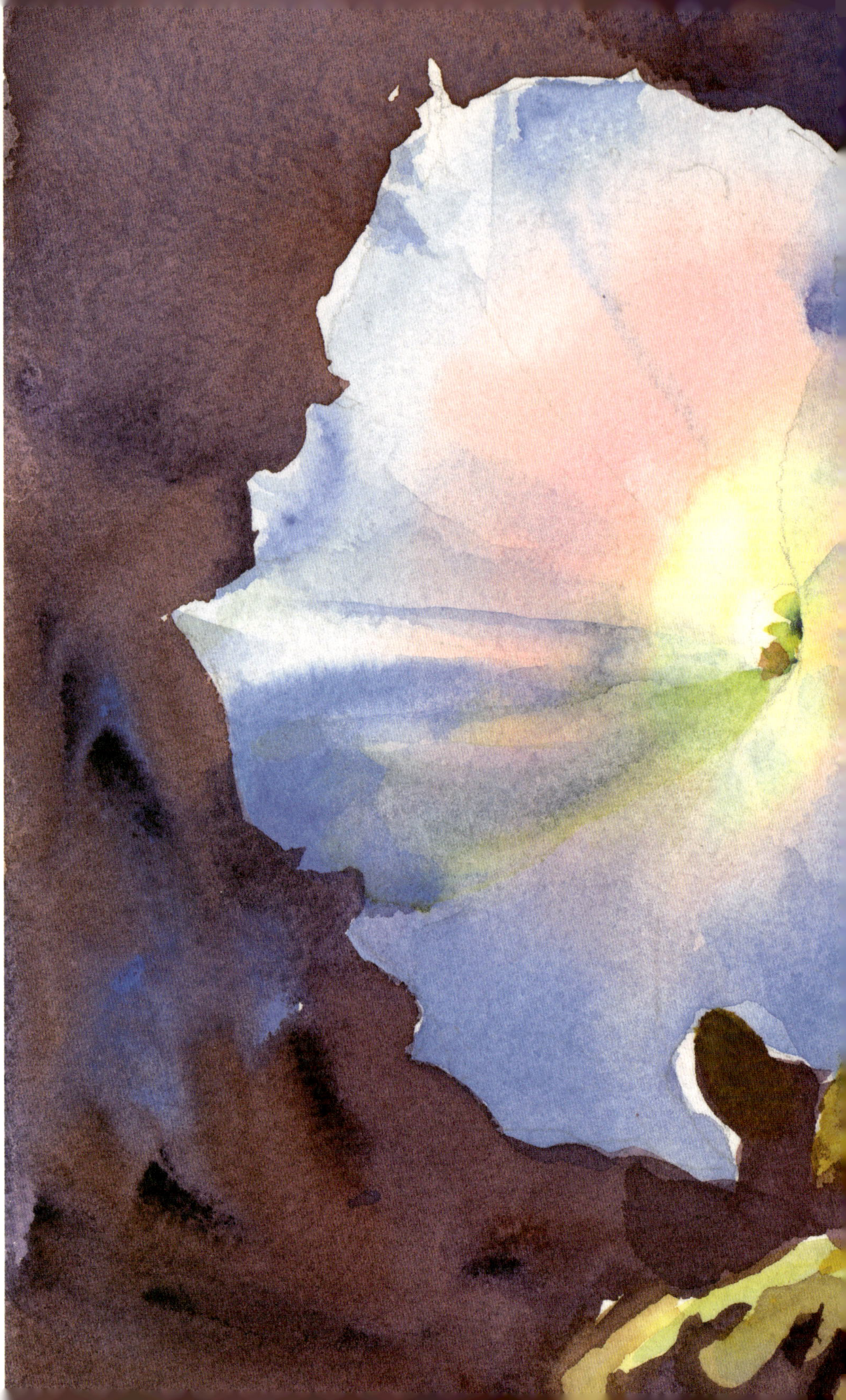

Petunias

The simplicity of these white flowers was captured by reserving areas of the white paper for the highlights and using soft washes of aureolin yellow and rose madder genuine to describe the flush of color and glow in the flower centers. Cobalt blue was dropped in using wet into wet and hard-edge techniques to explain the frilly edge of the petals. The rich background is a combination of all three colors with a loose granulating wash of napthamide maroon.

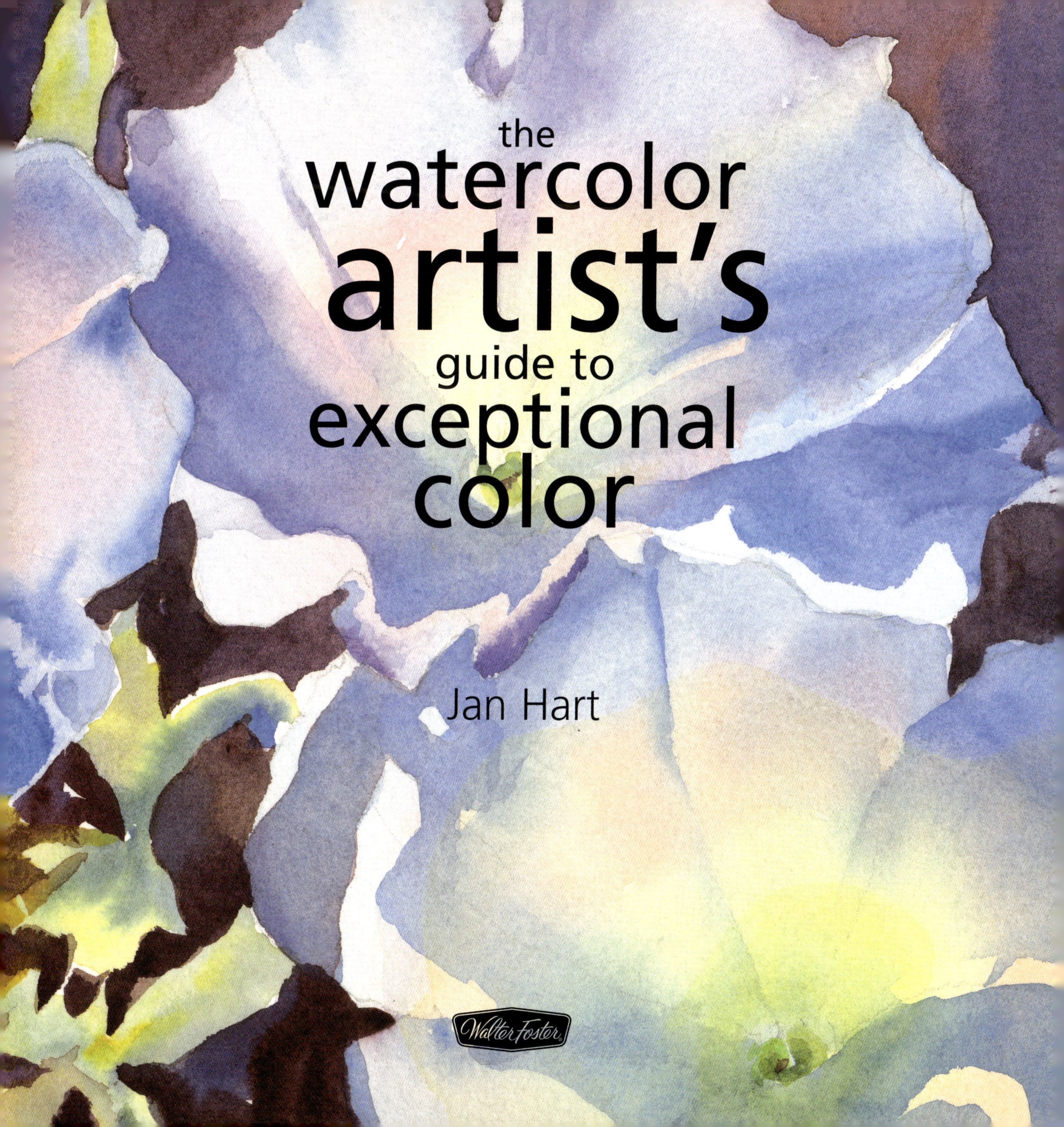

the watercolor artist's guide to exceptional color

Jan Hart

Walter Foster

A QUARTO BOOK

First edition for North America
published in 2007 by
Walter Foster Publishing, Inc.
23062 La Cadena Drive,
Laguna Hills, CA 92653
www.walterfoster.com
Walter Foster is a registered
trademark.

ISBN-13: 978-1-60058-052-9
ISBN-10: 1-60058-052-1

Conceived, designed,
and produced by
Quarto Publishing plc
The Old Brewery
6 Blundell Street
London
N7 9BH

QUAR.WGC

Senior Editor Liz Pasfield
Copy Editor Sally MacEachern

Designer Tanya Field
Photographers Phil Wilkins and
Jan Hart
Illustrator John Woodcock
Proofreader Helen Maxey
Indexer Pamela Ellis
Picture Researcher Claudia Tate

Art Director Moira Clinch
Publisher Paul Carslake

Manufactured by Modern Age
Repro House Ltd, China

Printed in China by SNP Leefung
Printers Ltd.

9 8 7 6 5 4 3 2 1

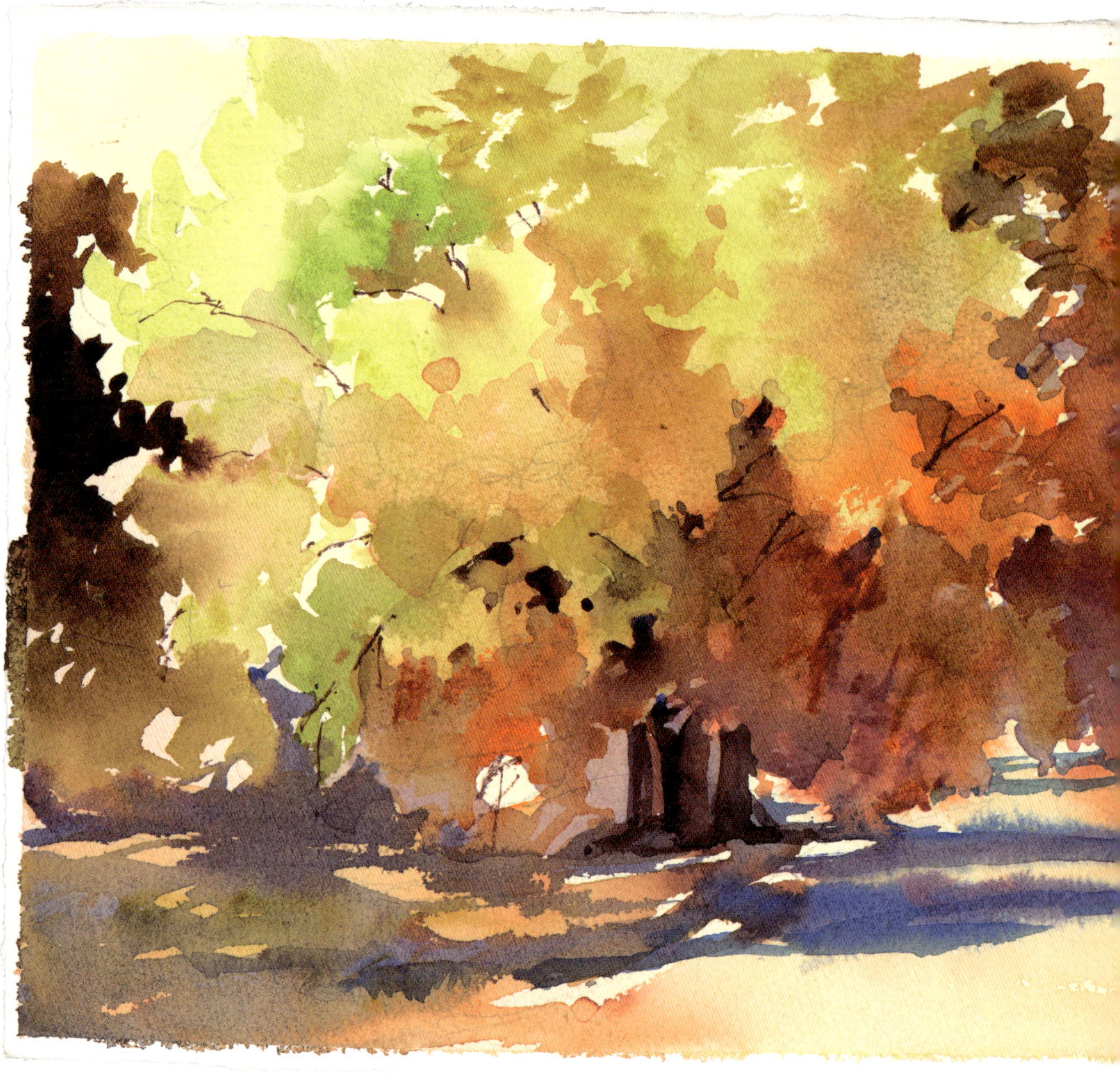

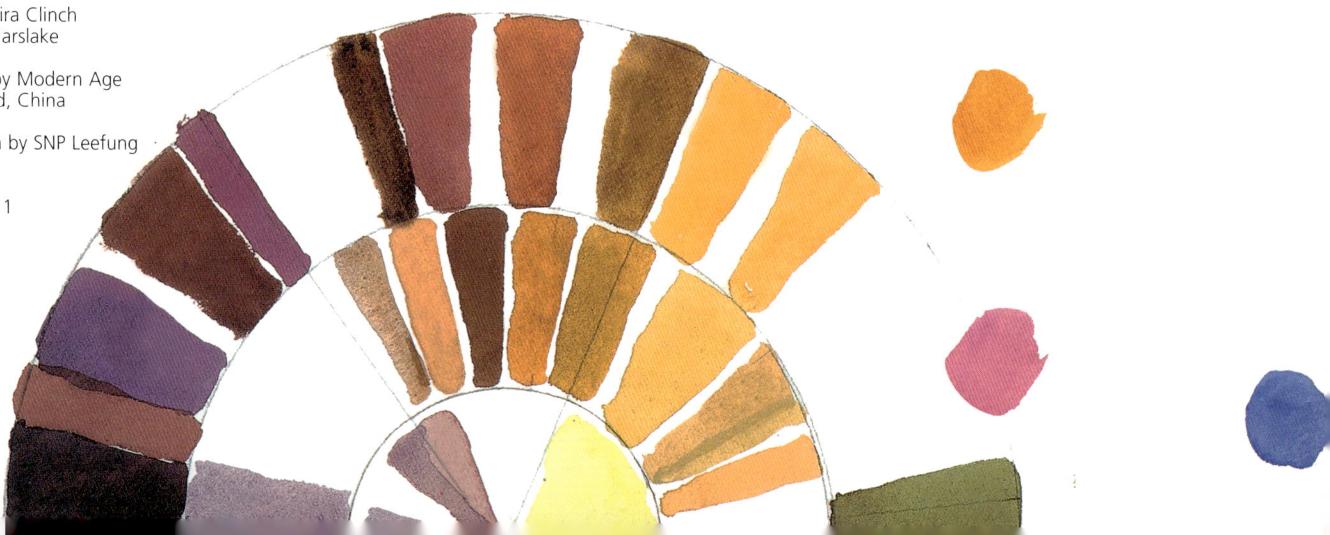

contents

introduction

There they are, all your selected colors—transparents alongside opaques, cool blue to warm red—waiting in individual wells in your palette. All you need now is some water and a brush to bring them to life. The sleeping pigments within each paint awake, ready to flow, granulate, and sparkle! Each time you paint you are setting in motion all sorts of chemical dances—and you, as the artist, have a front-row seat. But how much do you really know about your paints?

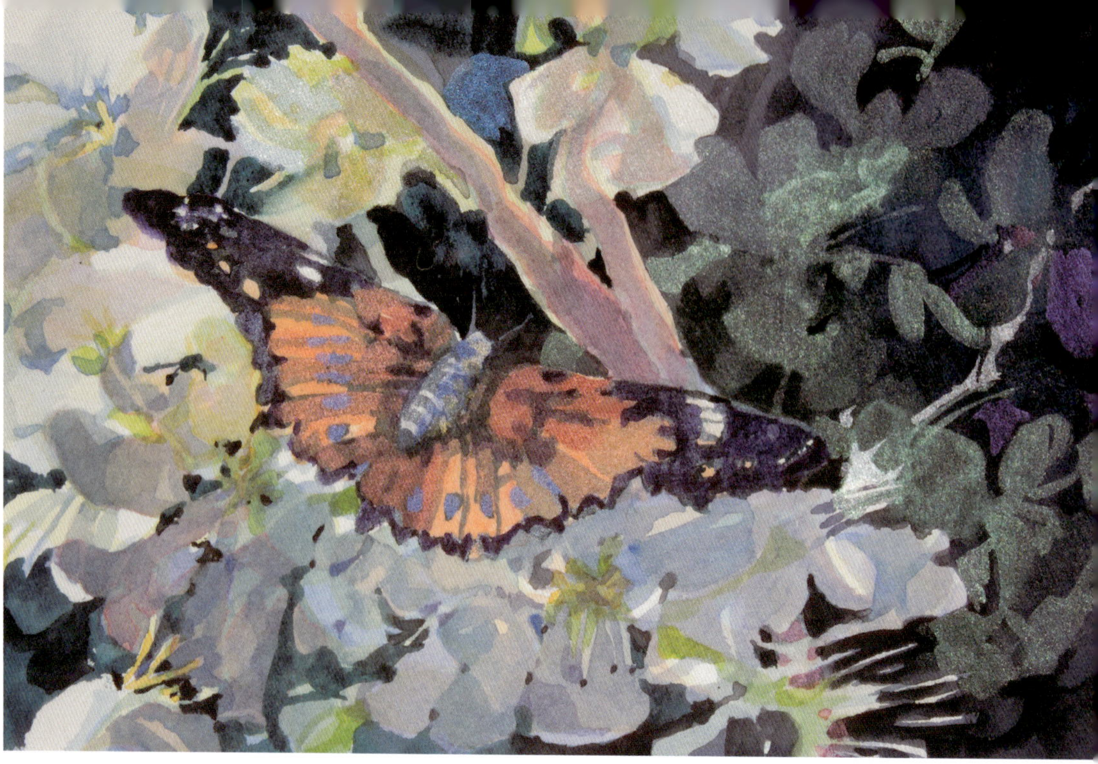

Butterfly Moment
Apple blossoms offer a perfect opportunity for optically layering the transparent luminous pigments, combined with some shimmering iridescents on the butterfly's wings.

Watercolors were, for many of us, the first paints we used as children. It was so easy—all you need is a brush, paint, water, and paper. This accessibility makes watercolor an attractive medium but not necessarily an easy one. The watercolor artist employs skills that go far beyond mere familiarity with the medium to bold actions and daring experiments! Those of us who love watercolor thrive on the challenges and accept the idea that we may never truly master it.

All visual artists use their colors and values to create shapes that culminate in a unified, harmonious whole. The knowledge and skill of the artist is apparent in the finished work. With most media it is the paint vehicles—oils, acrylics, pastels, crayons—that keep the pigments contained and consistent. In watercolor, it is water that releases the individuality of the pigments. Faced with what can seem like unruly children, the watercolor artist's first instinct may be to control. If you confine the pigments to certain areas or "correct" them with more paint, you can coerce individual pigments into acting like other media. But if you seek adventure you need to get to know the individual pigments and find ways to use their personalities for the creative benefit of the whole. In this way, the watercolor artist is like a musical director.

Knowledge begins with respect. Like musicians in an orchestra with individual skills and talents, the paints in the palette contain pigments that can contribute and collaborate with the others to produce a beautiful result.

Creating a watercolor painting is like playing jazz, where an underlying theme may be repeated and syncopated, with improvisation always a possibility. The staining pigments are encouraged to play a strong background rhythm, which still can be heard under the layers of additional music. They are asked not to overpower, but to provide a consistent framework. The sedimentary/opaques are star performers in their own right, and must be coaxed into lovely but careful combinations that disguise their grandstand ambitions. Some granulate to emphasize texture. Some diffuse to dramatize a passage. Others play harmoniously with the stainers, adding their personalities to the strength. All the while, the delicate luminous pigments are encouraged to glide over the soft passages—sometimes layered as solo performers and sometimes mixed together in glowing transparency.

This is a book about color and watercolor—from the simplicity of a three-paint palette to the bewildering array of colors and paints available. Within these pages, an incredible adventure is just waiting for a little water and a willing spirit.

JAN HART

KEY TERMINOLOGY

- **Chroma** Relating to the purity of a color or hue. The measure of the brightness or strength of a color.
- **Color, hue** a given color created by a specific wavelength of light.
- **Color index number** page 8
- **Complementary color** page 54
- **Color temperature** page 12
- **Color wheel** page 15
- **Direct painting** page 13
- **Glaze** page 36
- **Gouache** page 25
- **Granulation** page 28
- **Flocculation** page 28
- **Local color** page 80
- **Lightfastness** The chemical stability of a pigment under long exposure to light.
- **Luminance, brilliance** page 124
- **Negative painting** the process of painting a darker tone to create a "left over" lighter positive shape. A technique for layering vegetation.
- **Neutral color** page 70
- **Opaque** page 24
- **Optical mixing** page 36
- **Palette mixing** page 13
- **Permanence** page 22
- **Physical mixing** page 36
- **Pigment** Colored powder that is the component in paint that produces the color.
- **Primary color** page 48
- **Saturation** The intensity of a color. A highly saturated color is bright and a low-saturated color is more muted.
- **Sedimentary** page 24
- **Secondary color** page 48
- **Shade** page 80
- **Tertiary color** page 60
- **Tint** White (or water in watercolor) is added to a color. Pink is a tint of red.
- **Tone** Gray is added to a color.
- **Transparent** page 20
- **Tuck** A technique where the artist deliberately darkens a corner or juncture where two adjacent shapes appear to come together.
- **Value** page 66
- **Value scale** page 66
- **Wash, flat** and **graded** page 119

ABOUT THIS BOOK

SECTION 1 PIGMENT PROPERTIES PAGE 16

Explains the physical ways different pigments react on paper when mixed or painted.

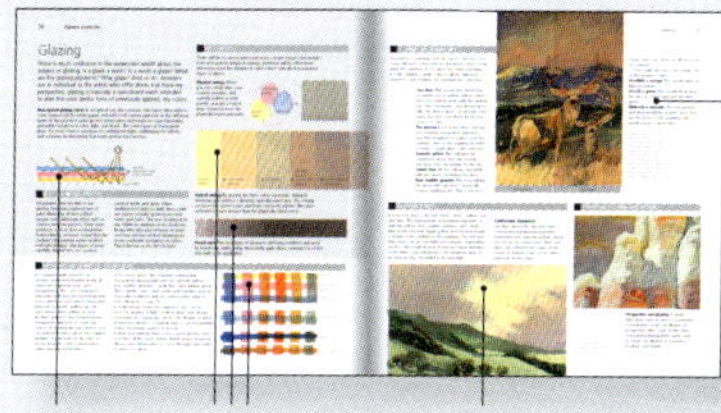

SECTION 2 PIGMENT AESTHETICS PAGE 40

Explains color theory, as well as the visual and aesthetic ways different pigments combine when mixed or painted.

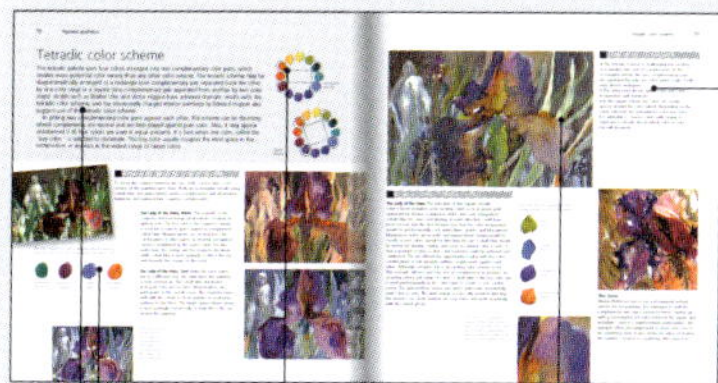

SECTION 3 CHOOSING PIGMENTS FOR PAINTING PAGE 76

Demonstrating the theory from sections 1 and 2, the author and other artists choose exceptional colors for specific subjects.

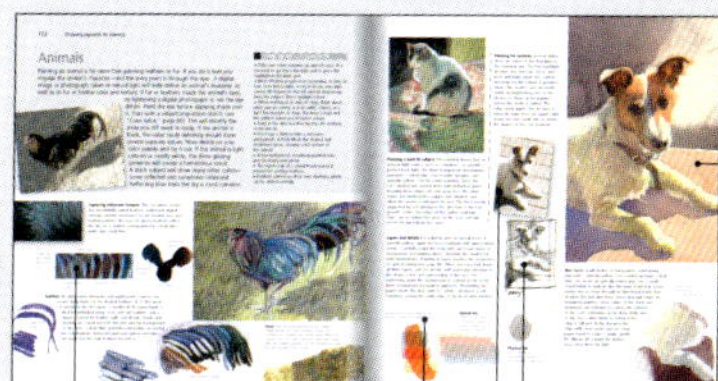

Paints and pigments

Your first paints were likely to have been given to you or recommended by a class teacher. Let's say you go to an art supply store to look for "cerulean blue." You are confronted with myriad choices and no good way to compare—cerulean, genuine cerulean, cerulean blue chromium, cerulean blue GS. Because paint manufacturers can name a paint anything they want, many choose the name they think artists are most likely to buy. As an artist you need to know more about the paints you buy and use.

ORGANIC AND INORGANIC PIGMENTS

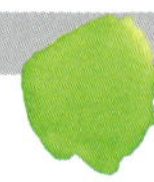

organic pigments phthalo green and quinacridone magenta

Watercolor pigments are divided into two basic, but very different, groups: organic and inorganic.

Organic pigments are usually bright, pure, and light in weight; they tint richly, and they are transparent. Most are manufactured in the laboratory.

Synthetic organic pigments include phthalos, quinacridones, and azos. The organics tend to flow freely when introduced into a wet wash. The only natural organic pigment in general use today is rose madder genuine.

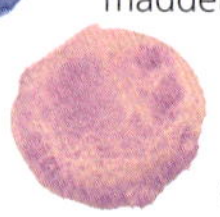

inorganic pigments cobalt blue and cobalt violet

Inorganic pigments are made of distinctively shaped particles with inherent color, which originates as iron oxides and hydroxides of copper, chromium, or aluminum, along with various amounts of clay, chalk, and silica. They can be transparent, sedimentary, or opaque. Synthetic inorganics contain fewer impurities and have smaller particles than their natural counterparts. They also tend to be smoother in washes. Many are beautifully granulated. Synthetic organics include cobalt blue, cobalt violet, manganese violet, cadmium yellow, and zinc white. These metals are often heavy and tend to drop on the paper when introduced into a wet wash.

WHAT IS PAINT?

Paint is the physical substance in a tube consisting of pigments (that give the paint its color) suspended in a binder. A paint can be single pigment (containing one pigment only) or a "convenience mixture" composed of more than one pigment (the colored powder within the paint that produces the color). Single pigment paints are preferable because they are purer and more lightfast. A paint labeled as a "hue" (such as cadmium red hue) is a mixture of relatively cheap pigments that is intended to match the color appearance of more expensive ingredients.

Understanding the label

According to ASTM (American Society for Testing and Materials) standards for paint labels, the generic name, common name, and color index number of the pigment(s) contained must all be listed on each label. Your tube of phthalo yellow green is labeled with the following information:

Common name or manufacturer's name: phthalo yellow green
Color index generic name: phthalocyanine green + arylide yellow
Color index number: PG 7 + PY 3 (P = pigment; G = green; 7 + P = pigment; Y = yellow; 3) = the precise chemical composition of the paint.

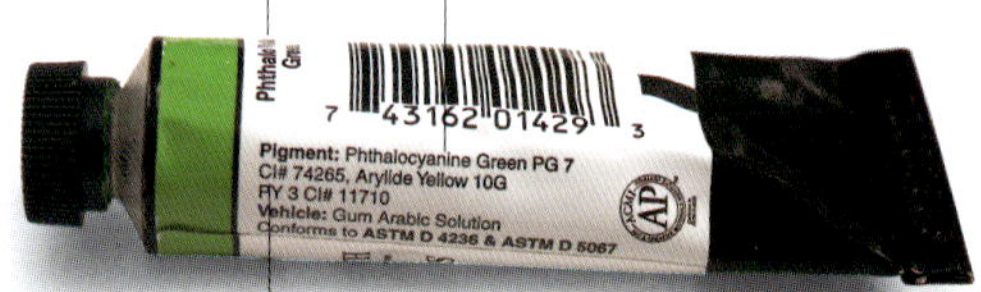

If there is just one series of numbers, the paint is a single pigment paint, which can be compared to any other paint with an identical color index number. Note that some paints that have the same color index number are further treated in the laboratory to produce variants in color (i.e., PBr 7 is the color index number for raw sienna and raw umber as well as their "burnt" or calcined counterparts, burnt sienna and burnt umber.)

Further investigation yields additional paints with the same color index number—PB 36—and color index name—cobalt chromium oxide—that are named cobalt turquoise, cobalt green deep, and cerulean blue by different manufacturers.

COLOR GROUPS

Each color group has a different mood and can be used for varied purposes. Here we look at the groups themselves and key paints from each group. Note: the color name is only the first indication of what a paint is. Check the index number to be sure.

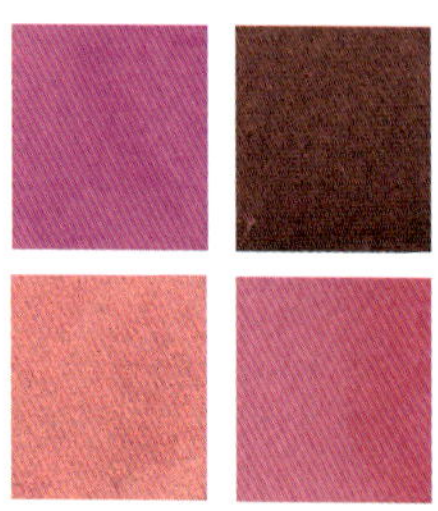

Clockwise from top left: quinacridone magenta, napthamide maroon, opera rose (W&N), rose madder genuine

The magentas

Magenta is the color of rhubarb and pomegranates—not red and not purple, but the color in between. Magenta is a subtractive primary color that is indispensable to four-color processing. The red-violet hue range rarely occurs in inorganic pigments and the natural organics are almost always impermanent. The artist needs to take care and do some research.

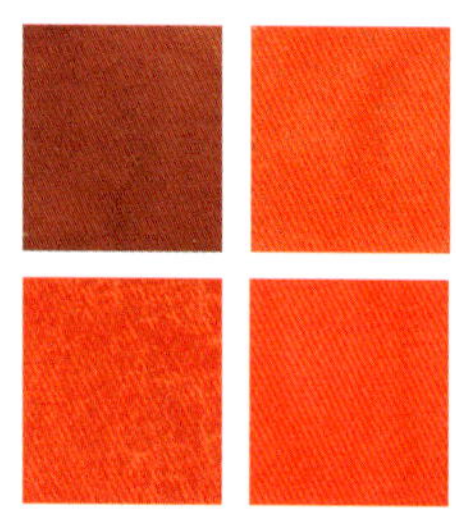

Clockwise from top left: perylene maroon, perylene red, vermilion, cadmium red

The reds

Red is hot and strong and can signal conflicting emotions from passionate love to raging violence. It may take some experimentation to find a favorite true red.

Testing pigments

These three painting tests (two follow on next pages) were carried out to explore and compare certain paint colors and mixes. Choices were made and then researched further. Some initial choices were ruled out after further investigation.

A selection of pigments available within the color family groups on Hart's color wheel (see page 15).

Yellows and yellow-greens

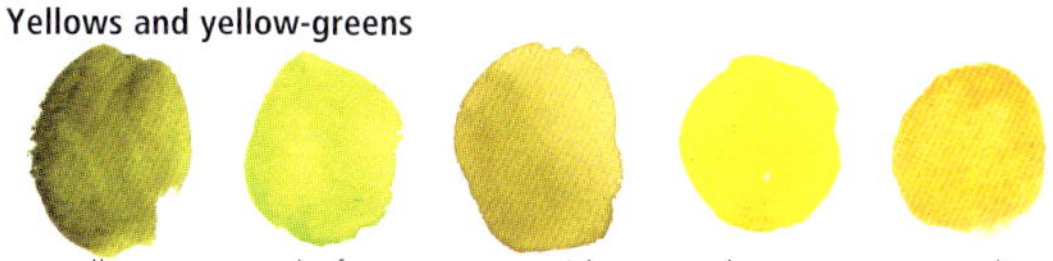

yellow green azo, leaf green, greenish yellow azo, lemon yellow, aureolin yellow

Magentas and red-violets

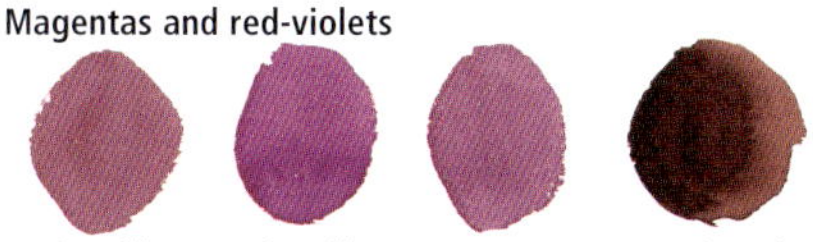

quinacridone violet, quinacridone magenta, permanent magenta, napthamide maroon

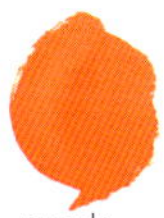

pyrrole orange

Green-blues, turquoises, and cyans

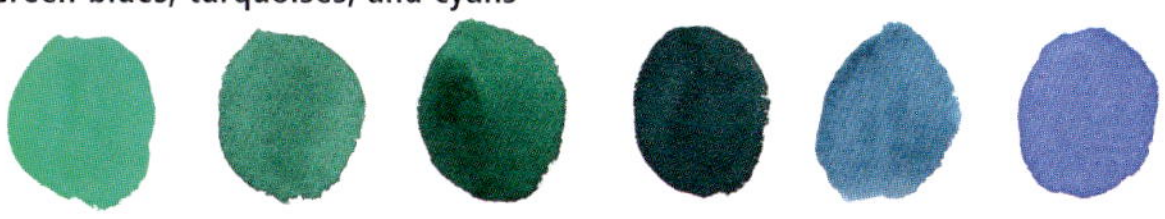

cobalt turquoise light, cobalt turquoise, ultramarine turquoise, phthalo turquoise, cerulean blue, cobalt blue

Parrots color study

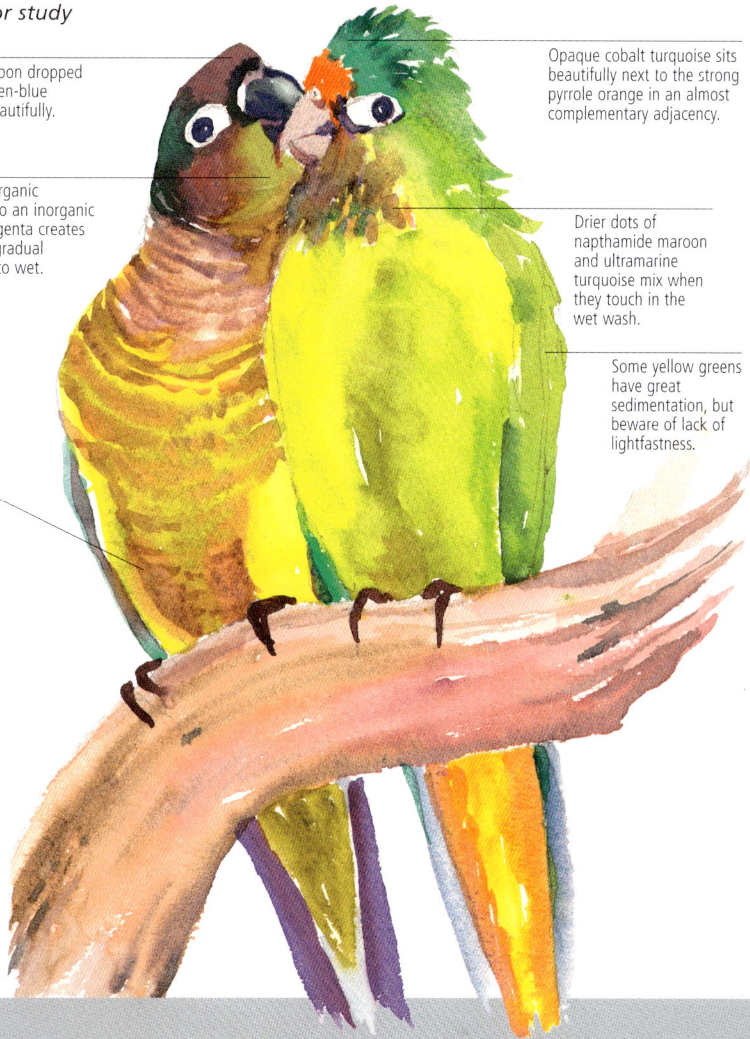

A small round brush is useful for dotting in a dry application of cobalt violet into a wet wash of greenish yellow azo. The cobalt violet displaces the yellow-green to create a feathered look.

Napthamide maroon dropped into the dark green-blue organic works beautifully.

A yellow-green organic azo placed next to an inorganic quinacridone magenta creates a soft edge and gradual transition, wet into wet.

Opaque cobalt turquoise sits beautifully next to the strong pyrrole orange in an almost complementary adjacency.

Drier dots of napthamide maroon and ultramarine turquoise mix when they touch in the wet wash.

Some yellow greens have great sedimentation, but beware of lack of lightfastness.

Clockwise from top left: pyrrole orange, cadmium orange, Winsor orange, quinacridone sienna

The oranges

Orange is vibrant and shares attributes of both red and yellow. It suggests emotions that are less aggressive than red and is calmed by the cheerfulness of yellow. Orange is most useful in fall landscape paintings. There are some interesting choices in paints between red-orange and yellow-orange.

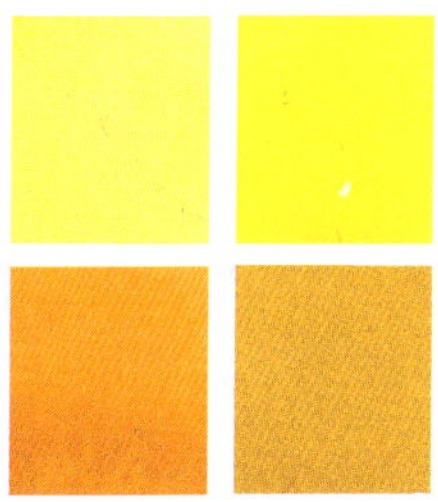

Clockwise from top left: azo yellow (aureolin), lemon yellow, new gamboge, cadmium yellow

The yellows

Sunny, bright yellow is energizing, hopeful, and upbeat to Western minds and is one of the primary colors in Native American art. Yellow can represent illumination, inspiration, and sometimes trouble. Landscape artists often use the color but beware—people generally either love or hate yellow.

Iris color study

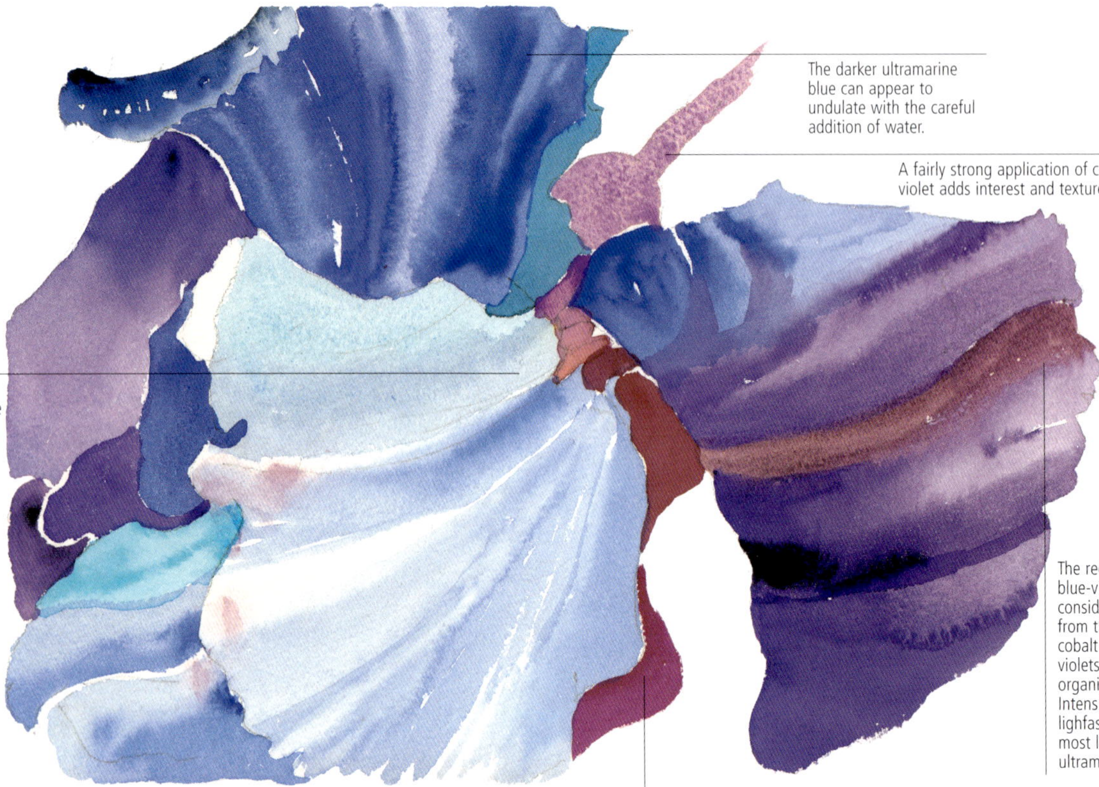

The darker ultramarine blue can appear to undulate with the careful addition of water.

A fairly strong application of cobalt violet adds interest and texture.

The subtle sedimentation in the pale soft cerulean blue adds a cooler accent to the adjacent cobalts.

The red- and blue-violets vary considerably in intensity from the lighter, paler cobalt and manganese violets to the synthetic organic dioxazines. Intensity does not ensure lighfastness. One of the most lightfast violets is ultramarine violet.

A selection of pigments available within the color family groups on Hart's color wheel (see page 15).

Some testing of reds, violets, and magentas in the painting yields the vibrant and lightfast quinacridone magenta.

Blue–violets and red–violets

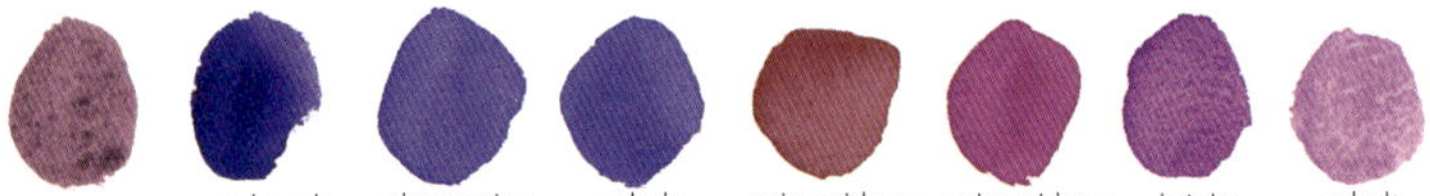

manganese violet | carbazole violet (diozanine) | ultramarine violet | cobalt violet deep | quinacridone violet | quinacridone magenta | bright violet | cobalt violet

Cyans and middle blues

cerulean blue | cobalt blue | ultramarine blue

Color groups

Clockwise from top left: rich green gold, phthalo green, chromium green oxide, viridian green

The greens

Green is life! It can be soothing and calming, or it can convey jealousy. Although the greens shown here provide an adequate color range, many artists mix their greens instead of trying to find a suitable premixed or convenience green. It is a great idea to do a mixing exercise (see "Green exercise," page 106). With yellows and oranges on one mixing axis and blues and blue-greens on the other, you can see what greens your existing paints produce. Some are dull. Some are vibrant. Most of the vibrant ones can be tamed with a bit of a complement, such as quinacridone rose or burnt sienna.

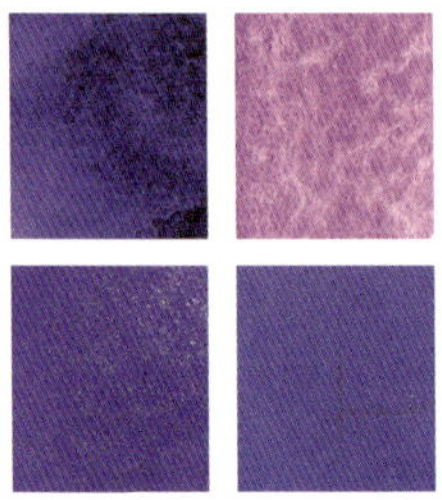

Clockwise from top left: dioxazine violet, cobalt violet, carbazole violet (dioxazine), quinacridone violet

The purples

Purple is regal, wise, and spiritual. As a complement to yellow-green, it is an appropriate color for spring landscapes, as well as mountains and long winter shadows. Use the red-violet hues for a warm color scheme and the blue-violets for a more somber, cool scheme. Lavender can suggest the feminine, while eggplant purple can suggest the masculine.

Cacti color study

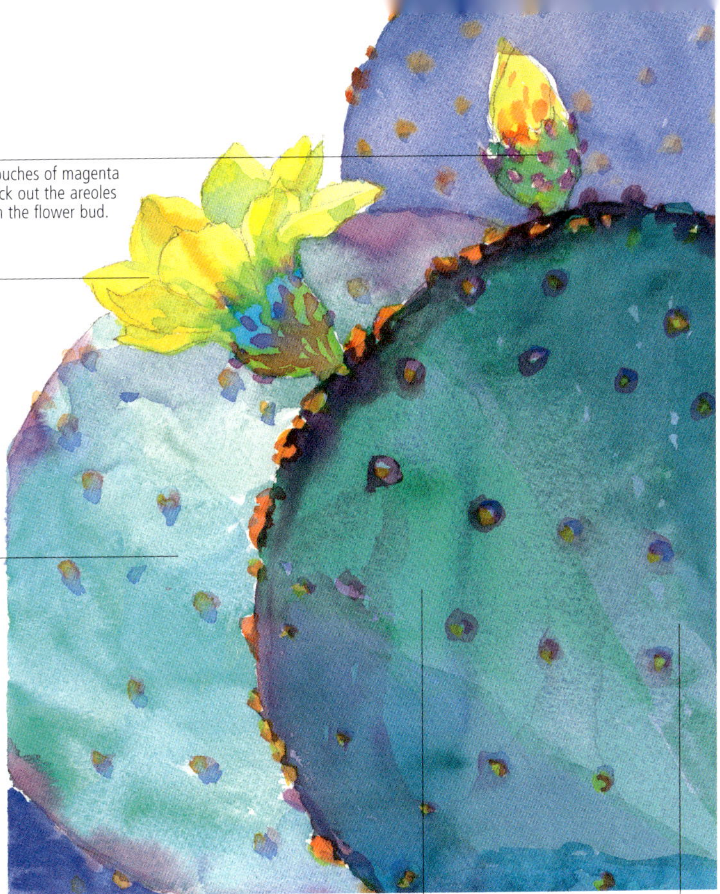

Touches of magenta pick out the areoles on the flower bud.

Both of the yellows sparkle with intensity and transparency. Testing of aureolin yellow concludes that it may change in color toward brown over time. Good substitutes are azo yellow (aureolin), hansa yellow, or lemon yellow.

Paler green–blues for delicate washes.

Mixtures of blues and green-blues are tested on the shaded area.

A glaze of transparent cobalt blue adds depth and a color shift.

A selection of pigments available within the color family groups on Hart's color wheel (see page 15).

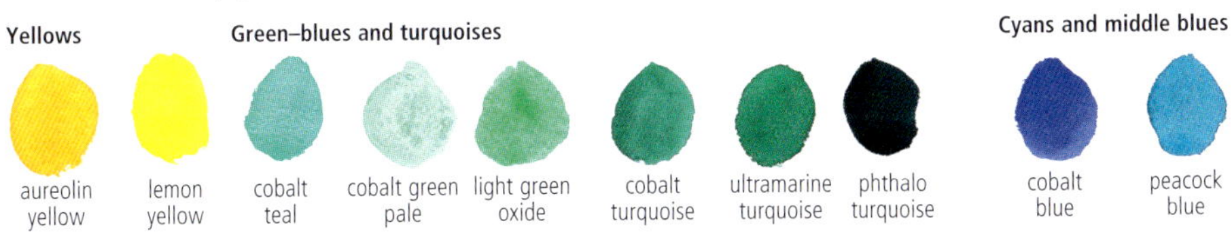

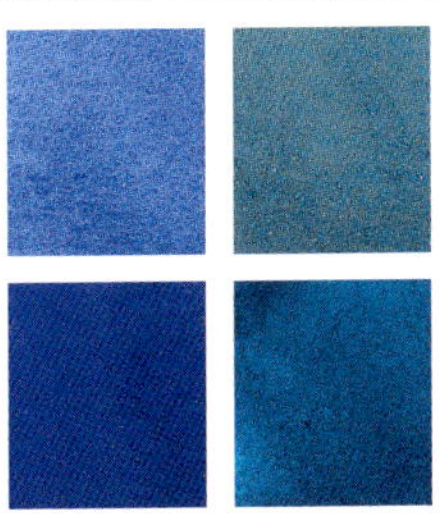

Clockwise from top left: cobalt blue, cerulean blue, peacock blue, ultramarine blue

The blues

As one of the primary colors, blue is important for mixing both greens and purples. It also is the coolest color on the color wheel, representing calm, stability, and cold. Ranging from blue-green to blue-violet, this color is complementary to red-orange, orange, and yellow—and always can be counted on to grab attention when placed in a counter position in painting. So many words conjure images of blue hues—azure, beryl, cerulean, cobalt, indigo, navy, royal, sky, robin's egg, cyan, cornflower, midnight, slate, steel—and that is a particular problem in paint manufacturer's naming!

THE ALCHEMY OF INORGANICS

Natural inorganic pigments are among the oldest used by humans. Improvements in the technology of grinding metals and minerals mean that there is a much wider range available to us today. The mineral origins of many favorites may surprise you.

Cobalt produces the most diverse range of pigments currently used in artists' paints. From cobalt violet through cobalt blue, turquoise, cobalt green, and yellow, it has been used since the late Middle Ages.

Copper compounds are the basis of many blue or green pigments, including malachite and azurite.

Iron oxides are the basis of the natural red, yellow, and brown earth colors. They also are present in synthetic oxide mixtures under names such as Venetian red, Indian red, and Prussian blue.

Magnesium was very important in the production of Indian yellow but has been replaced by the cadmiums and gamboge.

Manganese was mostly represented in manganese blue, but because of its highly polluting manufacturing process, it has been replaced by manganese blue hue, which is really phthalocyanine.

Mercury was found in the mineral cinnabar and in vermilion and scarlet lake.

Sulfur is in many pigments, but its most important contribution is to ultramarine blue.

Titanium dioxide is the supreme white pigment and is produced as titanium oxide. It is found in buff titanium and also is an ingredient in some of the beautiful range of light-valued cobalt greens and turquoises, such as cobalt teal.

Zinc oxide is Chinese white.

SOME THINGS TO CONSIDER

- As an artist you need to make decisions about the pigments that you select. Instead of following a color chart, do some research before you buy. There are books and internet resources that tabulate testing. Be sure to look for lightfastness ratings.
- The vast array of watercolors available can be overwhelming. Keep a palette just for test pigments. Only transfer a pigment to your personal palette when it has proved indispensable.
- Pigment preferences change over time, and new pigments are continually coming on the market. Look for special trial offers, and share information with other artists to find what suits you.
- You always can remove a paint from your palette if you find that you are not using it anymore.
- When choosing your palette paints, be sure to consider a pigment's personality as well as its color!

Basic mixing

The first thing a watercolor artist learns is how to mix water with watercolor pigments, which are suspended in a water-soluble binder. Next is learning how to mix paints together to get the color and characteristic you desire. It takes a while to get used to the amount of water to use with each color. One thing is certain: the watercolor artist gets plenty of mixing practice!

MIXING FUNDAMENTALS FOR 12 COLORS

The paints suggested for Hart's color wheel (see page 15) are all high-chroma, permanent, and high-intensity hues that generally mix well with one another to produce strong colors. Most of the paints suggested (at the top of each listing) are single pigment paints to prevent any unintended consequences of mixing too many pigments together. The exceptions are ultramarine turquoise and quinacridone sienna. Lower chroma, more neutral-colored paints such as the earth pigments—burnt sienna, raw sienna, Venetian red, Indian red, and PrimaTek® pigments—have been excluded from Hart's color wheel because they will "kill" the high intensity color mix. They can be used more effectively in other ways (see "Sedimentary and opaque paints," page 24 and "Neutrals," page 70).

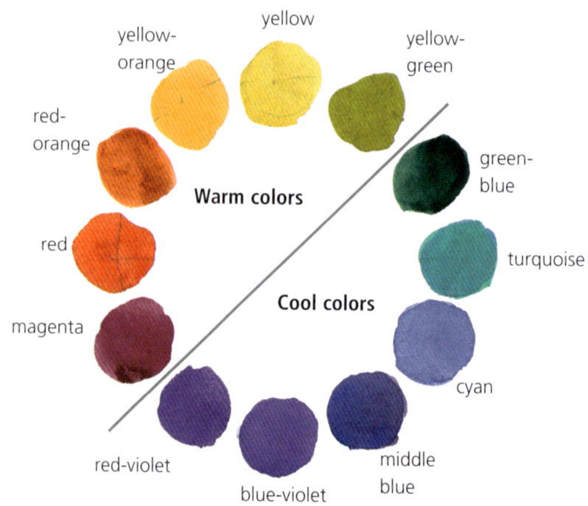

SOME THINGS TO CONSIDER

- The most intense and purest colors are mixed from the colors that lean toward the color you want to achieve. The farther apart the two colors are on the wheel, the more neutral the mix. Neutrals can be powerful accompaniments to pure colors of a lighter value, creating the impression of glow.
- Mixing three or more pigments together increases the likelihood of creating mud.
- If you mix a high-chroma brightly colored pigment with a low-chroma subdued pigment, you get a low-chroma mix.
- Direct painting is a wonderful way to allow the individual characteristics of pigments to interact on the paper.

CREATING THE COLOR YOU NEED

1 Think of the color you want to make; e.g., bright orange.
2 Use Hart's color wheel to select your mixing colors.

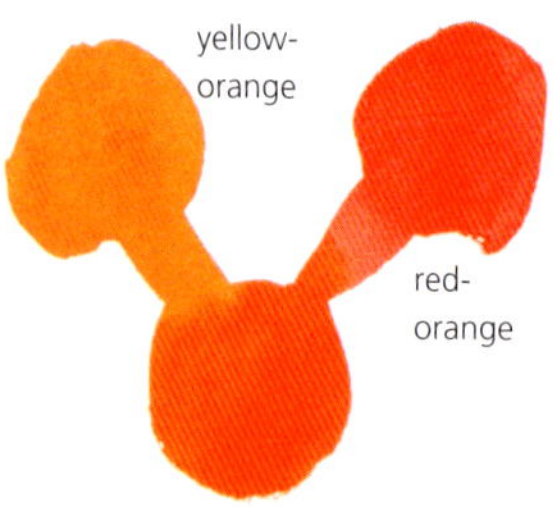

A bright orange lies between a yellow-orange and red-orange on the wheel. It can be mixed from combining paints in those adjacent color locations—for example, nickel azo mixed with scarlet lake.

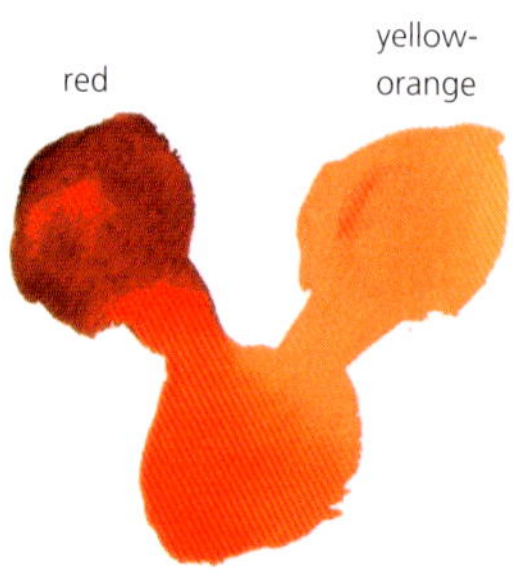

See what happens when paints separated by one color step are mixed—for example, a yellow orange, such as new gamboge, mixed with a red, such as perylene scarlet. The result is a nice orange, but it's not quite as vibrant as the first example.

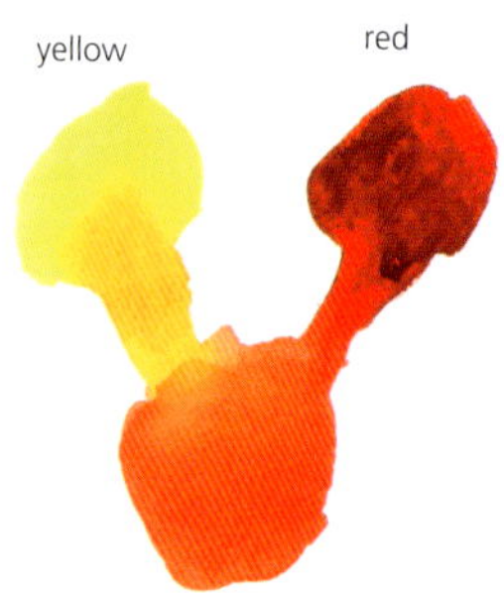

See what happens when you mix colors separated by two color steps, such as a yellow and a red. When azo yellow (aureolin) is mixed with perylene scarlet, the result is a more subdued orange.

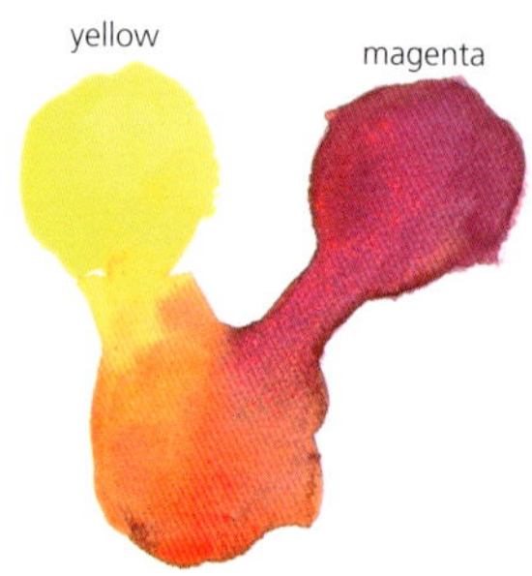

If you go another step farther away in either direction, you are nearing the complementary relationship, which will produce a near neutral. Here magenta is mixed with yellow.

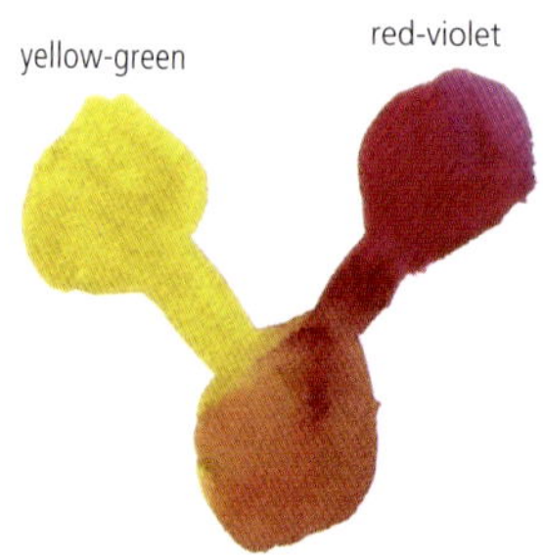

A yellow-green mixed with a red-violet (complements) creates a true neutral color.

IN THE PALETTE OR ON THE PAPER?

You can mix watercolor paints in the plastic palette or on the surface of the paper. Mixing on the paper is called "direct painting." Many artists use both methods, depending on their aim.

Palette mixing: Use a damp to wet brush to transfer your paint from its well to a clean mixing area of the palette. Begin with the lightest color. If your paint is fresh, be careful not to transfer too much. If your paint is dry, lightly spray it with water a few minutes before you paint, and then transfer it with a damp to wet brush. Create a puddle in your palette into which you can add the second color.

Direct painting: Mixing paints on the paper is one of most exciting parts of watercolor painting. Apply your first color to an area of the paper. Immediately add the second color with one or two strokes. If your paper is slanted, the paints will run together, which can produce some great effects. If your paper is flat, the paints will mix on their own, depending on the pigments. You can promote mixing by lightly nudging the colors with your brush. To avoid blossoms, make sure the paint you add is drier than the paint on the paper.

PALETTE-MIXING TIPS

- Try not to mix too thoroughly. Allow the separate pigments a chance to mix on their own and retain their individual personalities.
- Learn to judge how wet or dry your palette mix is from its appearance. If the mix separates in places and you see small white areas of your palette showing through, the mix is drier and therefore stronger or darker.
- Watercolor paint dries considerably lighter than it appears when you first apply it.
- Do not try to save your mixes. It may seem like a good idea, but the practice produces duller paint mixes and paintings.

Sample mixes
These four mixes demonstrate the difference between palette and paper mixes. The palette mix is on the left and the direct painting mix is on the right.

palette mixing | direct painting

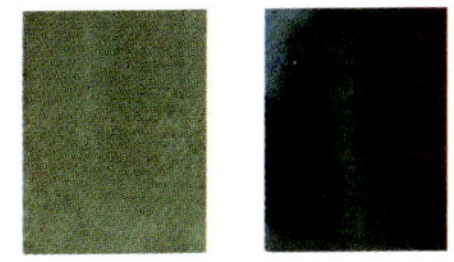

Ultramarine turquoise mixed with quinacridone burnt orange. Three color steps of Hart's color wheel separate this wonderful green mix, which is very useful for natural vegetation. Note the wonderful variations in the direct painting example. Burnt siennas also can be used in this mix.

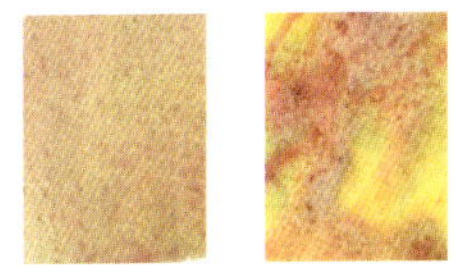

Azo yellow (aureolin) mixed with cobalt violet. This mix of near complements creates a beautifully granulated neutral palette mix, or an exciting dance of granulated violet in the sea of azo yellow (aureolin).

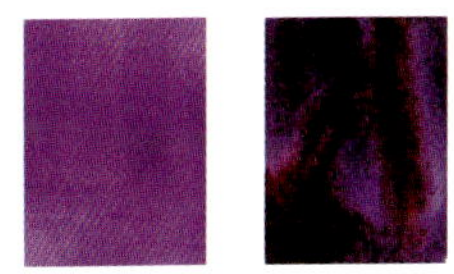

Carbazole violet (dioxazine) mixed with quinacridone magenta. Analogous (adjacent) colored pigments create a vibrant palette mix. The direct mix allows their individualities to show, which could be especially advantageous in a still-life background or for subtle variations in floral paintings.

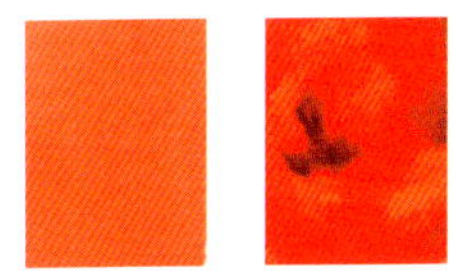

Perylene scarlet mixed with nickel azo. One step separates these two very different pigments. Both are synthetic organic pigments, which disperse well and mix together in the palette to create a nice orange. Adding nickel azo to the perylene scarlet in the direct mix demonstrates the characteristic shooting of the nickel azo, creating some interesting and varied effects.

3 The more colors you mix together, the duller and less pure the mixes become.

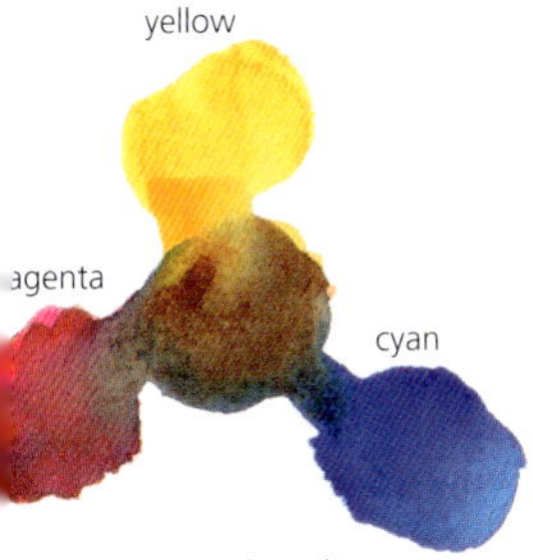

Mix together the three hue primaries—yellow, magenta, and cyan—to create an example of a neutral.

If you continue to add paints in an attempt to create a color that you have in mind, you will wind up with a drab mix known as "mud". In this example, burnt sienna and phthalo blue were added to the primary mix.

4 It is important to understand how much of each color to use in a mix. Start with the lightest pigment and add darker colors to the mix in your palette. Each time you mix, you gain insight for the next mix.

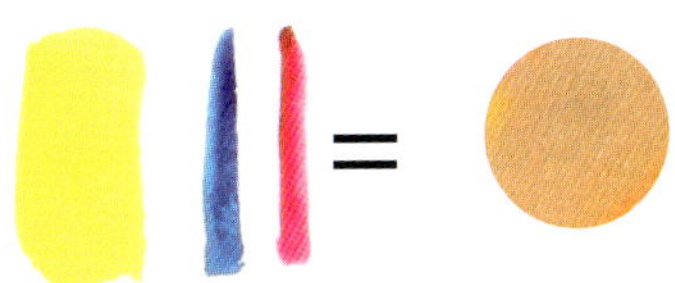

A lot of yellow and a little cyan and magenta.

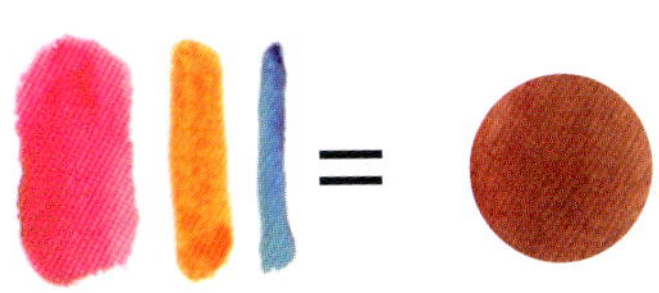

More magenta, less yellow, and very little cyan.

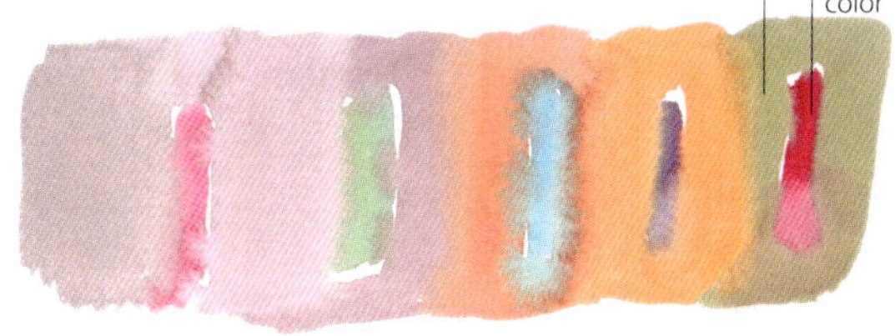

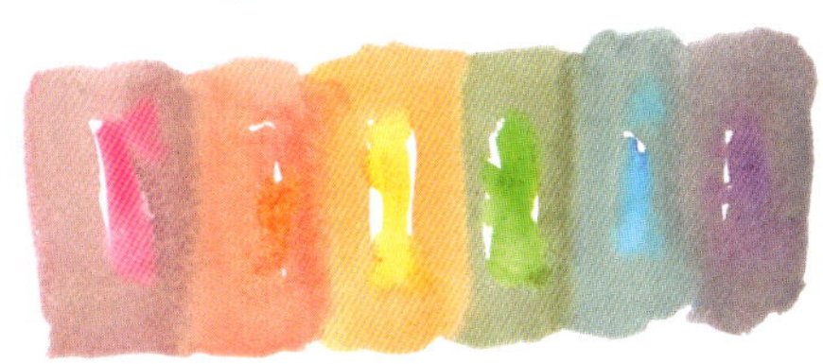

5 Mixed neutrals are valuable additions to a painting because they allow the pure colors to sing. Note especially that the pure colors begin to glow when surrounded by mixed neutrals that are analogous or complementary, especially if the pure color is a lighter value than the mixed neutral.

Color wheels

A color wheel is a schematic, ordered circle of hues that artists use to guide their color mixing and color design decisions. In the 18th century, Isaac Newton ingeniously joined two ends of the visual rainbow color spectrum to create what we can see as a color circle, or wheel. Although Newton cautioned that his circle applied only to mixtures from light, his theory was transferred to painting and paint mixing. Eventually, through much study and discussion, the idea of hue spacing came about. This explains why colors are not evenly spaced around the color wheel, and why colors of light and surfaces are perceived very differently. But—just when we think we can define, describe, and measure colors precisely—individual differences among different observers make any precision moot. But that doesn't stop us from trying!

SUBTRACTIVE AND ADDITIVE SYSTEMS

Artists mix pigments and create color wheels in one system (known as subtractive) and view them in another (called additive).To understand the dichotomy between subtractive and additive systems is fundamental to understanding color theory.

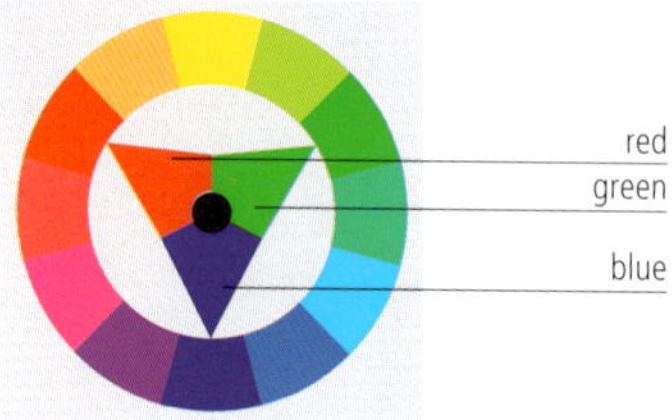

Simple Additive (RGB) System
This wheel describes how the eye and brain interpret wavelengths of light in creating color perception. This system is used only in devices that use light—such as television sets—and our eyes and brain. The primary colors are red, green, and blue, and all colors mixed together create white light.

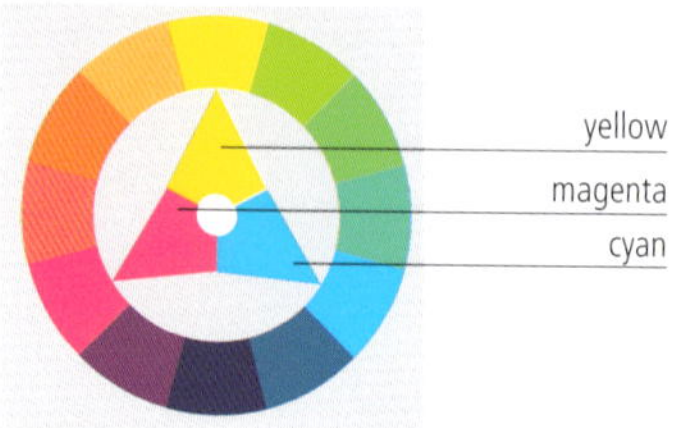

Simple Subtractive (CMYK) System
Most of the color wheels we are used to seeing are subtractive. As artists, we are accustomed to a system where all pigments mixed together create black or gray. Color mixing in this system occurs in the palette or on the paper. Artists now recognize that the three primary colors are cyan, magenta, and yellow.

LIMITATIONS OF COLOR WHEELS

Near-perfect wheels, like the additive one below that demonstrates Newton's theory, don't match the pigments that are available to the artist. Compare this wheel with the pigment wheel (right), designed by Bruce MacEvoy (see page 128), with high-chroma pigments on the outside and low-chroma to the inside. The large gaps where no pigments exist on the wheel are obvious. Because our final review of a painting is visual, some would say that the visual color system should be the framework for artists' color decisions.

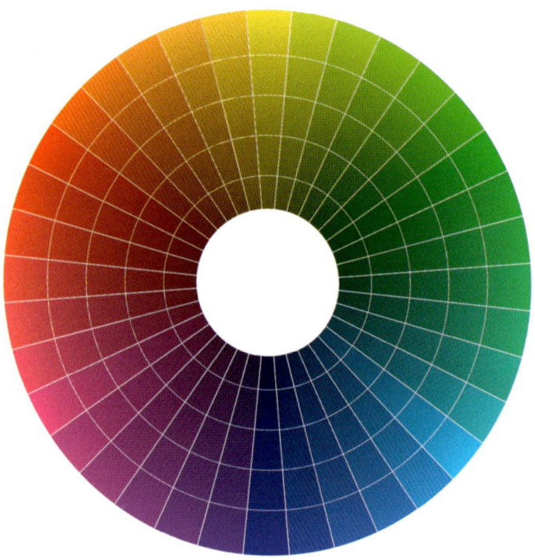

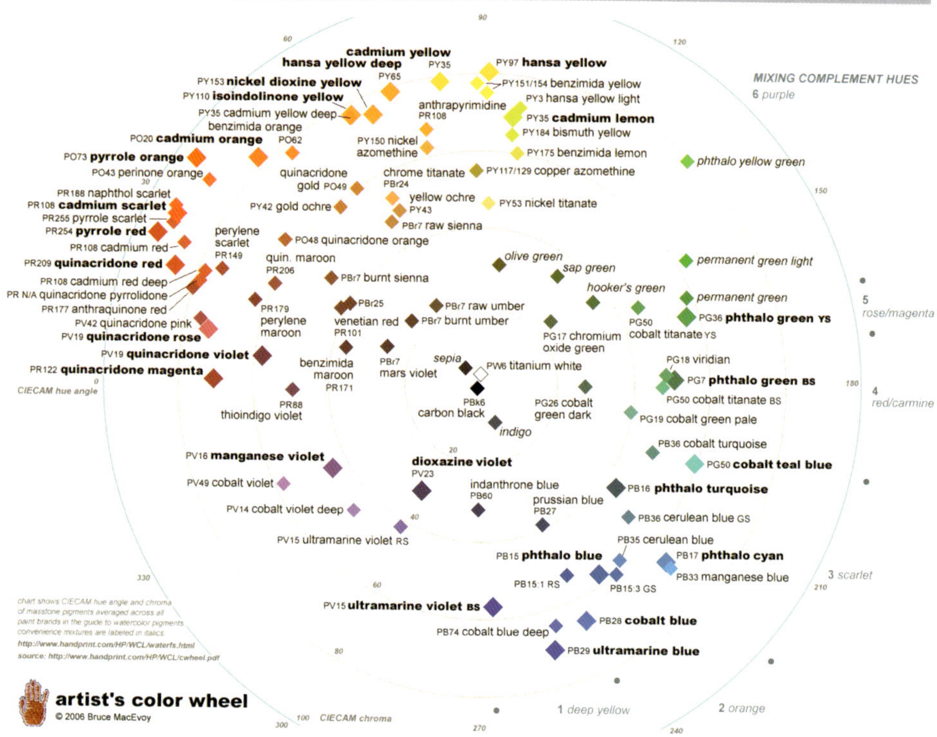

HART'S COLOR WHEEL

The author has created this color wheel in order to simplify a complex subject. This wheel is based upon personal paint preferences and personal experience. You can adapt it to fit any artist's choice of paints, as long as you retain the complementary color relationships and mixes.

The example shows a pigment for each of the 12 color positions on the wheel, and options are given in the chart below for you to replace or experiment with alternative colors. This 12-color wheel would give you an ideal palette, or you may wish to add some earth colors (see "Neutrals," page 70).

The wheel and the chart that correlates to it (below) list all of the paints used in the book, complete with pigment codes so that you can use this as your central pigment reference page. Remember that the pigment numbers are the best way to know what pigment(s) have been used in the paint. Often the paint name is misleading, with manufacturers assigning the same name to very different paints or assigning an enticing name that gives no information about the paint; e.g., orange lake. Paints by different manufacturers have been used throughout the book to explore them all.

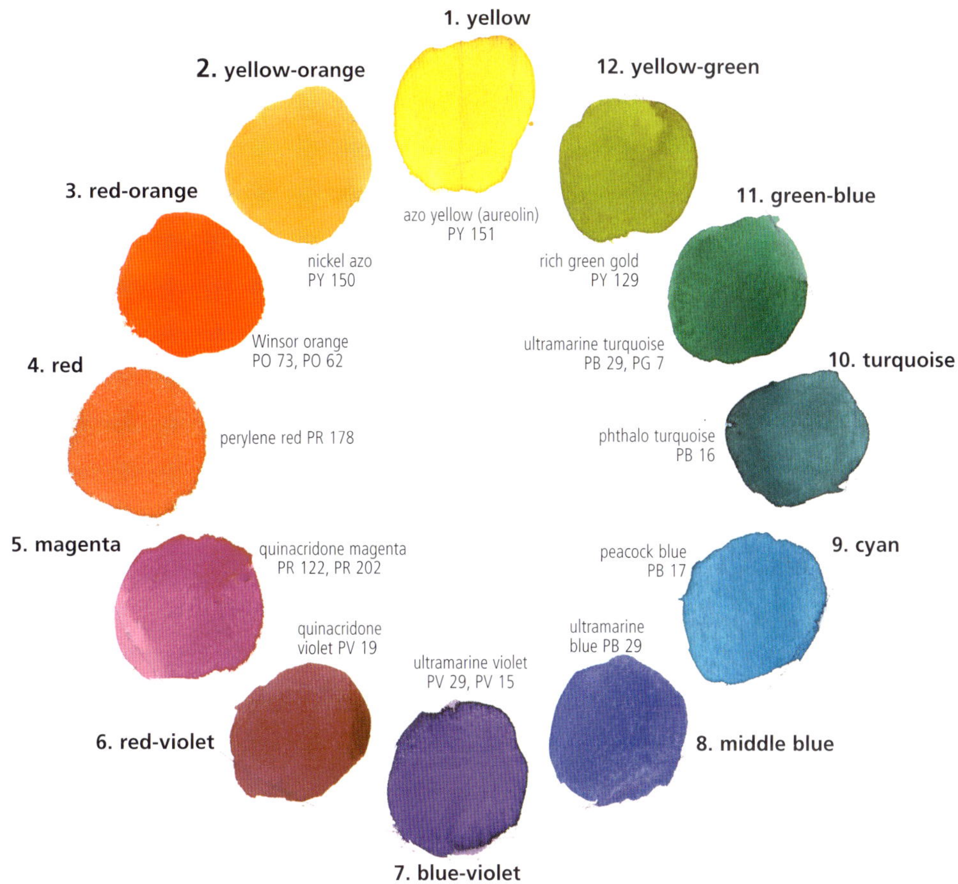

1. yellow
azo yellow (aureolin) PY 151
hansa yellow light PY 3
cadmium yellow PY 35
permanent lemon yellow PY 175
nickel titanate PY 53
lemon yellow PY 3
benzimida yellow (Winsor) PY 175
aureolin yellow PY 40
hansa yellow PY 97

2. yellow-orange
nickel azo PY 150
new gamboge PY 153
Indian yellow PY 153
quinacridone gold PO 49
permanent yellow PY 110
quinacridone burnt orange PO 48
permanent orange PO 62
cadmium yellow deep PY 35

3. red-orange
Winsor orange PO 73, PO 62
cadmium orange PO 20
perinone orange PO 43
orange lake PO 43
quinacridone sienna PO 49, PR 209
vermilion PR 108
quinacridone coral PR 209
cadmium red light PR 108
cadmium scarlet PR 108
cadmium red-orange PR 108
pyrrole orange PO 73

4. red
perylene red PR 178
perylene scarlet PR 149
napthol red PR 122
cadmium red PR 108
quinacridone red PR 209
anthraquinoid red PR 177
permanent red PR 112
pyrrole red PR 254

5. magenta
quinacridone magenta PR 122, PR 202
quinacridone rose PV 19
quinacridone burnt scarlet PR 206
opera (Holbein) PR 122 + BV 10
opera rose (W&N) PR 122 + BV 10
alizarin crimson PR 83
permanent magenta PV 19
permanent rose PV 19

6. red-violet
quinacridone violet PV 19
carbazole violet (dioxazine) PV 23
manganese violet PV 16
cobalt violet PV 49
bright violet PV 7, PV 15
Winsor violet (dioxazine) PV 23

7. blue-violet
ultramarine violet PV 29, PV 15
indanthrone blue PB 60
cobalt violet deep PV 14
permanent violet PV 23
Prussian blue PB 27
cobalt blue violet PV 19, PB 28
indanthrine blue PB 60
lavender PV 15, PB 29, PW 6

8. middle blue
ultramarine blue PB 29
phthalo blue PB 15
some cobalt blues PB 28
some cerulean blues PB 36
French ultramarine blue PB 29

9. cyan
peacock blue PB 17
some cerulean blues PB 36
some cobalt blues PB 28
manganese blue PB 33

10. turquoise
phthalo turquoise PB 16
cobalt teal PG 50
some cerulean blues PB 36
cobalt turquoise PG 50
cobalt green PB 50
cobalt turquoise light PB 50

11. green-blue
ultramarine turquoise PB 29, PG 7
phthalo green PG 7, PG 36
cobalt green pale PG 19
viridian green PG 18
light green oxide PG 50

12. yellow-green
rich green gold PY 129
phthalo green PG 7, PG 36
green gold PY 150, PY 3, PO 3, PY 129, PG 10
chromium oxide green PG 17
terre verte PG 23
leaf green PY 154, PG 7
greenish yellow PY 117

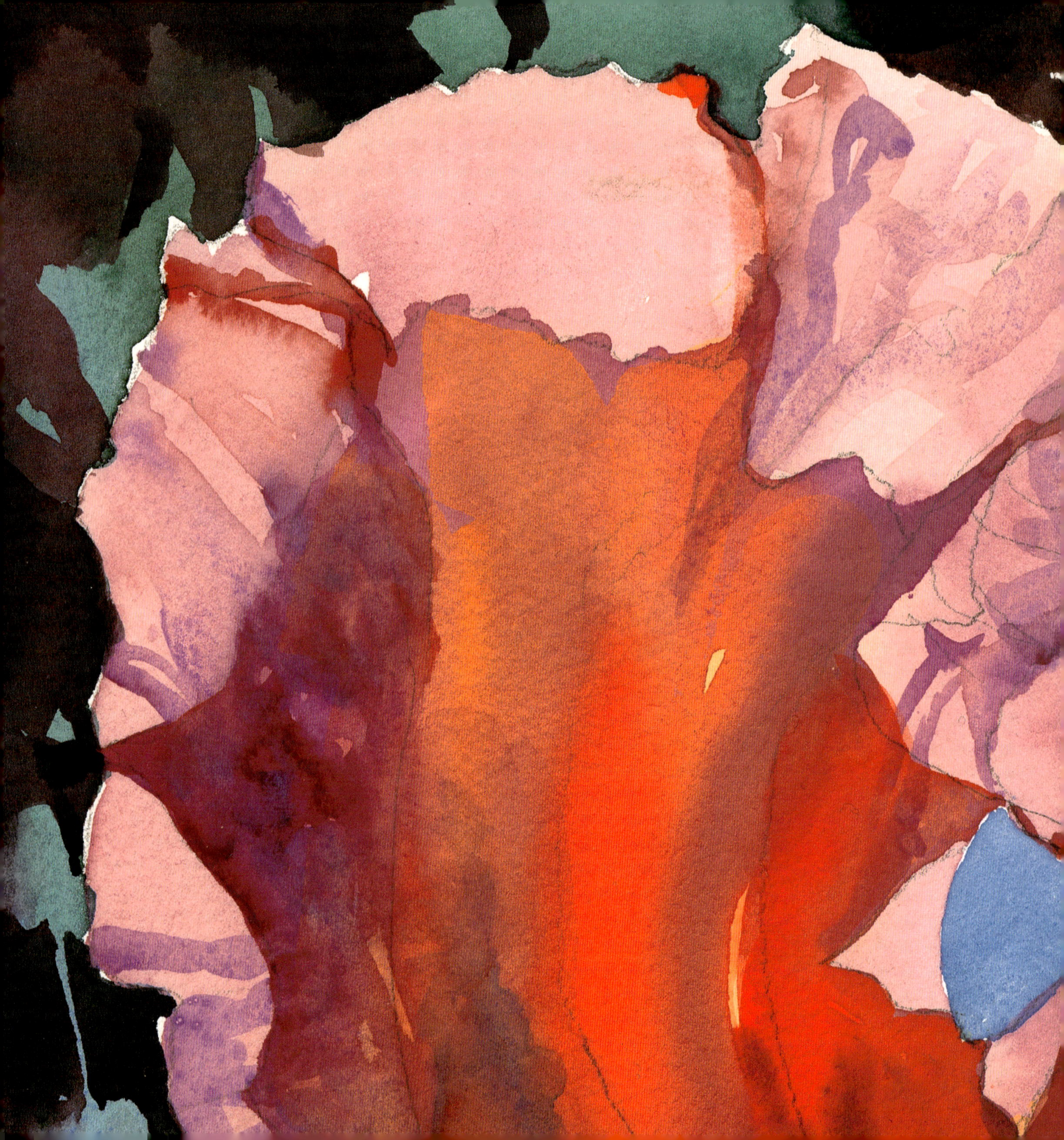

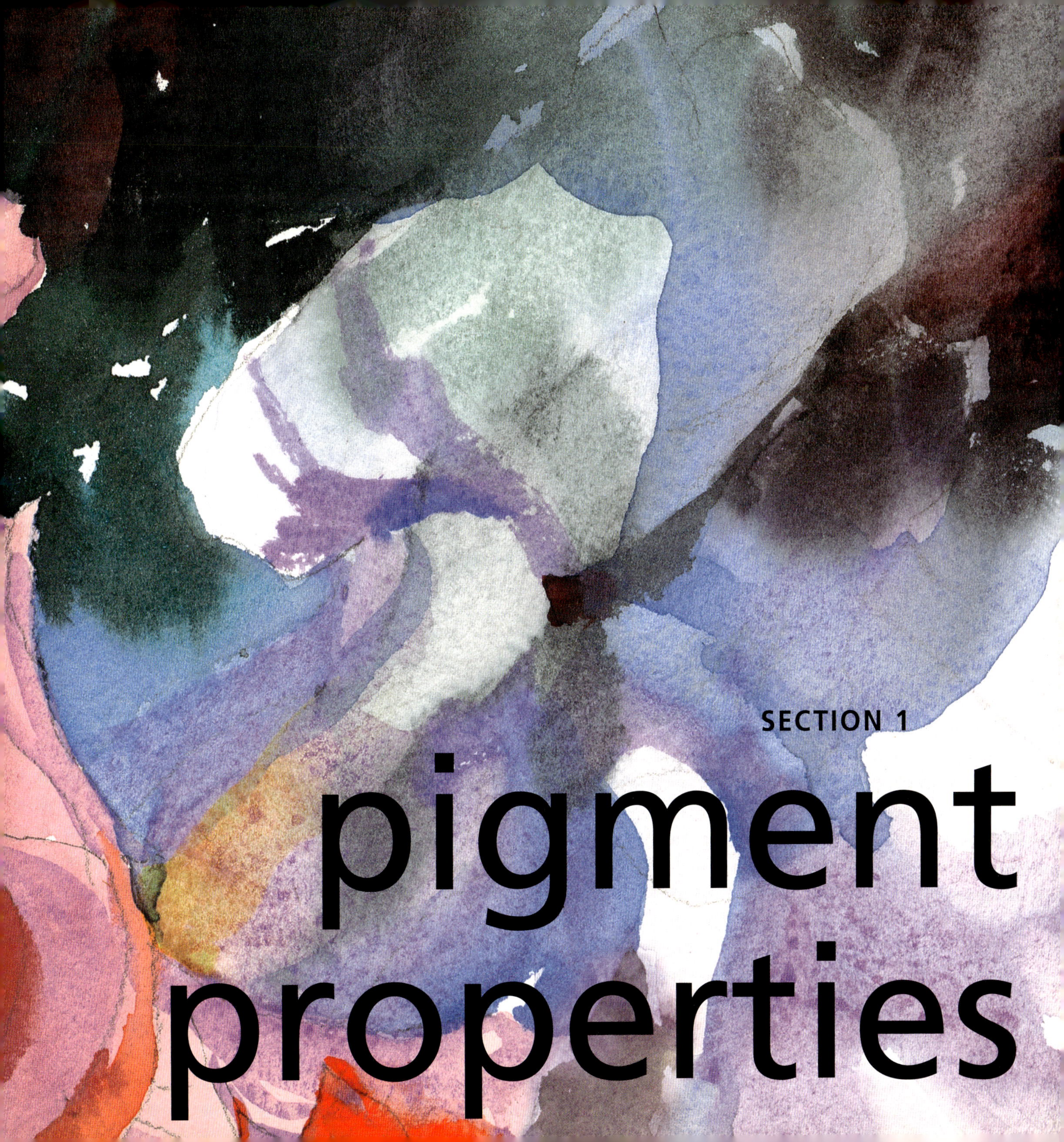

SECTION 1

pigment properties

Pigment properties

Watercolor pigments vary from strong, startling dyes that conquer anything they touch through granulating and/or opaque paints that add texture or softly blanket the gentle transparents that lie delicately, almost unseen. Creative artists find myriad ways—as shown in this gallery—to use and display the magic and unpredictability of watercolor pigments that often surprise even the most experienced painter!

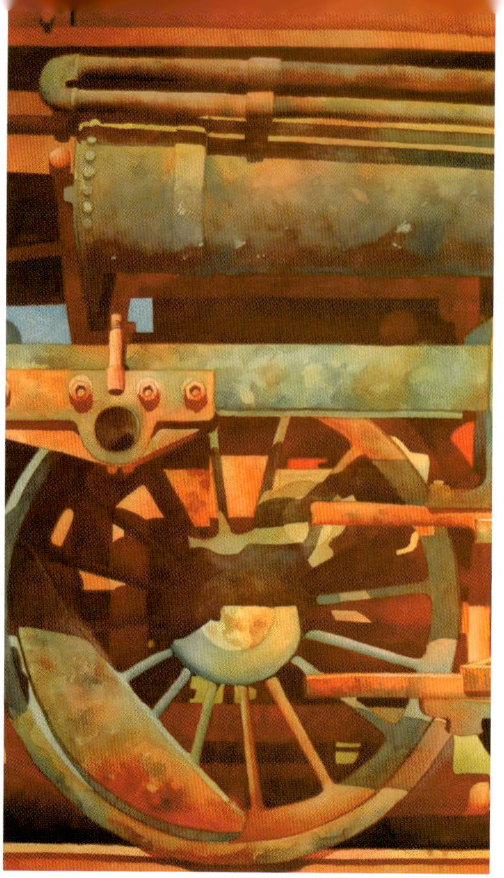

▶ *Glorious Grunge*
Dana Brown
The subject demanded a heavy use of watercolor, so the painting was built up wet on dry, in many layers of transparent color. A limited palette has been used, as the artist sees color harmony as the "glue" that holds her complex subjects together. Her usual palette consists of aureolin yellow, French ultramarine blue, and Winsor red, sometimes with cerulean blue added.

▼ *Sunlight and Shadows at the Big House* Julian Bray
As in Dana Brown's painting, this image has been built up in a series of transparent glazes. The shadows were laid over the brickwork with deep reds and blues. For the sky, opaque gouache or body color with various blues was laid over a yellow orange underpainting.

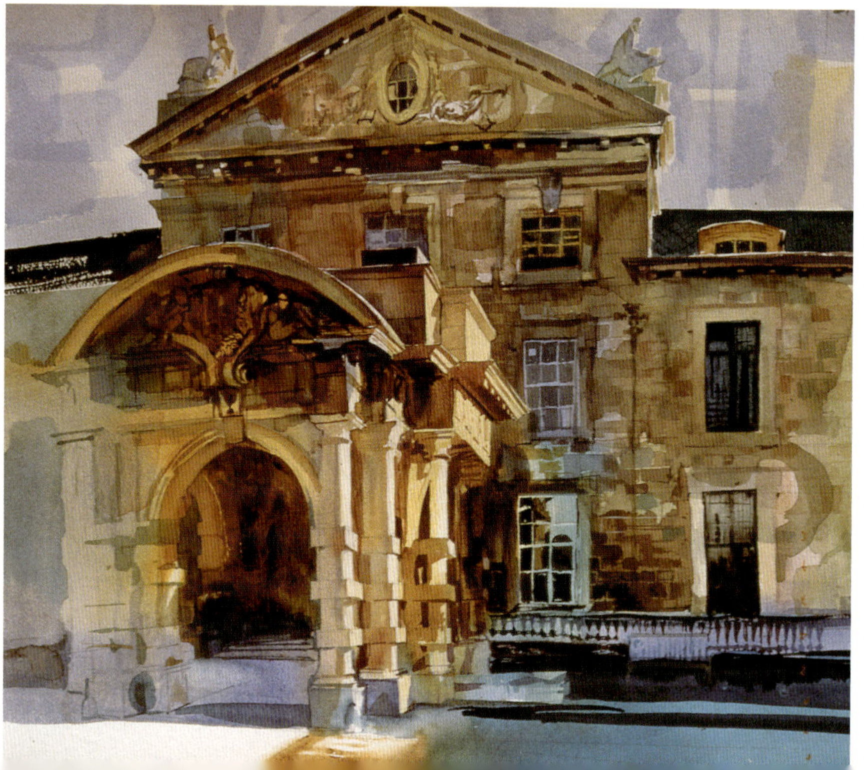

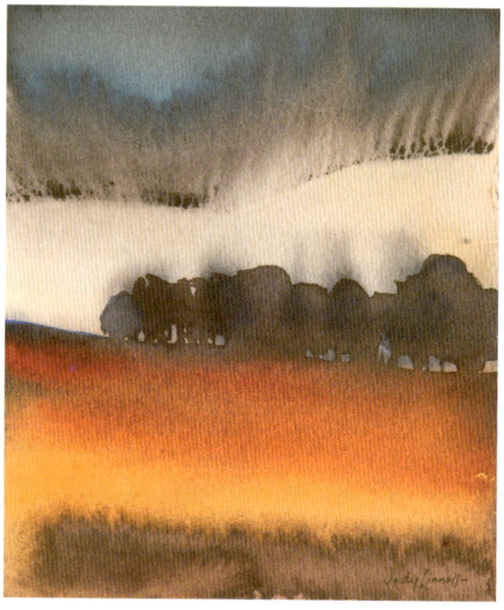

▲ *Trees on a Hill* Judy Linnell
The artist uses a controlled and selective wet-into-wet technique, allowing the paint to dry naturally in places so that it forms backruns. Drying time is crucial: the paper needs to be damp enough to let some colors flow into one another, but dry enough to define the shapes of trees and vegetation without the paint running into the sky above.

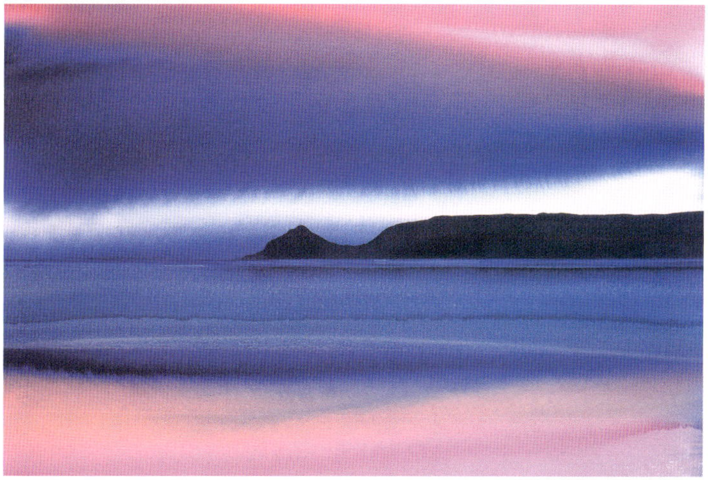

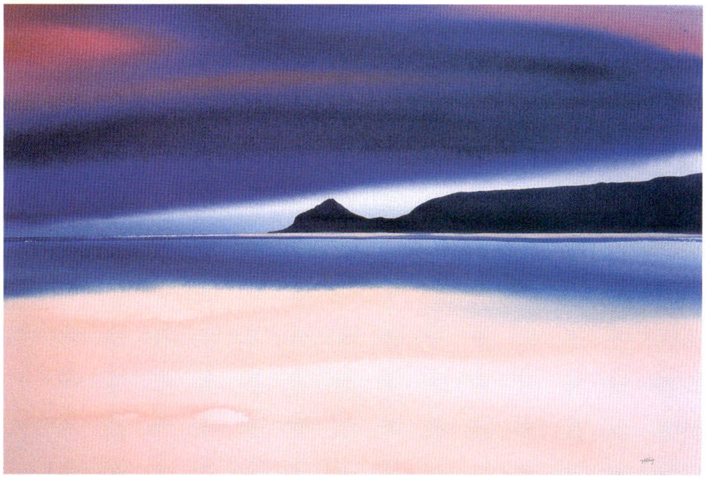

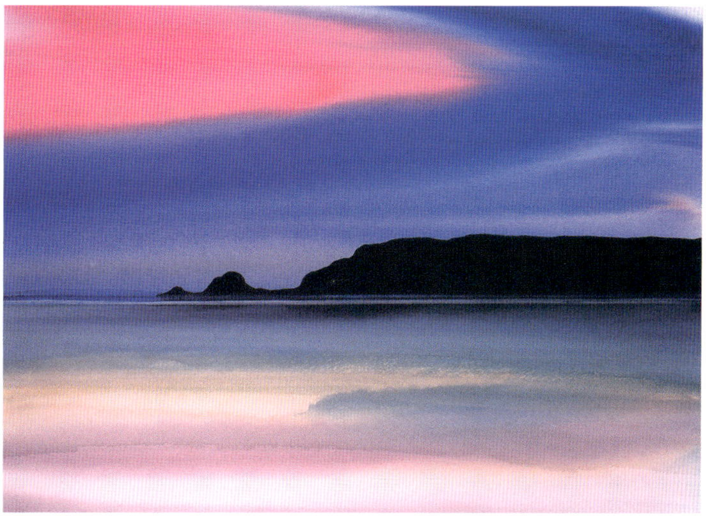

◀ ***Last Light (top), Distant Light (middle), Passing Storm (bottom)*** ROBERT TILLING
The artist has worked the same scene three times, softly laying and mirroring wet-into-wet horizontal washes of high-chroma paints to focus attention on the bands of light and reflection across the paintings. This demonstrates both the versatility and the unpredictable properties of watercolor and how varied atmospheres can be created through color choice and paint application.

▼ ***Hydrangea*** ANN SMITH
A sense of form and depth is achieved through using the transparent colors and layering techniques possible with watercolor. Shadowy shapes and forms are hinted at underneath built-up layers of glazes. Flashes of white reserved paper or weak washes of aureolin yellow create a compositional link with dappled highlights on the two analogous color scheme areas of magenta—violet and green-blue.

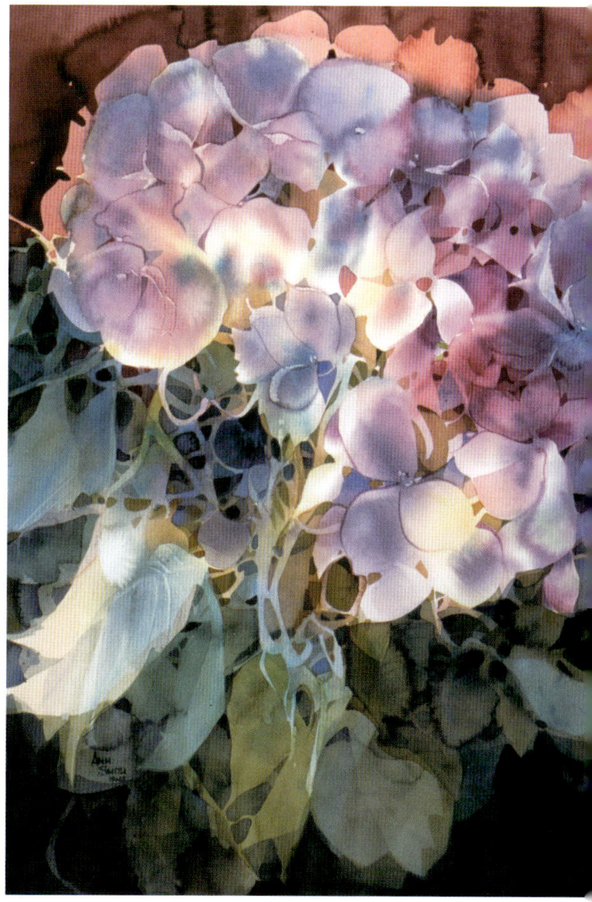

Transparent non-staining paints

Although all watercolors are transparent if the paint is sufficiently diluted, some colors are more transparent than others. Because the tradition of watercolor involved building up glazes, many artists look for the most transparent paints to emphasize this medium's delicate and luminous properties. Unfortunately, some of the most beautiful transparent pigments, such as rose madder genuine and aureolin yellow, are not always lightfast. Also, some paint manufacturers are moving toward synthetic replacements that may not be as transparent, so the artist is faced with a difficult choice.

TRANSPARENT PAINTS

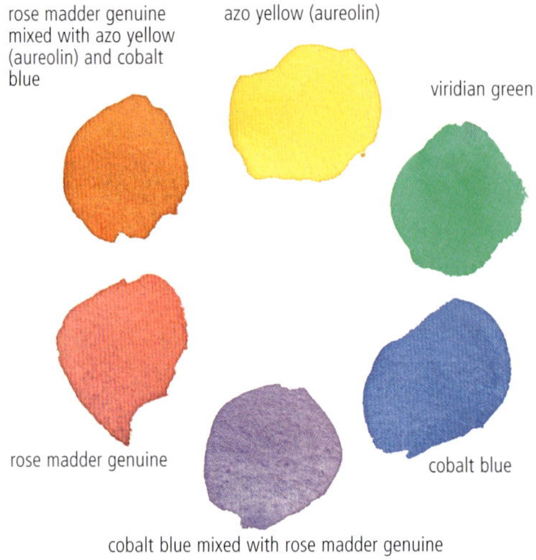

The transparent paints that are best used for glazing are sometimes called "luminous." These layered, softly transparent paints allow light to penetrate through to the white paper and then reflect back up through the layers again. Together they create the glow that makes watercolor so memorable. The luminous transparents are mostly non-staining.

The suggested palette on the left shows examples of luminous transparents.

WHAT ARE THE PROPERTIES OF THE TRANSPARENT PIGMENTS?

Glaze test Experiment with applying different pigment washes over a sketch to discover which colors will give a gentle glaze to your work. Apply one layer of wash, let it dry, and then apply another. Here mostly transparent paints were used to study potential shading possibilities. The luminous pigment mix of rose madder genuine and aureolin yellow and the hemetite genuine are the most effective at gently altering the color without overpowering the painting beneath.

- Luminous non-staining pigments are perfect for building up glazes to achieve glow in light-colored subjects such as white roses and snow.
- Pure nonstaining transparents can fine-tune a painting. You can even use some staining transparents—carefully and not heavily. If you find that your background is too busy and unconnected, a glaze of cobalt blue may solve the problem. If your painting lacks color unity and appears too dull, warm it up with a glaze of rose madder genuine, aureolin, or an appropriate substitute.
- Shadows on light-colored subjects can be painted with combinations of these pigments. Consider a morning snow scene. You glaze the snow with the pale yellow of morning light and paint the long shadows in a cobalt blue and rose madder genuine mix.

rose madder genuine/aureolin yellow mix The luminous mix glazes beautifully and softly. It is a nonstaining glaze that can be lifted.

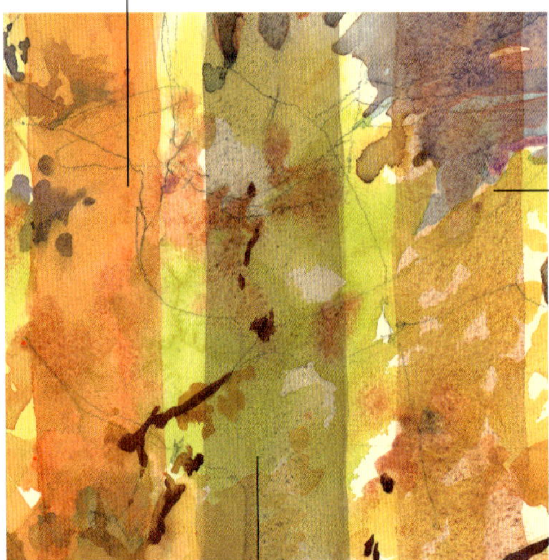

Iridescent garnet This pigment has transparency and some granularity. The sheen of the Iridescent is interesting up close. Because the pigments appear to drop immediately into the paper texture and quickly diffuse some of the underlying pigments, take care when applying as a glaze.

hemetite genuine One of Daniel Smith's PrimaTek pure minerals, its transparent binder allows visibility; the granulating minerals add texture.

phthalo blue Definitely not a glazing pigment, even though it is essentially transparent. It overpowers whatever is beneath it and is permanent. Much of the underlying painting is lost.

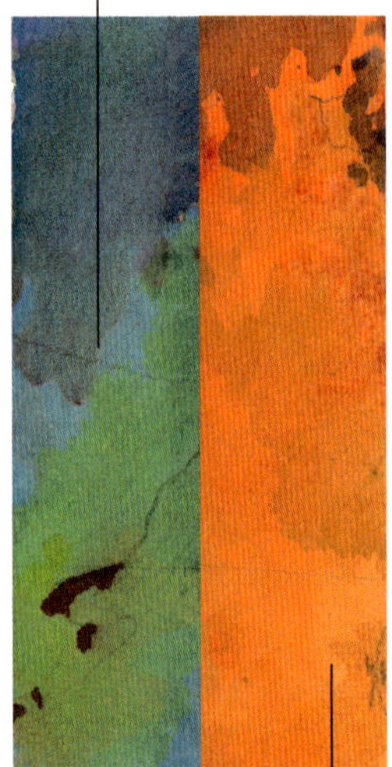

quinacridone burnt scarlet Two glazes of this strong staining pigment obscure most of the warm details in the foliage.

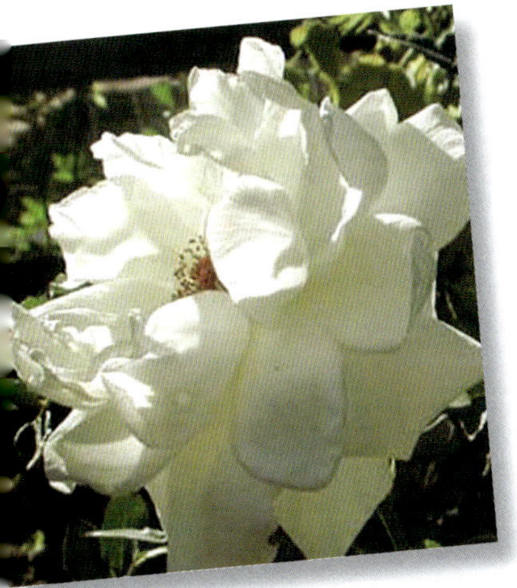

White Rose Study Luminous paints are perfect for this white rose study and other light-colored subjects, as they provide gentle glazes that allow the subject matter to glow.

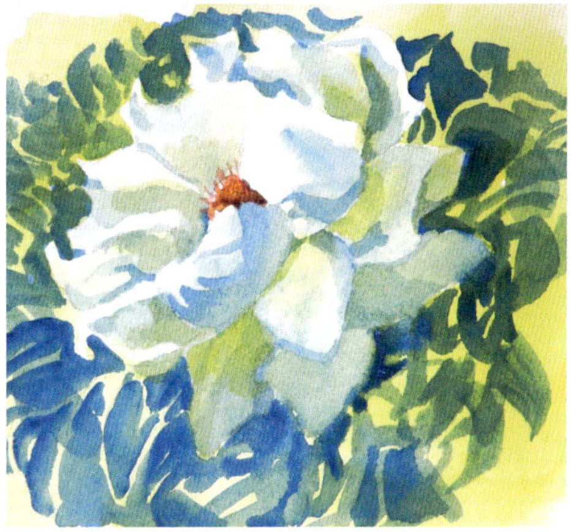

1 With an aureolin yellow wash around it, the white rose begins as shapes painted first with aureolin yellow and then, when dry, with cobalt blue and an orange center. Apply cobalt blue shapes around the rose shapes in a dizzying array.

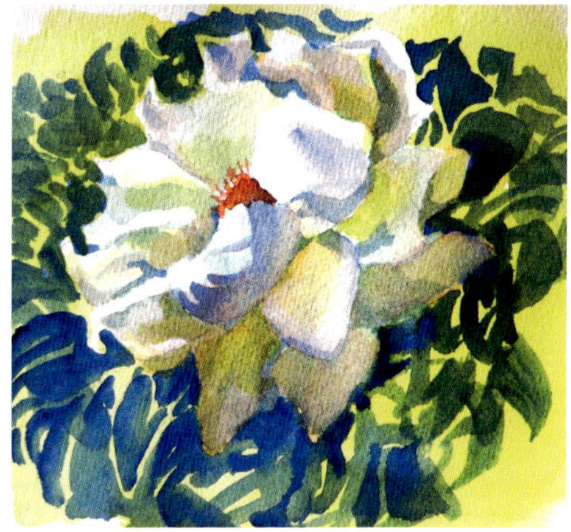

2 Glaze rose madder genuine onto parts of the rose. When influenced by the underlying blue and yellow, it becomes a transparent luminous neutral.

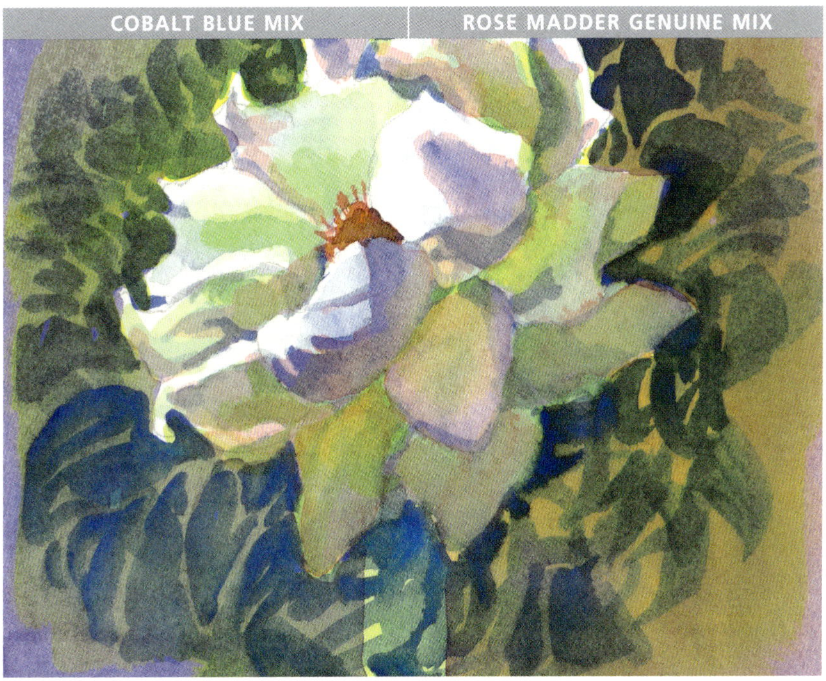

3 Use two glazes to subdue the frenetic background. Both are cobalt blue mixed with rose madder genuine, but the left side contains more blue, and the right contains more rose madder. Notice the pronounced effects. On the left side, the blue-violet subdues the yellow and makes it more green. On the right side, the rose madder neutralizes the greens and subdues and warms the yellow. Both glazes push the background back and allow the rose to glow.

SOME THINGS TO CONSIDER

- Transparent, nonstaining pigments can be very useful for fine-tuning a landscape painting—pushing back, pulling forward, color harmony, unity, etc.
- The quinacridone pigment family, composed of seven intense colors from deep yellow to vibrant violet, is transparent and bright. They are stainers, but they can be used beautifully as glazes if diluted. Use quinacridones when you want warm glazes.
- Use the luminous paints to create any color of glaze you desire. You can build up to mid-value or darker by drying between each glaze.
- The PrimaTek pigments are not considered transparent, but the binder between the granules of some granulating pigments allows a modified transparency. Consider the granulating PrimaTeks for unusual glazing possibilities.
- Avoid glazing with phthalo blue or green.
- Decide on your transparent pigments for glazing after researching and personal testing for lightfastness. Make your own transparency chart and pin it to your studio wall for handy reference.

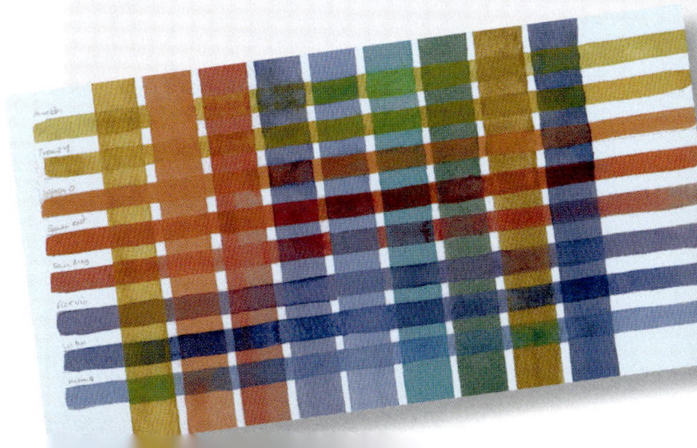

Permanent staining pigments

Stainers are strong, synthetic, organic, or inorganic pigments that have been ground to submicron particle size. These "warrior" pigments will adhere to just about anything, from your pristine white paper to plastics such as synthetic papers. Stainers can be intimidating until you know how to use them. Think of them as tigers. While they are wet, they are in their cub stage—easily lifted, washed down, and moved about. Once dry, they are fully grown and will defy any attempt to remove them. They also will show through later glazes with beauty and strength.

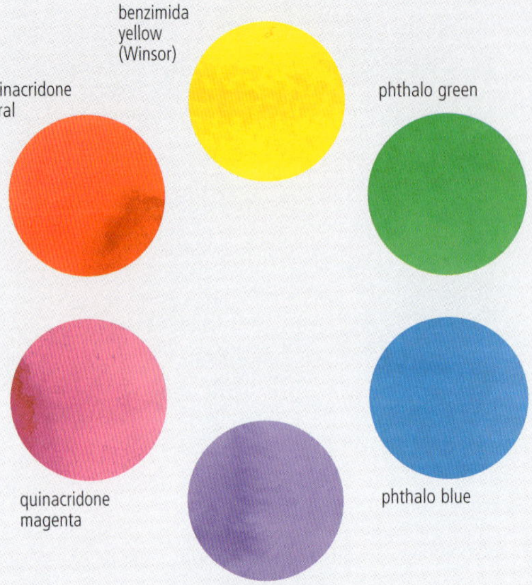

Other staining pigments
These pigments also work well as stainers:

quinacridone magenta
quinacridone sienna
quinacridone burnt scarlet
quinacridone gold deep
quinacridone rose
quinacridone violet
carbazole violet (dioxazine)
ultramarine turquoise
phthalo blue
nickel azo
cadmium orange
cadmium red light
azo yellow (aureolin)
ultramarine violet
opera (Holbein)
permanent lemon (yellow)
peacock blue
permanent violet
Permanent yellow lemon
Winsor orange
benzamida yellow (Winsor)
phthalo turquoise
Winsor violet (dioxazine)
green gold

CAN A STAINING PIGMENT BE LIFTED?

Any pigment can be lifted if you do a little planning before you paint. Use a tiny brush with stiff bristles. You can buy lifting brushes from art supply stores, but take care not to damage the paper when scrubbing.

Use an appropriate paper Some watercolor papers are more receptive to lifting. Because of sizing or other ingredients, brands like Fabriano appear to let go of the pigment particles more easily than other brands. Compare the bottom three paper samples.

Lift before it dries While the staining pigment is still wet you can easily lift it, no matter what the paper, as demonstrated in the top three paper samples.

Do a color swatch test If you want to learn more about your paint and paper liftability, try a color swatch test. Obtain samples of three or four different watercolor papers and test them. Compare the masked, lifted areas on the three papers shown below. The surface of the Lanaquarelle paper appears to break down before the Fabriano Artistico and Arches samples.

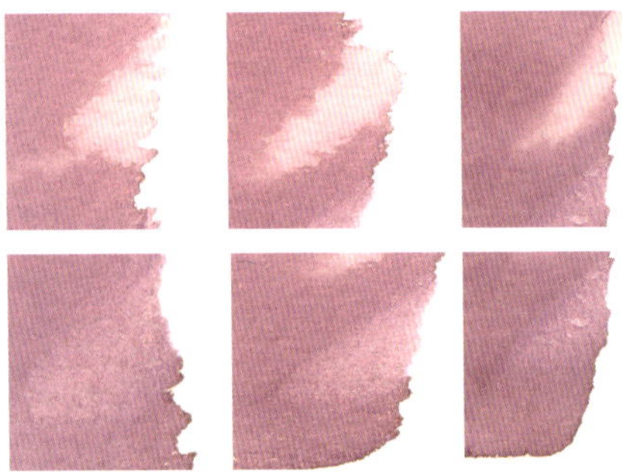

Arches CP Fabriano Artistico Lanaquarelle

AS A FIRST WASH

When you know you want a strong, dark value in a passage, use a staining pigment in your first wash. Stains love to be first! They disperse, flow, and can even be lifted if still wet. Once dry, they stay where you left them, will not move when you add subsequent washes, and can show through subsequent glazes and shifts in hue. The strong quinacridone magenta and phthalo blue go down well and continue to influence the later washes. They can also be mixed together to create an effective lavender wash (see page 23).

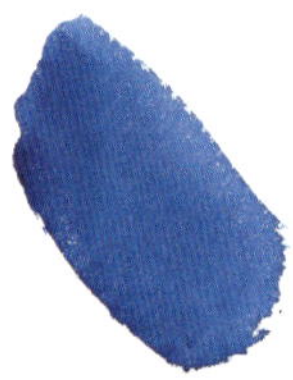

phthalo blue

quinacridone magenta

NEGATIVE CHARACTERISTICS

Stainers can be flat or overpowering. If stainers have been mixed strongly and then overworked or glazed over each other, they tend to lose their liveliness. Mix them only once and allow them to move into the wet paint on their own. If the passage looks flat and slightly muddy (top right), rewet with water and add dense, pure staining pigment directly onto the paper. Allow the paint to flow with just a nudge from your brush (below right).

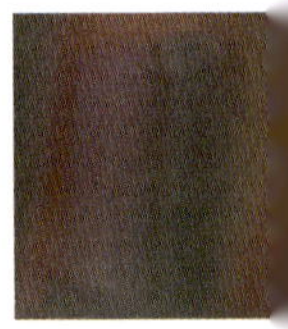

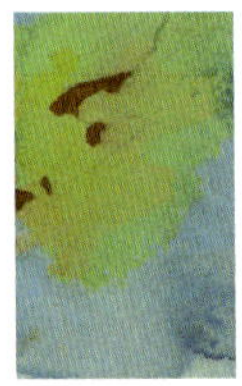

phthalo blue

Don't use them as a glaze A saturated staining pigment such as phthalo blue shouldn't be used as a glaze—it kills the undercolor.

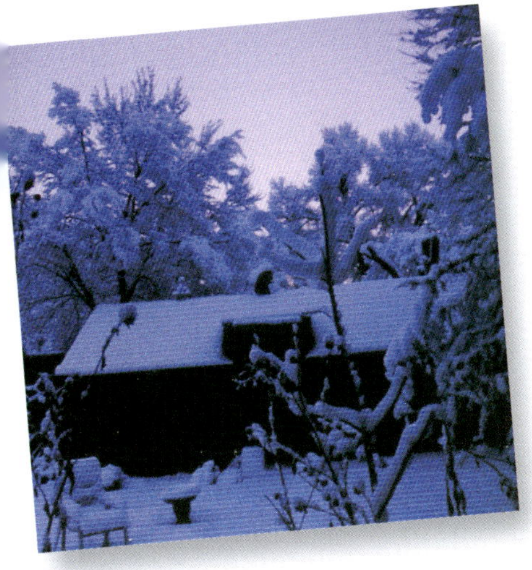

Snowy Morning The stainers make beautiful darks and can be used to build a low-key painting all on their own. This photograph was taken early in the morning. Notice how the values appear to change in relation to each other as the painting progresses. In step 3 when the darkest darks are painted in, the snow-covered roof appears lighter than in the previous step—yet it has not been touched.

1 Begin with quinacridone magenta. A graded wash establishes the early morning sky and provides a subtle underwash for the rest of the painting.

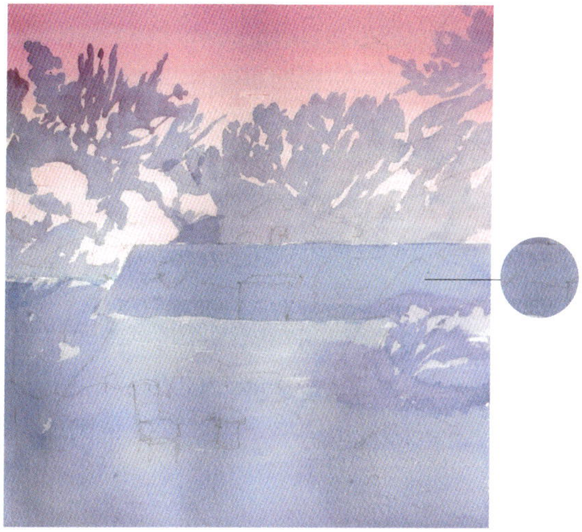

2 Mix phthalo blue with quinacridone magenta and water to create a cool lavender wash. Apply this wash several times in varying places, allowing each layer to dry between applications.

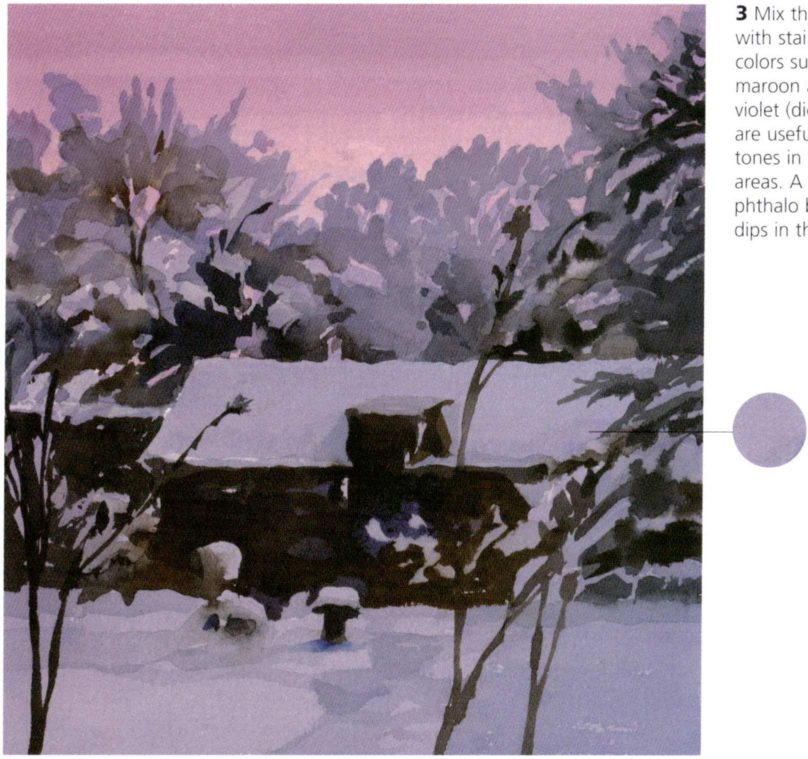

3 Mix the darkest darks with staining analogous colors such as perylene maroon and carbazole violet (dioxazine), which are useful for warmer tones in the darkest areas. A pale wash of phthalo blue accents the dips in the snow.

SOME THINGS TO CONSIDER

- Whether a pigment stains depends on the pigment manufacturing, the paper it is painted on, and even individual paints. Testing is the best way to find out. Some manufacturers produce staining pigments that are more liftable. Old Holland, Rembrandt, and Holbein pigments tend to stay on top of the paper longer, giving you more time for lifting. Daniel Smith, M. Graham, Winsor and Newton, and MaimeriBlu pigments tend to stain more aggressively.
- As you build up a painting from light to dark, be patient and wait until you have your darkest darks in before you evaluate your lightest lights.
- You can use a stain in a small area to provide a strong finishing dark. Staining pigments, because of their ability to disperse, make effective tucks in corners, as shown in the eyes of these parrots.

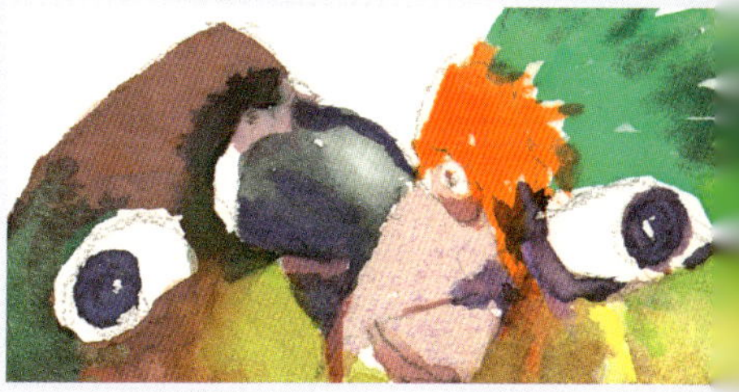

Sedimentary and opaque paints

Watercolor paints that contain sediment, exhibit granularity, separate out, move, drop, or shoot are called "sedimentary" or "opaque." While other paints lay down a foundation or provide a finishing shift in hue, sedimentary and opaque paints add textures, create the nuances of a rock surface, establish an illusion of leaves and twigs, or soften harsh passages. These "workhorse" pigments create excitement beyond color! Cobalt violet, for example, despite its weak, gummy demeanor, can sparkle to life when added directly into a duller mix. And, although reputed to be transparent, some cobalt blues are slightly sedimentary and will dive for the paper if introduced into a wet wash.

WHAT CAUSES SEDIMENTATION AND OPACITY?

Watercolors are made from ground pigment particles. A highly transparent pigment allows light to pass through widely spaced, small particles, bounce off the white paper surface, and reflect back to the eye. A sedimentary pigment has larger particles and may also have a specific gravity (weight) that makes the particles heavier than water. The effect is something like looking through large drops of rain during a storm. The space around the drops of water allows some visibility. An opaque watercolor pigment contains very small, densely packed particles that allow little space for light refraction.

A sedimentary palette (you can substitute some colors with other properties if you wish)

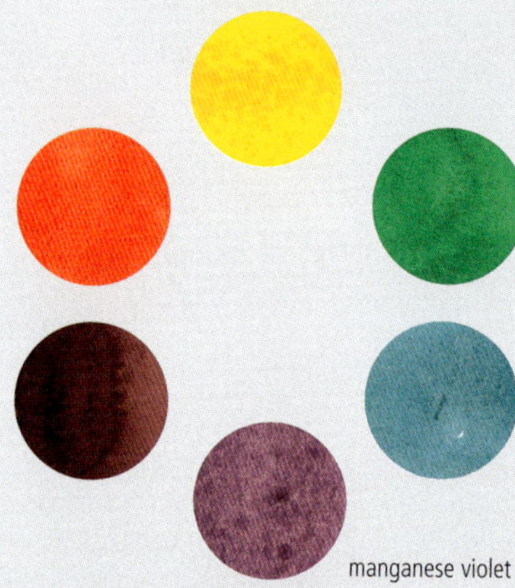

Pigments don't always fit neatly into either sedimentary or opaque, so this suggested palette has examples of both.

SEDIMENTARY WATERCOLOR PAINTS

Cobalts This group ranges from pure transparents to sedimentary pigments, with some beautiful examples of granulation and flocculation.

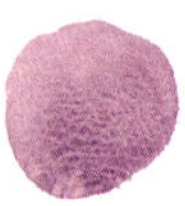

cobalt violet A favorite paint. Notice the beautiful granulation and flocculation.

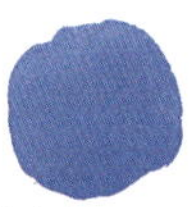

cobalt blue Some slight granulation is visible.

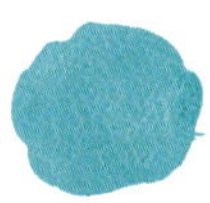

cobalt turquoise light Beautiful, sedimented.

cobalt teal Opaque if used strongly.

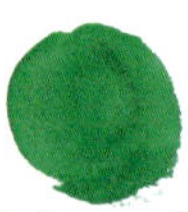

cobalt green Make sure you choose the pigment code PG 50. Some versions are a mix of other pigments.

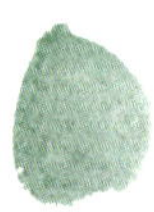

cobalt green pale

Sedimentary pigments The group of pigments listed below offers some powerful choices.

burnt umber

ultramarine blue

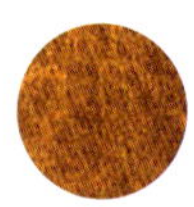

raw sienna

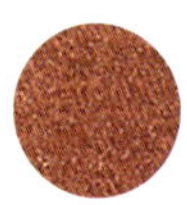

Potter's pink

cobalt turquoise

Mars brown

Lunar Series (*Daniel Smith*) This group of sedimentary colors forms reticulated patterns resembling the moon surface. Lunar black, lunar violet, lunar earth, and lunar blue all contain iron oxide black (also referred to as Mars black). Its magnetized iron particles produce etched granulation.

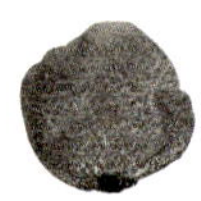

lunar black: Mars black Both granulation and flocculation can be seen in the reticulated patterns.

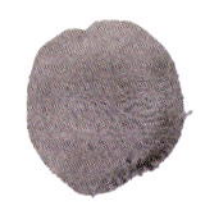

lunar violet: ultramarine violet and Mars black Mars black with ultramarine added.

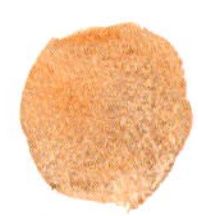

lunar earth: magnesium ferrite and Mars black A versatile pigment as an additive to other paints and as a textured earth color.

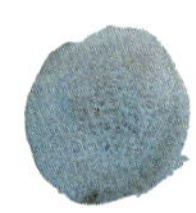

lunar blue: phthalo blue and Mars black Mars black with phthalo blue added; note evidence of some flocculation.

THE GOUACHE–WATERCOLOR CONTROVERSY

The line between gouache and transparent watercolor is sometimes blurry—in terms of usage as well as definition. Both contain the same basic ingredients, but the addition of opaque white gives gouache, or body color, its characteristic opacity. Before 1832, watercolor painting involved applying layers of transparent washes, with the paper itself reserved for the lights. Then Henry Newton and William Winsor introduced a dense zinc white, that they sold as Chinese white. This opaque paint made it possible for the English School of Watercolor to emulate and compete with oil painting. Watercolor purists, however, still reserve the white of the paper.

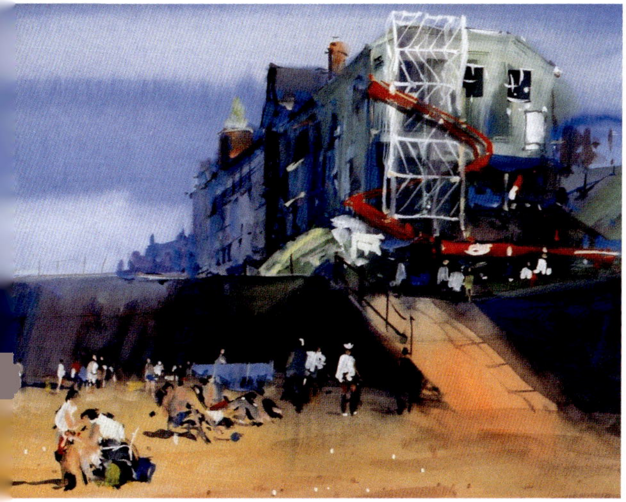

Is white watercolor really gouache? Nearly every manufacturer includes Chinese white in the transparent watercolor inventory and zinc or permanent white in the gouache inventory. It is probably safest to say that gouache is an opaque watercolor and that it differs from traditional watercolor in the following important ways:

- Gouache is thicker than watercolor. Adding more layers of gouache does not change the color.
- Gouache colors are lightened by adding white pigment instead of water.
- Gouache paints are not applied in glazes or layers.
- Gouache paints are not absorbed into the paper, remaining on the surface in a thick layer.
- Gouache paints create flat color areas more easily than watercolors.
- Gouache can be used like oil paints to apply lighter colors over dark.

Cromer Beach
Alan Oliver added the details and highlights with opaque white used raw or mixed to create a variety of body colors.

OPACITY TEST

Try doing an opacity test on your own choice of pigments. Sedimentaries provide texture, so use them as a base or in a mix. If they contain large pigment granules or if they flocculate, use them for a textured glaze. Use opaque pigments in flat colors or in mixes with other pigments where you desire opacity.

Make a vertical stripe of a staining pigment, such as carbazole violet (dioxazine). When dry, brush over several sedimentary and opaque paints. Allow to dry. You can see the strong opaques—cadmium orange, buff titanium, titanium white, Venetian red, and cerulean blue—and the delicate sedimentaries—zoisite genuine, cobalt violet, lunar black, lunar earth, and maybe even Chinese white.

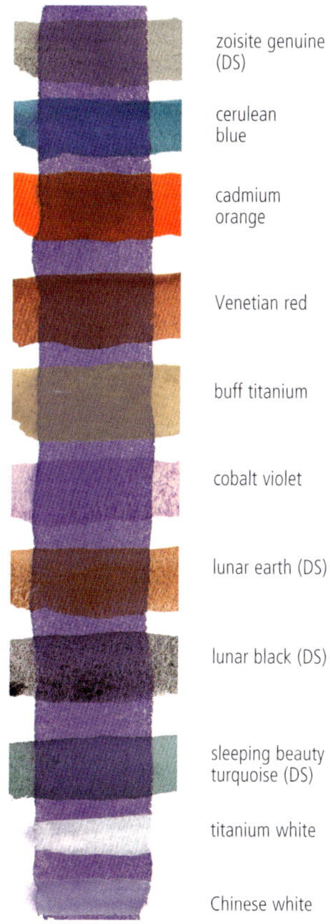

OPAQUE WATERCOLOR PAINTS

Earth pigments These pigments are all variations of iron oxides. Most are opaque or finely granulated. They include burnt sienna, raw sienna, yellow ochre, raw umber, burnt umber, Venetian red, and lunar red rock. The earth pigments can provide a soft background for small touches of intense color. They are easy to wet, rewet, and use to create easy color harmonies. Note the very subtle granulation in the samples shown below.

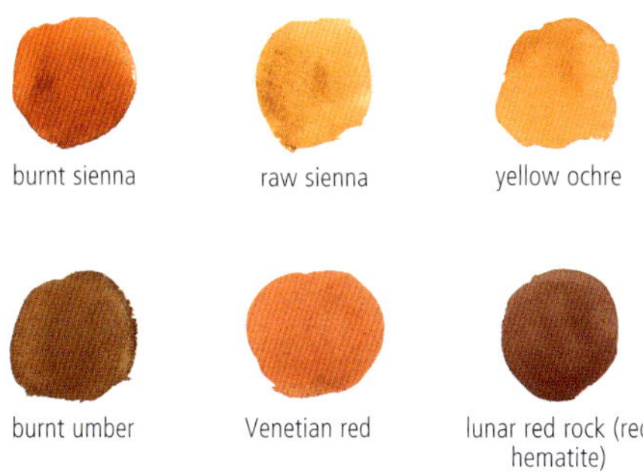

Other opaque paints Chromiums and cadmiums are all opaque.

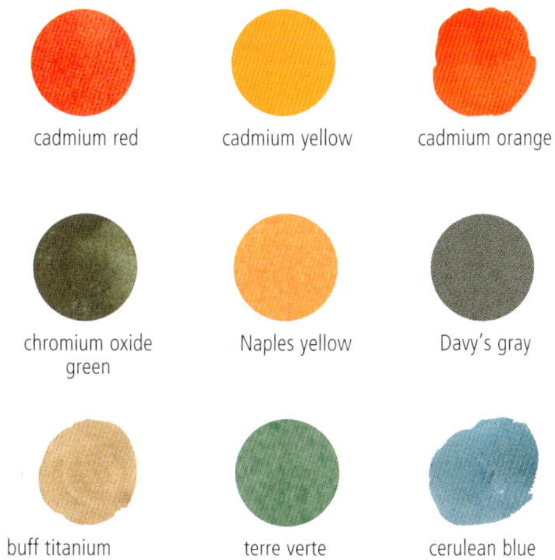

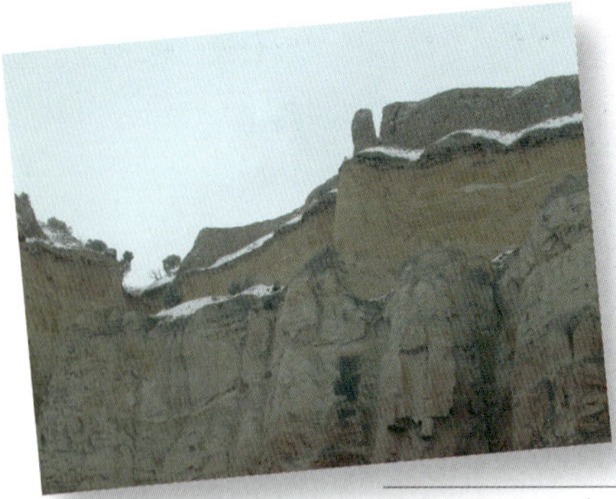

Canyon Snowfall Opaque and sedimentary pigments are perfect for an overcast, snow-covered cliff.

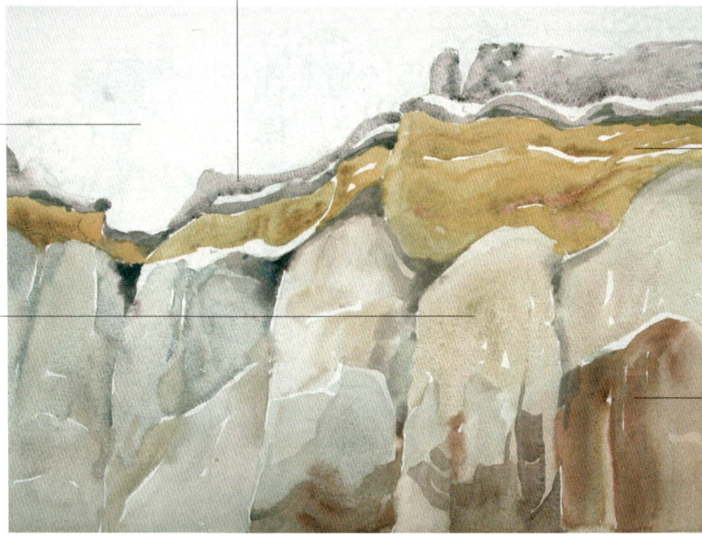

Gypsum top In the photograph this is a dense, crumbly gray. Because the yellow sandstone below can provide a dominant hue, the artist decided to "see" the gypsum above as complementary purple-lavender "gray." A look through the PrimaTeks (for granulation) yields purpurite. Hematite and lunar black add interest and dull the strong purple. Applying clear water first in a few places at the top helps lose some edges to the sky. Without mixing too thoroughly, neutralized purple is painted around the white snow shapes.

Underpaint A mix of sedimentary manganese blue, cobalt turquoise, and cerulean blue is used to underpaint, creating some delicate granulation in the sky and a base for the rest of the painting.

White pillar tops Buff titanium is used as a base, adding some cerulean blue and purpurite to push the neutral slightly toward blue and lavender. Care is taken to create a few sharp ledges and crevices.

Yellow sandstone Soft, textured sandstone cries out for opaque color. A buff titanium base with quinacridone gold and sedimentary goethite works well with horizontal brushwork. The earth pigments could work as well. Again, some cobalt violet is dashed in for fun!

Red sandstone base A mix of cerulean blue, Venetian red, and hemetite seemed just right. Look at the beautiful granulation and the sharp-edged strokes.

AVOIDING MUDDY MIXES

The lifeless noncolors that artists call "mud" are usually the result of improper mixing. Sedimentary colors are more prone to turning into a dull muddy mix, so take care! To avoid making mud, you first need to understand what is not mud.

- Brown color in a pigment isn't mud; you can see life in the pigments below.

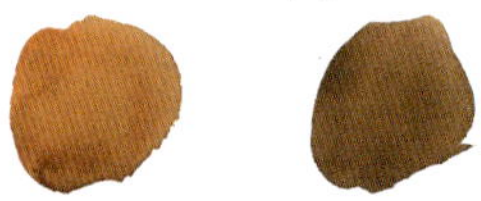

burnt sienna — burnt umber

- When you mix two complementary colors such as cobalt blue and quinacridone sienna together, allow one of the paints to dominate.

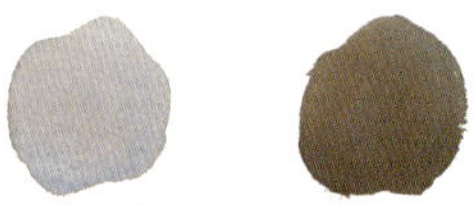

more cobalt blue than quinacridone sienna — more quinacridone sienna than cobalt blue

- Avoid mixing three primaries together unless they are transparent and luminous, as opaque and staining pigments are more difficult to handle. Compare the luminous mix at right with the mix below. Below, the paints are applied in a layer and then overmixed, creating dull mud in places.

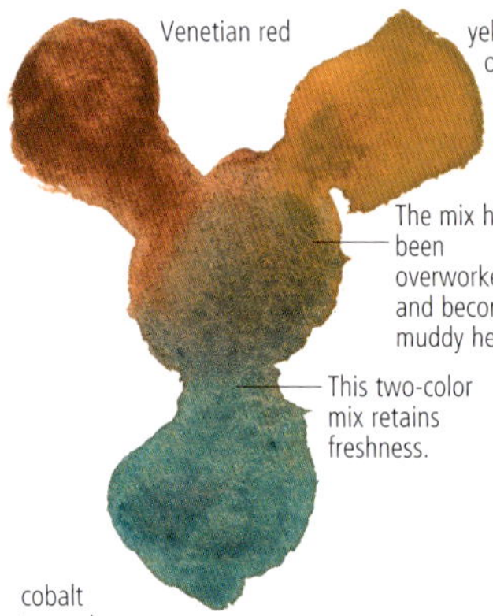

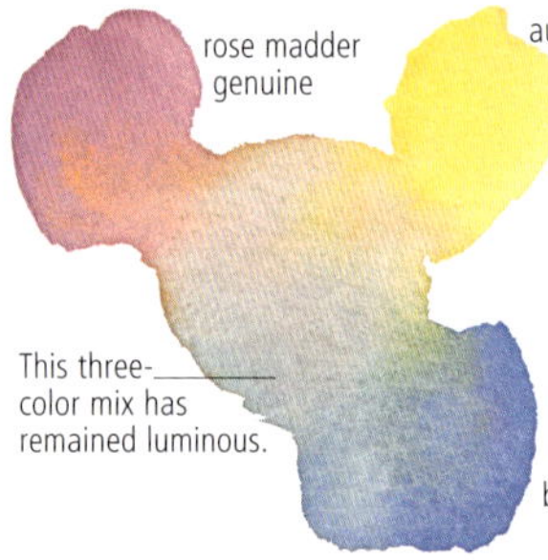

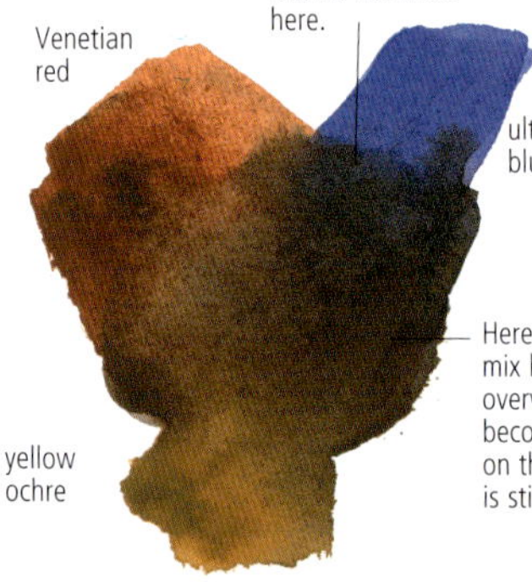

- Avoid mixing more than two opaque/sedimentary colors together. Here two opaque/sedimentary colors are allowed to mix. The cobalt blue settles beneath the burnt sienna, creating a soft neutral mix that is not muddy.

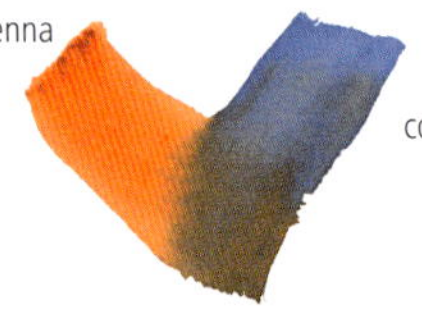

- When three paints (see below right) are allowed to mix, it creates a more lively neutral than the overbrushed mix (see below left).

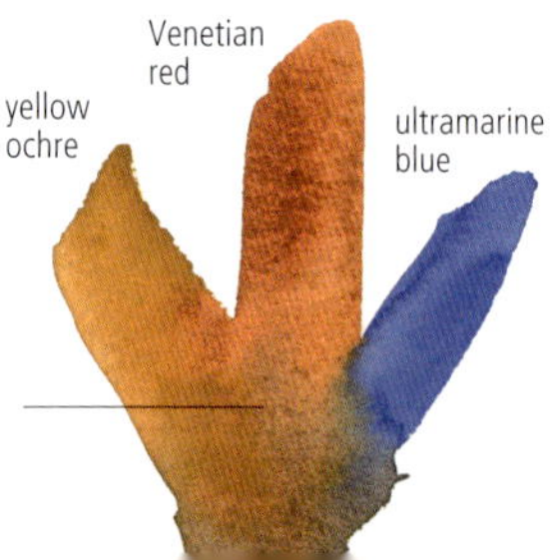

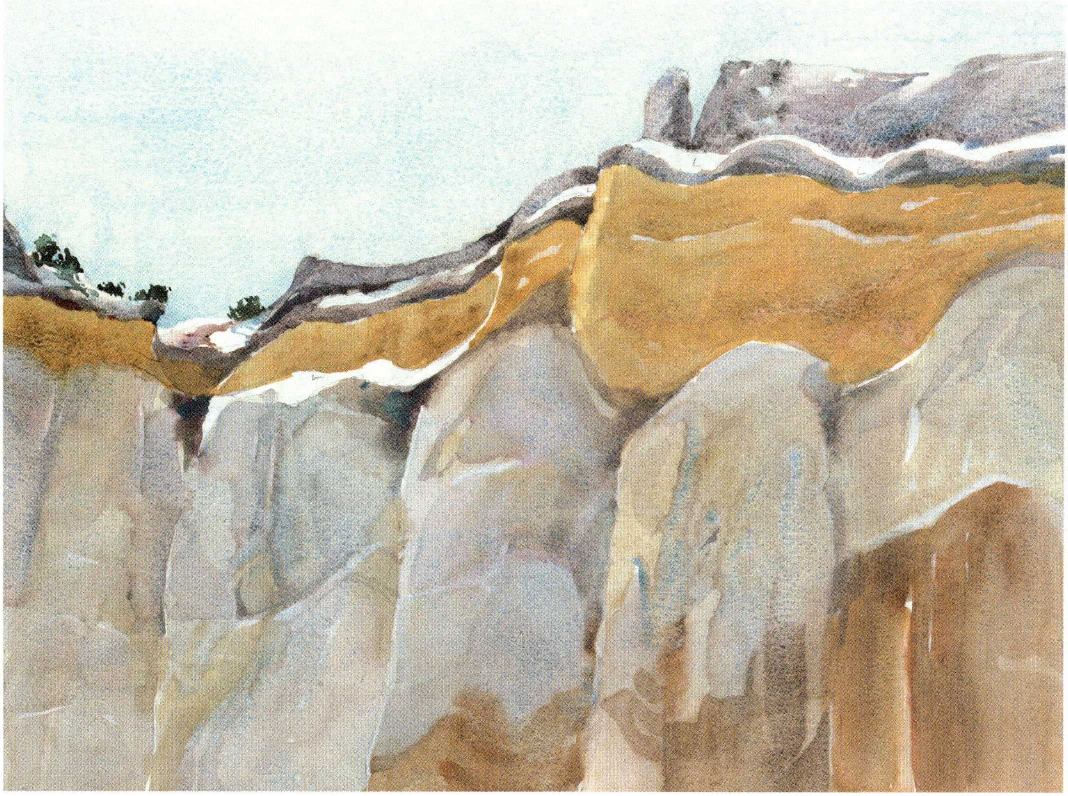

Finishing glazes The sky can be repainted to expose the snowcap, and another glaze of a sedimentary painted over the rocks may soften some edges and add more granulation. The artist added manganese blue to the sky and glazed everything else but the snow with manganese blue and rose madder genuine mix. (Just add some tree details—and it feels done.) One tuck in the lowest spot in the sky creates the snowcap! Look closely at the lovely manganese blue sedimentation in the glaze.

Play sheet A "play sheet" can help the artist to discover the things a pigment can do in addition to its color. Some pigments push others aside; some drop into a wash. The play sheet below was done to find out what some sedimentary/opaque pigments would do in a wet wash. Using clear, transparent pigments and a dancing brushstroke, various shapes were applied directly to the paper. Sedimentary/opaque pigments were dropped in one by one to study their actions.

SOME THINGS TO CONSIDER

- Sedimentary and opaque paints can provide wonderful textures and effects that are difficult to attain with smooth paint and brushes alone.
- Use sedimentary and opaque pigments when you want to paint richly—once. Let them dry completely. If you mix too much on the paper, you will interfere with the granulation process—and risk stirring up mud.
- Avoid mixing more than two opaque pigments together.
- If you add sedimentary or opaque pigments to an already wet wash and let them mix, you will never create mud. The pigments will mix according to their relative weights and settle out separately.
- You can safely mix a sedimentary/opaque paint with a staining or luminous transparent paint.
- Avoid sedimentary/opaque paints that contain more than one pigment.
- Take care when applying a glaze or layer to an already dry mixed wash. Try lightly covering the already painted area with a layer of water, then dropping in the subsequent color.
- Continued brushstrokes, if applied heavily, can stir up the paints beneath, creating mud.

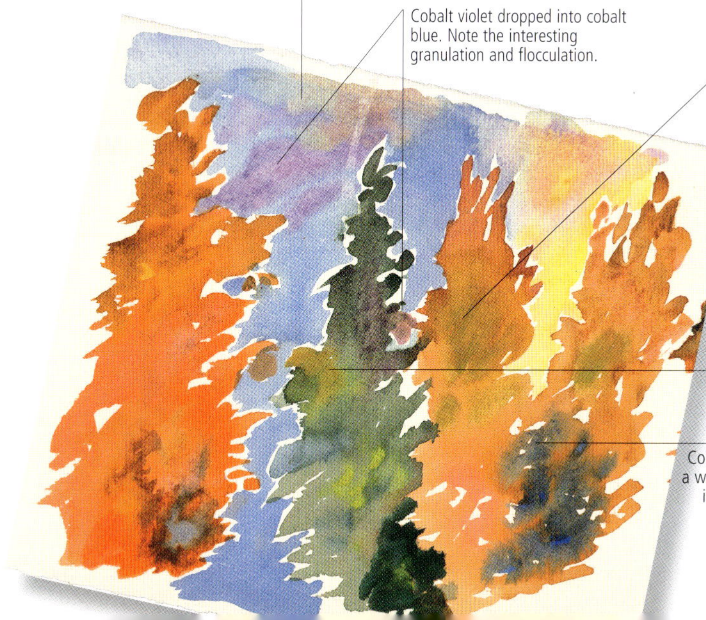

Buff titanium added into cobalt blue and cobalt violet. It tends to move other pigments aside.

Cobalt violet dropped into cobalt blue. Note the interesting granulation and flocculation.

Green gold and nickel azo shoot into the quinacridone burnt scarlet, softly infiltrating the scarlet.

Aureolin yellow dropped into green. It dives for the paper.

Cobalt blue dropped into a wet wash of scarlet and into some white areas.

Granulation

If a pigment mixed into water separates into tiny particles, it is called a "granulating" or "sedimentary" pigment. Granulation is a natural property of some denser pigments, such as ultramarine blue and cobalt violet. Granulating colors are usually composed of one or more inorganic pigments that contain metal. The pigment drops out of the binder/water solution and settles into the valleys of textured watercolor paper. A cold-pressed or rough watercolor paper works best, although some pigments also will granulate on smooth paper.

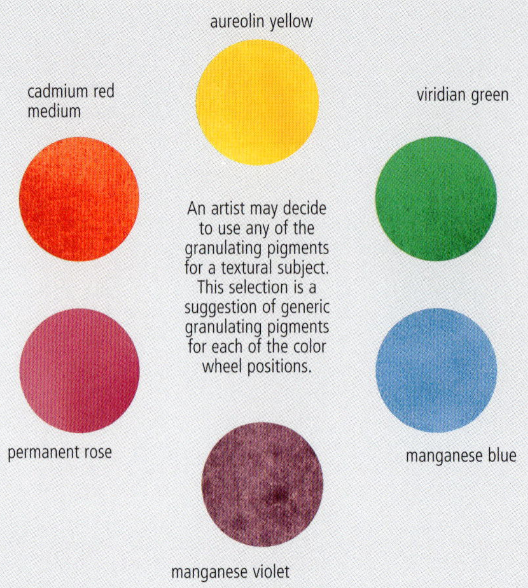

An artist may decide to use any of the granulating pigments for a textural subject. This selection is a suggestion of generic granulating pigments for each of the color wheel positions.

FLOCCULATION

Flocculation is a term used to describe a kind of granulation in which the particles stick together, or clumps, to create flakes or spots of pigment color. Usually this is because the particles have electrical attractions to each other. Ultramarine blue illustrates this ability to form flakes or to flocculate.

ultramarine blue

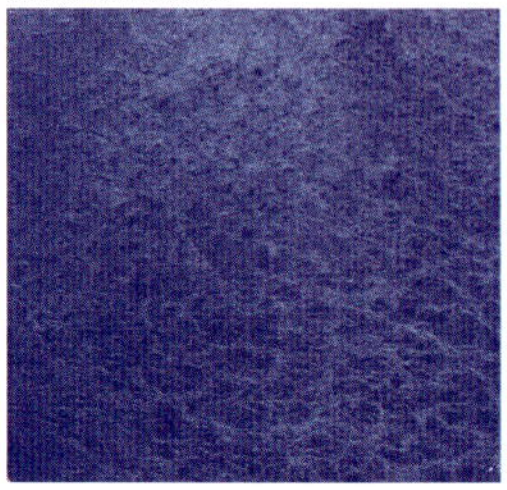

HOW TO USE A GRANULATING COLOR

- A granulating color is useful as a flat wash for textured or mottled subjects. Remember that the way a pigment behaves depends upon the brand of paint. Each manufacturer uses different recipes, so pigments with the same names may behave quite differently.
- A granulating pigment can be used as a glaze if it is transparent enough to allow the underlying paint to show through.

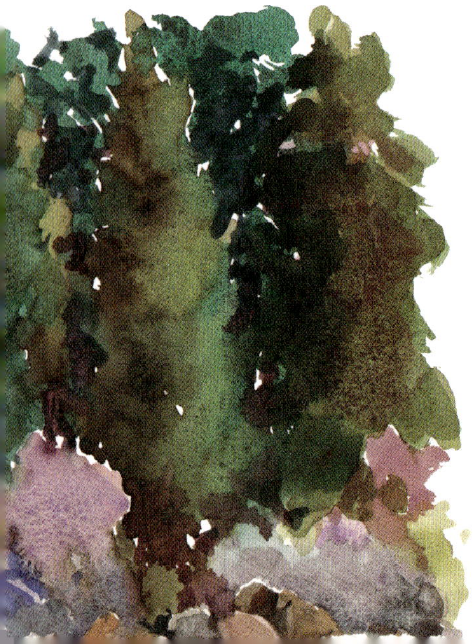

Cobalt violet has been glazed over the tree on the right and some of the foreground for added texture and interest.

INCREASING GRANULATION

Use textured paper The amount of granulation you can expect to see varies according to the texture of the paper, the amount of water used, and the pigment. Although some pigments granulate on smooth, hot-pressed paper, the effect is increased if you use textured paper, as shown in the examples below. The effect of textured paper is most apparent with smooth pigments such as cobalt blue.

Use distilled water The lack of electrically charged ions allows metal particles in the pigments to fall out of the solution more easily. Compare the cobalt blue and lunar black distilled water samples with the control samples. The use of distilled water slightly increases the granulation.

Add granulation medium A granulation medium gives a mottled appearance to non granulating paints, or it further enhances natural granulating effects. Compare the cobalt blue granulating medium sample with the distilled water sample. Mixing granulation medium instead of water with the paint creates strongly noticeable granulation and flocculation.

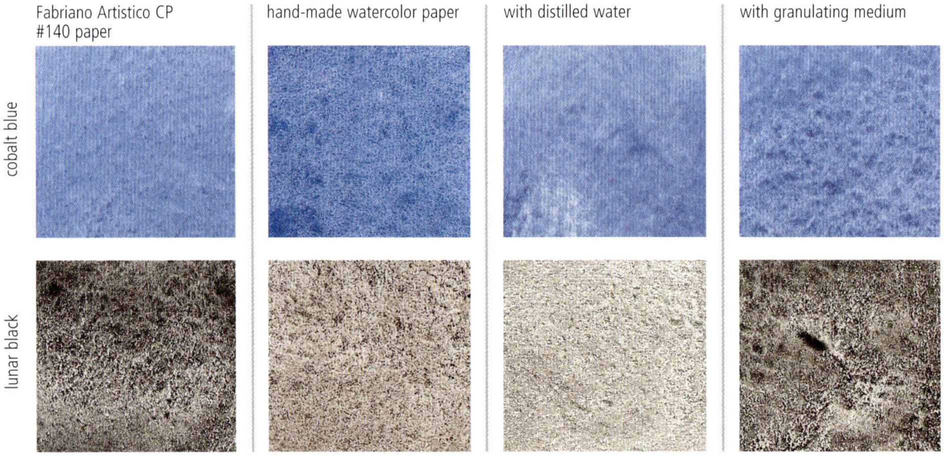

WHEN TO USE GRANULATING PIGMENTS

You can use granulating pigments whenever you want to depict or express a textural surface. These three examples show how effective granulation can be for a mottled, textured subject; granular rock and earth surfaces; and storm clouds. But you can also consider using granulation for abstract paintings utilizing textural qualities, adobe or stucco buildings, wood, vegetation, and shadows cast over a textured surface.

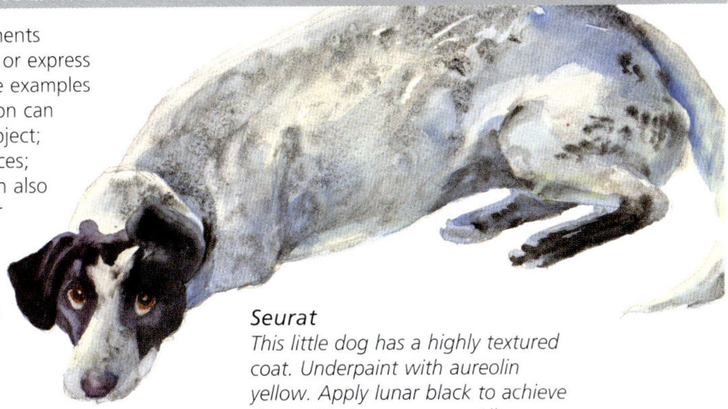

Seurat

This little dog has a highly textured coat. Underpaint with aureolin yellow. Apply lunar black to achieve the mottled appearance. Allow some areas to granulate freely by adding water. On other areas, like the rump, apply lunar black with the tip of a round brush and allow to settle into the wash. Glaze cobalt blue over the dry lunar black. Lay down a first wash of cobalt blue on the black head areas, and then mix with lunar black.

Chinle Badlands

The Chinle Badlands are an arid area with clay-rich soil that has been eroded by wind and water, resulting in beautifully colored striations. Allow the granulating pigments to spread and diffuse, wet-into-wet. When dry, add a glaze of cobalt violet mixed with rhodonite or azurite. Suggest erosion channels by dampening the trail and adding an touch of napthamide maroon along one edge. Paint the sky upside down, starting with a layer of aureolin yellow. Follow immediately with successively darker layers of cobalt blue.

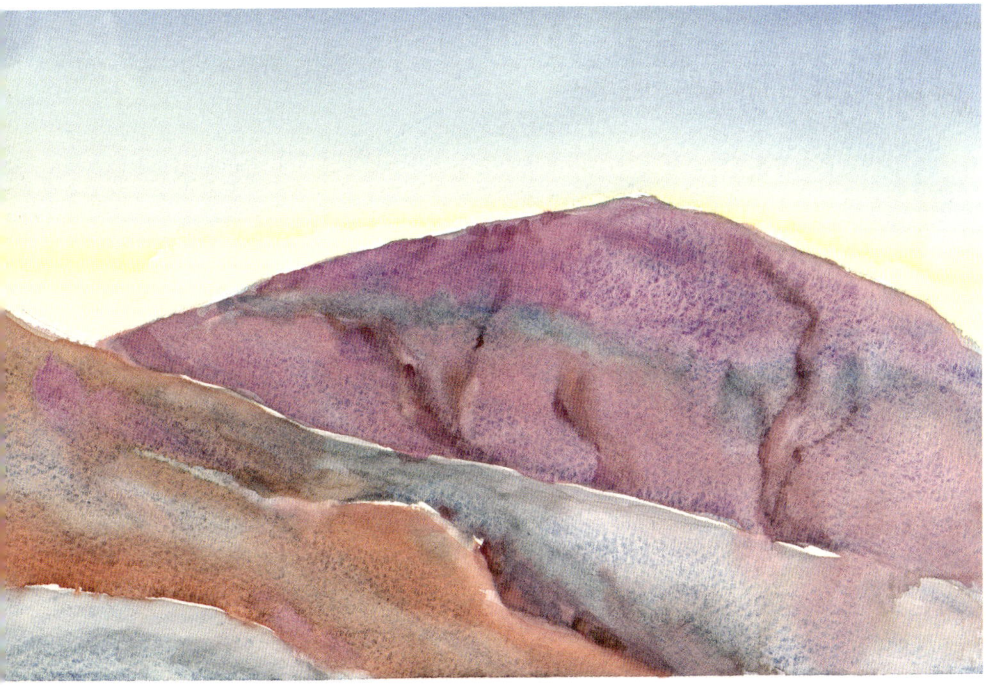

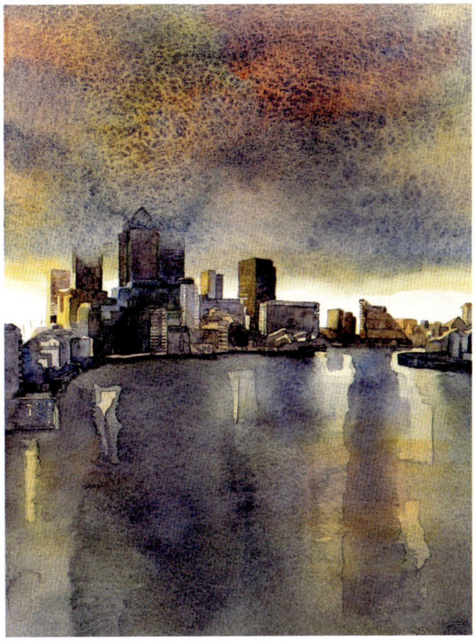

Stormy Sky

The artist used granulating ultramarine blue and moonglow (DS) to capture the gritty, leaden sky. Warm undertones were created by washes of new gamboge and quinacridone red (allowed to dry), followed by an ultramarine blue wash with moonglow dropped in wet into wet.

SOME THINGS TO CONSIDER

- There are so many subjects in the landscape that warrant texture but not detail, making them ideal for granulation: vegetation, earth, rocks, distant mountains.
- The granulating pigments teach the artist about letting go. Add them to a wet wash and watch. Do not touch them again until they are dry.
- Granulating and flocculating pigments create some beautiful patterns in a wash, but they will be destroyed if you mix them too much on the paper.

Wet-into-wet pigment actions

The gentle flows and complex effects that result when paint is applied to wet paper or into a wet wash on the paper are unique to watercolor. No other medium flows so freely in water or reacts with such originality to create back runs, pigment granulations, diffusion, and color mixing. J.M.W. Turner brought wet-into-wet techniques to the public's attention in the early 1800s. His vibrant representations of sunsets, mists, and water reflections expanded artists' understanding of wet-into-wet, diffuse color mixes. Many modern watercolor artists have also discovered the joy of using wet techniques and the compelling action of watching the process.

Diffusion Any concentration of paint diffuses well into pure water, and a thicker concentration of paint will diffuse into a thinner concentration. Use diffusion to tuck, or darken, a corner or soft shadow area. First wet the corner; then drop in a denser paint and allow it to diffuse out. The synthetic, inorganic pigments with small, light pigment particles work best to achieve an even diffusion. Use diffusion on soft flower-petal edges. For example, add quinacridone magenta just outside the wet area and allow it to diffuse by gently linking it into the wet area. Using the same method you also can gently fuse two colors, such as ultramarine violet and aureolin yellow, together.

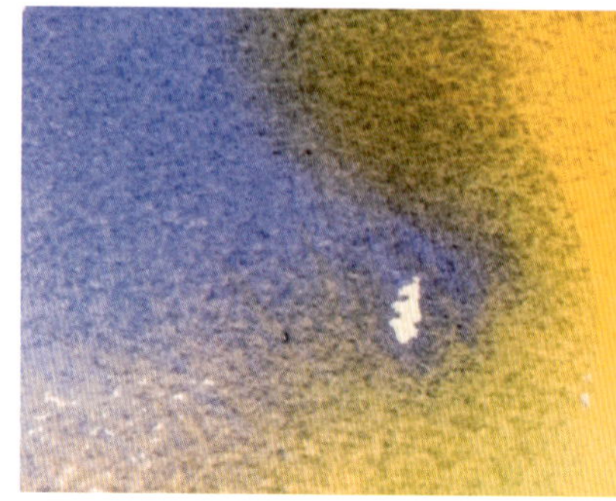

WHY PAINT WET-INTO-WET?

Learning Wet-into-wet processes teach more than technique. Give up control and allow the paint to suggest new directions—in the process, you will get to know individual pigments. The range of effects shown here seem similar but will give subtle differences.
Creativity Painting with water can be both exciting and terrifying. With each painting, you will work through the fear into the creative.
Great beginnings Starting a painting wet-into-wet is pure excitement and adrenaline! After the planning and sketching, charge into the painting with the trust that anything in the pigment play can be modified later, if needed. Taking the risk of sloshing deep magenta into the field of green and then dropping in some nickel azo to see it shoot, can open the door to exciting work!
Integrity A painting shows integrity when it demonstrates the characteristics of the medium used to paint it. The fresh, expressive brushstrokes of a wet-into-wet painting exemplify the watercolor medium.

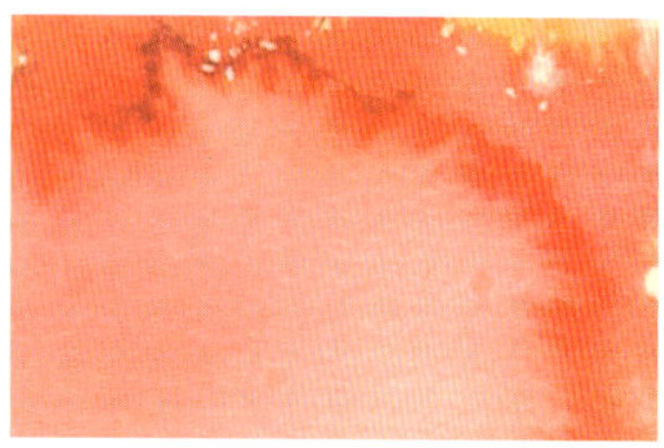

Back runs A back run appears when a too-wet area runs back into a drying area, carrying pigment along its edges. Called "blossoms," "blooms," or "oozles," the back run moves in the opposite direction from diffusion. On a tilted surface painted with a uniform wash, an edge of water forms at the bottom. If allowed to stay there while the rest is drying, a back run will move into the drying area. Intentional back runs can be effective in floral paintings.
Flow patterns Gravity flow moves the granulating or flocculating pigments from a high to a low area on the paper's surface, creating a flow pattern in the wash. It also can occur on a flat surface when you add water into a granulated wash; the water will move to the denser area to equalize the pigment to water ratio.

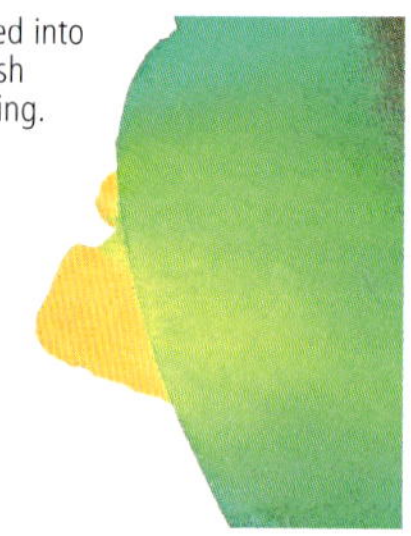

Nickel azo introduced into a phthalo green wash demonstrates shooting.

Shooting Shooting is a rapid form of diffusion. It often is caused by the wetting agent, or dispersant, added to a pigment by the manufacturer to prevent it from clumping in storage. The most apparent examples are nickel azo and green gold, which contains nickel azo. Some artists believe that nickel azo is difficult to mix with other paints, but it really depends on how you do it.
Granulation and separation of pigments Some pigments granulate or flocculate in a wet wash. (See "Granulation," page 28.) Some paints containing two different pigments separate out in a wash. The heavier pigments drop to the paper while the lighter pigments stay near the top.

strong weak

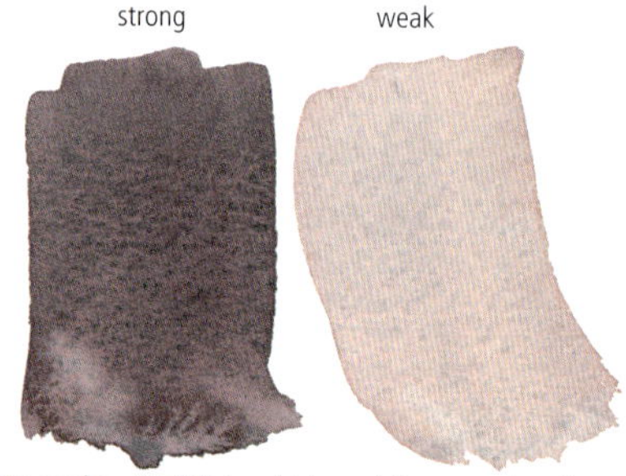

Moonglow (DS) This paint is a subtle separation of pigments: viridian green, ultramarine blue, and anthraquinoid red.

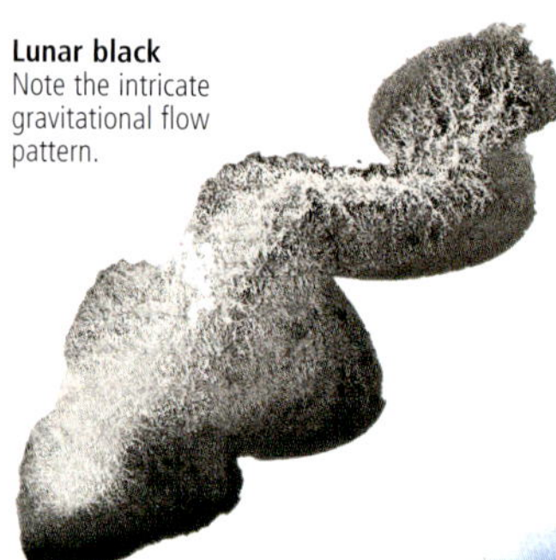

Lunar black
Note the intricate gravitational flow pattern.

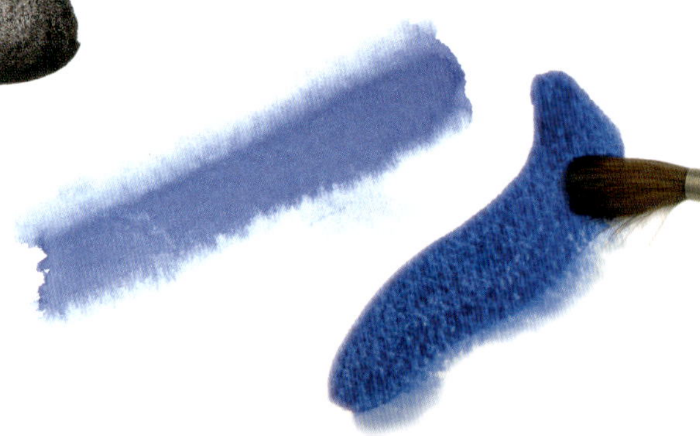

Ultramarine blue
Water added into the wash creates feathers.

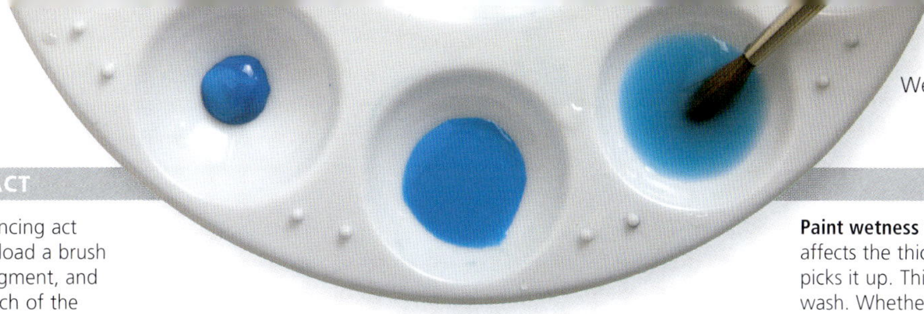

A BALANCING ACT

There is an intricate balancing act going on each time you load a brush with water, dip it into pigment, and apply it to wet paper. Each of the three has an important role to play in the process.

Paper wetness When paper is thoroughly wet, it is shiny. As the water begins to evaporate, the surface takes on a satin appearance. You can safely use the wet-into-wet technique with shiny or satin surfaces. If you cannot see either type of surface, test the paper with the back of your fingers, (your fingertips may transfer oil to the paper, acting as a resist). If the paper feels cool, it is still damp, but most likely not damp enough. For best results, wait until the paper is dry; then rewet.

Brush wetness If the brush is wetter than the paper, it dilutes the receiving wash. This creates a darkened edge or a back run. If the brush is dryer than the paper, the introduced pigment tends to stay where you put it with softened edges.

Paint wetness The wetness of the paint in the palette affects the thickness of the paint and how the brush picks it up. Thicker paints will diffuse into a thinner wash. Whether you use fresh paint each time you paint or rewet your dry palette paint, develop an awareness of what works for you.

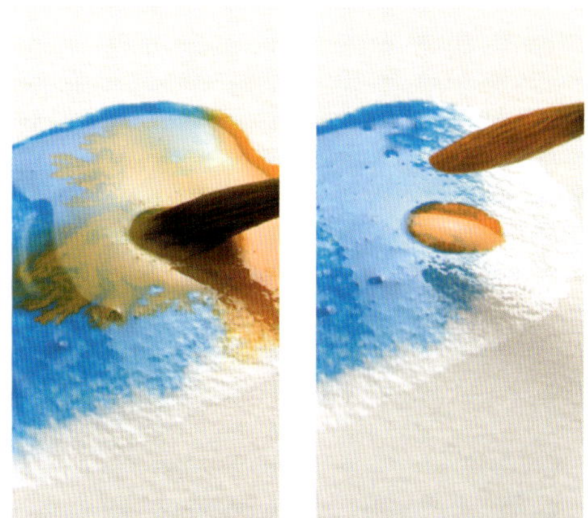

DROPPING IN

Drop a color into a wet area and allow it to react as its nature determines. You can brush or dab the paint in. It may diffuse, feather, bleed, creep, drop, or shoot, depending on the introduced pigment and the density of the receiving wash. In these examples, carbazole violet (dioxazine), a concentrated, dark organic pigment, receives inorganic and organic pigments very differently.

Heavy pigments—synthetic inorganics
The heavy pigments drop into the wash, often leaving a strong-edged "footprint."

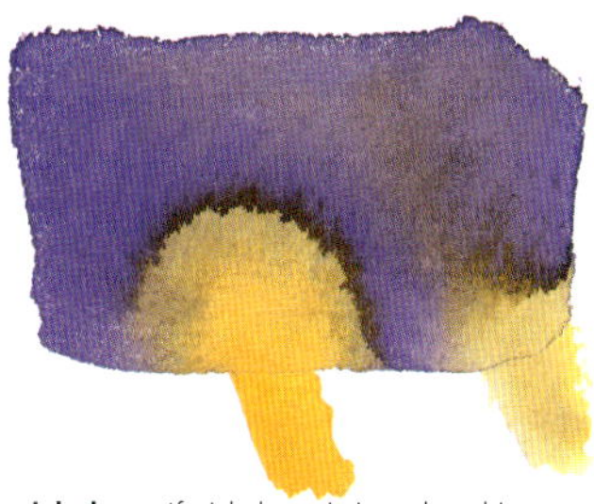

nickel azo If nickel azo is introduced into a lighter-weight wash, it shoots wildly. (See page 30.) If the receiving wash is not wet enough, it drops to the paper.

cobalt violet This beautifully granulating pigment dives for the paper.

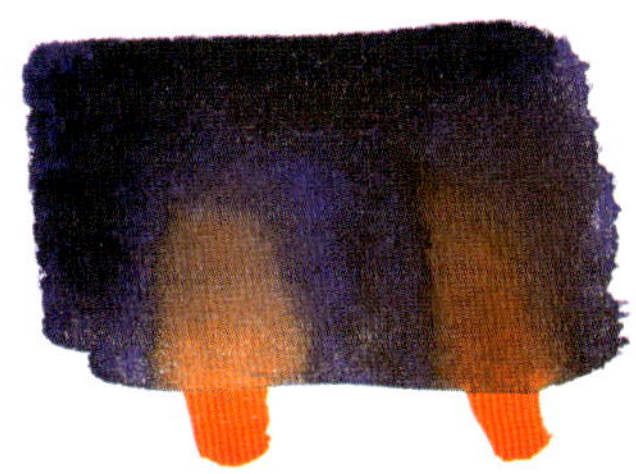

cadmium orange See how this heavy pigment dives in and spreads out into the lower layers of the wash, altering the color.

Light pigments—synthetic organics
These pigments mix into the wash, resulting in soft or feathery "footprints."

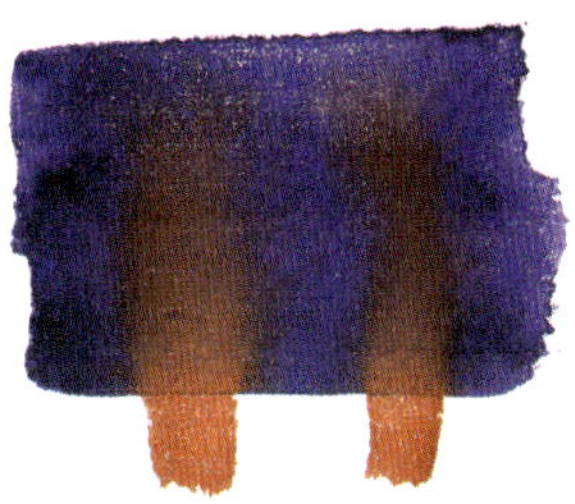

perylene maroon This beautiful pigment appears to fuse with the wash it enters.

ultramarine blue Just look at this ghostly soft infiltration.

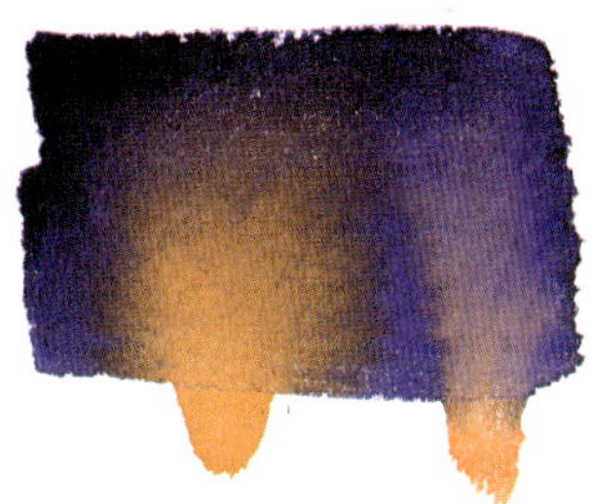

quinacridone gold Displays a feathery edge in the carbazole wash.

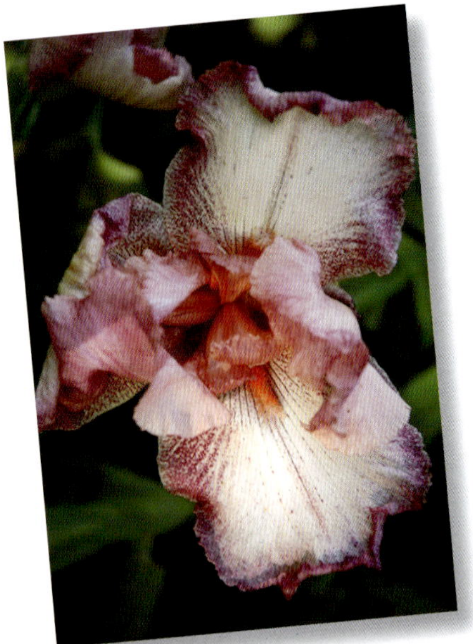

WORKING WET INTO WET: IRIS FLAME

The softly feathered coloration at its petal tips makes this beautiful iris an ideal subject to be painted in sections, wet into wet. This petal-by-petal method allows you plenty of time to play and experiment. Because you are painting only in a prewet area, the wet-into-wet process is kept somewhat under control.

Painting the flower Working petal by petal, prewet with water or a diluted wash before adding the colors. Select pigments for color and action: cobalt violet for mottled petal work; quinacridone magenta, carbazole violet (dioxazine), and ultramarine blue for edge diffusion; cobalt blue and rose madder genuine for glazing and finishing; cadmium orange, cadmium red-orange, and napthamide maroon painted wet-into-wet for center colors. The flower is complex, so gestures that imply direction are useful.

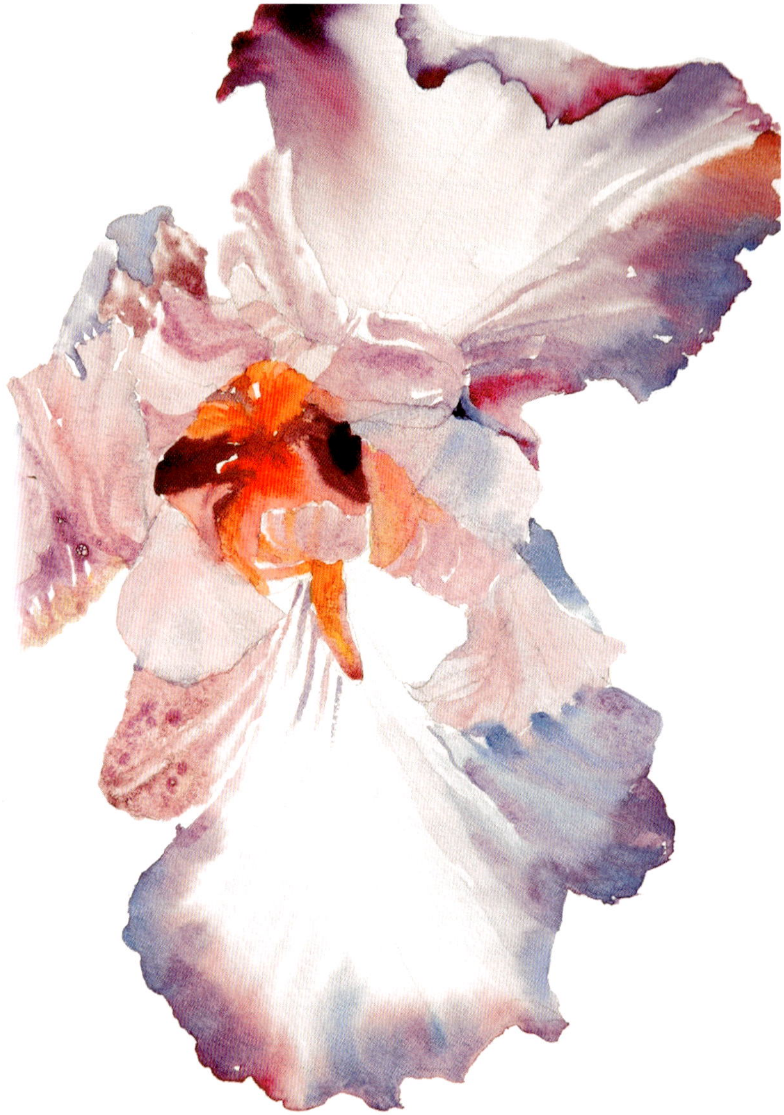

Petal colors

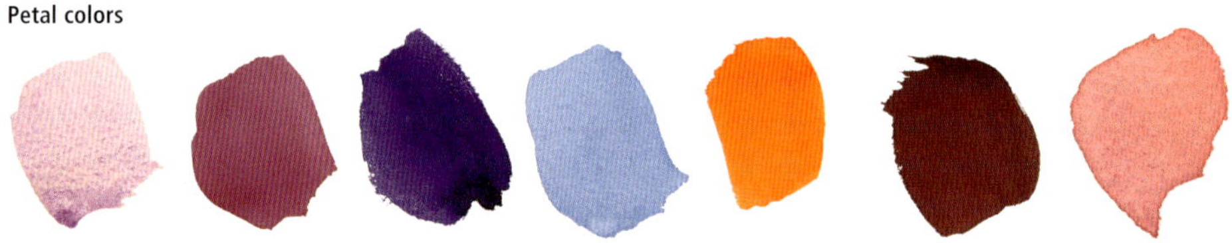

cobalt violet | quinacridone magenta | carbazole violet (dioxazine) | cobalt blue | Winsor orange | napthamide maroon | rose madder genuine

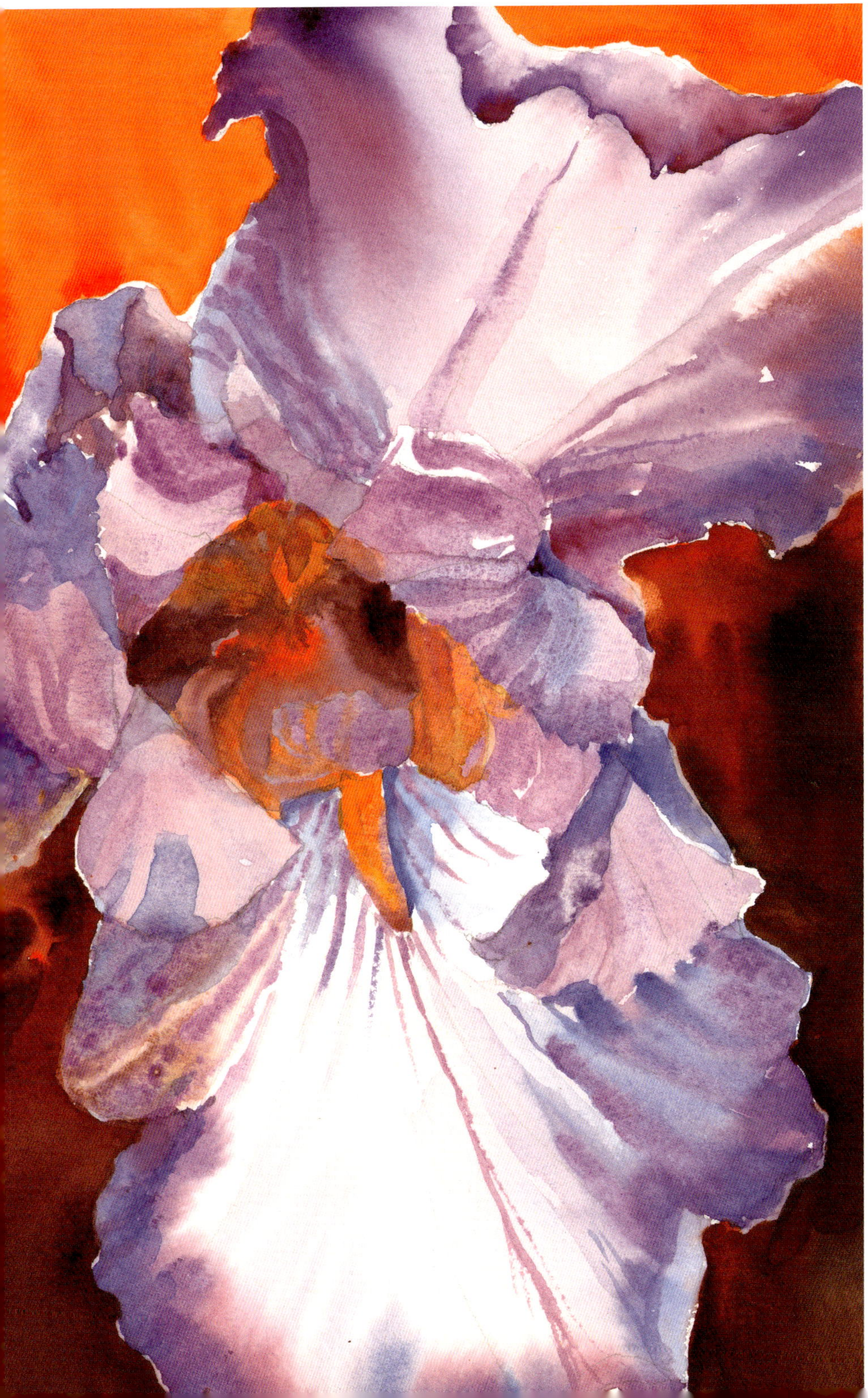

Painting the background The vibrancy of the flower center pleads for an analogous background. (See "Analogous Color Palette," page 52.) Just for the fun of it, and because of the beauty of the center, a warm/hot background moving from orange to maroon was chosen. Organic pigments such as quinacridones (magenta, gold, scarlet), perylene maroon, napthamide maroon, and carbazole violet (dioxazine) make beautiful dark mixes. Heavier, inorganic pigments such as Winsor orange, cadmium orange, and cobalt violet can be dropped into these mixes to add punctuations of color. Tilt the paper to encourage the gravitational flow.

Background colors

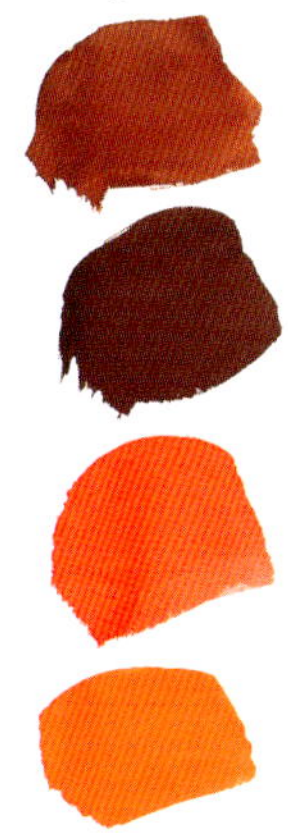

perylene maroon

napthamide maroon

cadmium orange

Winsor orange

SOME THINGS TO CONSIDER

- There is a significant difference between "dropping in" and mixing pigments. The first is a wet-into-wet process when a paint is directly brushed onto an already-wet surface. The latter is a mix of two or more paints in a palette. The mix is then applied to paper.
- You can use a wet-into-wet technique over the entire paper or just in sections for more control. Testing how your pigments react to wet-into-wet techniques is time well spent. You get to understand the pigments as personalities.
- You can use clear water or a watercolor wash to wet the paper.
- Choose pigments to match your purpose. The light inorganics are bright, strong, and easy to use as washes. The heavier organics behave wildly—shooting, dropping, and pushing against the others. Together they create a symphony of color!

Underpainting

An underpainting (or underwash) is an initial layer of paint applied to the surface of the canvas or paper that serves as a base for subsequent layers of paint. Although the process is generally associated with oil painting, a number of watercolor artists use underpainting in their work.

Underpainting always has been an essential part of the oil painting process. European artists such as Vermeer and Leonardo da Vinci employed white underpainted areas as a backdrop for brighter, lighter colors, which would then appear much more brilliant than when painted over darker undertones. An underpainting of umbers and siennas provided the base for the darker areas of the composition. Over time, painters of other mediums also began to use underpainting.

USING COLOR BLOCKS

Judi Betts uses underpainting to create an independent and underlying network of color blocks upon which the major design elements of the painting are later applied. The result is a painting with an exciting depth and rhythm, as well as a touch of mystery.

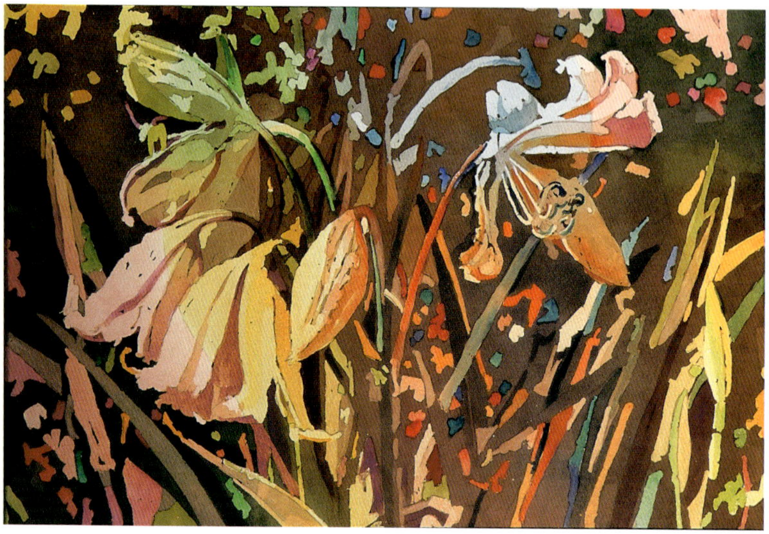

GRISAILLE

Grisaille is a traditional technique that uses a range of grays or browns to build up the tonal values of a painting. It can be left as a monochrome, or color can be added by glazing. Traditionally grisaille was used with oil paints or tempera, but the technique is suitable for use with a range of media, including watercolor. It is important to use permanent pigments for the underpainting.

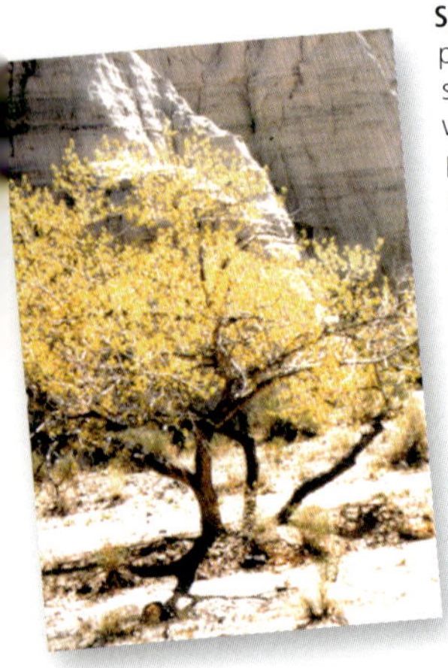

Spring in the Arroyo Looking at the photograph left, the author began by selecting a permanent gray pigment that would not lift off when glazed. A proprietary neutral tint was chosen and applied according to the values found in the photograph. Notice that the lower part of the painting has not been overpainted.

The main task was to decide whether to go darker or to allow the grisaille beneath to carry the values alone. The neutral tint was a great choice—it was easy to use and it stayed down through several glazes.

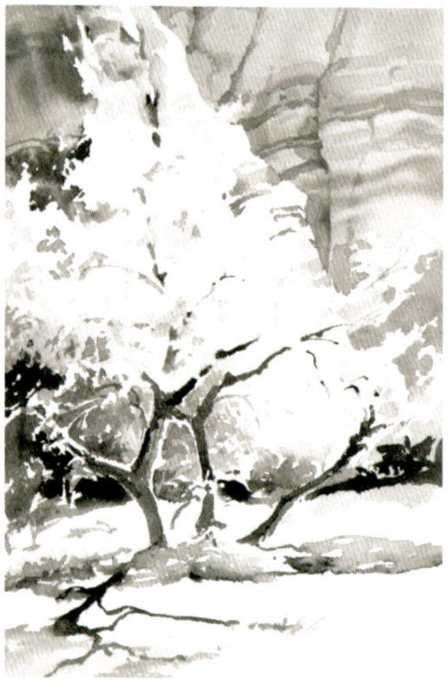

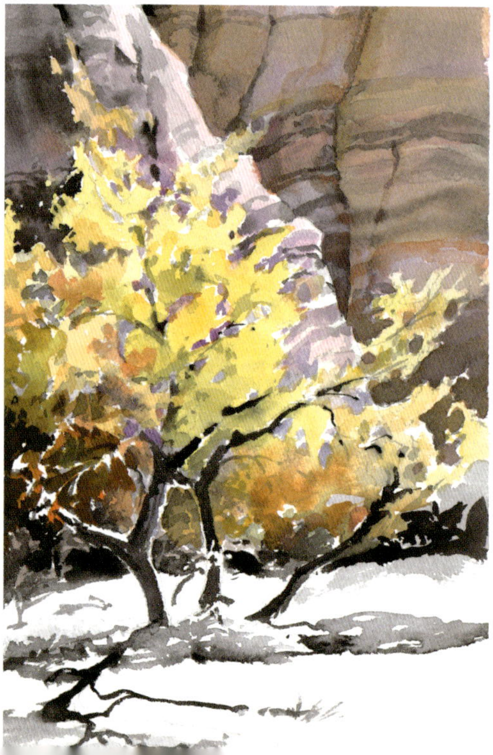

ATMOSPHERIC UNDERPAINTING

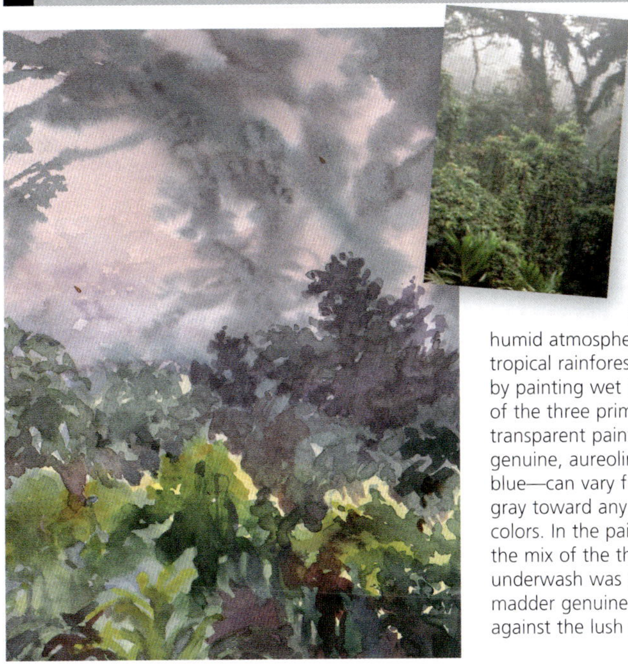

Underpainting can enhance the atmosphere in a landscape painting. An underwash of yellow can establish the impression of dry heat and warm sunshine in a high altitude locale. Conversely, the humid atmosphere of coastal fog or tropical rainforest is best suggested by painting wet into wet. A mix of the three primary non staining transparent paints—rose madder genuine, aureolin yellow, and cobalt blue—can vary from a luminescent gray toward any of those three colors. In the painting shown, the mix of the three colors for the underwash was pushed toward rose madder genuine in order to play against the lush foliage.

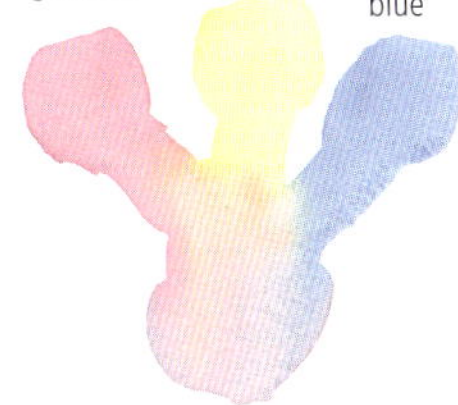

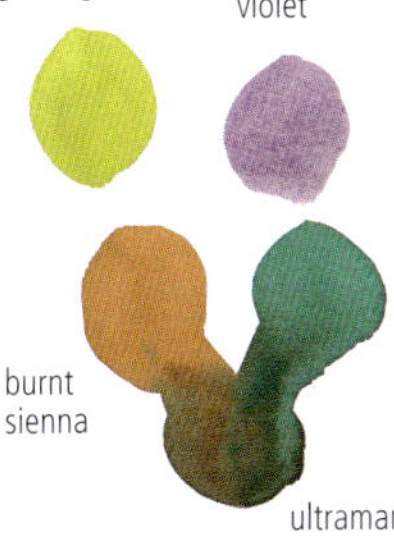

SOME THINGS TO CONSIDER

- An underpainting can help set the mood for a painting.
- Do not worry too much about the effect of a yellow underwash on your subsequent colors. It all depends upon the strength of the next layer.
- Be sure to let the underwash dry completely before you paint over it, unless you begin with areas that can use the soft edges of wet-into-wet painting.
- Use staining, permanent pigments that will not lift off for underpaintings that will receive more than one glaze.
- When using underpainting for a vegetative subject, try a mixed purple, e.g., phthalo blue and a permanent red. Then, for those areas that you intend to be green, push the underpainted purple toward blue with the intention of applying a yellow to achieve green.

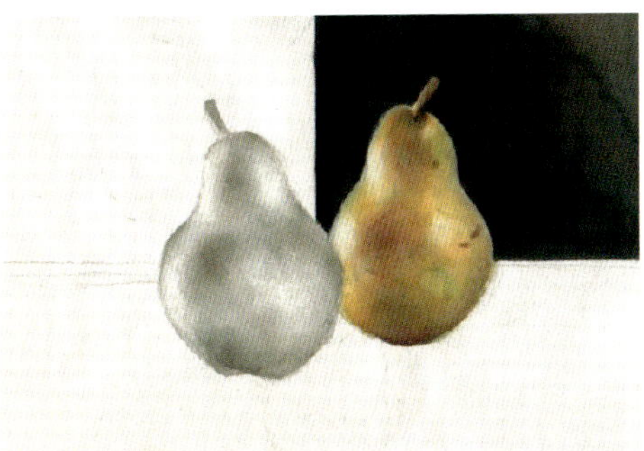

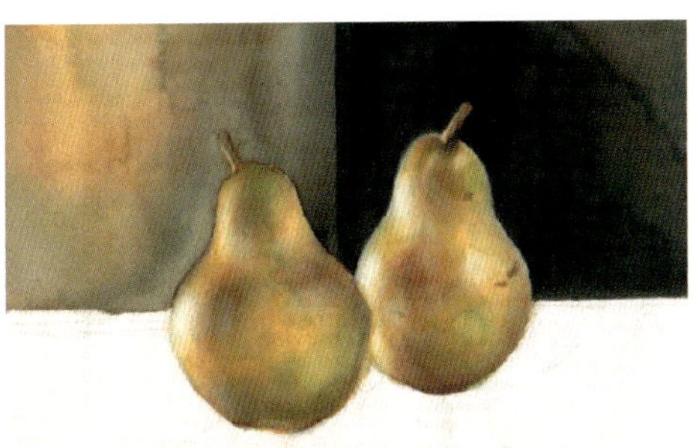

Two Pears Aselka Syzdykova experimented with the grisaille technique when underpainting this still-life composition of two pears. Looking to achieve soft, natural effects, she found purple or blue underpainting to be too harsh. She decided to try gray underpainting by mixing Prussian blue and burnt umber to create the gray she required. This technique allows her to establish tonal values in advance by underpainting them and then glazing with flat, transparent washes. The transparency of the watercolor is not lost due to the specially mixed gray underpaint.

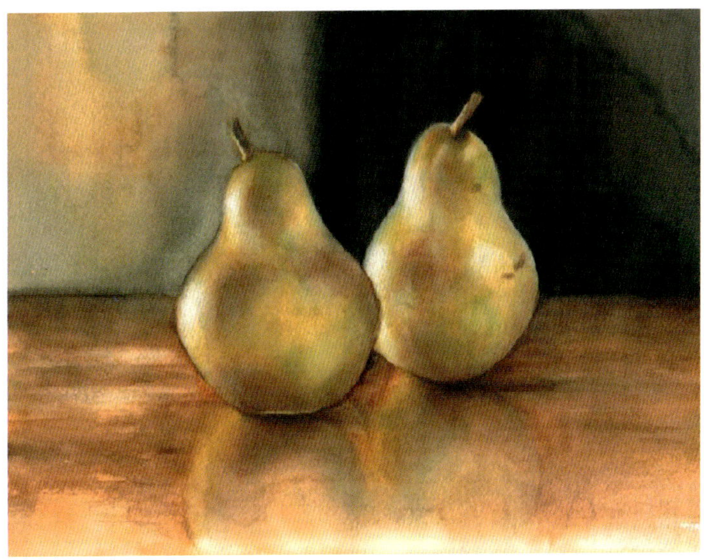

Glazing

There is much confusion in the watercolor world about the subject of glazing. Is a glaze a wash? Is a wash a glaze? What are the glazing pigments? Why glaze? And so on. Answers are as individual as the artists who offer them, but from my perspective, glazing is basically a specialized wash intended to alter the color and/or tone of previously applied, dry colors.

How optical glazing works In an optical mix, the separate, thin layers allow light to enter, bounce off the white paper, and reflect off various pigments in the different layers. In the process it picks up new information and results in many interesting and subtle variations in color, light, and depth. The more layers of transparent glaze, the more chances you have of catching the light, multiplying the effects, and achieving the luminosity that made watercolors famous.

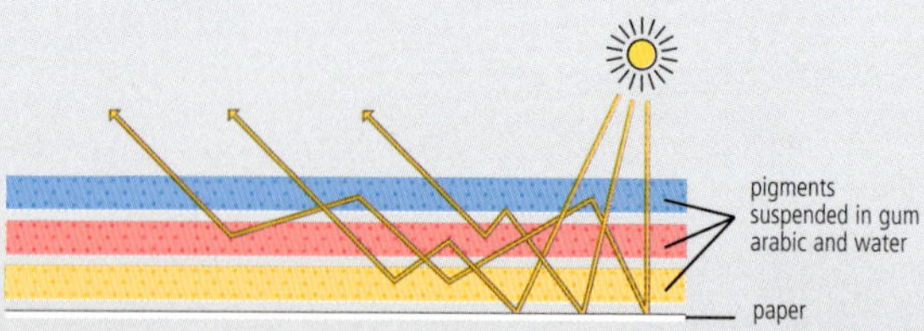

HISTORICAL PERSPECTIVE

Oil painters were the first to use glazing, brushing a layer or two of paint diluted by oil over a dried opaque base. Although artists such as Vermeer used the process, there were problems, such as dust accumulation. Watercolorists, however, found that the medium's transparent nature worked well with glazing—thin layers of wash carefully applied over one another created depth and glow. When working from light to dark, they could use glazes to build up luminous mid-tones and darks. This was developed in the 1800s by students at the École des Beaux-Arts who placed layers of wash over less and less of their drawings to create masterful gradations in values. This is known as the *French Style*.

WHY GLAZE?

There will be occasions when you want a simple mixed color straight from your palette (physical mixing), and there will be other times when you want the intrigue of colors mixed optically in transparent layers or glazes.

Physical mixing When you mix cobalt blue, rose madder genuine, and aureolin yellow in your palette, you get a mixed gray composed from the physically mixed pigments.

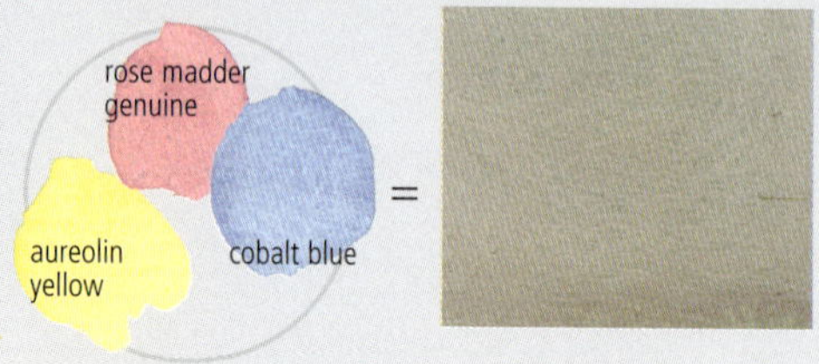

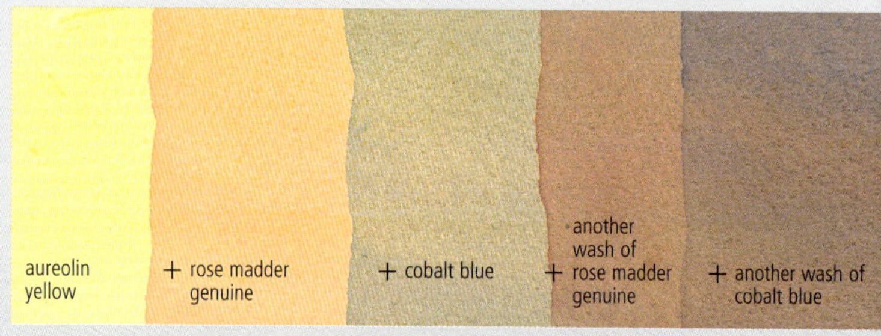

Optical mixing By glazing the three colors separately, drying in between, you achieve a glowing, optically mixed gray. The mixing occurs in the viewer's eyes and brain, not in the palette. The glow achieved is much stonger than the physically mixed colors.

French style This technique of glazing is still being modified and used by watercolor artists today. Repeatedly apply glaze, covering less of the strip with each application.

PIGMENTS TO CONSIDER FOR GLAZING

- Compared with gouache (an opaque, water-based paint) nearly all watercolor pigments have some transparency. The most transparent pigments work best for layered glazing. Some artists use permanent transparent pigments to avoid "pulling up" the layer below when adding the new.
- Others prefer to use nonpermanent transparent pigments to avoid any chance of staining the layer below. You can find information about the staining qualities of pigments on the tube or by checking the paint manufacturer's online pigment information.
- For many artists, the standard nonstaining transparent glazing pigments are aureolin yellow, rose madder genuine, cobalt blue, and viridian green. These gentle, pure colors work well together and are especially useful for delicate and/or white subjects. (See "Neutrals," page 70.)
- Sedimentary watercolor pigments also can be used for glazing. A light cerulean glaze over distant mountains in a landscape creates the illusion of aerial perspective distance. Cerulean blue's cool temperature makes mountains appear to recede.
- Note that phthalo blue is not a good glazing choice as it dyes all the layers below. Burnt sienna, however, allows some information to come through and could be used as a glaze.

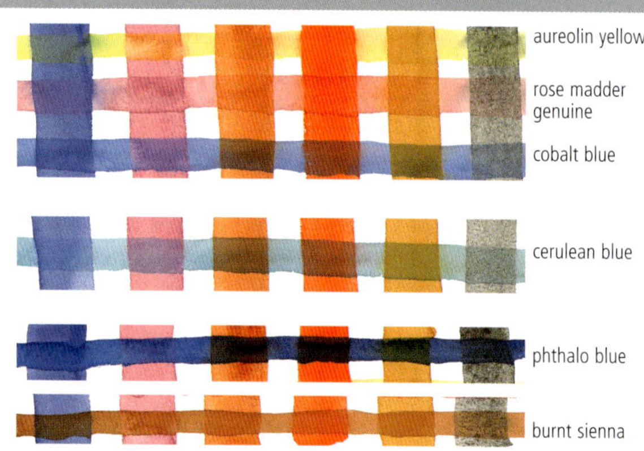

CORRECTING COLOR KEY

Sometimes a painting ends up out of color key—too many different colors with no dominant color to help unify the painting. If you glaze the entire painting, it is like adding a single color to all the disparate pigments, and it brings the painting into color key.

Two Deer This watercolor sketch has an undercoat of golden yellow, which does not entirely work with the pinkish sky, blue mountains, and distant green hills. An allover glaze can provide color unity, but you must think about your choice of color.

The options Each of the three primary non staining transparent pigments was first imagined as a glaze over the existing colors in the painting in order to make a single glaze color selection.

Aureolin yellow This will turn the mountains green and add orange and gray (over the purple) to the sky.

Cobalt blue All the yellows and golds will turn green, including the deer.

Rose madder genuine This may subdue the green hills but won't drastically change anything else. This is the best choice and may create an allover sense of a sunset.

You could also use a secondary mix of the previous colors:

AY+RMG = orange This would gray the blue mountains.

AY+CB = green This would likely gray the sky too much and turn the deer green.

RMG+CB = lavender The foreground and deer would be grayed. Since they are the focus of the painting, this would not be a good idea.

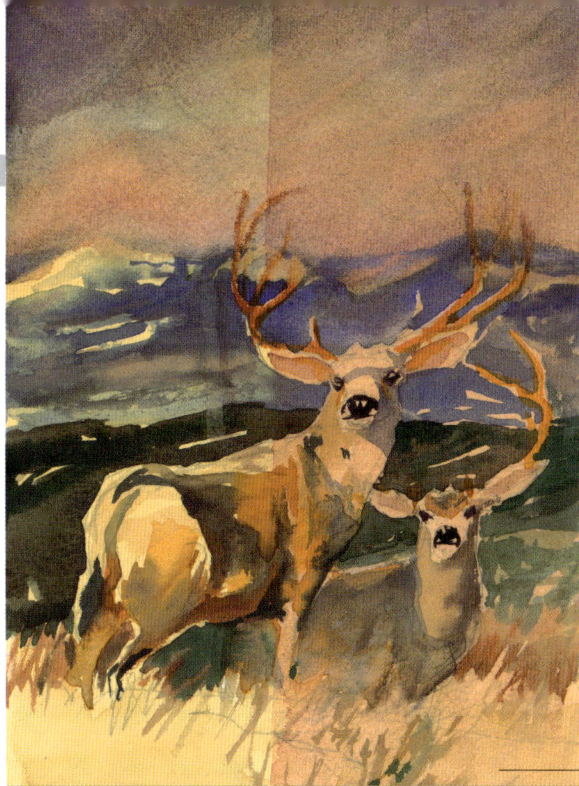

without glaze | with glaze

Applied very carefully, just to the right side of the sketch, rose madder genuine darkens the bright yellows of the foreground grasses and the deer. Overall the colors are more unified and back in color key. Note how the application of the rose madder genuine glaze tempers all of the colors—unifying and softening.

GLAZING A SKY

It is best to glaze a sky with three colors—yellow, red, and blue. The transparent, nonstaining pigments of aureolin yellow, rose madder genuine, and cobalt blue work very well. Apply yellow first for best results. Consider it the sunlight in the painting. The red and blue layers can be very light or moderate, depending on the color result desired. If you use equal densities of the three, you will produce the luminous gray of an overcast sky—beautiful in its own right.

California Dreamin'
Jan Hart glazed the sky with three nonstaining transparent pigments, beginning with aureolin yellow, which she left as the cloud color. With each layer, she softened the edges of the clouds to feature some of the other pigments at the edges.

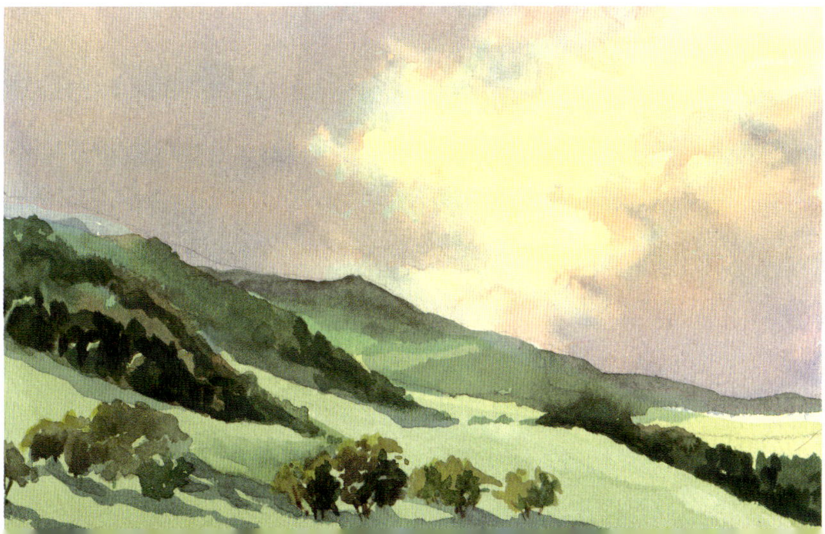

CREATING VOLUME AND DEPTH

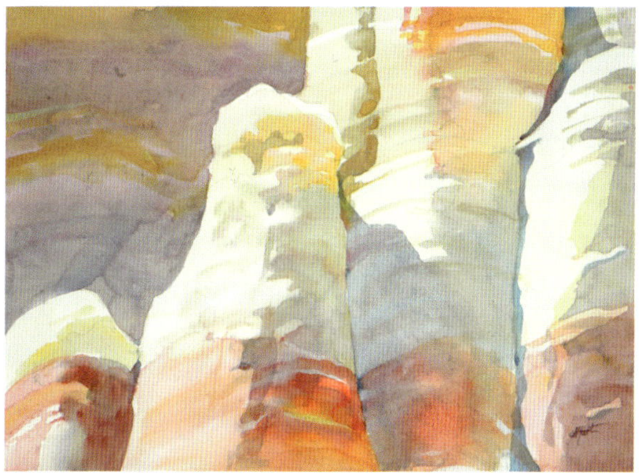

Cerulean blue was used as a glaze for the distant hills to push them back.

Perspective and glazing A single light glaze over an area of a painting immediately creates an illusion of perspective. Here each of the three nonstaining transparents were used to create the illusion of roundness, shadow, and depth.

HOW TO GLAZE

Glazing requires care. A glazing mix is mostly water, but it must contain enough pigment to cover and change the appearance of the dry paper or the colors beneath.

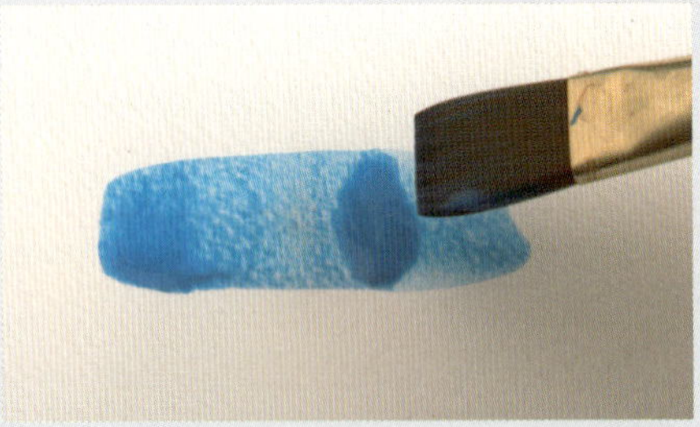

1 Apply the glaze with a soft, wide, fully loaded brush, barely touching the slanted surface. Think of the paper surface reaching up to grab the pigmented water.

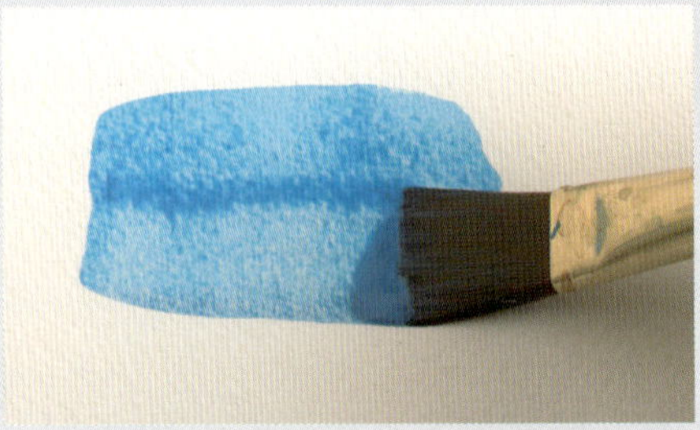

2 As a bead of glaze gathers at the bottom of the previous horizontal stroke, reload the brush and repeat the action, picking up the bead along the way. Allow to fully dry before going back.

Multiple glazes Here glazes of cobalt blue, rose madder genuine, and aureolin yellow have been applied, demonstrating their effectiveness as gentle glazing pigments. Aureolin yellow was applied first and shows through the final glaze.

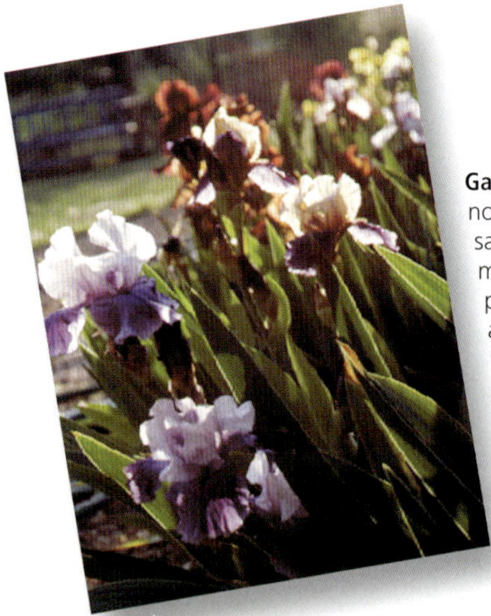

Garden Glade In this watercolor sketch, the author used transparent, nonstaining pigments to glaze specific parts of the painting, saving the lights while building up the transparents and darks. You may hear that someone has applied 57 glazes in the course of a painting. It may not mean that the entire painting was glazed over and over, just parts of it. It is less important to count than to plan the process and to anticipate the outcome before beginning. Here the author decided that any underwash of yellow would work well, giving a sunny lift to all the overglazed colors of the flowers. The large proportion of green in the composition would benefit from the added interest of blue glazed over the top rather than just adding straight green.

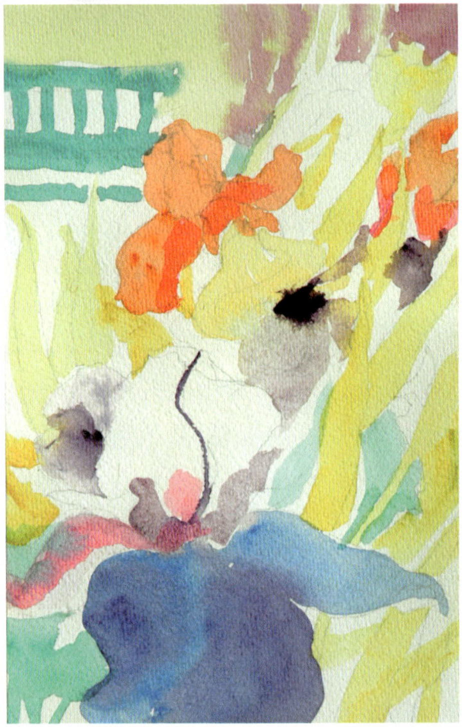

1 The author began with an overall underwash of aureolin yellow over the drawing on watercolor paper.

The underlying colors of the flowers, foliage, and background are painted in. They will serve as the base colors for additional glazes. Strong emphasis is given to yellows with the knowledge that blue glazes will overlay and produce green.

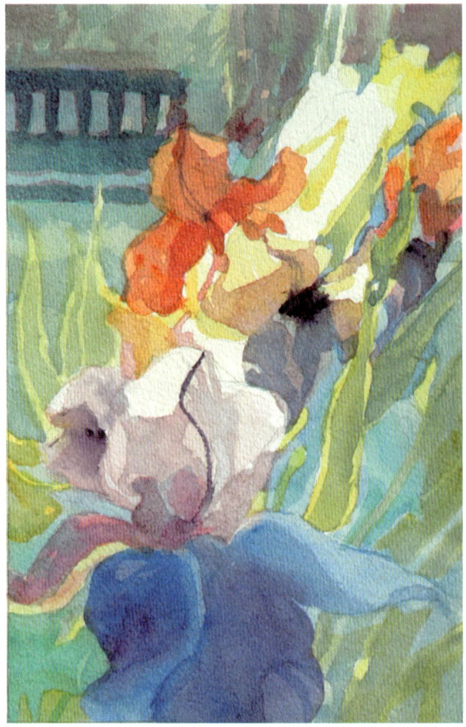

2 When the paint is completely dry, a cobalt blue or lavender (cobalt blue and rose madder genuine) glaze is applied selectively over the background, through the centers of the leaves, and as shadows on the iris petals. The cobalt blue glaze over the background creates the sense of depth.

Rose madder genuine is now applied as a glaze over parts of the background and the irises. Note how the flowers are beginning to glow as layered shapes are added. Then go back to cobalt blue to add special nuances, layered shapes, and little accents near oranges, just for delight.

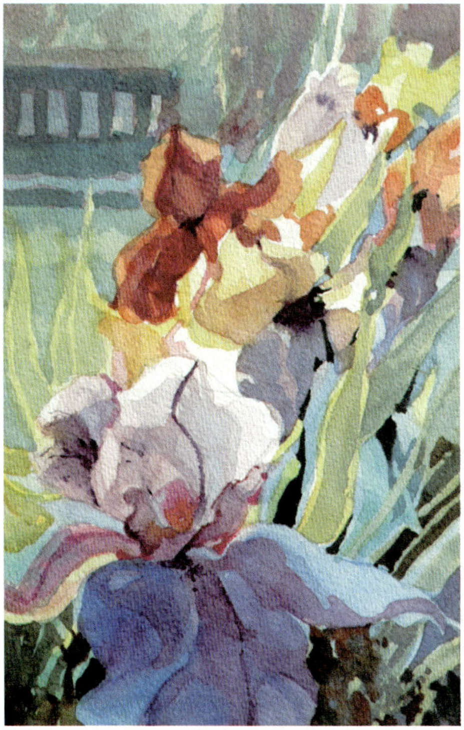

3 A dark green mix is applied very carefully behind the petals and leaves in the lower half of the painting, keeping in mind the ideas of making interesting shapes, creating a path of connection, and adding emphasis. Other colors used in the painting can be added for emphasis and details.

4 Building a painting with glazes requires planning and patience. Think about colors in layers. A strong initial pink layer becomes lavender when transparent blue is later glazed over it, and yellow leaves will become partially green. Let each layer dry completely before applying the next.

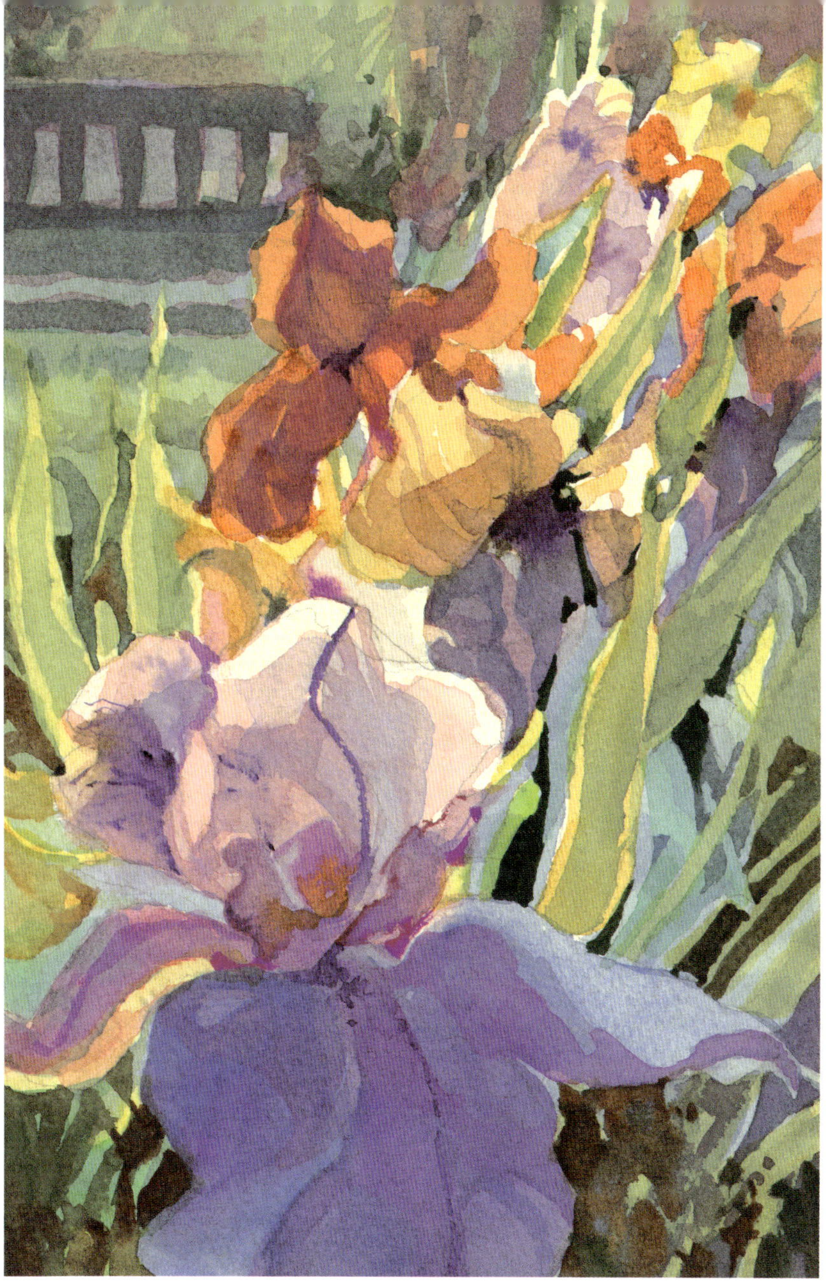

Colors used

opera (Holbein)

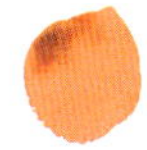

quinacridone sienna

Glazing colors

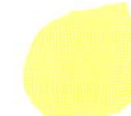

azo yellow (aureolin)

rose madder genuine

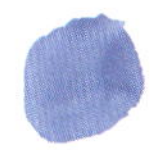

cobalt blue

Dark green mix

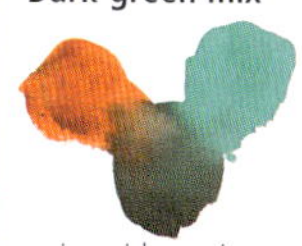

quinacridone sienna

ultramarine turquoise

SOME THINGS TO CONSIDER

- Apply a glaze on a completely dry area. Do not go back over it while it is wet, even if you think you can "fix" something.
- Glaze with transparent pigments. They can be permanent or nonstaining transparents.
- Leave some of the layer underneath peeking through. This adds interest and depth.
- There are degrees of transparency and opacity to consider in every pigment. Although cobalt blue is used for glazing, it does have some sediment and a tendency to stain at the edges.
- Avoid applying a staining pigment as a glaze over anything you want to see after the glaze has been applied.
- Colored transparent glazes can finish or fix a painting. A warm glaze can bring the foreground forward, a cool glaze can "push" a background backward, a glaze in the same colors as the painting can darken slightly, and an allover glaze can correct an "out of key" painting.

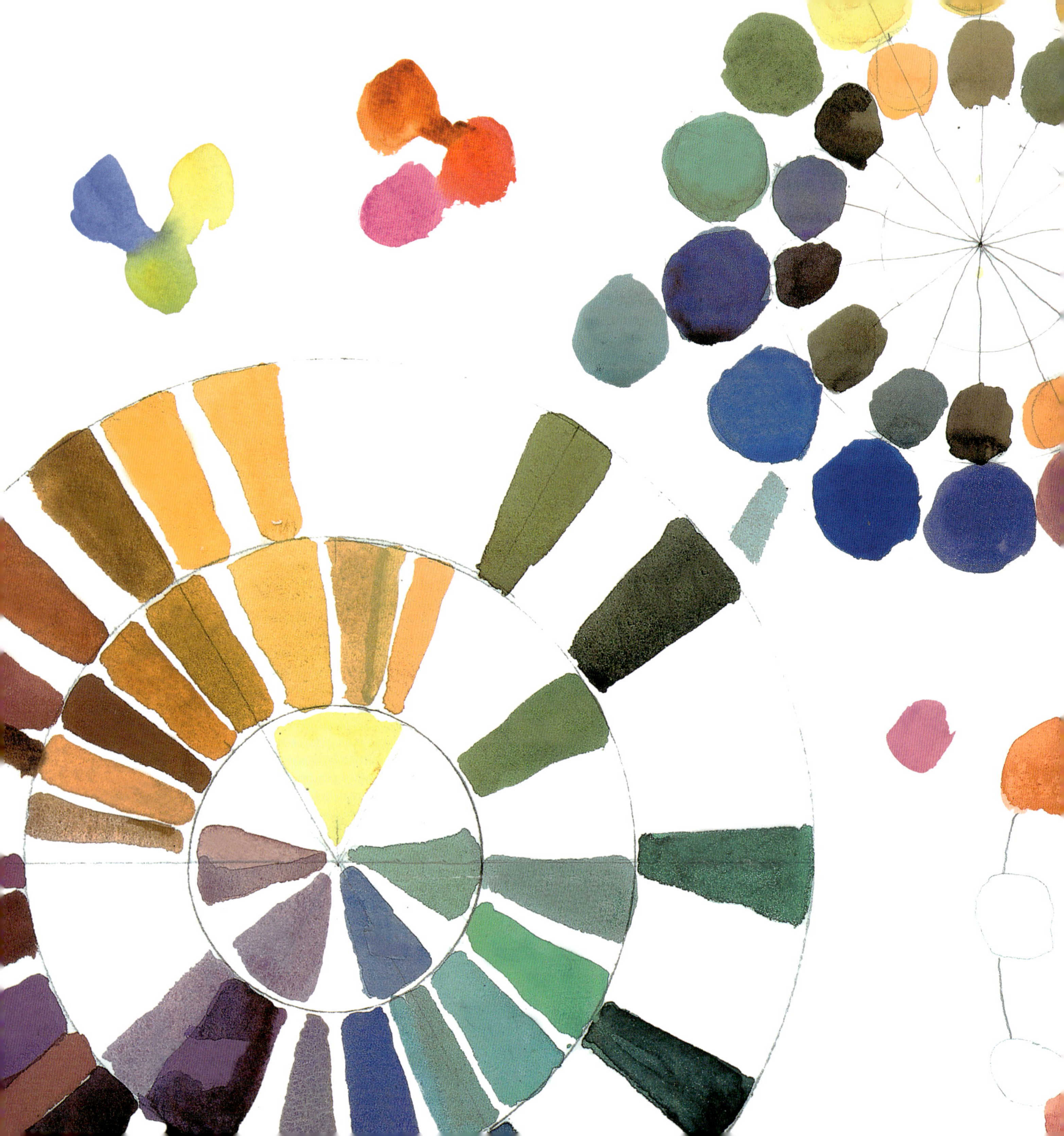

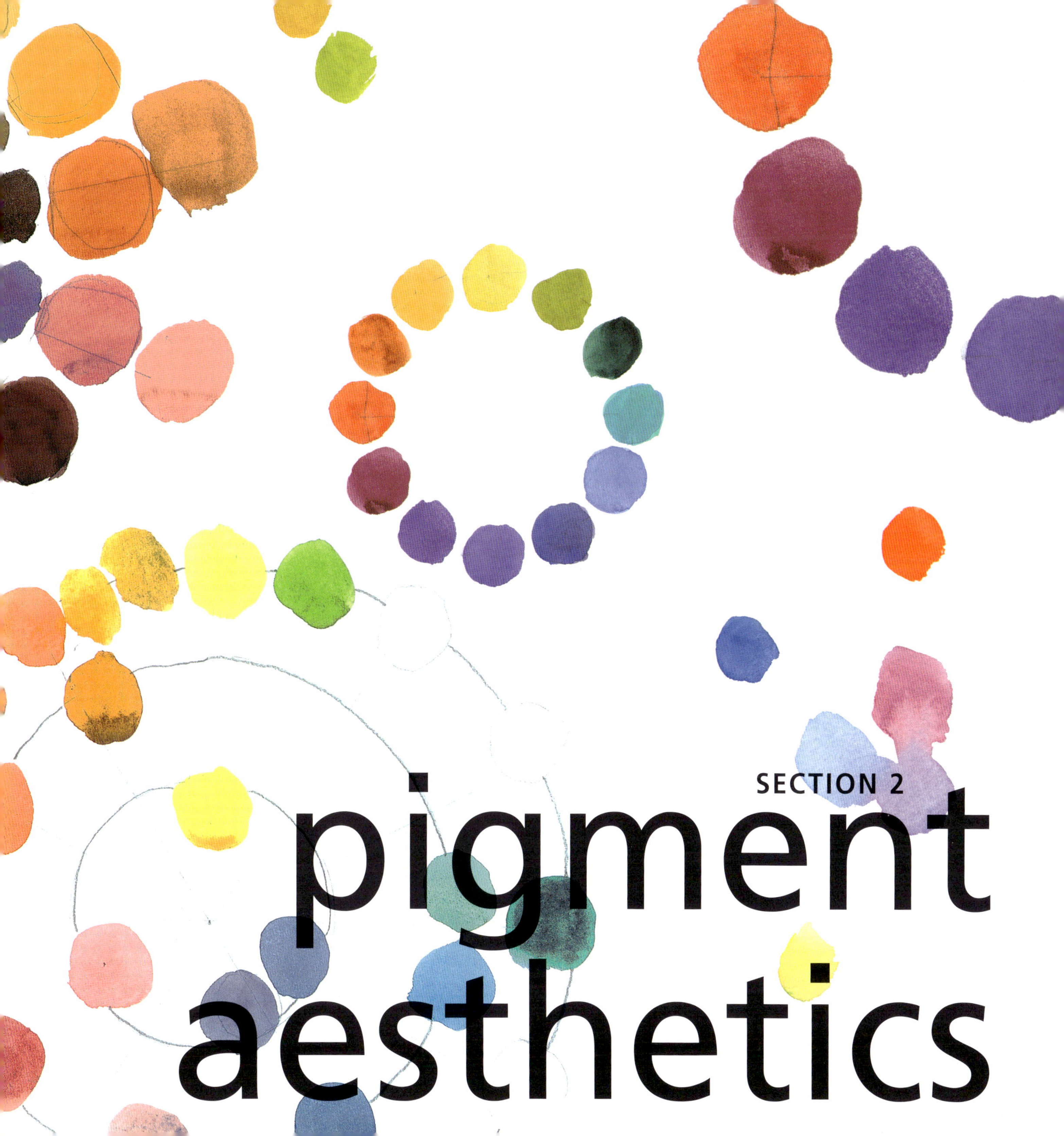

SECTION 2

pigment aesthetics

Pigment aesthetics

The choice of colors to use for a painting is one of the most fundamental and important decisions in enabling the artist to communicate a feeling, idea, or mood. From active, upbeat reds, oranges, and yellows to quiet, somber blues, colors communicate. Artists must consciously select a color scheme that will best portray their intent. Color key, pigments, and values then can elaborate.

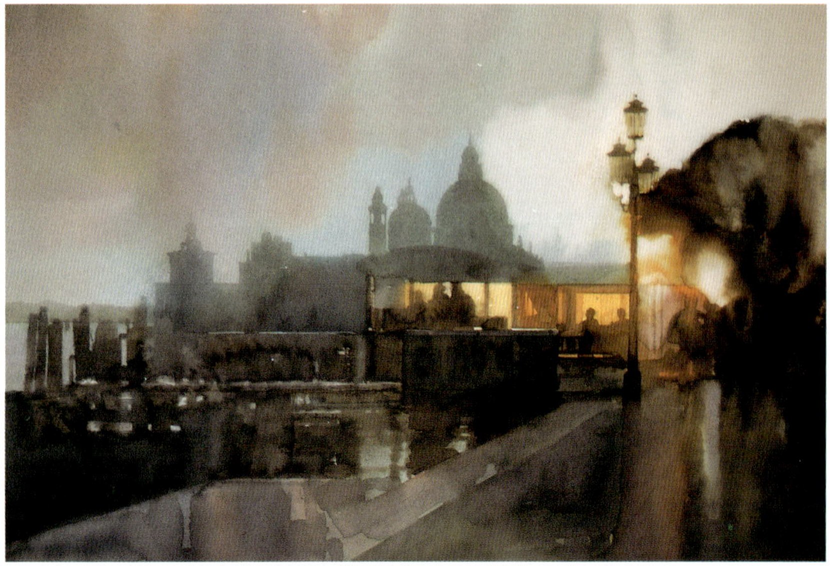

▲ *Rain, Venice* Peter Kelly
The artist effectively uses low-chroma and low-key neutrals to showcase the glow of light. The split-complementary color scheme demonstrates the visual appeal of neutralized mixes of analogous red-violets (carmine), blues (cobalt), and cyans (cerulean) playing opposite high-chroma yellow-orange (yellow ochre). The higher chroma paints were mostly neutralized by the addition of indigo blue and burnt sienna.

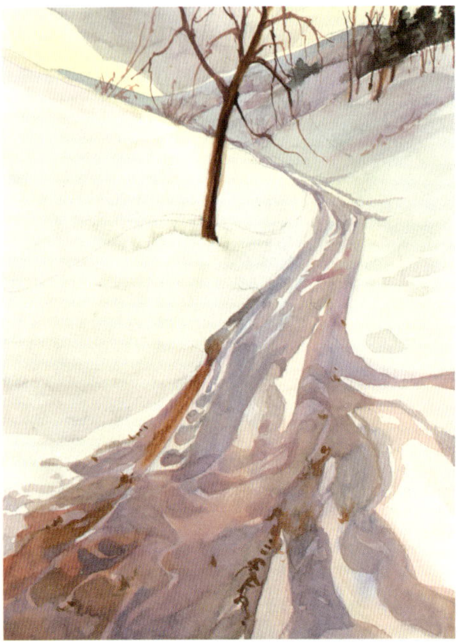

▲ *Winter Track* Jan Hart
A primary color scheme of transparent, luminous paints (rose madder genuine, cobalt blue, and aureolin yellow) was selected to portray an overcast winter scene with a suggestion of light beyond. Some mixed neutrals were added for distant trees. The soft neutral tones in the snow are actually glazed layers of the three paints. Note the foreground.

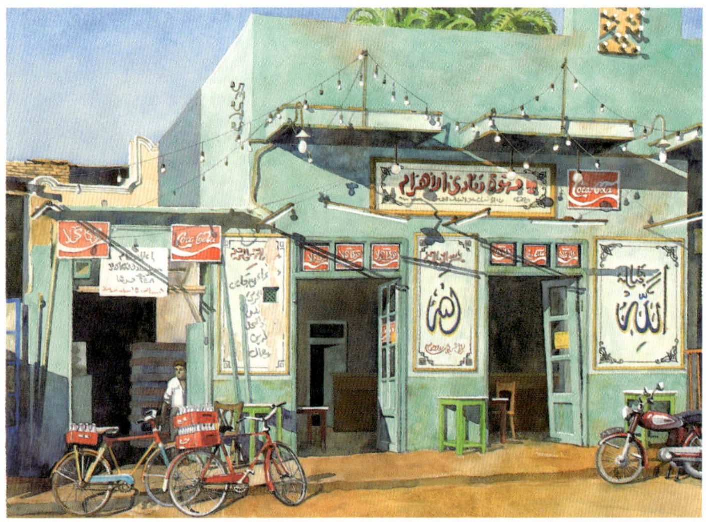

▲ *Coca-Cola* Moira Clinch
The artist was attracted to the accidental complementary color scheme provided by the Egyptian shop. Washes of cobalt teal provided the basis for the building with the complementary spots of quinacridone red for the signage and bicycles. Washes of ultramarine blue, indanthrone blue, and dioxazine violet were added wet on dry to create interesting shadows.

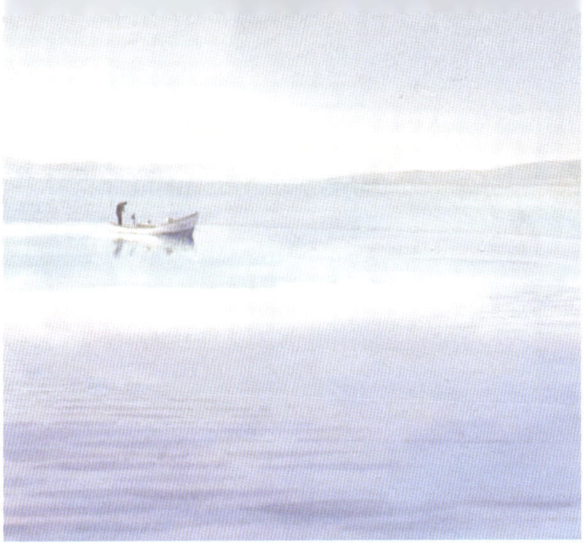

▲ *Early Morning in the Aegean* Garth Allen
The artist depicts the soft glow of morning in this high-key painting using a limited palette of just three strong paints—phthalo blue, permanent rose, and a bit of raw sienna. While most of the painting is analogous with light washes of the permanent, transparent warm blue and cool red in mixes, the complementary hint of morning light captures a misty moment.

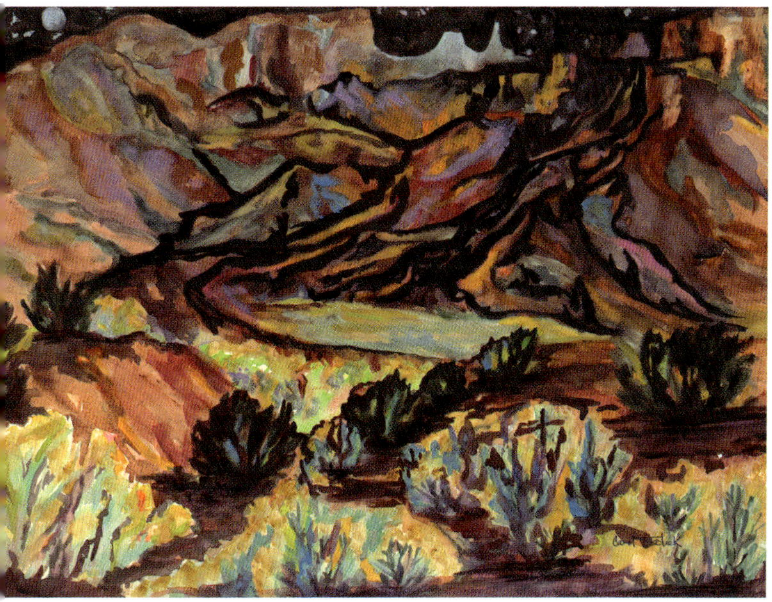

▲ *Desert Night* Carol Tasheck
In Carol Taschek's expressive painting, the night is slowly swallowing up the desert light. The foreground bushes glow against the backdrop of dark shadows, still simmering with vibrant colors. Notice how the artist uses intense colors in her dark areas but usually glazes them to lower the contrast of values.

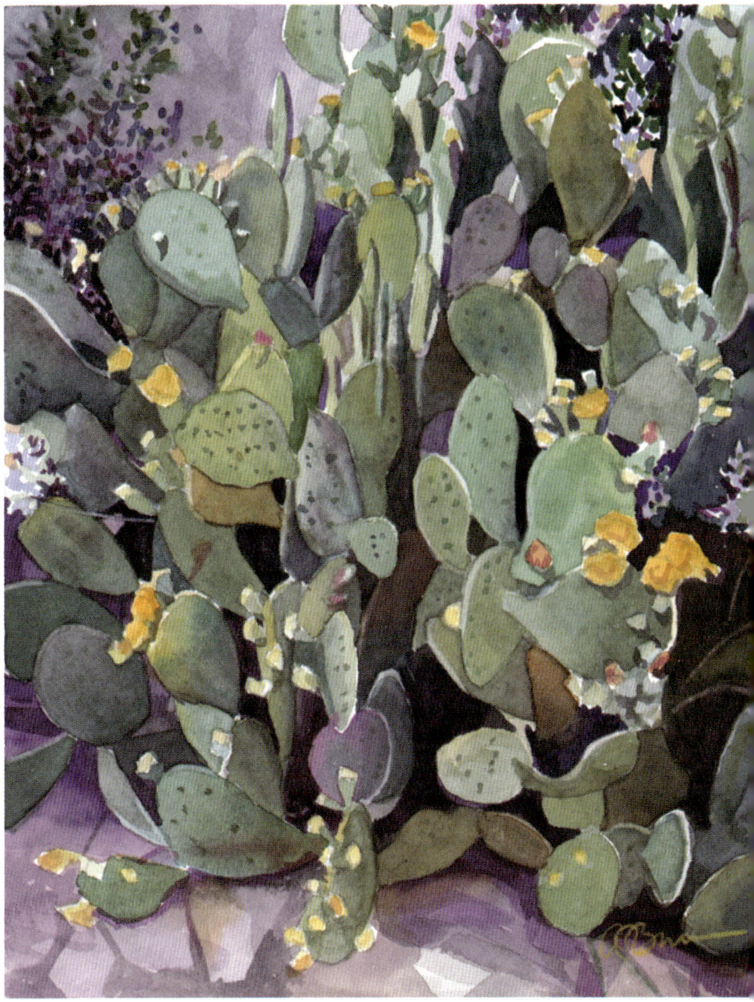

▲ *Light and Cactus in the Open Air* Allen Brown
Allen Brown selected the square tetradic color scheme using Daniel Smith paints: nickel azo, ultramarine blue, ultramarine turquoise, and quinacridone pink. His cacti subject asked for greens, which he was able to mix using nickel azo with a warm and cool blue. Although his neutral greens dominate the composition, the higher chroma pink violets and bright yellows add excitement and emphatic color accents.

Comparing color schemes

A color scheme is a specific choice of colors based on their relationship to each other on the color wheel. The scheme may comprise two to six colors, or hues, which are then redefined as pigments. It is helpful to use high chroma, intense, and fully saturated pigments, such as those in Hart's color wheel (see "Color wheels," page 14). A specific color scheme can simplify and unify the work and help you to express emotional tone. These studies illustrate how the artist's choice of color scheme affects the mood and emphasis of the work.

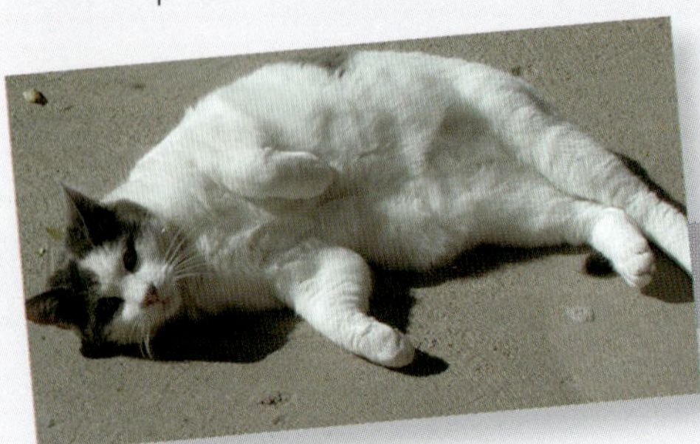

SOME THINGS TO CONSIDER

- Many artists resist color schemes—until they try one. Using a color scheme is an effective way to extend your understanding of colors and color relationships.
- Use the Velázquez, monochromatic, and complementary palettes to learn about value/tone relationships and/or as value studies for another painting.
- Two of the palettes—the six-color palette and the tertiary palette—contain six pigments. Both offer three sets of complements, which means that the pigment selection is based on personal choice.
- The more colors used in a painting, the more difficult it is to achieve color harmony. Try putting tape over the paints in your palette that you intend not to use in your color scheme.
- To personalize your color wheel, replace colors on Hart's color wheel (see "Color wheels," page 14) with your own choice of similar pigments.

Monochromatic scheme Using a single color in variations of lightness and saturation makes for easy viewing and can establish an overall mood. However, it may be difficult to highlight the most important element of the painting. Choosing just one pigment is a good way to establish the values and can even be called a value study. Here manganese violet was selected as much for its texture as for its color. Note how the granulation provides additional interest.

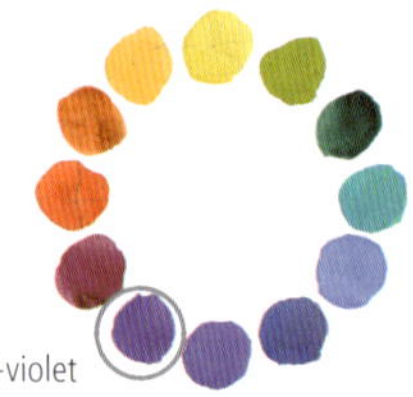

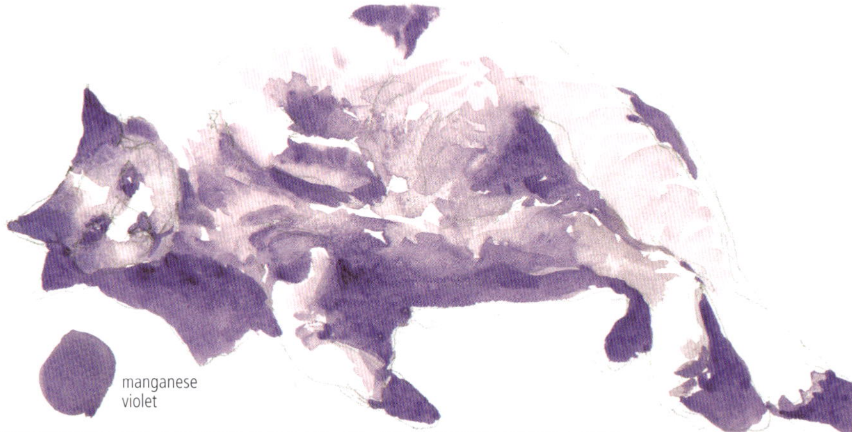

COLOR SCHEMES OVERVIEW

Six-color scheme (see "Six-color palette," page 50) This palette offers plenty of opportunities to achieve colorful neutrals. With three sets of complements, neutrals from brown to gray to black are possible, and each can be "pushed" toward the pure color for accents.

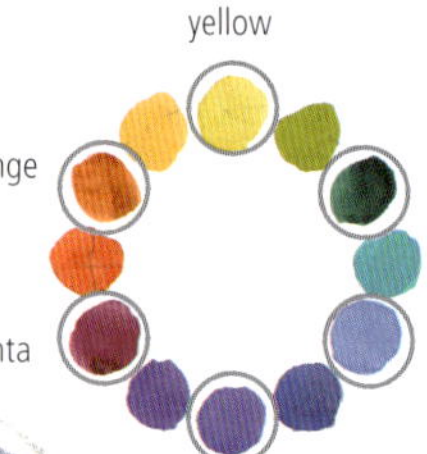

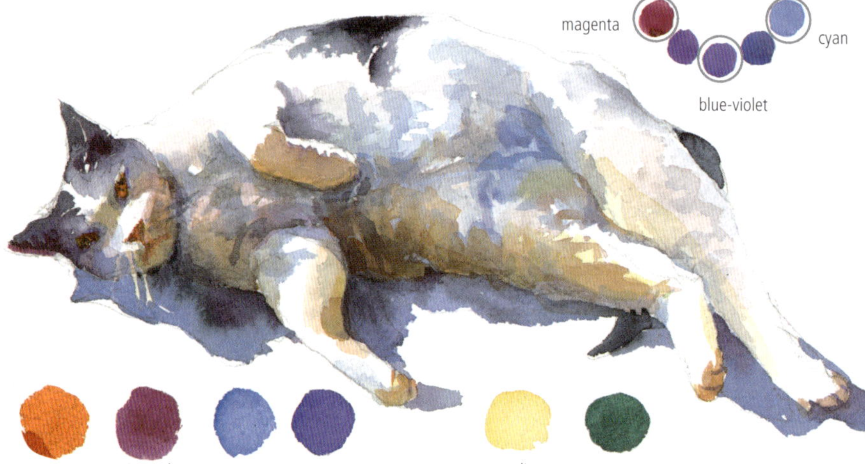

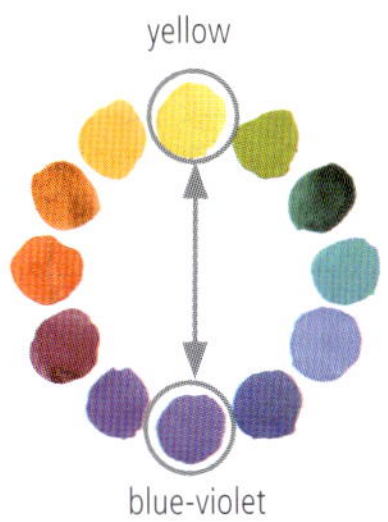

Complementary scheme (see "Complementary palette," page 54) Using pure color opposites enables you to present a stronger contrast than in any other color scheme, thus drawing maximum attention. For the best results, place cool colors against warm ones, or vice versa. The predominance in the amount of one color over the other creates the intended mood. A night painting, for example, may start as a complementary color scheme. Note the strong contrasts in this cat study.

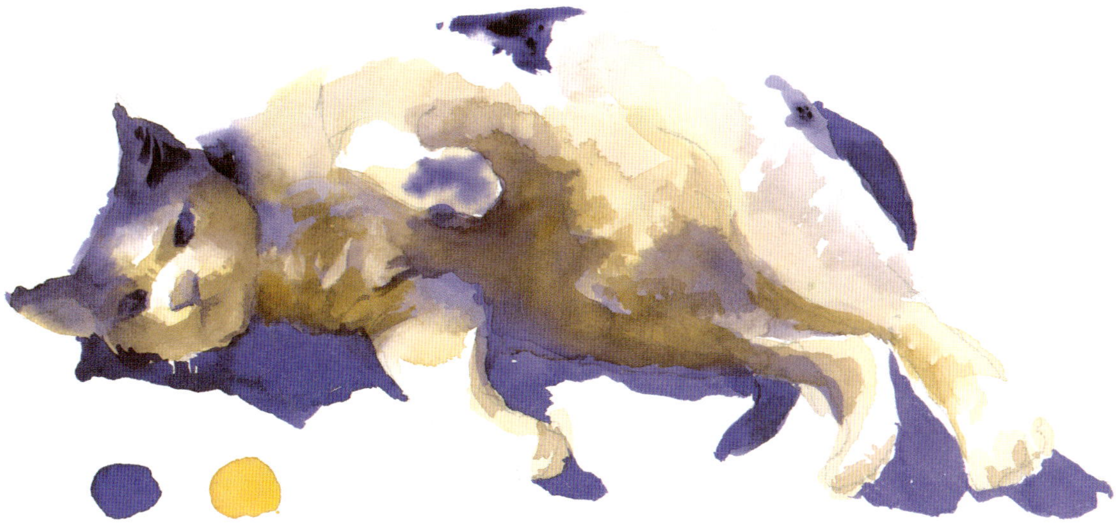

carbazole violet (dioxanine) aureolin yellow

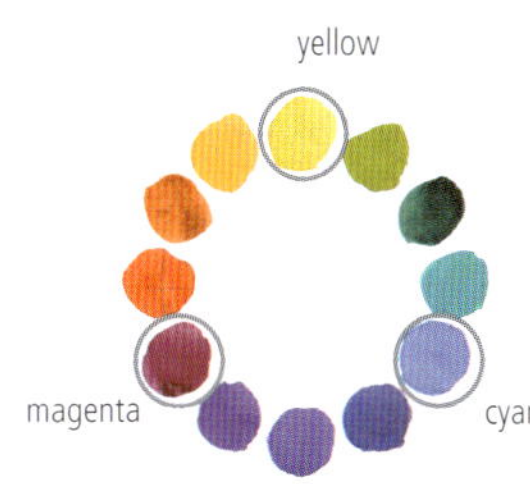

Primary color scheme (see "Primary palette," page 48) Because this scheme uses the three primary colors (which produce all other colors), it may offer the widest range of color possibilities. Nevertheless, the choice of just three pigments as the base helps produce unity and harmony in the painting. The primaries can be the magenta, yellow, and cyan of the standard color wheel, or the red-orange, blue-violet, and green of Hart's color wheel (see "Color wheels," page 14). Using only the three primary colors to mix the secondary colors produces a less vibrant, more neutral painting (see "six-color palette," page 50).

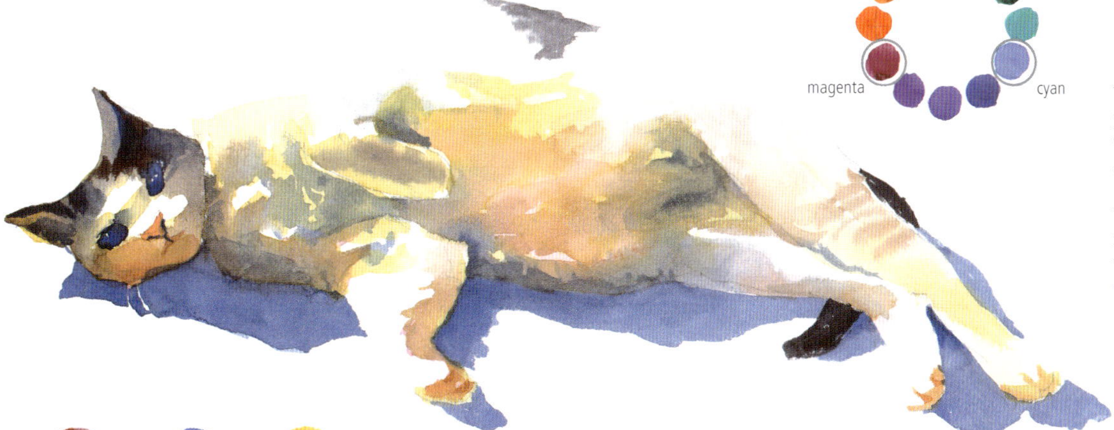

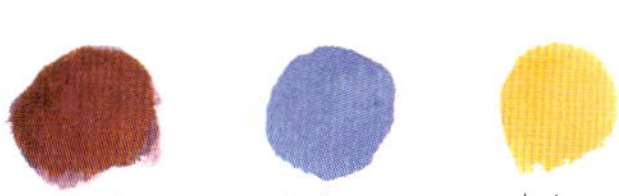

quinacridone magenta cobalt blue cadmium yellow

Split-complementary scheme (see "Split-complement palette," page 56) The split-complementary scheme extends the capabilities of the complementary pigment relationship. You can emphasize a single warm color by placing it against three oppositional cool colors—for example, yellow placed against a warm blue, a blue-violet, and a violet. Note the liveliness of the cat study palette, which combines the attributes of the analogous palette with the contrast of the complementary palette. The complementary pair are usually located in the center of the analogous trio.

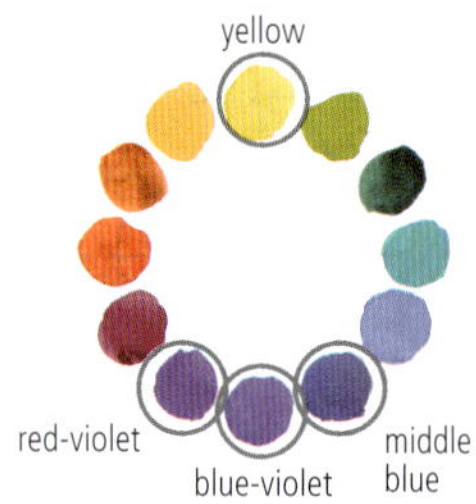

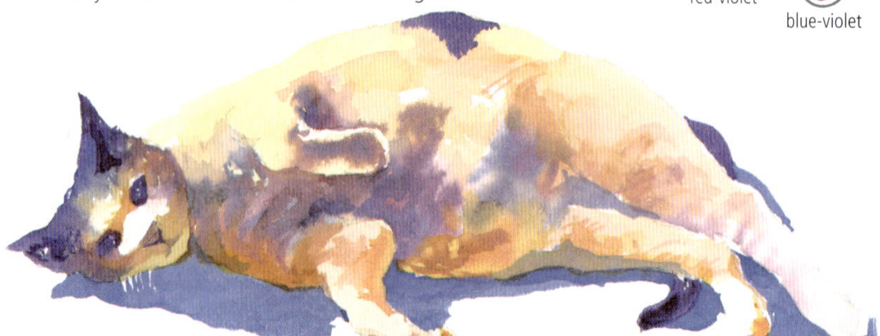

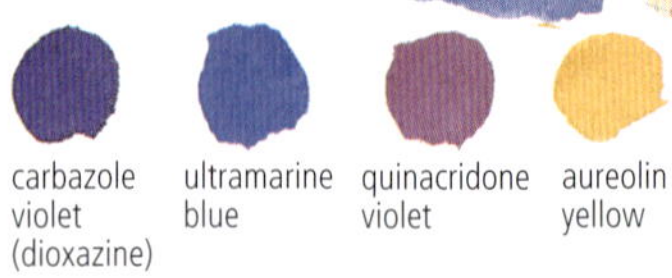

Velázquez color scheme (see "The Velázquez palette," page 62) The Velázquez color scheme uses a limited palette of three to four pigments that were available to the old oil-painting masters. The yellow ochre, burnt sienna, and ultramarine blue combine to create soft neutrals and glowing lights, as shown below. Modernize the palette by substituting quinacridone gold for yellow ochre and quinacridone burnt orange for burnt sienna. Ultramarine blue remains a longtime favorite of many artists and a staple of their palettes.

You can achieve a wonderful glow with these pigments. The pale green is achieved by mixing yellow ochre and ultramarine blue. Although ultramarine blue and burnt sienna cannot create lavender, the neutral achieved is most useful.

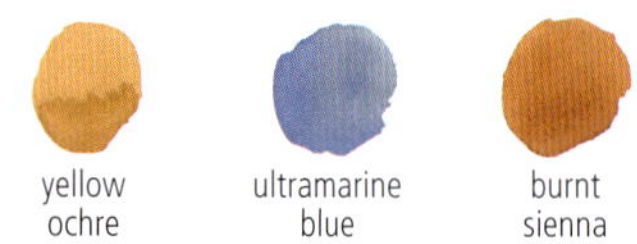

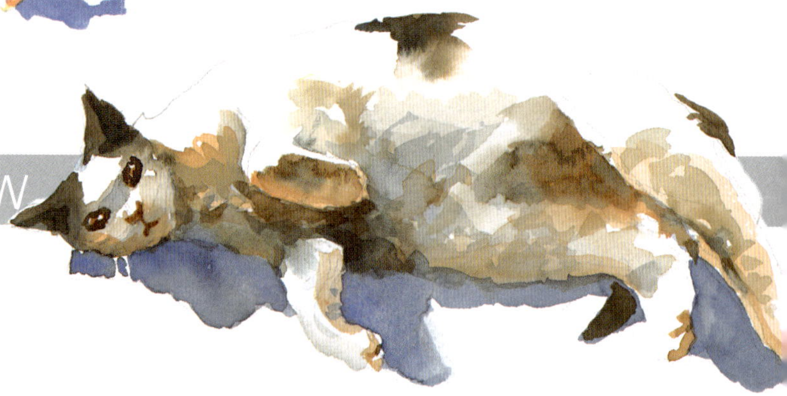

COLOR SCHEMES OVERVIEW

Tetradic scheme (see "Tetradic color scheme," page 58) This is the richest color scheme because it uses four colors arranged into two complementary color pairs. This creates variety while remaining fairly simple. The color scheme may be arranged as a rectangle or a square, examples of which are shown below. A complex yet potentially beautiful scheme, it may appear unbalanced if all four colors are used in equal amounts. It is best when one color is selected to be dominant, or three of the four colors are more subdued.

Note the relative richness of the color scheme in this cat study. With two sets of complements, some beautiful neutrals can be created, as well as some incredible pure color notes.

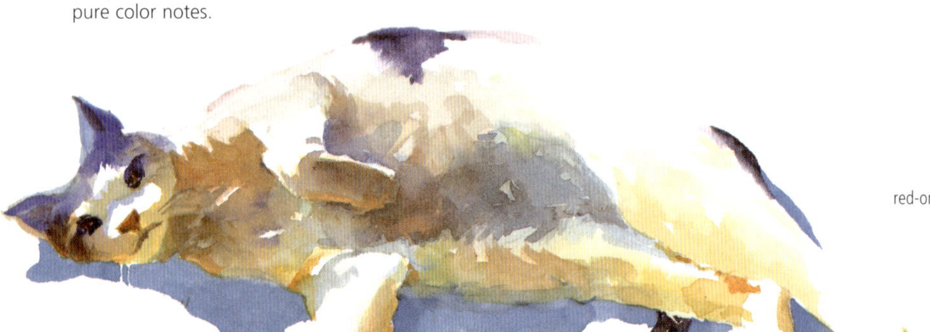

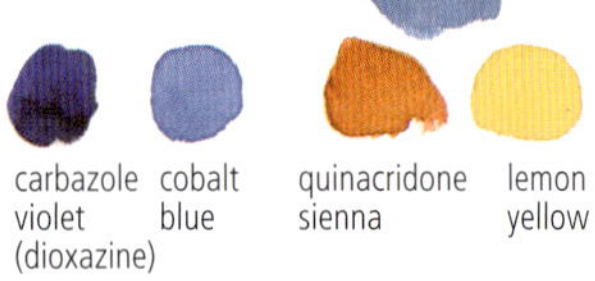

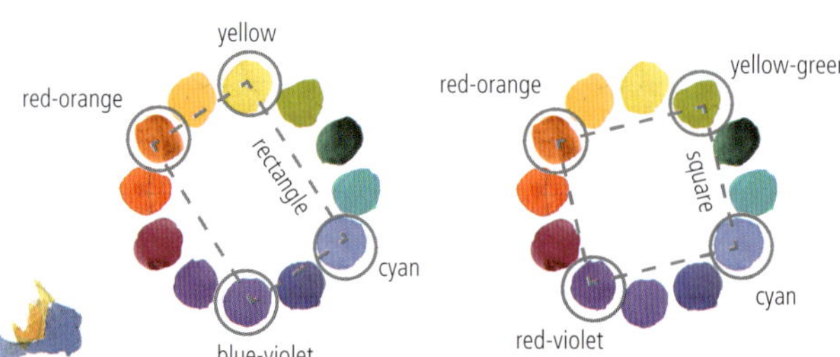

Analogous scheme (see "Analogous color palette," page 52) This color scheme offers the strongest potential for creating unity and a particular mood. It is as easy to use as the monochromatic scheme, but it looks richer. Using paint colors that are immediately adjacent to one another creates a singular boldness. There is no color contrast. A painting done in an analogous scheme can encompass all cool colors for a somber or nighttime scene, or all warm colors for a lighter portrayal. For best results, avoid combining warm and cool colors in the same analogous scheme.

It is possible to select immediately adjacent hues for a "tight" study, or hues that are separated by one color step for a "loose" study. It also is possible to select analogous pigments that are located in more neutral positions on the color wheel, such as greens or red-violets, for more neutral mood possibilities. Above all, this color scheme encourages you to step out of your comfort zone.

Tight palette

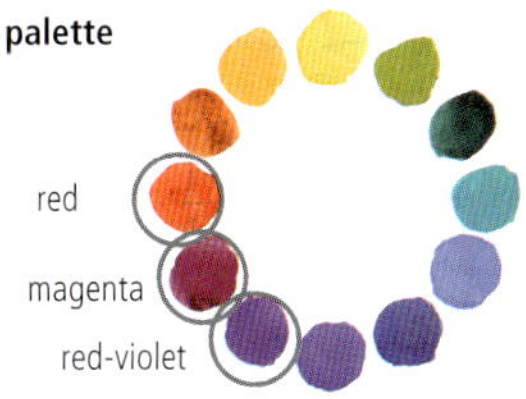

Loose palette

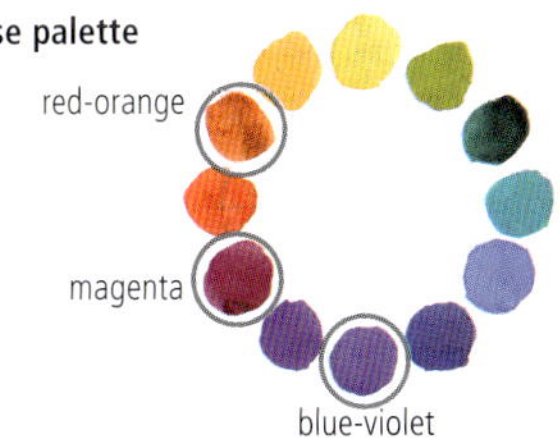

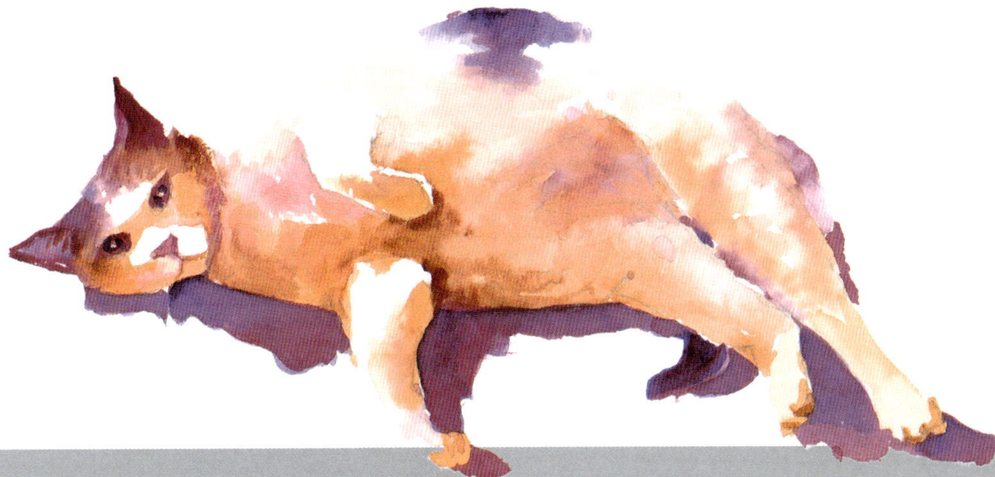

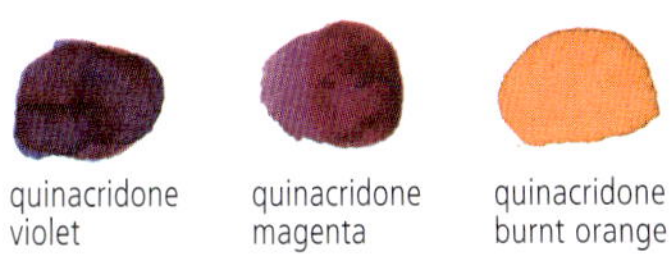

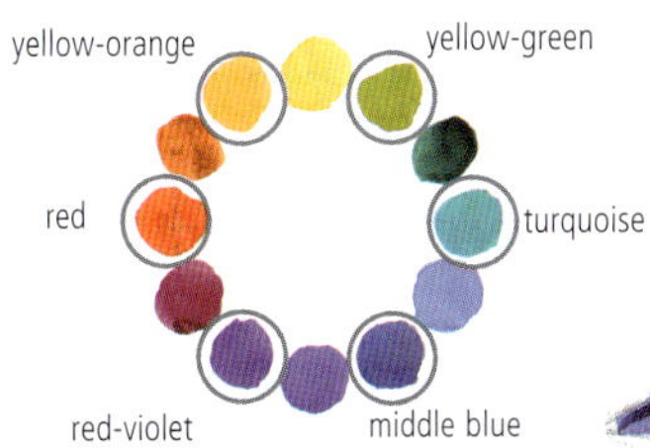

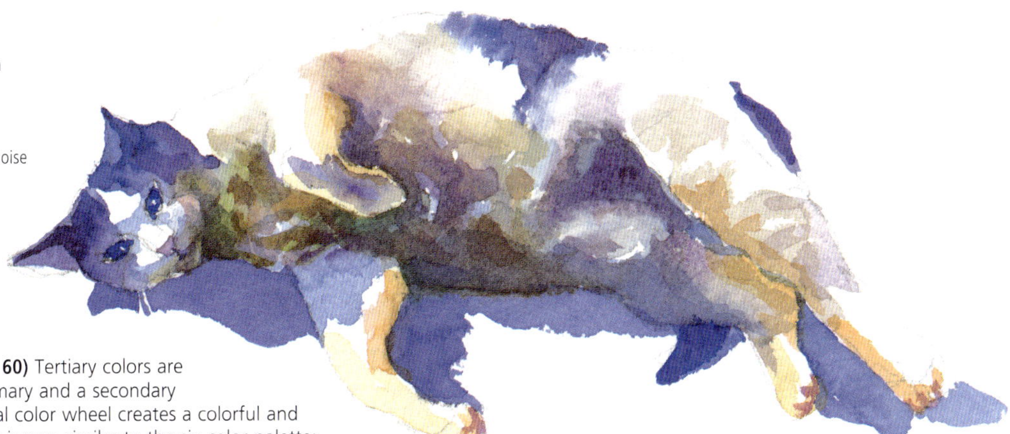

Tertiary palette (see "Tertiary colors," page 60) Tertiary colors are currently defined as those mixed from a primary and a secondary pigment. Mixing the tertiaries from the visual color wheel creates a colorful and unusual assortment of six hues. This scheme is very similar to the six-color palette; it is just one color note counterclockwise on the color wheel. As such, the tertiary palette also contains three sets of complements, making it useful for achieving colorful complementary neutrals with accents. As this study shows, when bright green gold and cobalt teal are used with manganese violet and quinacridone red, they create some great neutrals. A predominantly warm or cool bias in color selection works best for this color scheme.

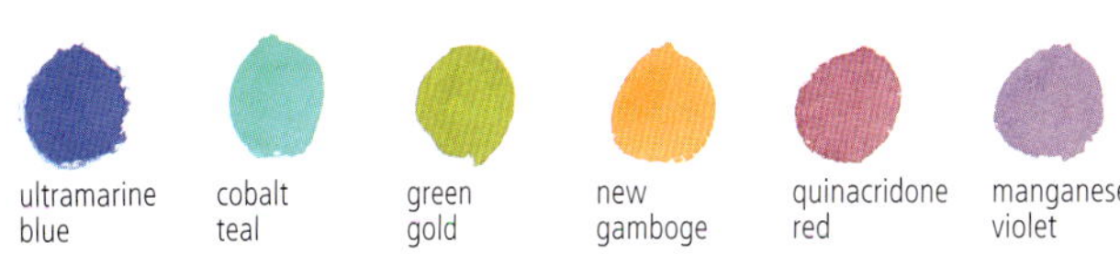

Primary palette

Primary colors depend upon whether you are seeing them through light, as in a television or on a computer screen, or as inks and paint pigments. There are basically two kinds of primary colors: light or additive color primaries, and pigment or subtractive color primaries.

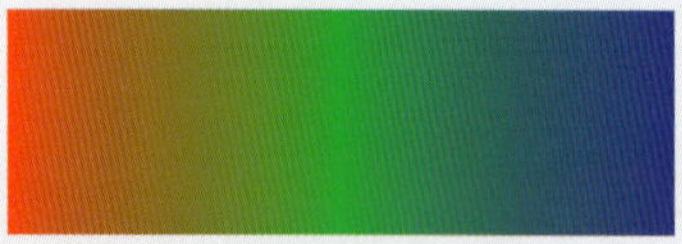

Light or additive color primaries When we mix colors of light, the more we mix the brighter the color gets. Colors add to each other. By mixing just three colors of light—red, green, and blue—we can make any color we want. These are the primary colors used to make the millions of different colors we see on television and computer screens.

Pigment or subtractive color primaries Paints and pigments absorb different colors of light, subtracting from what you see. The more pigment is added, the more light is absorbed and the darker the combined color becomes. It is nearly the opposite of mixing light. The primary colors for paint or pigments are cyan, magenta, and yellow. Mixing the three pigment primaries produces black or gray, as well as all other pigment colors.

RELATING LIGHT AND PIGMENT COLORS

If two colors from one primary group are combined, they make a primary color from the other group. The primary colors of light are secondary colors for paint and pigments—and vice versa.

Light **Paint**

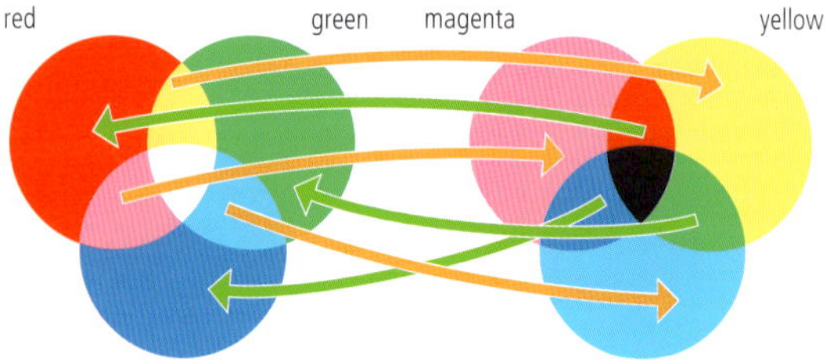

red + blue = magenta
blue + green = cyan
green + red = yellow

magenta + yellow = red
yellow + cyan = green
cyan + magenta = blue

Artists need to consider both types of primary colors when painting. Colors are mixed according to the subtractive pigment primaries, and then our eyes evaluate the colors we use through the additive light primaries.

HART'S COLOR WHEEL

This color wheel attempts to accommodate both systems. It uses quinacridone magenta, aureolin yellow, and cobalt blue as primary colors. Admittedly the cobalt blue is not a true cyan, but neither is cerulean, phthalo, manganese, or ultramarine. Cobalt blue mixes well with other pigments, which some would say partially makes up for its limitations. See page 14 for more on the color wheel and alternative colors for each of the numbered color postions.

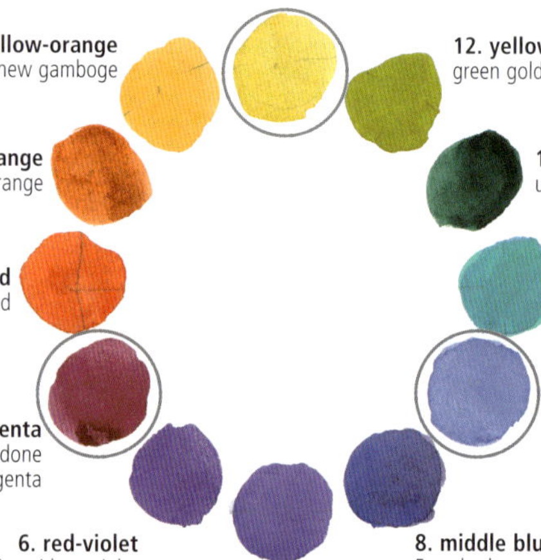

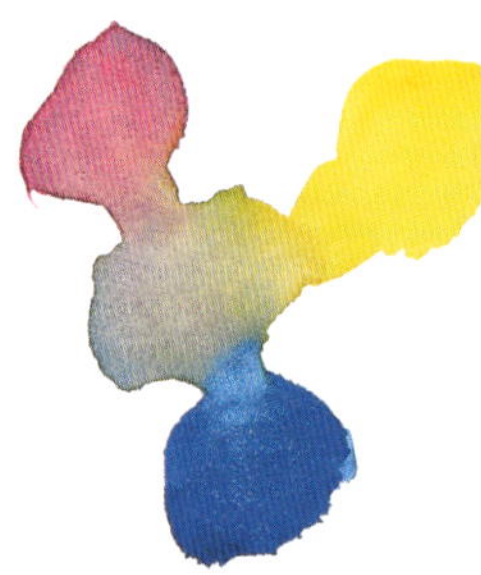

Primaries mix to gray The three primary colors mixed together make gray.

Primaries mix to secondaries Two primary colors mix together to make a secondary color. Primaries with secondaries provide a full range of colors.

magenta + yellow = orange

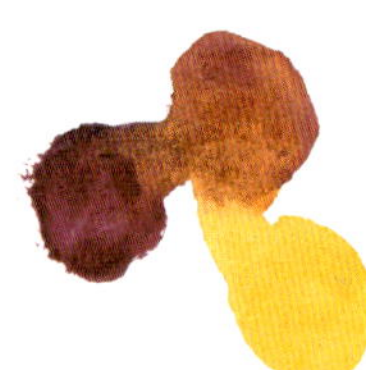

yellow + cyan = green

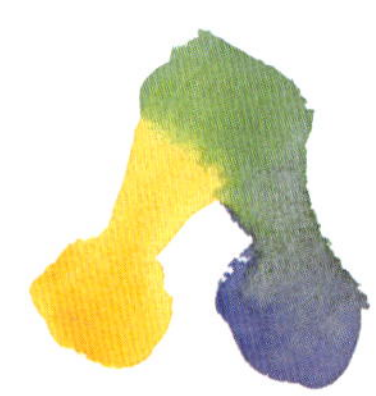

magenta + cyan = blue-violet

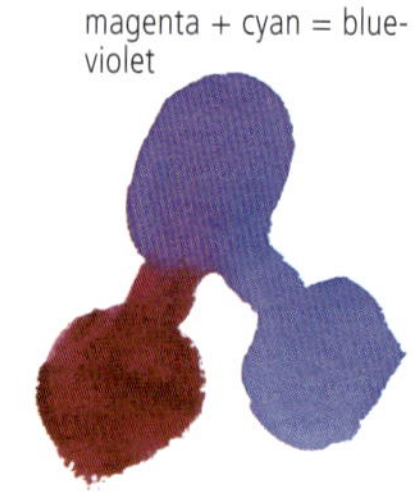

WHAT CAN YOU DO WITH A PRIMARY PALETTE?

Because primary colors mix to create all other colors, an artist can use just three pigments for a painting. These three studies of the same subject use only primary colors of different kinds of watercolor pigment. (See "Pigments," page 8.)

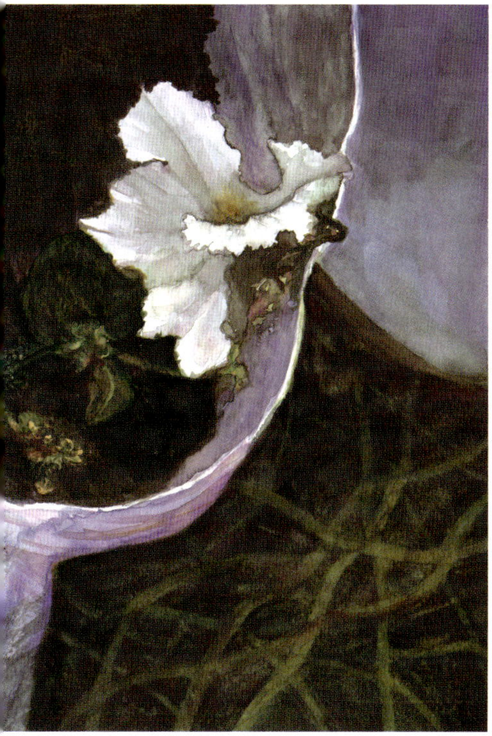

Permanent, staining pigments John Deyloff selected three permanent, staining primaries for his study: phthalo blue, Holbein's opera, and quinacridone gold. Note the very dark darks that he was able to mix from these three pigments—as well as some lighter grays. Transparent washes are more difficult to obtain with these strong pigments.

phthalo blue

opera (Holbein)

quinacridone gold

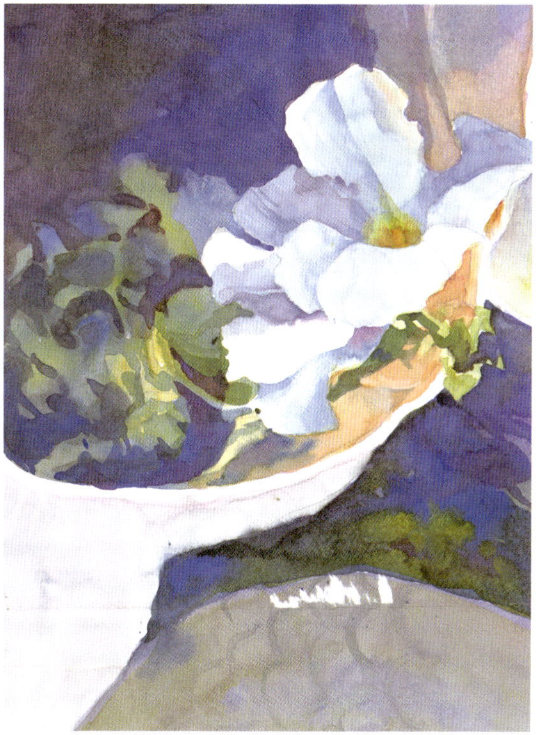

Transparent, non-staining pigments The author played with three of her favorite pigments, which demonstrate a bit of granulation (in the cobalt blue), transparency, and nice variation in colors. Note that achieving very dark darks is not as easy with this palette of primaries. The colors chosen were: cobalt blue, rose madder genuine, and aureolin yellow.

cobalt blue

rose madder genuine

aureolin yellow

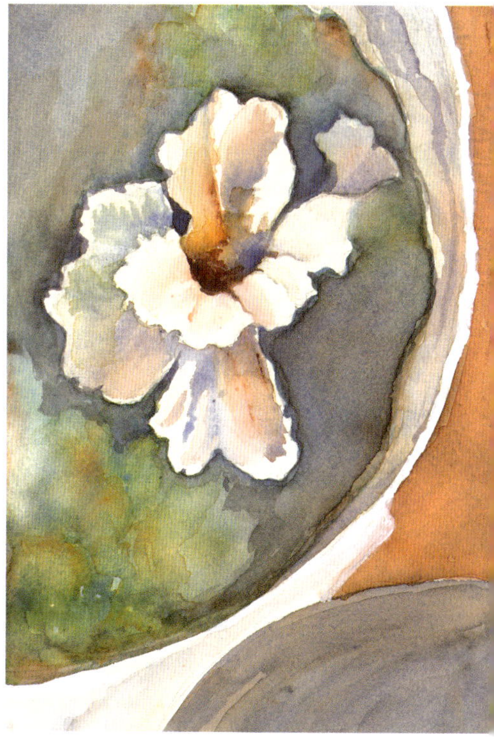

Sedimentary or opaque pigments Karen Norris chose three sedimentary or opaque pigments for her study. Her selection enabled her to create some interesting textures and pigment mixtures, as well as some sense of transparency. Quinacridone burnt scarlet is not a sedimentary pigment, but the artist chose to include it with the two that are—ultramarine blue and new gamboge.

quinacridone burnt scarlet

ultramarine blue

new gamboge

SOME THINGS TO CONSIDER

- It takes only three pigments to create a painting. Choose three primaries that have the characteristics you want—and go!
- If you want a little more variety and power, try out a six-color palette (see "Comparing Color Schemes," page 44) that includes the secondaries.
- Use the primary palette or the Velázquez palette (see "Comparing Color Schemes," page 44) to learn color mixing and how to achieve a good range of values.

Six-color palette

A six-color palette may be the answer to many artists' prayers! Carefully selected and individualized pigment choices reduce the number of pigments you need and can cover all, or nearly all, the color bases. Remember that the standard primary palette consists of a magenta, a cyan, and a yellow. A six-color palette includes secondary colors produced from mixing the primaries. Because mixed pigments lose some of their chroma and intensity, a real paint palette is shown that substitutes the mixed secondaries for real paints to produce even more visual power.

Six-color palette: Paint primaries and mixed secondaries In the paint primary group (see Primary palette, page 48), the primaries are magenta, cyan, and yellow, which produce the following mixed secondaries:
cyan + yellow = green (secondary)
cyan + magenta = blue-violet (secondary)
magenta + yellow = red-orange (secondary)

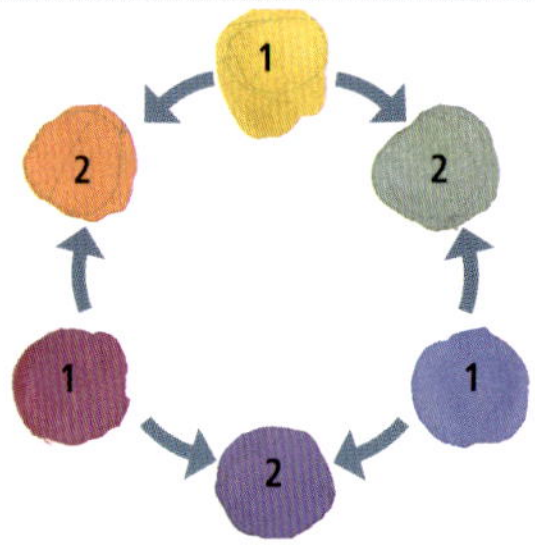

Six-color palette: Paint primaries and paint secondaries When real manufactured secondary pigments are used instead of mixed secondaries, the six-color palette gains mixing power and intensity. This is because mixing pigments causes a reduction in tinting strength in the mixed secondary. Compare the results of both palettes. It is the artist who makes these pigment choices.

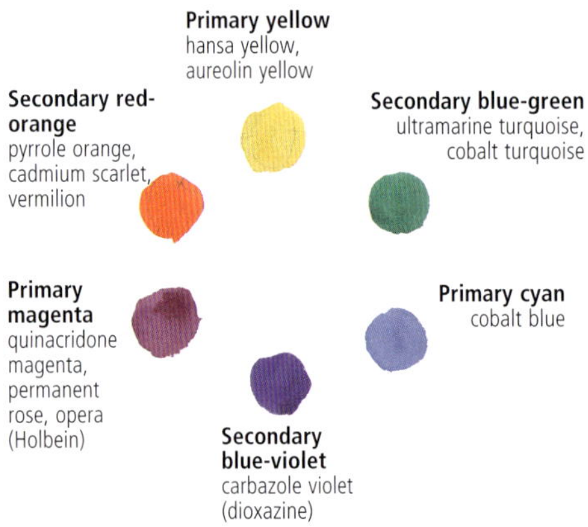

SOME THINGS TO CONSIDER

- A six-color palette can provide most, if not all, of the colors or hues needed for a color-harmonious painting.
- If you desire certain pigment characteristics in addition to color, add other pigments (e.g., pigments for granulation, sedimentation, transparency, or iridescence).
- A primary or six-color palette is great for simplifying color choices and learning about mixing pigments.
- Build your own six-color palette based on the information given and your own preferences in pigments. For instance, a pigment choice for a yellow-orange could be any of the following: nickel azo, Indian yellow, or new gamboge.

Split-primary six-color palette Here, your choice of primary has an effect on the mixed secondary (see "Working Across the Mixing Line" below). In this palette, each primary pigment is split into a pair of colors, each leaning toward one of the other two "primaries." For example, a single primary yellow is replaced by a warm (deep) yellow that leans toward red and a cool (light) yellow that leans toward blue. The artist can select the warm and cool version of each primary color. This selection may include:

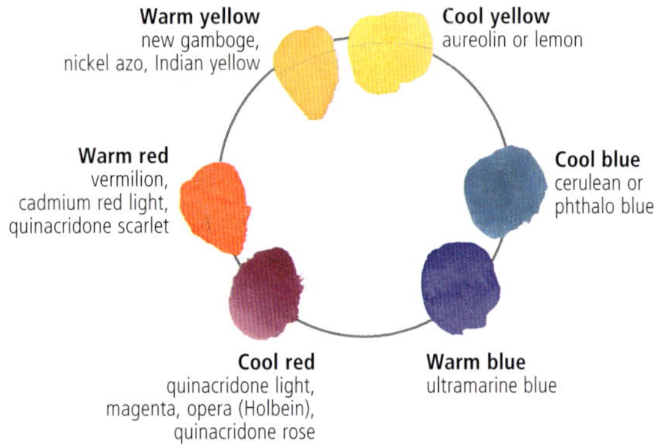

WORKING ACROSS THE MIXING LINE

Split-primary purple mix example Note the gradual transition from vibrant purple mix (1. cool red and *analogous* warm blue) to the semineutral purple-gray (2. warm red and *complementary* cool blue). The dashed lines divide the warm and cool version of each primary color. Notice that mixing paints that are close together on the color wheel (analogous) results in vibrant color mixes. As you mix primaries that are farther apart, the resulting mix is less vibrant. Mixing paints opposite each other (complementary) produces a semi-neutral result. Once familiar with the theory, you can decide what you prefer.

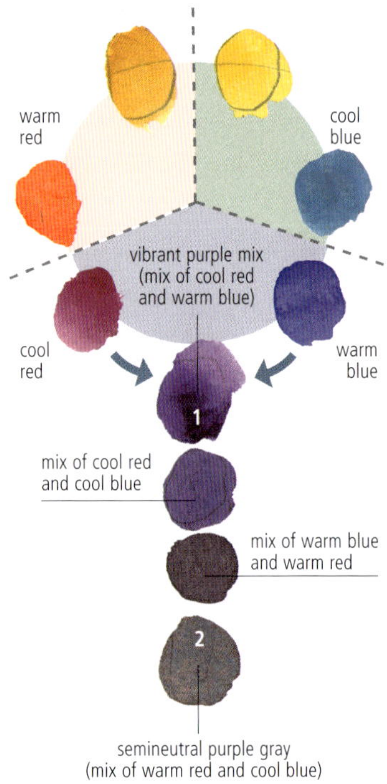

WHAT CAN THE SIX-COLOR PALETTE DO?

These paintings by the author help show the essential differences between the specially selected six-color palette and a full palette of individually chosen pigments. In comparing the two paintings, you can see that the six-color palette is able to cover virtually all the color and value ranges obtained by a full palette, proving that a limited palette can be successful colorwise. The most important difference between the two palettes, however, is what individual pigments can do beyond color—qualities such as granulation or shooting.

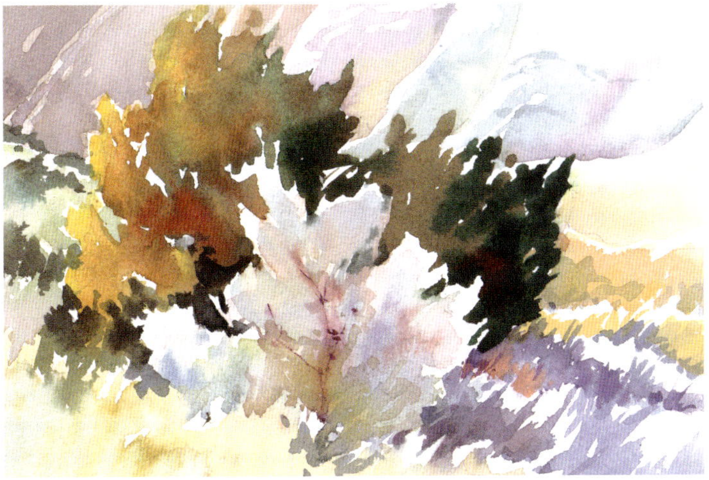

Six-color palette: primaries and secondaries The artist has used the six-color palette. Mixes are obtained by mixing the six paints. Just about every color can be produced.

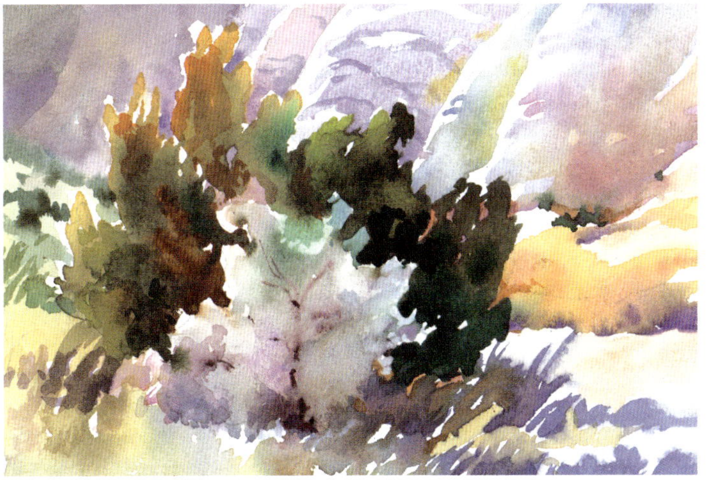

A personal palette Here she has used her favorite paints, which include quinacridone burnt sienna, ultramarine turquoise, nickel azo, cobalt violet, cobalt blue, napthamide maroon, aureolin yellow, buff titanium, quinacridone gold, rose madder genuine, and manganese violet. Many are sedimentary or opaque, suggesting the vegetation.

USING SPLIT-PRIMARY MIXES

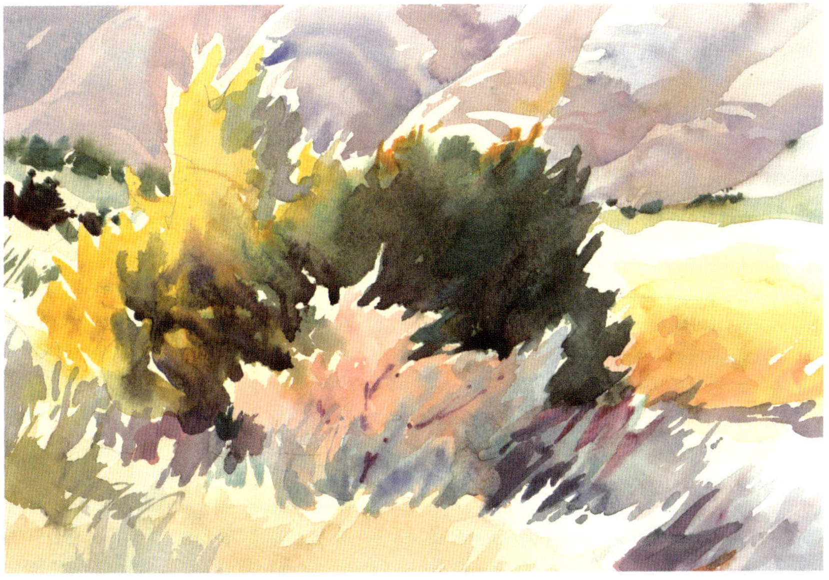

Split-primary mixes In this study, the author used the split-primary colors for her mixes. In order to achieve some of the dark gray-greens and semineutral lavenders desired, she worked across the mixing line (see opposite). The mixes with one asterisk * did not cross the mixing line; those with two asterisks ** did. The color harmony is beautifully apparent in the painting despite the lack of some pigments known for texture, shooting effects, etc.

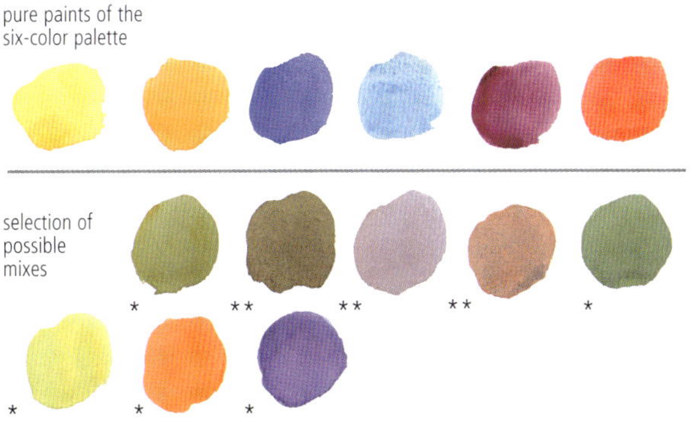

Analogous color palette

One of the most beautiful palettes, the analogous color scheme offers the artist adjacent, closely related pigments that combine in perfect harmony. Each pigment contains a part of its neighbor, which makes them all related. Many people who grew up in the "dyed to match" culture of the 1950s, when orange and red "clashed," only learned years later to appreciate the rich harmony of the analogous hues. Choose a minimum of three adjacent colors to explore the interesting ways in which this palette can be used to promote the desired feeling and mood. A pigment map, or pigment wheel, or color map—whatever it may be called—can help with some of the pigments not on the color wheel for high-chroma pigments.

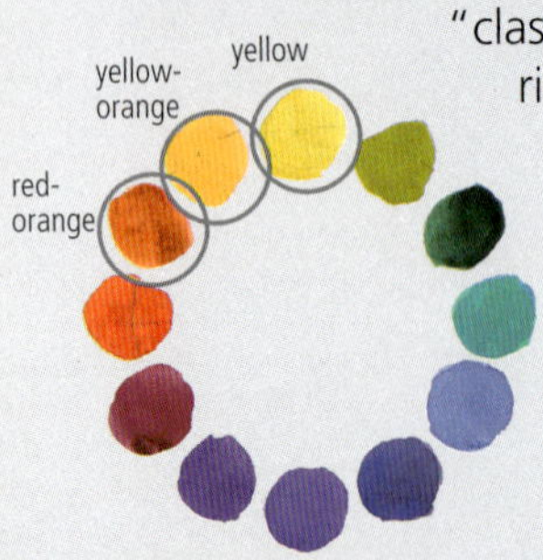

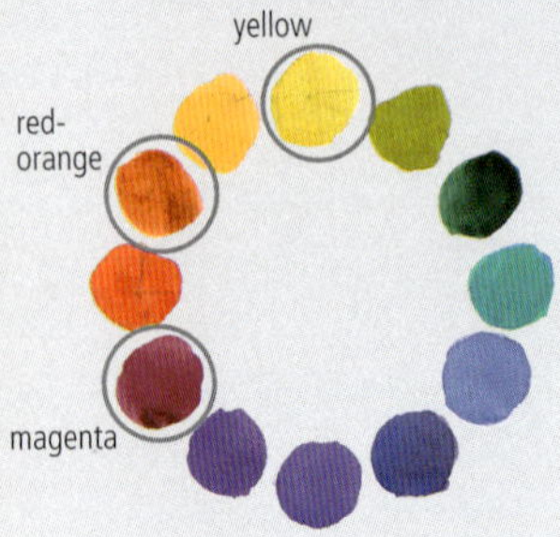

Close or loose relationships The top pigment wheel shows close analogous color relationships, and the bottom pigment wheel shows one step or looser relationships. Try both and see the different possibilities.

SOME THINGS TO CONSIDER

- The analogous color scheme is inherently harmonious.
- Use this color scheme to explore some analogous hues, in high and low chroma. With the combined force of an analogous grouping, the choice of an appropriate subject matter is all-important.
- When it comes to greens the analogous color scheme is fully visible in nature. Remember this in your next summer landscape.

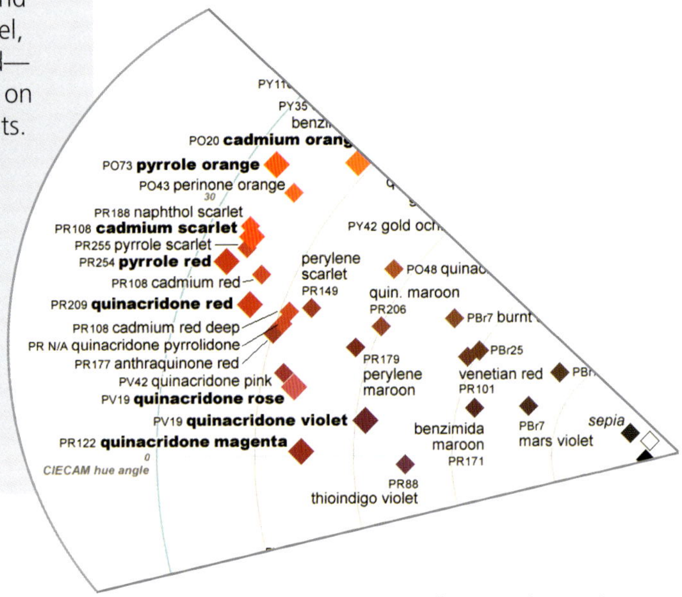

Color pigment map Manufactured pigments are arranged on this color pigment map by Bruce MacEvoy (see page 128) so that those with the highest chroma are located on the outer edges, whereas the low chroma pigments are closer to the dark center. All of the pigments within a pie-shaped wedge bounded by three high-chroma analogous pigments can be used to add variety and subdued relief to the composition. These semineutrals can be manufactured paints or mixes of the analogous rim pigments with their respective complements. There are many semineutral, low-chroma paints available that are capable of creating deep tones.

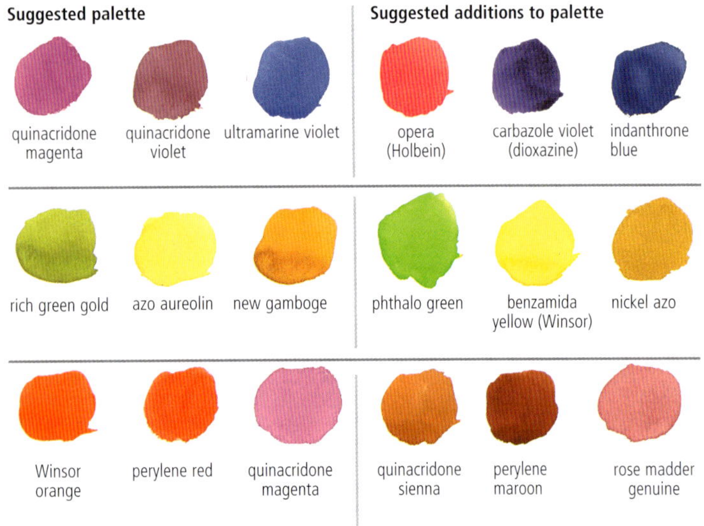

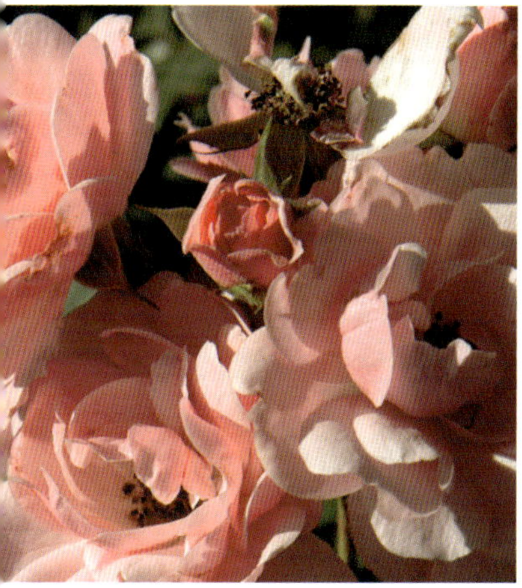

ROSE STUDIES

These studies of a pink rose demonstrate the various effects that the analogous palette can produce.

High- and low-chroma pigments Some artists enjoy combining high- and low-chroma pigments within the analogous scheme. Note the rich, dark mixes of napthamide maroon and purpurite genuine that serve to increase the contrast and add rich accents, reminiscent of chocolate and raspberries.

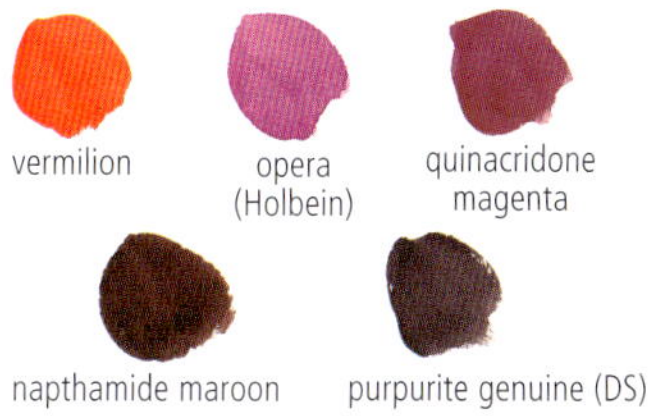

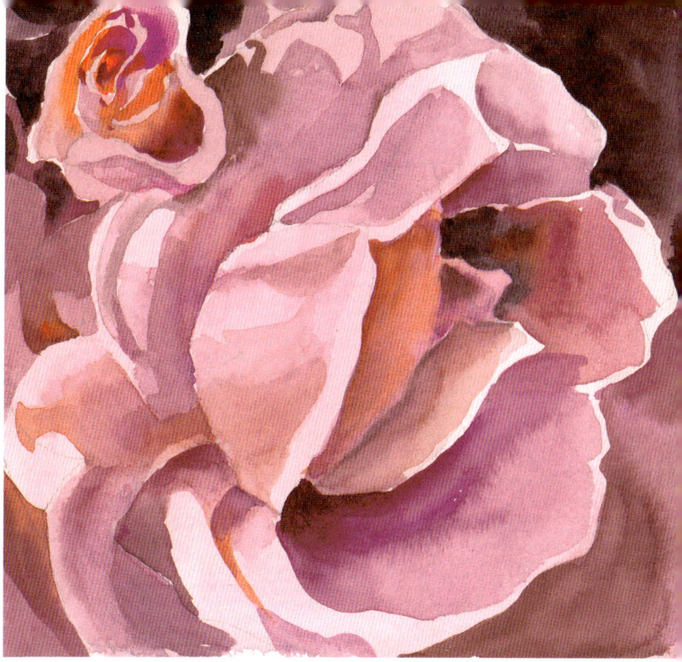

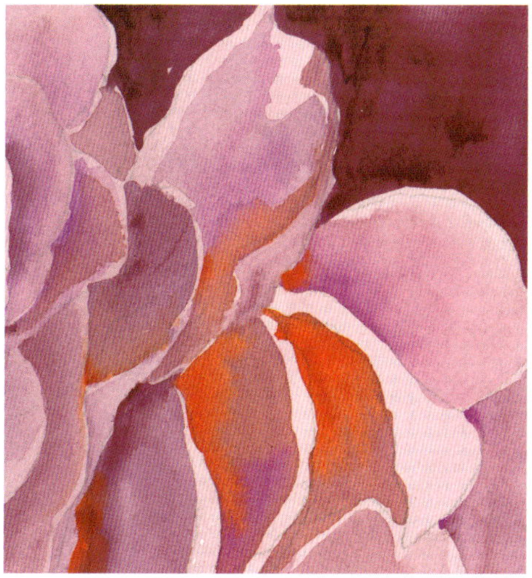

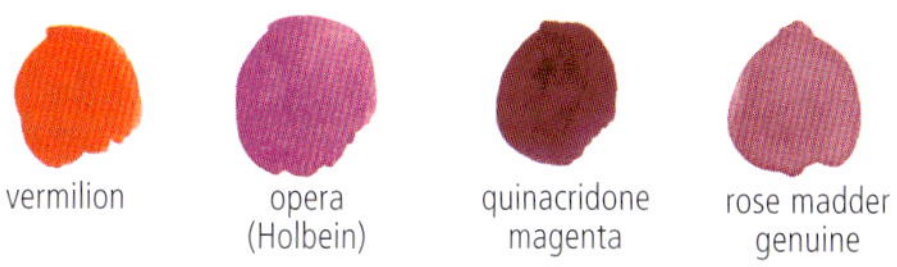

Pure, high-chroma pigments The use of three or four adjacent high-chroma pigments on the visual color wheel certainly grabs attention with its sizzle. It can overwhelm the eye if the high-chroma pigments are used purely and at full strength. Even mixes of these intense pigments create a vibrant painting. Here the quinacridone magenta provides some relief in the background. Rose madder genuine was used as an underwash.

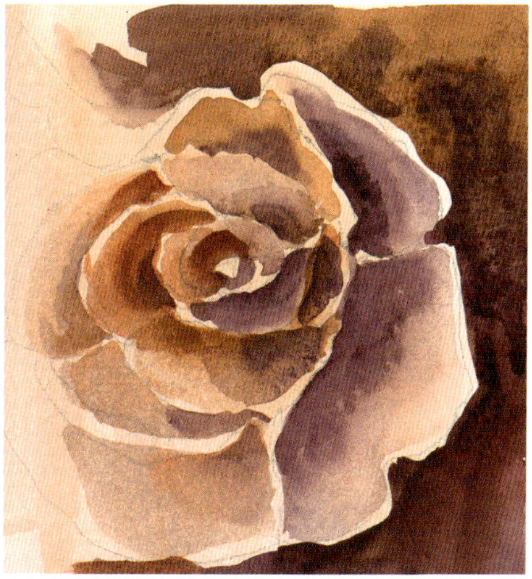

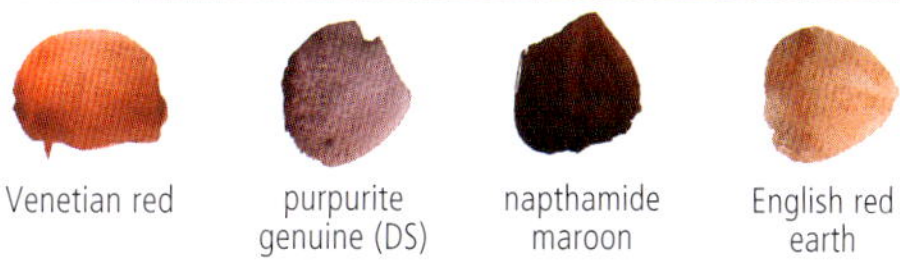

Low chroma, semineutral Each of these pigments is located away from the high chroma rim of the pigment map. Together they comprise "neutralized" violet, red, and red-orange, along with some wonderful granulations. A distinctive mood of mystery, or cloaked danger, is evoked by these semineutrals. Note the rich creeping and granulating in the mixes. An underwash of pale English red earth helped to set the somber mood.

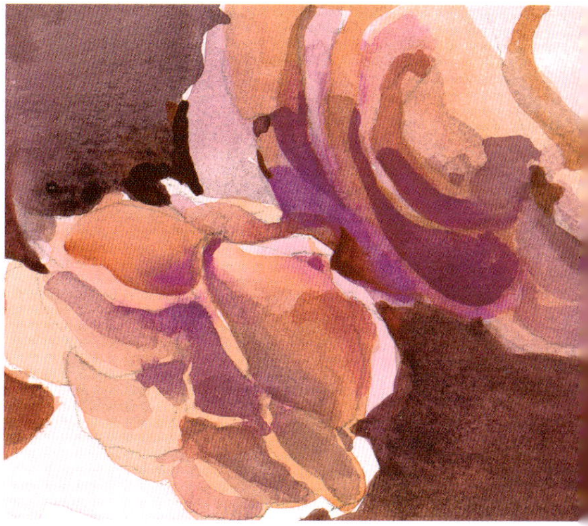

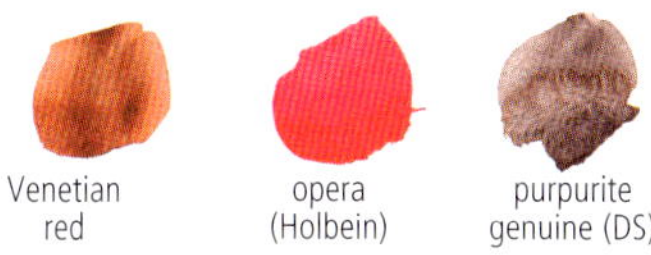

Variations of high and low You can combine two high-chroma pigments and one low-chroma, or two low and one high, as shown. A simple, elegant color scheme can consist of three carefully selected analogous paints—two of low chroma and a single high-intensity pigment. Here the dusky purpurite genuine and smooth Venetian red were selected as the red-violet and red-orange, respectively. The central magenta position was claimed by the vibrant opera—a "hot pink" that is really cool in temperature.

Complementary palette

It is said that no color is more beautiful, more exciting, or more vibrant than when it is placed next to its complement—its partner—across the color wheel. On the color wheel, the complement of a primary color (magenta, cyan, or yellow) is the combination of the other two primaries. So mixing a color and its complement is the same as mixing all three primaries together.

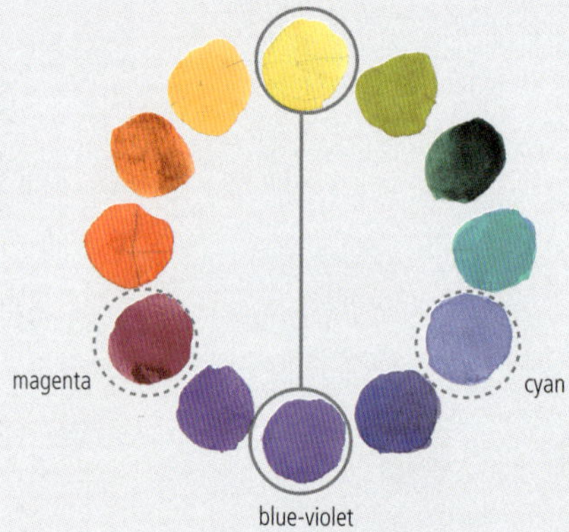

Yellow's complement, blue-violet, is a mix of magenta and cyan. Blue-violet plus yellow = dark gray or black.

FINDING A VISUAL COMPLEMENT

Compare the selected pigments below to find a visual complement. A visual complement is a complementary color found using the additive light wheel (see "Primary palette," page 48). Vermilion, for example, is surrounded by ultramarine turquoise, cerulean blue, and cobalt blue. Look at the vermilion, then at one of the other colors, and go back to the vermilion. Repeat for each of the blues. Your eyes will respond excitedly when they encounter close visual complements. You also can try mixing the two colors together and seeing which gives the most neutral or unbiased gray. You can make the choice.

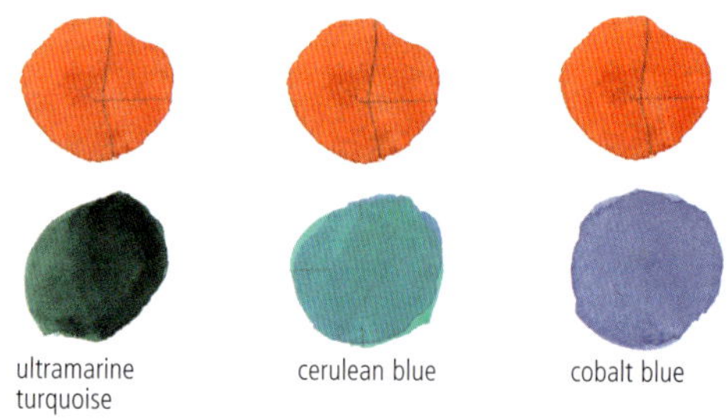

Dove Flight The author selected cobalt blue-violet and Indian yellow in order to combine visual complements in a simple composition. Note the extensive use of soft, varied, mixed blue-violet/yellow grays. Pure colors are saved for a few accents placed near some mixes. The color bias subtly leans toward the warmer yellow, allowing the blue-violet notes to sing even more harmoniously. Unsaturated, grayed yellows could have deadened the composition and were used with conscious care.

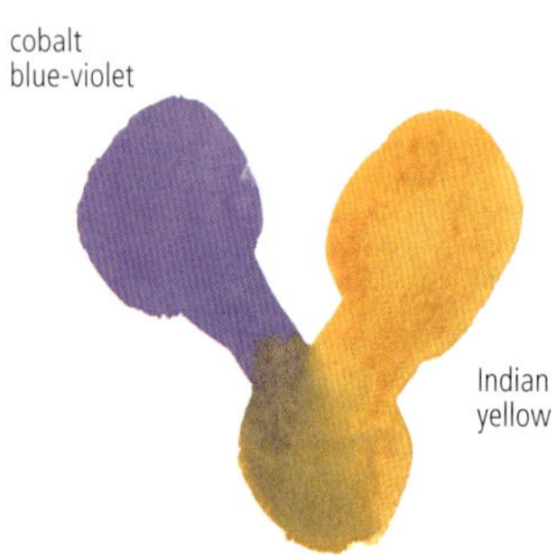

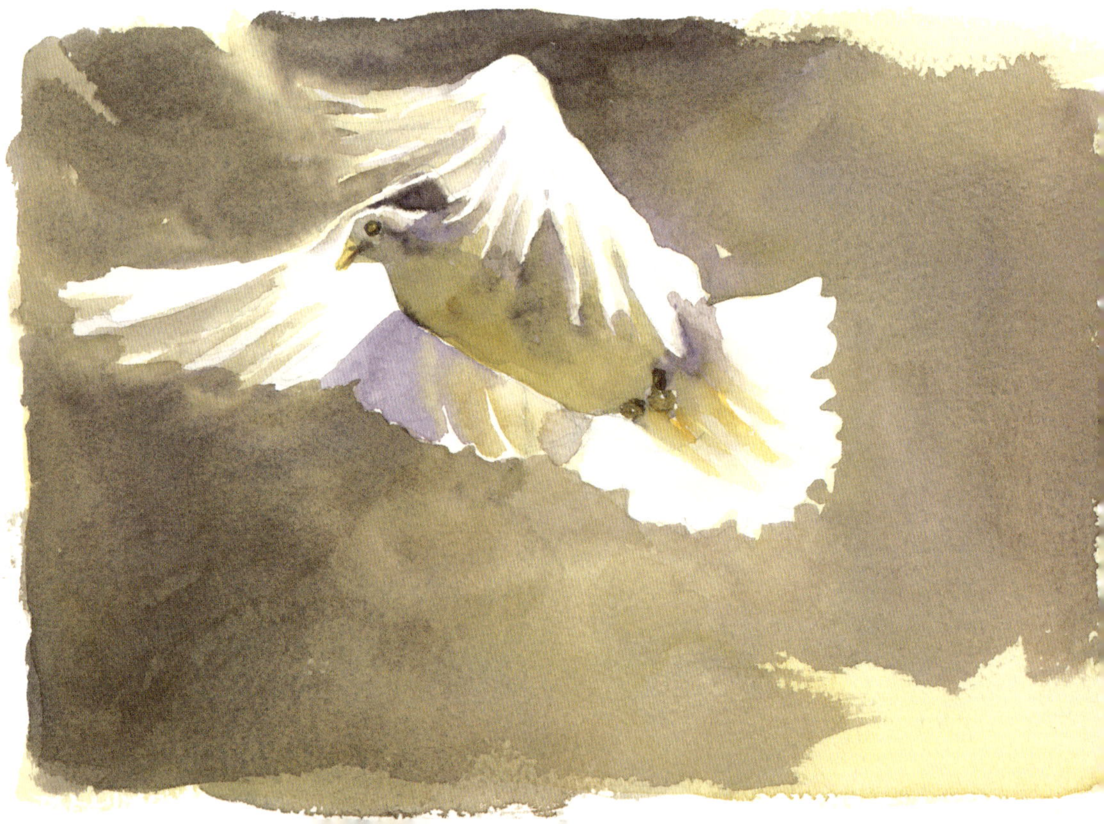

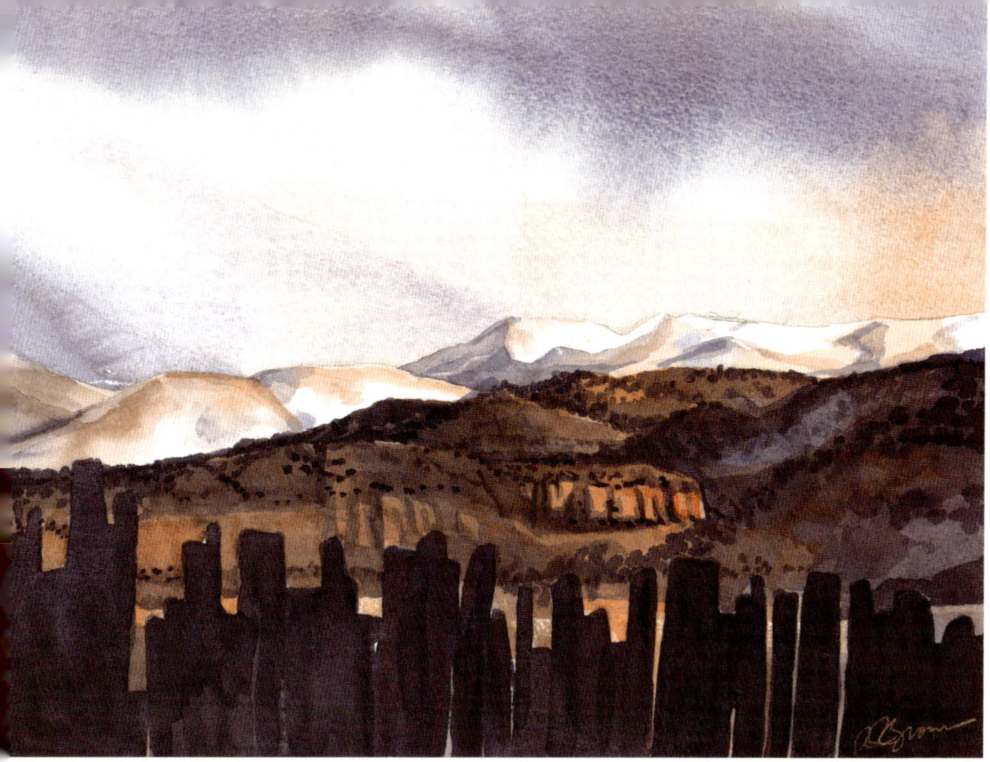

Beyond the Coyote Fence Allen Brown selected cadmium orange and ultramarine blue as complementary colors for his painting. His color choices appear to be consistent with the pigment color wheel. Although he used pure cadmium orange very sparingly and pure ultramarine blue even more sparingly, his deft use of both for mixing colorful neutrals is quite apparent. He made a conscious choice to use more ultramarine blue than cadmium orange to give the cool bias his winter landscape needed.

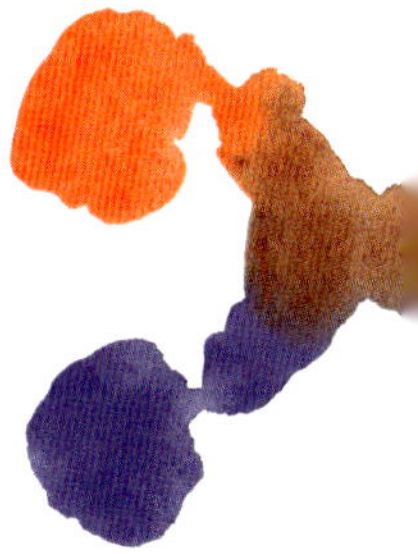

HISTORICAL COLOR THEORY

According to 18th-century color theory, complementary colors acted as color opposites, creating a new kind of color relationship—color contrast or color antagonism. Color contrast was demonstrated when these oppositional colors were shown side by side, while color antagonism was mostly inferred because the mixing of the two complements produced gray. It was said that the complementary colors destroyed each other. Modern understanding of color complements enables us to view each color participant more magnanimously, in the knowledge that it is the wavelengths of the colors that combine to produce white light.

Design harmony is affected not by the mixing of the color but by the viewers of finished color. Visual complementary colors, therefore, are the most relevant to color design and were advocated by Chevreul, Rood, and other classical color theorists.

The mixing complement (found by mixing colors) and the visual complement (found by viewing colors) may be similar or quite different from each other because of substance uncertainty in the pigments, different color wheels, color harmonies, etc. This means that the artist has to use the information available to make a choice. It is, therefore, a good idea to get used to making your own decisions about what colors "work best together." You can trust your eyes!

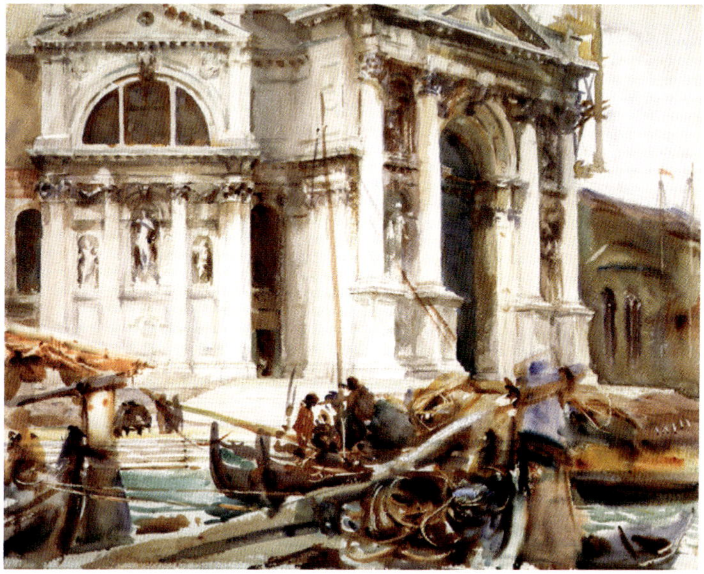

SOME THINGS TO CONSIDER

- The complementary palette is a simple, easy-to-use color scheme with potential for the strongest color contrasts.
- The strongest color choice is a warm and a cool for the complementary scheme.
- For best results choose a dominant color that will appear directly and in mixes. Use the other color for accents.
- Consider using a warm, pure color (red or orange) as an accent placed opposite unsaturated cool colors to emphasize the warms—or vice versa.
- Avoid overuse of unsaturated warm colors such as brown or dull yellow. Overuse tends to create a deadening effect.

Santa Maria della Salute
John Singer Sargent often used complementary colors to help illustrate the warm reflected light and cool shadows on sun-drenched white buildings or statues. Look at the use of the yellow-orange raw sienna against the middle-blue ultramarine blue in this 1904 painting.

Split-complement palette

The split-complement palette extends the capabilities of both a complementary and an analogous color scheme. It also offers the artist strong color contrast for emphasis. In the usual split-complement palette, three analogous colors are opposed by the complement of the middle color. The center color of the three is called the "key color."

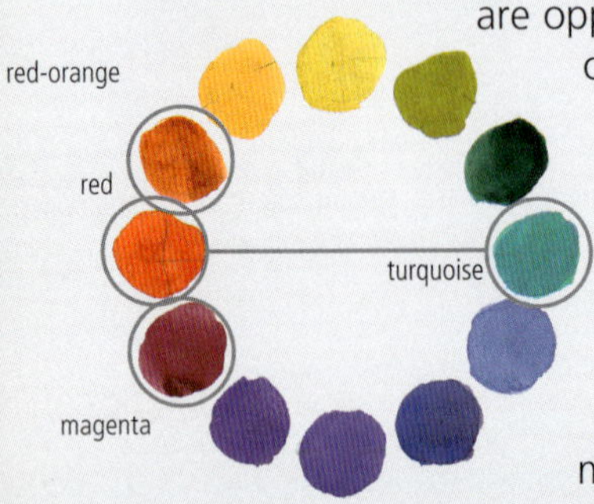

Using predominantly warm or cool analogous colors establishes a strong mood. The selected complementary color is useful for accents and emphasis. The predominantly warm analogous colors create a lively, hot, or invigorating feeling with some startling, cool punches. A predominantly cool analogous trio promotes a feeling of cold, sadness, or quiet, which is then startled by complementary warm notes.

Some artists who use the split-complement color scheme avoid the center color of the analogous group. Its use as a direct complement to the single color opposite it adds perceptive pigment strength (because of the visual vibration they produce together), but it is considered difficult to use. This is because direct complements produce mixed neutrals, which can deaden a color composition unless used carefully.

CANDLE STUDIES

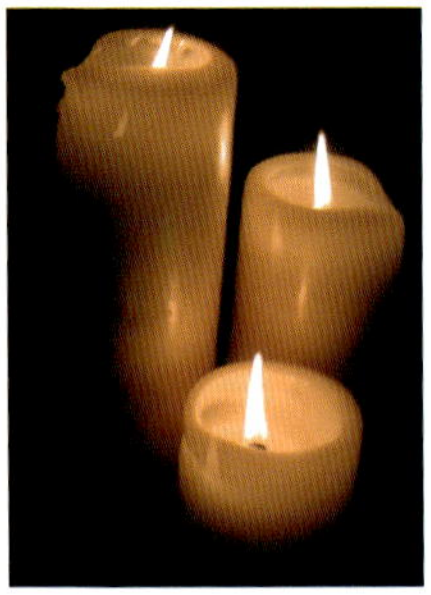

These candle studies are all examples of split-complementary paintings.

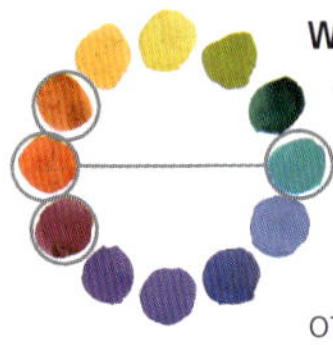

Warm The use of the warm analogous trio (right) with the cool complement of the central warm color demonstrates the strong contrast this color scheme offers. The mood expressed by the warm dominance is welcoming. However, the strong use of mixed neutrals in the background and the low color key (see page 64) suggests a more somber theme. If the intent is a festive mood, a higher color key could help reinforce the idea. When you make color choices, be careful to avoid contradictory effects.

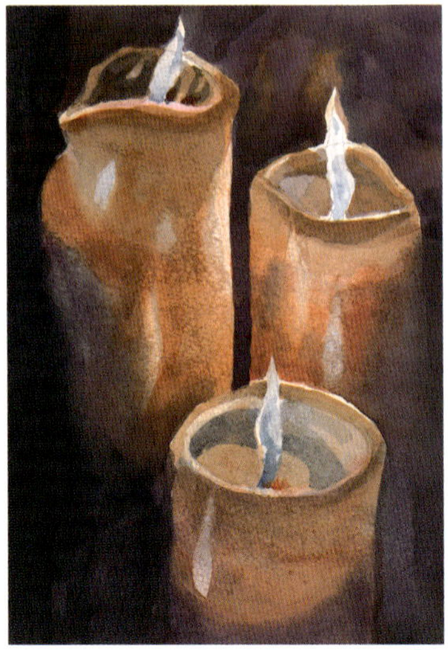

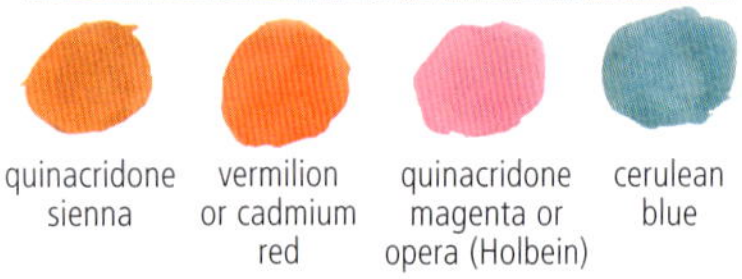

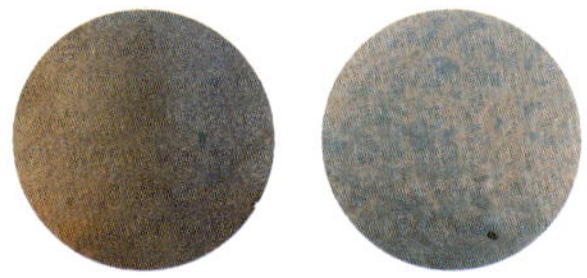

Note the delicate sedimentation in the vermilion/cerulean mixes.

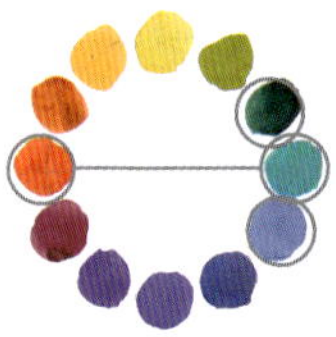

Cool The three predominant cool blues are cobalt blue, cerulean blue, and ultramarine turquoise. Although there is some indication of warmth in the subdued background, most of the effect is cold and dark, suggesting a winter night. The complementary candle flames flicker warmth in the midst of cold. The low color key and the predominantly cool color temperature work together to communicate a reflective, somber mood.

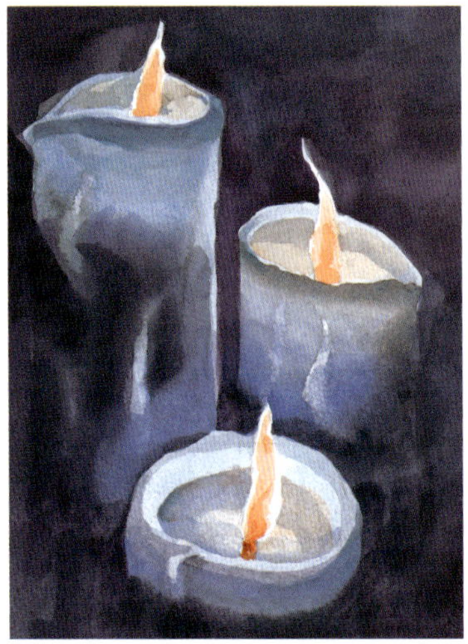

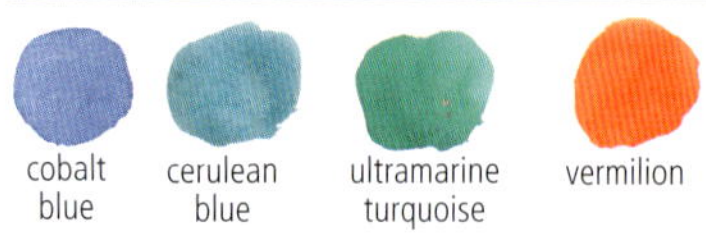

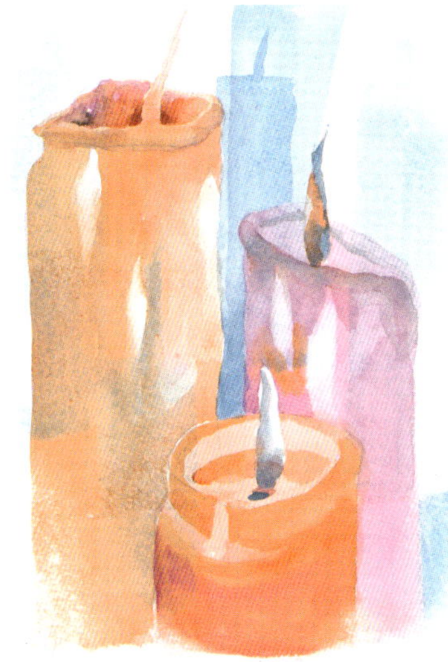

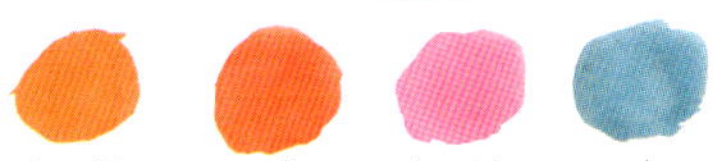

quinacridone sienna | vermilion or cadmium red | quinacridone magenta or opera (Holbein) | cerulean blue

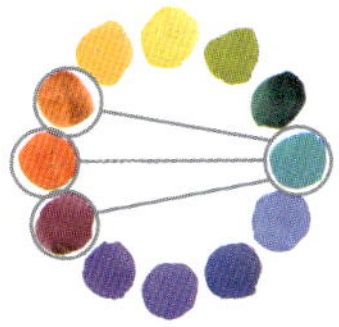

High color key Using the same paints as in the "warm candle" swatches (three warms, one cool center complement), this high key play of color effectively expresses a festive mood. The use of purer colors together with fewer mixed semineutrals promotes the color vibration of the orange/blue complements.

MIXING NEUTRALS

In the warm and cool candle studies, the direct complements of each color were used, producing mixed neutrals with a less colorful result. For example, mix cobalt blue with quinacridone sienna to produce a new neutral. And mix a bit of ultramarine turquoise with quinacridone magenta to obtain its neutral.

This method is a little more painstaking as you must remember to mix in the direct complements. Take care that the dull browns created from warm pigments and their complements do not overwhelm the composition.

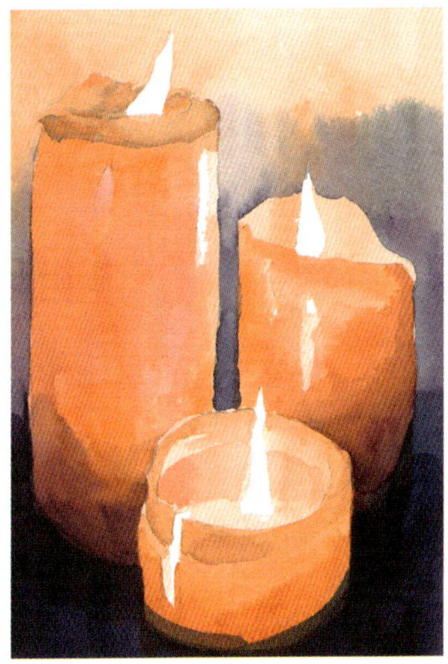

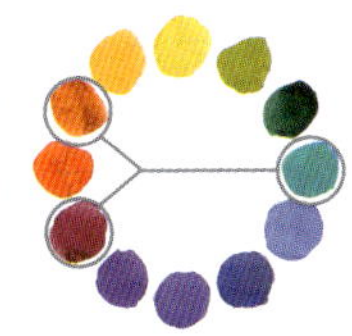

Warm, full color key Three strong pigments—warm red-orange, a cool magenta, and a turquoise complement to the mixed red of the other two—make the most colorful split-complementary triad. The mixed neutrals from these paints are not quite direct complements and therefore not quite so neutral or brownish. Over an initial underwash of quinacridone sienna, the mixes create a colorful ensemble. Using a full range color key from very light to very dark, the overall color temperature is decidedly warm, which punctuates the notes of pure blue.

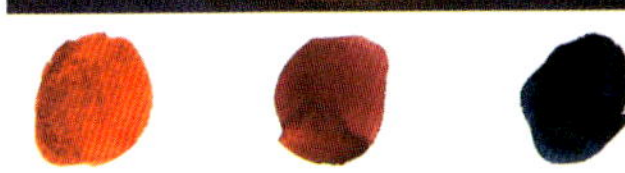

quinacridone sienna | quinacridone magenta | phthalo turquoise

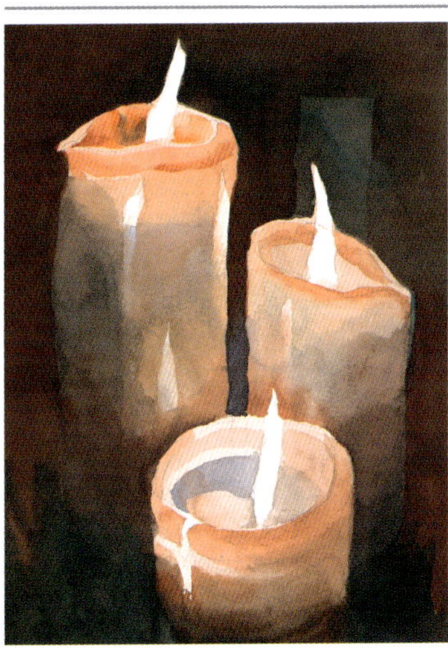

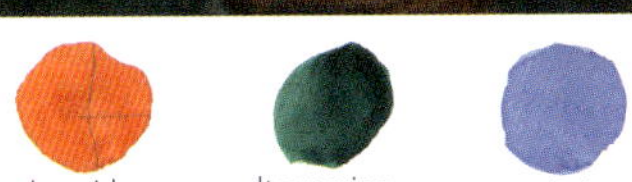

quinacridone burnt scarlet | ultramarine turquoise | cobalt blue

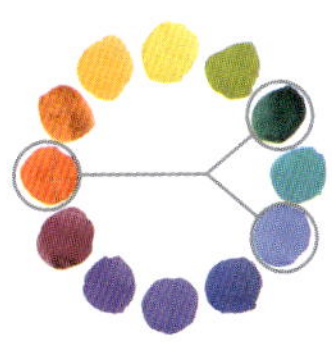

Low color key Using just three paints—ultramarine turquoise (strong, green-blue), cobalt blue, and quinacridone burnt scarlet (strong red)—is the most limited palette possible in the split-complementary scheme.
The absence of a direct complement is theoretically overcome when the two other analogous paints are mixed together. The artist's selection of pigments will strongly affect the success of this variation. Here the selection of strong paints demonstrates variety and simplicity. Note the high color and value contrasts. The selection of cobalt blue provided delicate glazing for the candles.

SOME THINGS TO CONSIDER

- The split-complementary color scheme offers the artist the strongest color contrast, combining the analogous and the complementary color schemes.
- Be careful when mixing the semineutral warms, which may deaden the composition or create imbalance.
- Mixing direct complements in the standard color wheel produces a semineutral gray, brown, or black.
- Three-pigment split complements are easier to use than four-pigment split complements.
- Consider applying the key color and its analogous hues only in darkened mixtures. Then use the single complement as an accent in very small, saturated areas.

Tetradic color scheme

The tetradic palette uses four colors arranged into two complementary color pairs, which creates more potential color variety than any other color scheme. The tetradic scheme may be diagrammatically arranged as a rectangle (one complementary pair separated from the other by one color step) or a square (one complementary pair separated from another by two color steps). Artists such as Walter Ufer and Victor Higgins have achieved dramatic results with the tetradic color scheme, and the emotionally charged interior paintings by Edward Hopper also suggest use of the tetradic color scheme.

In pitting two complementary color pairs against each other, this scheme can be daunting. Mixed complements are neutral and are best played against pure color. Also, it may appear unbalanced if all four colors are used in equal amounts. It is best when one color, called the "key color," is selected to dominate. This key color usually occupies the most space in the composition or appears in the widest range of mixed colors.

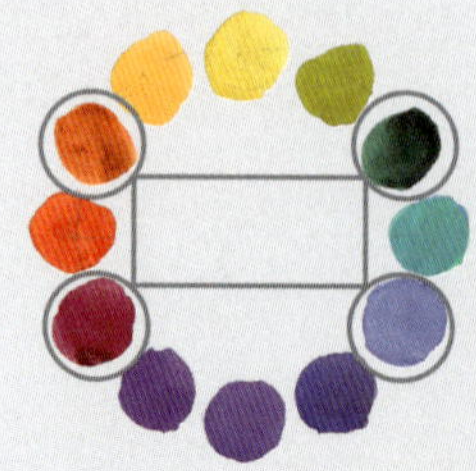

rectangular tetradic

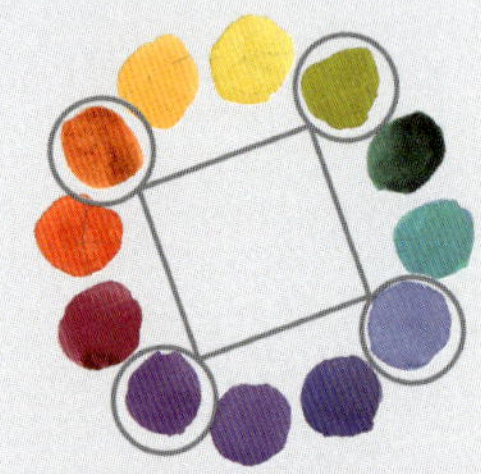

square tetradic

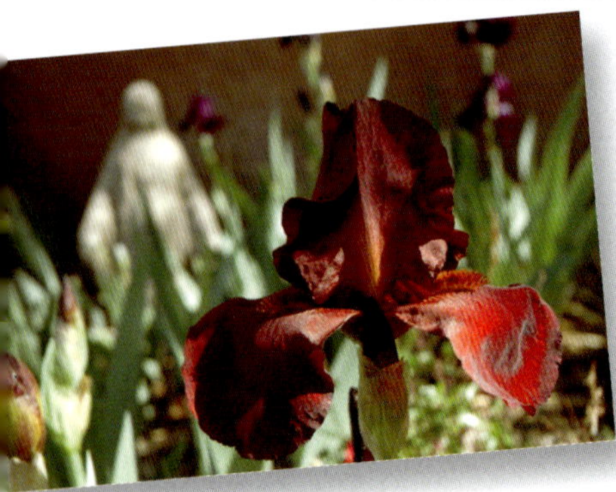

The color choices for both rectangular tetradic paintings (Note the mixes that can be produced from these colors):

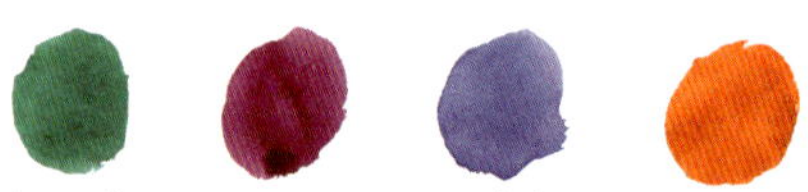

ultramarine turquoise | quinacridone magenta | cobalt blue | quinacridone sienna

USING A RECTANGULAR TETRADIC PALETTE

To show the contrast between the two, both a warm and a cool version of this painting were done. Both are rectangular tetrads using cobalt blue and quinacridone sienna (complements) and ultramarine turquoise and quinacridone magenta (complements).

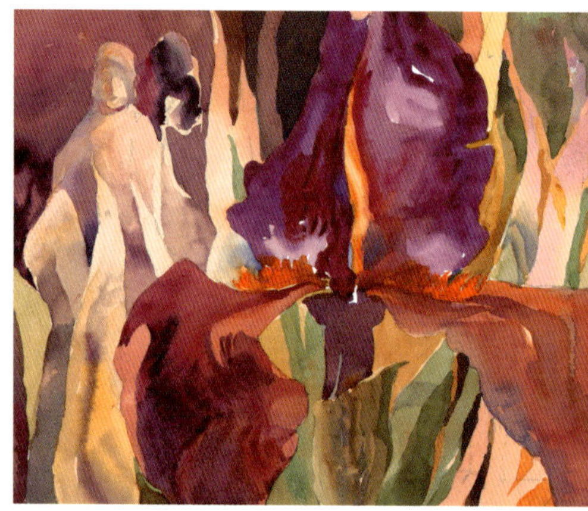

Our Lady of the Irises, Warm The warmth of the magenta and red-orange predominate, creating an upbeat note. The key color is the magenta; orange is used for accents to place against its complement, cobalt blue. Neutral greens are created from the combination of other paints. A cheerful and upbeat mood is established by the warm colors. For this warm bias, the orange and the magenta dominate, while cobalt blue is used sparingly to direct the eye and intensify the orange on the petal.

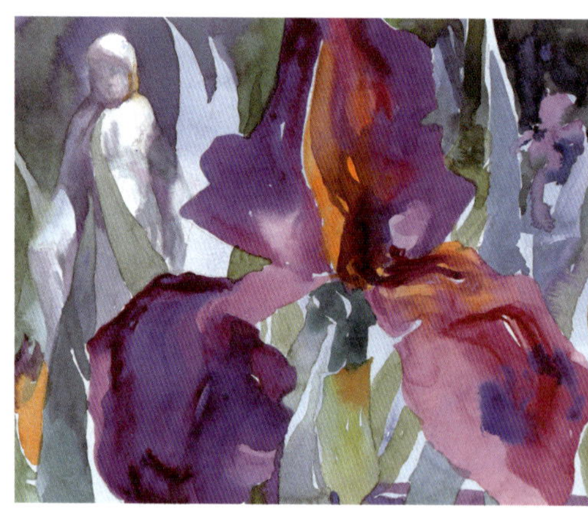

Our Lady of the Irises, Cool Using the same paints, but in a different way, the artist gives this painting a more somber air. The cobalt blue dominates in its pure form and in mixes. Neutral green also participates in the overall mood. The magenta mixes well with the cobalt to create purples as analogous partners to the blues. The bright quinacridone sienna is used sparingly, but usefully, to help direct the eye around the painting.

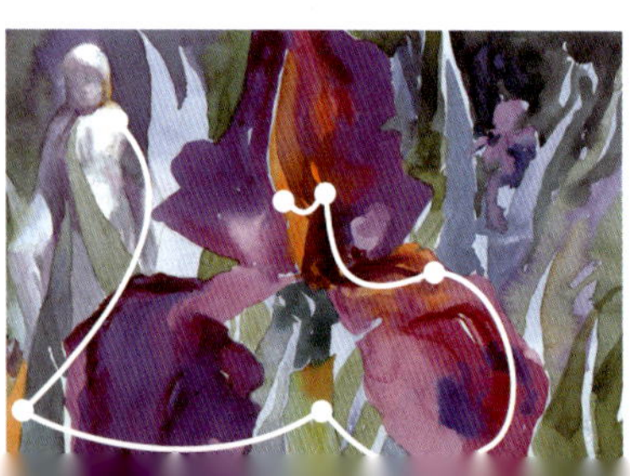

Note the intentional juxtaposition of the orange near complementary blues and its use to subtly nudge the viewer's eyes around the work.

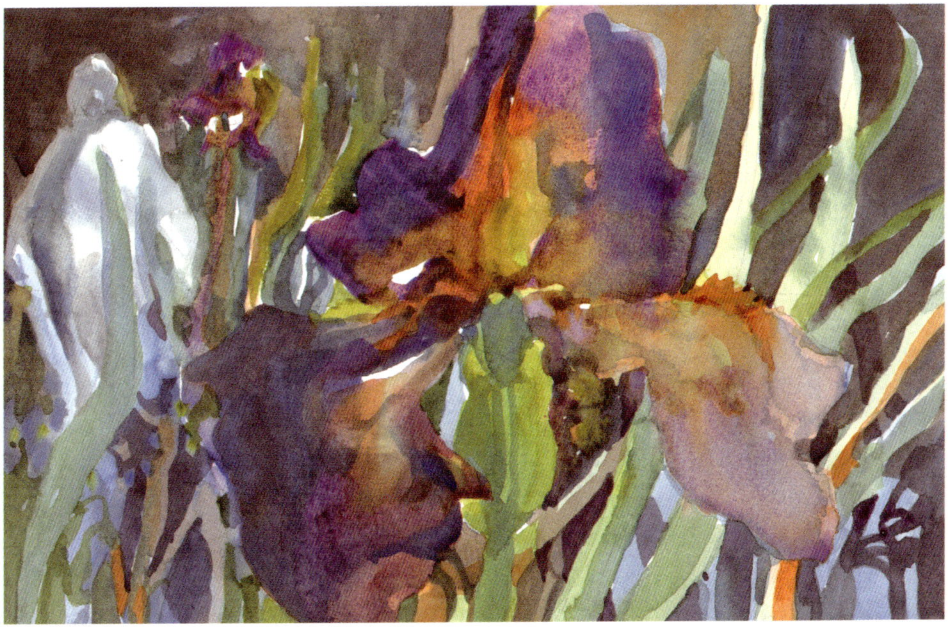

SOME THINGS TO CONSIDER

- The tetradic scheme is challenging but exciting, as it involves two sets of complements. In the rectangular tetrad, the two complementary pairs are separated by only one color, which makes both ends almost analogous.
- The artist must decide which color and color temperature will dominate.
- In the square tetrad, the colors are evenly spaced around the color wheel. Depending on the colors selected, the potential for color war exists. It is advisable to choose colors with mixing in mind and to decide ahead which color or color mix will dominate.

USING A SQUARE TETRADIC PALETTE

Our Lady of the Irises The selection of this square tetradic color scheme included some exciting colors such as green gold; quinacridone sienna; manganese violet; and cool, transparent cobalt blue for mixes and glazing. A warm direction could have been chosen, but the first decision was that the color temperature would be predominantly cool, using blues, violets, and blue-greens. Manganese violet, green gold, and quinacridone sienna would be mostly accent colors, useful for directing the eye. Cobalt blue would be useful for glazing, mixing, and some occasional color accents. It was important to plan so that color harmony could be achieved and celebrated. The iris offered the opportunity to play with the color combinations in full strength, pitting complements against each other. Although complex, this is an exciting color scheme to try. This example still uses just two sets of complements to produce an amazing variety and range of colors. Cobalt blue is the key color and is used predominantly in the color mixes to create a cool, somber mood. The quinacridone sienna and green gold make wonderfully vivid color accents. The vivid orange is especially useful in directing the viewer's eye. Dark neutrals are easy mixes and work beautifully with the mixed greens.

These are the pure pigments for the square tetradic version of the painting.

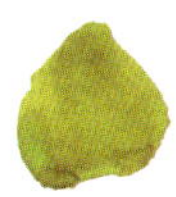
green gold

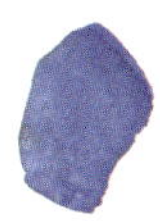
cobalt blue

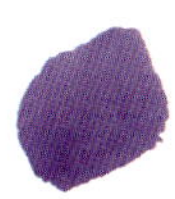
manganese violet

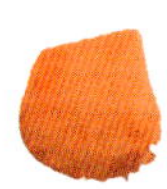
quinacridone sienna

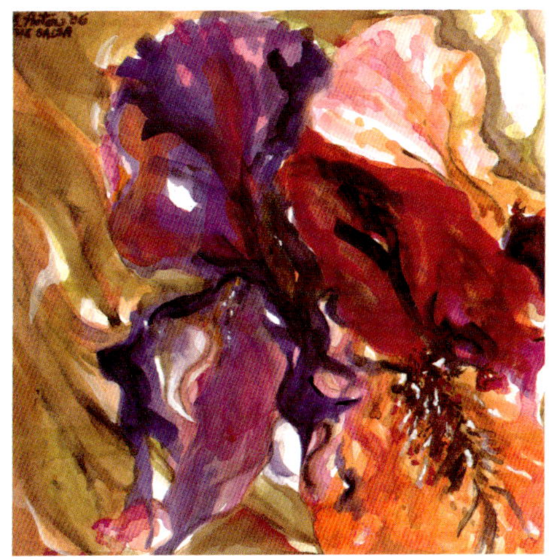

The Salsa

Sharon Porter set out to use a rectangular tetradic palette for her painting. She managed to shift the complements one step counterclockwise, ending up with a combination (of sorts) between the square and rectangle—and no complementary relationships. Her example offers encouragement to those who love to try something new. It also shows the value of limiting the number of paints in a painting. And salsa it is!

One of the most interesting aspects of this color scheme was in the possible mixes. Note the wonderful sedimentation and granulation introduced by the use of manganese violet.

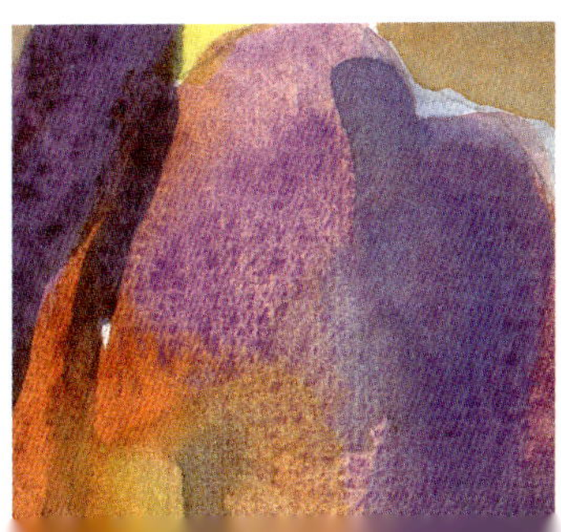

Tertiary colors

A tertiary color is currently defined as an equal mix of a primary color with the secondary color next to it on the color wheel. Up until the last century, however, a tertiary color was defined as a neutral mix of three primary colors or a primary and its complement created by mixing the other two primaries (see "Neutrals," page 70). These colors create an unusual and lively palette that sometimes harks back to an earlier time and was a favorite palette of French artist Henri Matisse.

STEPS TO MAKE YOUR OWN TERTIARIES

Primaries

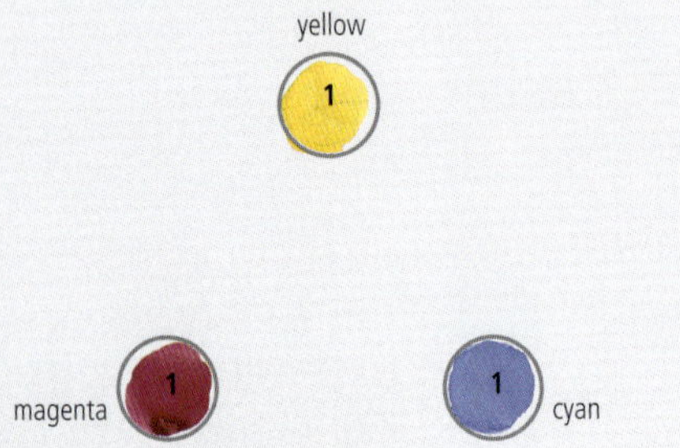

Primaries mix to make secondaries

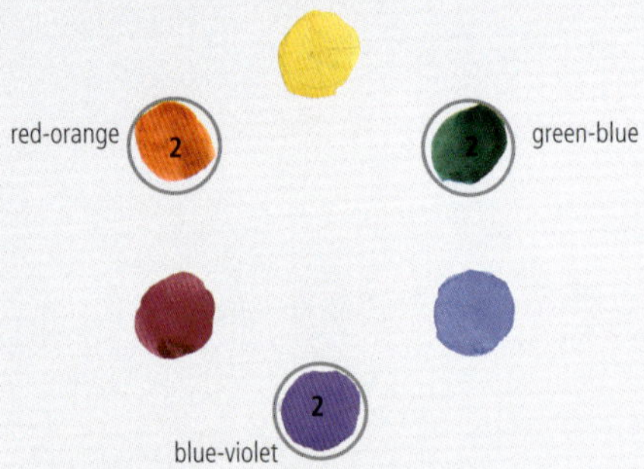

Secondaries mix with primaries to make tertiaries

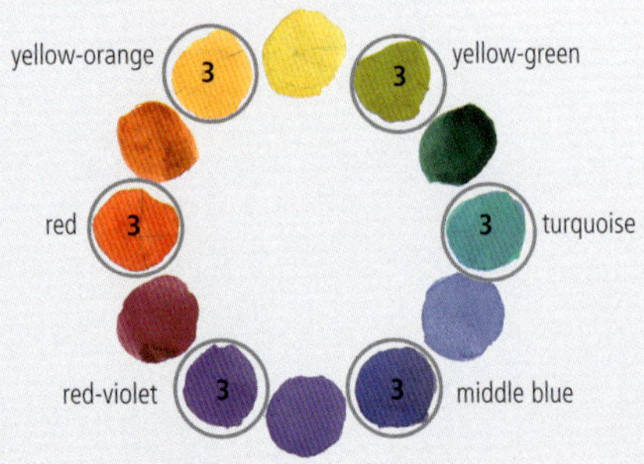

MANUFACTURED TERTIARIES

You can buy close pigment matches to the mixed tertiaries:

mixed tertiary	paint equivalent
yellow-green	green gold
blue-green	cobalt teal or cerulean blue
middle blue	ultramarine blue
red-violet	manganese violet or quinacridone magenta
middle red	cadmium red
yellow-orange	cadmium yellow deep, new gamboge, or Indian yellow

Jungle Flowers
Carol Taschek has used a limited tertiary palette. The result is an harmonious and atmospheric work.

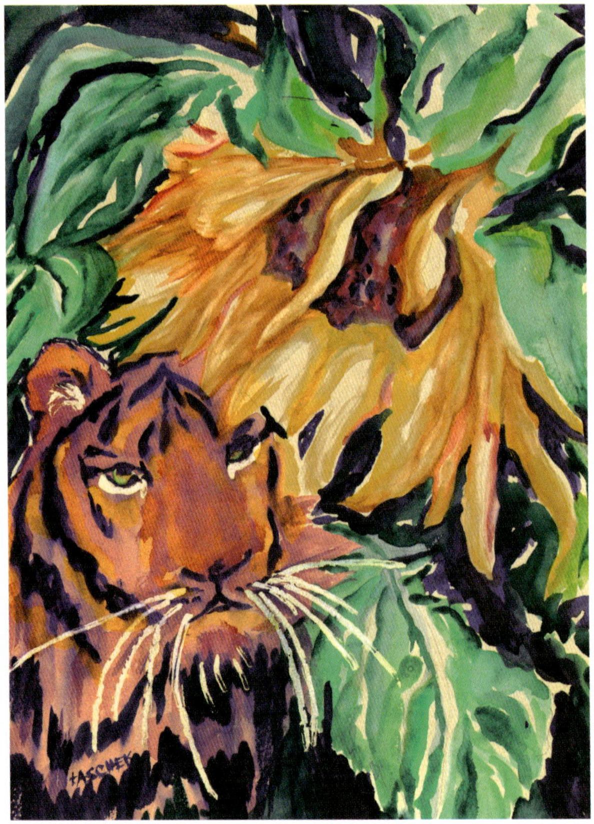

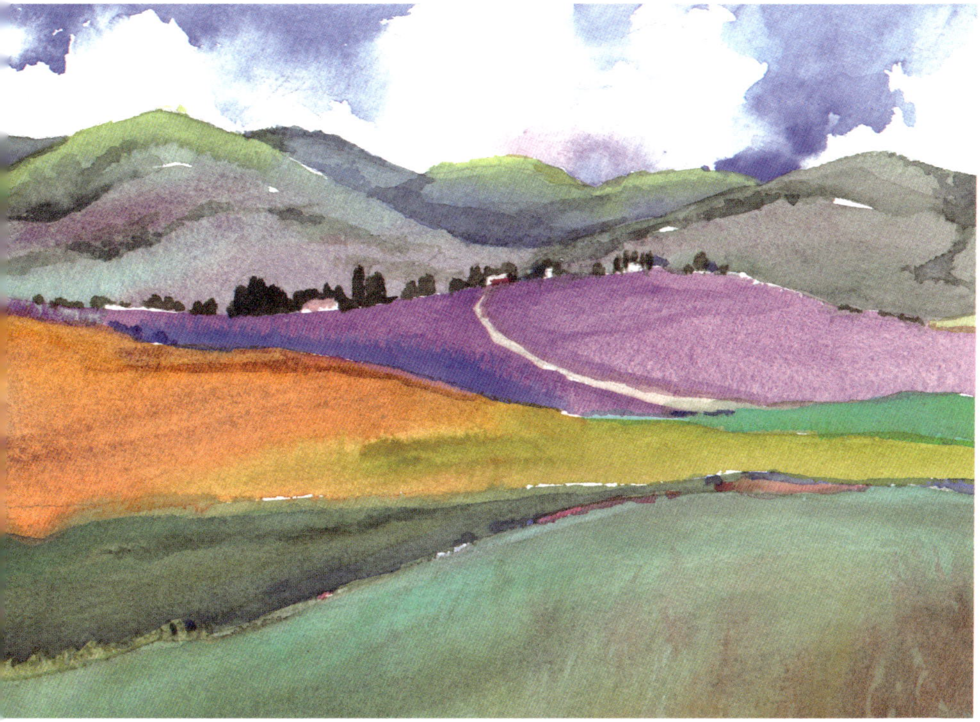

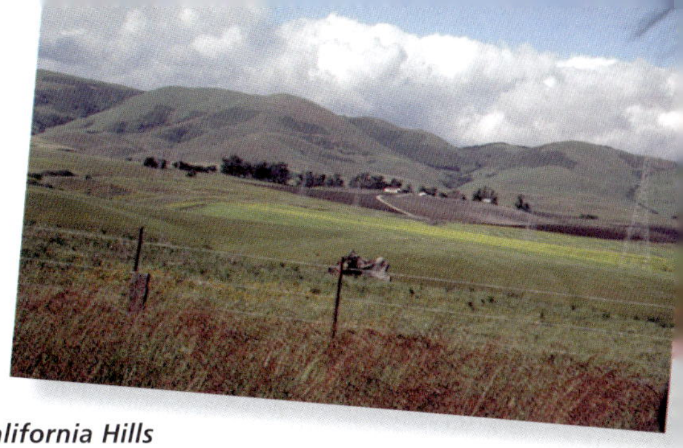

California Hills
The tertiary colors are an unusual and very exciting palette to explore. Simply because they are not the colors most artists are used to using, they can provide some real surprises. This painting of the California hills by the author offers fresh new ways to see and use color.

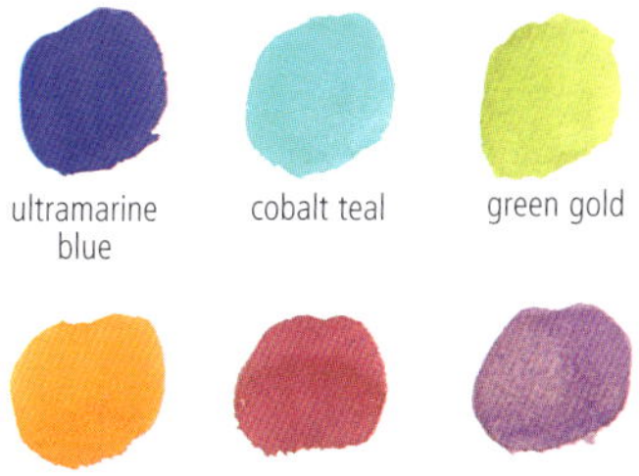

Prickly Pear and Parrot
The unusual colorations in this painting demonstrate some of the inherent beauty of this palette. The author used a mix of rose madder genuine and cobalt blue for the violet instead of manganese violet. The most intense and bright colors—yellow-green and yellow-orange—were used for the accents.

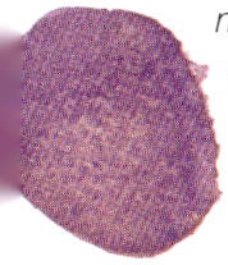

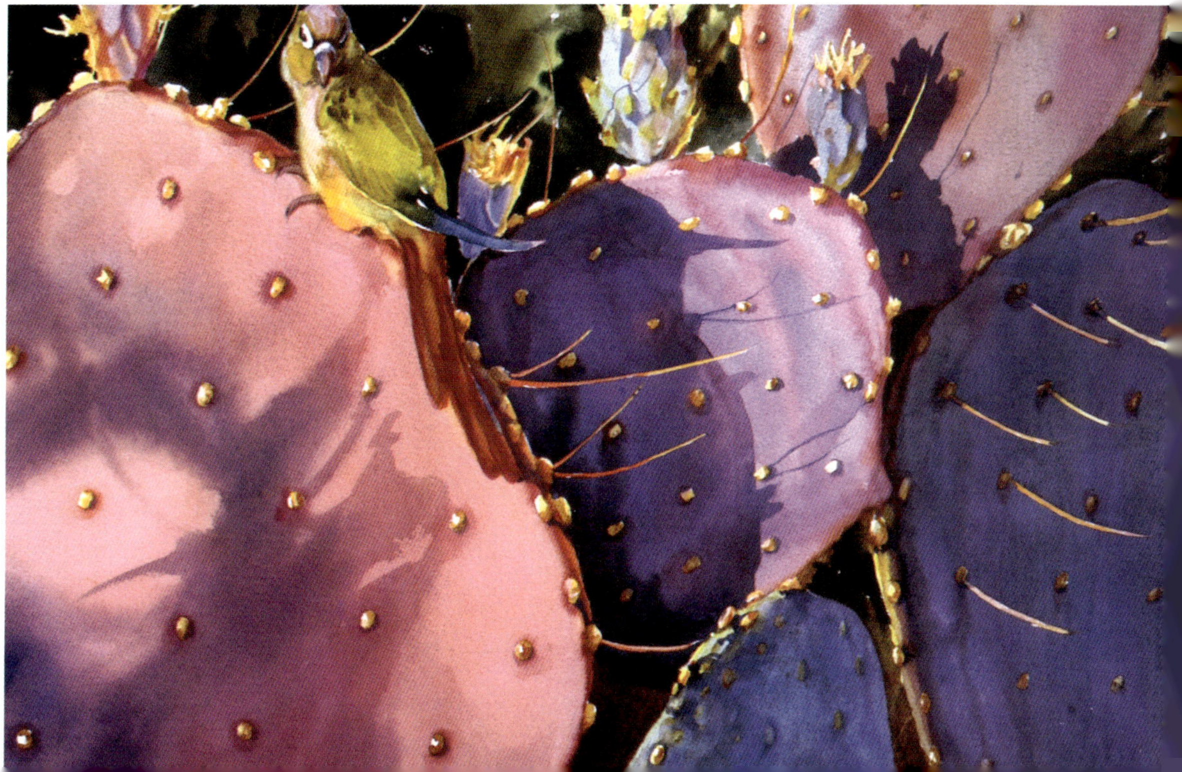

SOME THINGS TO CONSIDER

- The tertiary palette is an unusual group of six colors that have been used together for centuries.
- There is a subtle suggestion of Art Deco within the array of tertiary colors.
- In spite of the confusion in definitions, tertiary colors are not "mud." Mixing mud in watercolor is usually the result of mixing too many paints together and of overworking sedimentary or opaque paints on the paper (see page 26).

The Velázquez palette

The Velázquez palette, comprised of ultramarine blue and two or three earth pigments including yellow ochre and burnt sienna, is named for Spanish artist Diego Velázquez. Velázquez managed to use the limited pigments available in the early 17th century to merge color, light, space, rhythm of line, and mass. Because all were of equal importance to him in his paintings, he was known as "the painter's painter." The old masters modeled the values for their oil paintings by using a dark wood palette that matched the tone of their canvas. They built up values by beginning with a brown underpainting and finishing with dark brown shadows. Velázquez was the first to use the colors that he saw in those shadows—including the blues and greens. Because of his innovation and originality, he influenced many artists—including Edouard Manet, Camille Corot, Francisco de Goya, James McNeill Whistler, and John Singer Sargent—for centuries to come.

yellow ochre

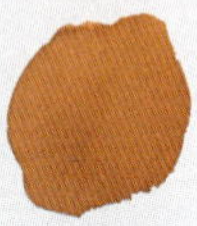
burnt sienna

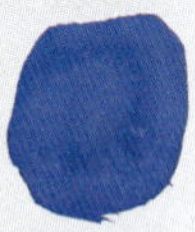
ultramarine blue

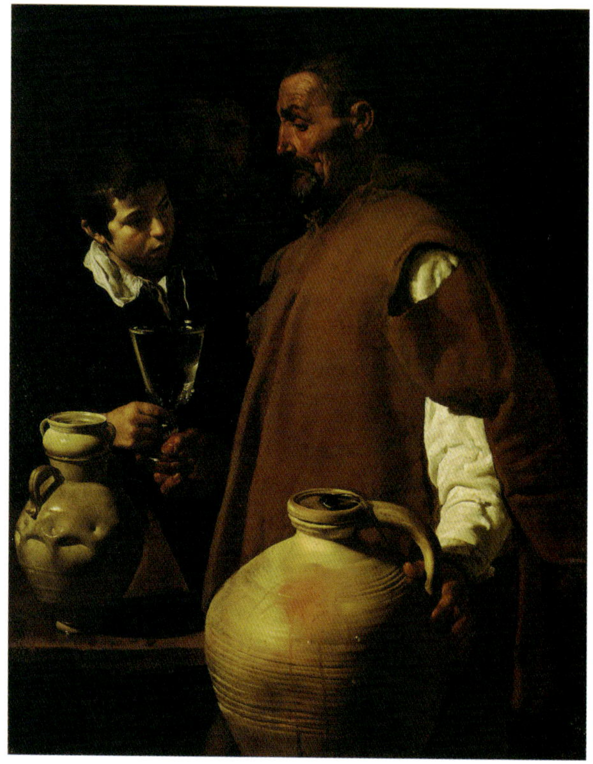

The Water-seller of Seville
This oil painting of 1623 by Velázquez demonstrates some of the inherent beauty of the palette he championed. An everyday activity is ennobled through an exploration of light and shadows, surface textures, and local, earthy colors.

A BEGINNER'S PALETTE

The limited Velázquez palette is perfect for beginning students. They can experiment safely with color mixing while paying close attention to the building of values. They also are spared the confusion often brought on by the bewildering array of available colors. They gradually can add the brighter and higher chroma pigments—one at a time—as their confidence grows. Alizarin crimson, cadmium yellow, and cobalt blue are often early additions to the palette.

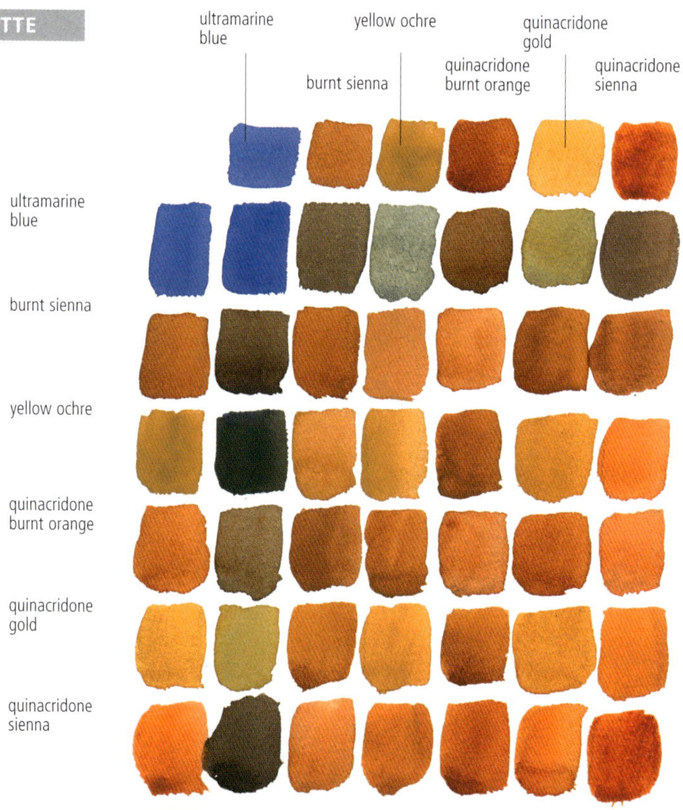

SOME THINGS TO CONSIDER

- The Velázquez palette offers consistently harmonious colors for any subject.
- The palette is ideal for beginners, the value possibilities are wide ranging, the paints work well together, and the subtle color is rewarding.
- Begin with the limited Velázquez palette. Once you are comfortable, add alizarin crimson and cadmium yellow. Then all colors are possible!
- Consider substituting quinacridone gold or raw sienna for the yellow ochre in the palette. This will add vibrancy and more color opportunities.
- The earth pigment map by Bruce MacEvoy (see www.handprint.com/HP/WCL/earthc.html) shows a pie-shaped wedge bounded by high-chroma yellows to reds (the outer edge of the circle corresponding to Hart's color wheel, see page 14). The lower-chroma earth pigments (some of which are used in the Velázquez palette) are placed nearer to the center according to the relative chromas and hues of the various paint manufacturers (see "Neutrals," page 70).

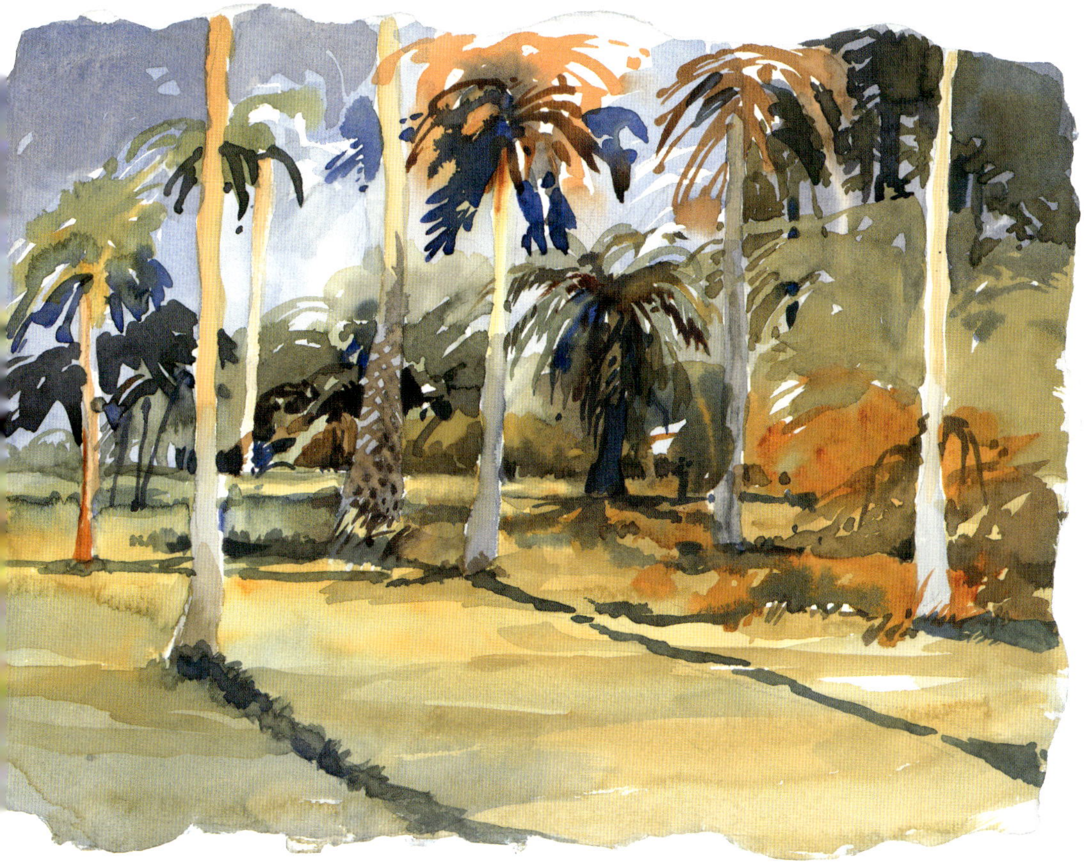

Costa Rica Morning
A more modern version of the Velázquez palette includes the brighter, more vibrant quinacridones. The author used just three paints: quinacridone gold, quinacridone sienna, and ultramarine blue. Note the vibrancy of the pure paints when surrounded by subdued versions of a near complement (for example, sienna against subdued green and blue-green).

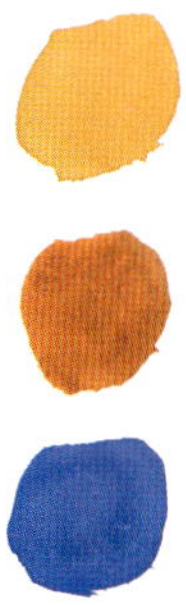

quinacridone gold

quinacridone sienna

ultramarine blue

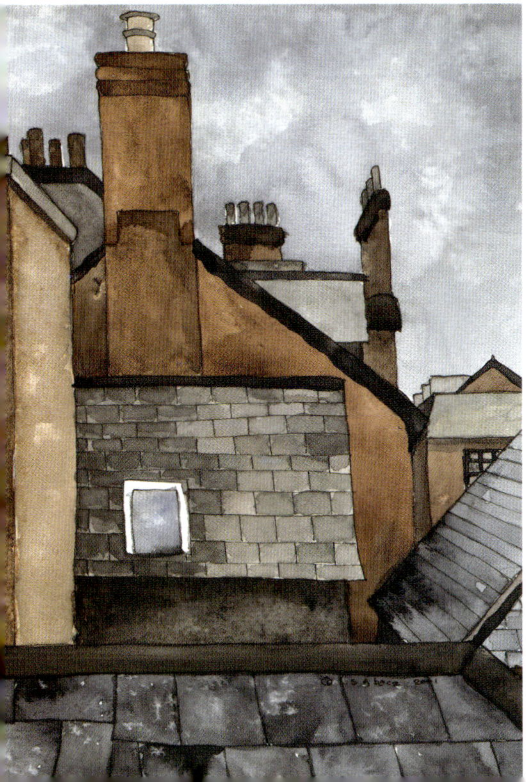

England
Sally Baca used ink line with neutral mixes of the traditional Velázquez palette to portray the gloomy overcast skies and neutral rooftops.

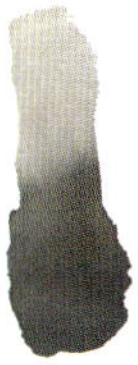

Taos Pueblo
Allen Brown demonstrates the beautiful fit of a slightly modified Velázquez palette and the desert of New Mexico by substituting yellow ochre with quinacridone gold and then glazing. This painting uses pure pigments with some accents added into the shadows and a light glaze of rose madder genuine.

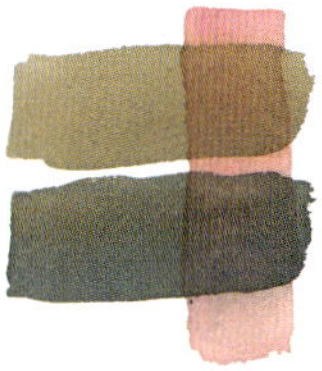

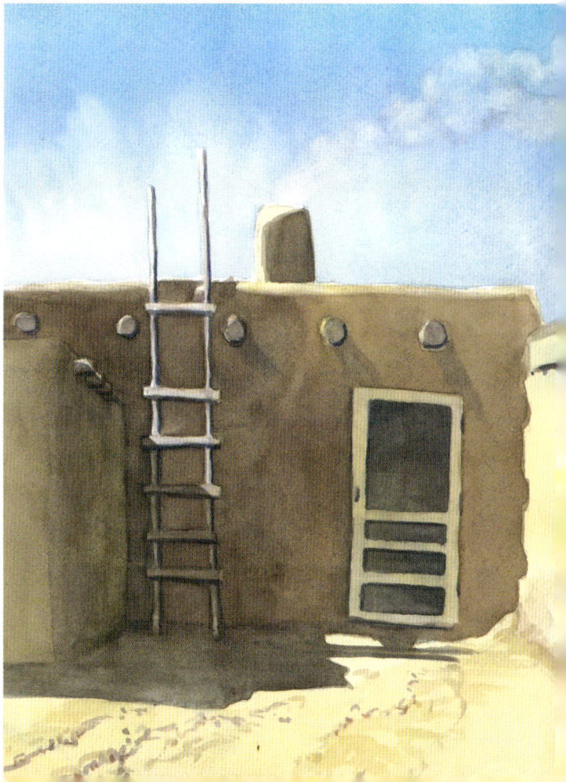

High and low color key

Color key, or tonal key, is a term that describes a painting's overall lightness or darkness. When you begin a painting, it is useful to think in terms of the intended key as a way of expressing the mood or desired feeling. Sketches in pencil will help you analyze the color key relationships of your subject. Note the different paints used in high- and low-key palettes. Low-key paints are generally lower chroma and/or painted heavily. High-key paints are usually transparent, high chroma, and painted lightly. In diluting the paints for a high color key, the white of the paper shines through, making them appear tonally lighter. Some colored paints, such as yellows and oranges, can never range darker than a mid-value color tone.

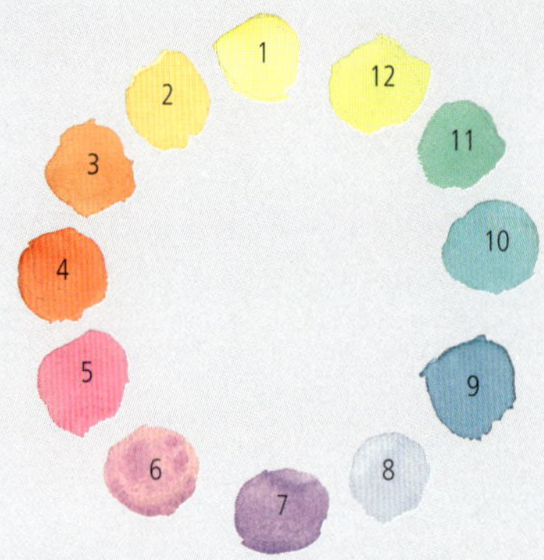

High key palette (left)
1. lemon yellow or raw sienna
2. quinacridone gold
3. burnt sienna
4. English red earth
5. napthamide maroon
6. manganese violet
7. ultramarine violet
8. ultramarine blue
9. indigo
10. phthalo turquoise
11. ultramarine turquoise
12. green gold

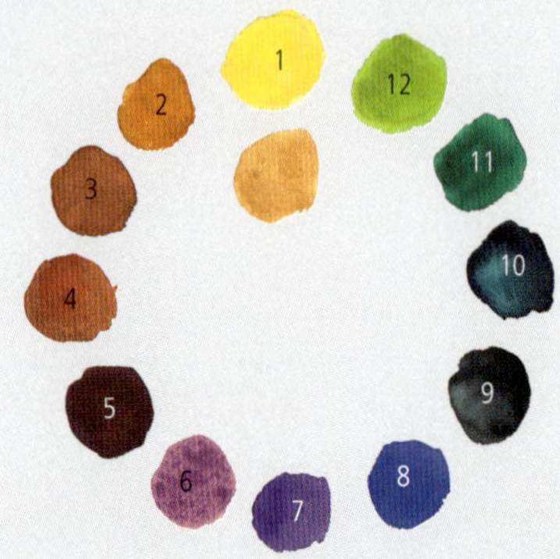

Low key palette (right)
1. aureolin azo yellow
2. nickel azo
3. quinacridone sienna
4. perylene red
5. opera (Holbein)
6. cobalt violet
7. ultramarine violet
8. cobalt blue
9. Prussian blue
10. phthalo turquoise
11. ultramarine turquoise
12. green gold

HIGH AND LOW COLOR KEY

All paints used in a painting have a tonal position that relates to a black-to-white graded scale for comparison. Squint your eyes to help translate color into grayscale, or make black-and-white photocopies of paint swatches. A specific paint's tonal position depends mostly upon how heavily it is applied.

Generally, a high-key painting represents bright illumination. The mood is often cheerful, although the emotional tone can vary with the subject. A high-key painting of heat and dryness may or may not be comforting and cheerful. Even the shadows in a high-key painting are usually of mid values. A high-key painting that contains mostly mid to light colors and values provides an opportunity for spotlighting a darker subject.

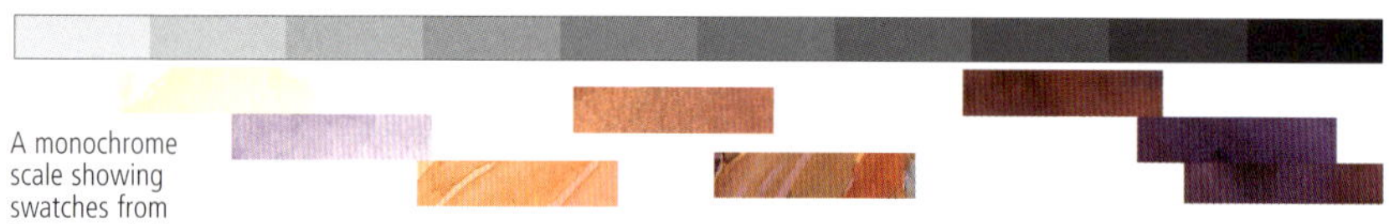

A monochrome scale showing swatches from the two paintings linked with their tonal values.

A low-key painting contains colors and values that are at the dark end of the value scale. The colors or pigments are generally low chroma or semineutral mixes of higher chroma pigments. Low-key paintings often indicate dim illumination, a somber mood, or darkened atmosphere. Night paintings are often low key. A bright or light subject can be featured very effectively in a low-key painting.

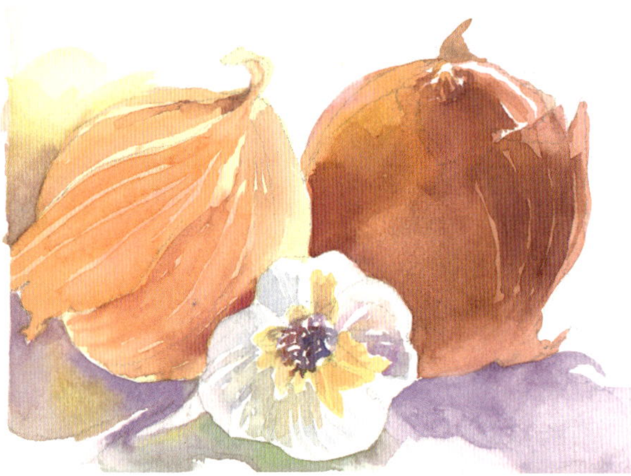

Onions and Garlic
The author's primary idea behind these paintings is to show the differences between high and low keys. In the high-key example on the left, the lights are delicate whites and pale neutrals. The shadows reach just to midtones. The darkest areas are the focal points away from the light featured strongly against the white. In the low-key example, the subjects appear drenched in dark shadows with the mid-tones of the blue garlic and complementary orange onion as focal points.

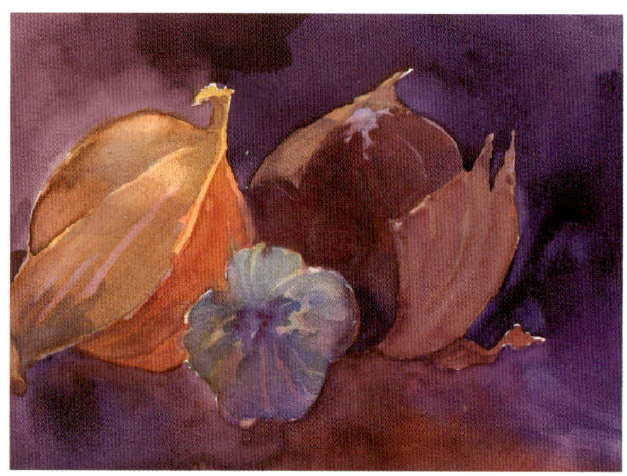

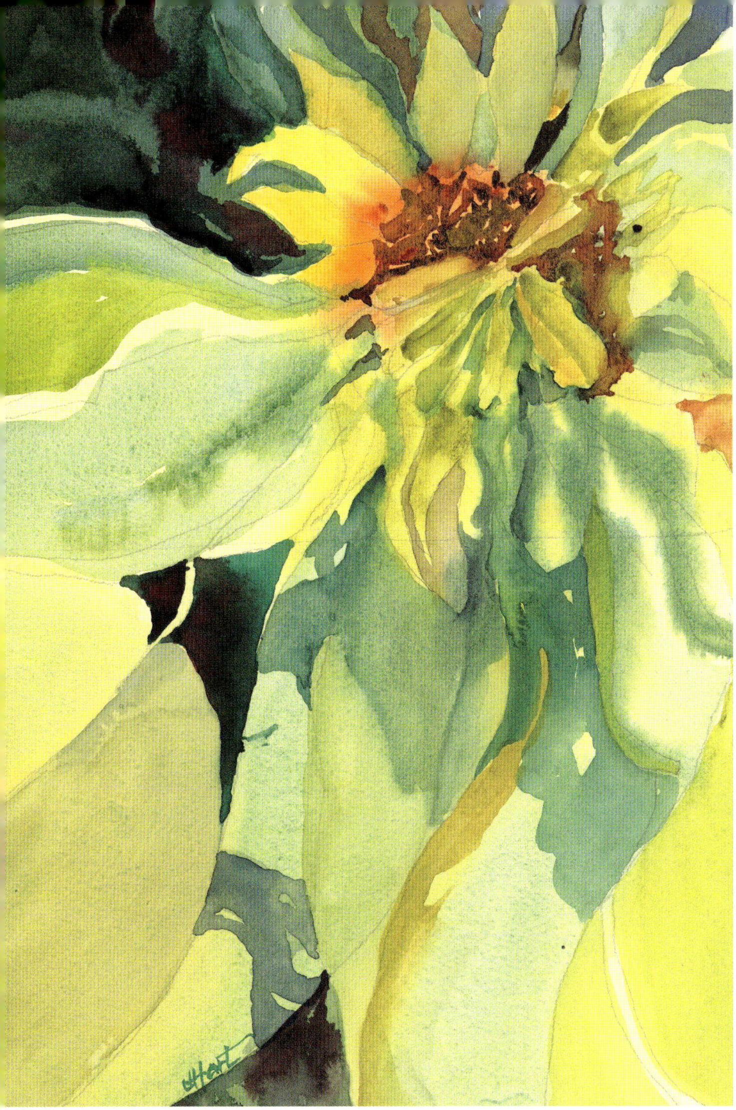

Sunflower
The author's choice of a yellow sunflower bathed in light provides the perfect opportunity for a high-key painting. Even the cobalt blue shadows allow the paper's white to show through to contribute to the overall high color key. The minimal darks add nice contrast.

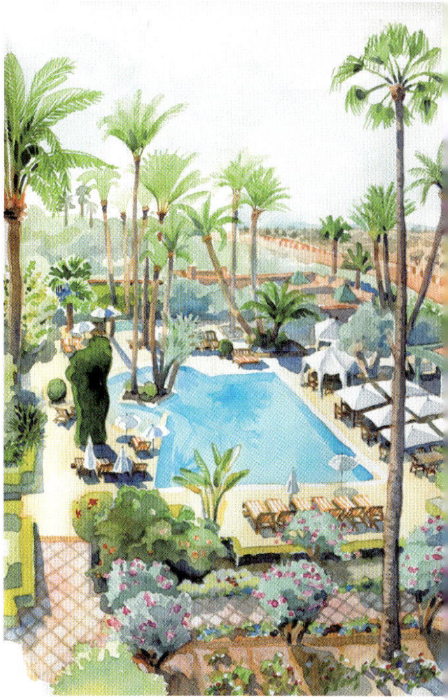

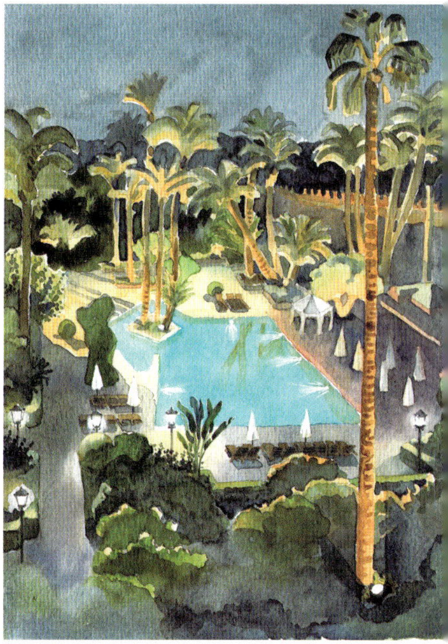

Day and Night
A perfect way to experiment with observing and painting high and low color key is to choose the same subject in bright sunlight and then at night. You almost have to think in reverse and reassess daytime decisons about light and shade. In this example, artificial lights create glowing areas that are normally in shadow.

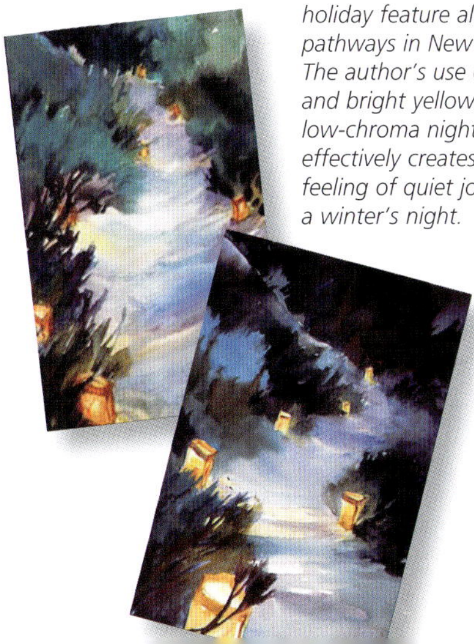

Farolito Pathway
These nighttime study sketches of farolitos (little lanterns) are a traditional holiday feature along pathways in New Mexico. The author's use of light and bright yellows in this low-chroma night scene effectively creates the feeling of quiet joy on a winter's night.

SOME THINGS TO CONSIDER

- A high-key painting works well for expressing summer, heat, and brightness.
- A low-key painting works well for nighttime subjects and dramatic or melancholy scenes.
- A low-key painting can use low chroma pigments. For best results, mix semineutrals or low chroma mixes from higher chroma pigments. Many low chroma pigments are really combinations of two or more pigments. Mixing two of these multi-pigment compounds together produces a mix of four or more pigments. This may be a recipe for "mud."
- High chroma reds, greens, blues, and purples can be used effectively with semineutrals in dark, low-key washes.
- If you have trouble achieving a dark value, wait until it dries. Rewet/dampen the specific area and add drier pigments directly into the wet area.

Color value

A value, or tone, indicates the darkness or lightness of a subject. Every color has its own value. Individual watercolor pigments also have values separate from their color, as shown on the Artist's Value Wheel (see right) by Bruce MacEvoy (see page 128) . The colors are plotted vertically according to their lightness or darkness, and from the center outward according to their chroma level. A pigment at full strength may have a value of three on a value scale (see below). When water is added, this value can change.

Value patterns dominate our visual experience, guide our eyes through a painting, and enable us to understand form and perspective. Many artists begin a painting by studying and designing the value composition as shown lower right.

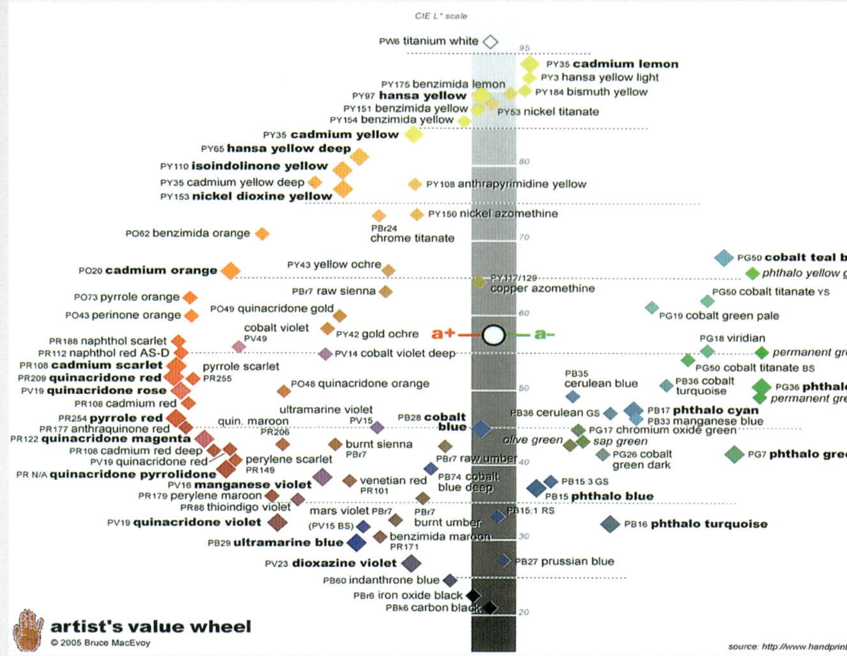

COLOR VALUE EXERCISE

Create a value scale from black to the white of the paper across your page. A nine-step value scale is commonly used. Place each of the fully saturated palette colors under the value scale at what you think is the correct point.

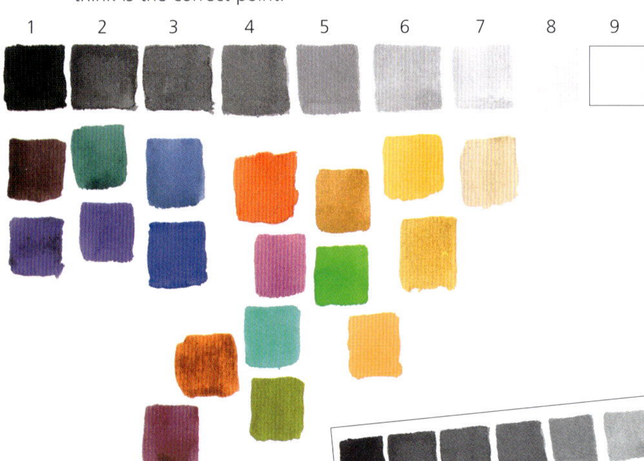

It may be helpful to do some comparison tests on another piece of paper before adding them to your chart. For instance, a pure hue of yellow would be positioned closer to the white end of the scale than a pure hue of blue. Squinting or photocopying (see page 64) will help you see value differences.

Then take a black-and-white photograph, or make a black-and-white photocopy of your scale and colors. See how close you got to the actual values. This is a difficult exercise because watercolor dries lighter and because a high chroma, bright color usually appears lighter to the eye than it really is. You are likely to think that the brighter pigments of opera (Holbein), cobalt teal, and phthalo green are darker than they actually are. As you would expect, the pigments that reflect a lot of blue are located at the darker end of the scale, and those that reflect yellow are at the opposite end.

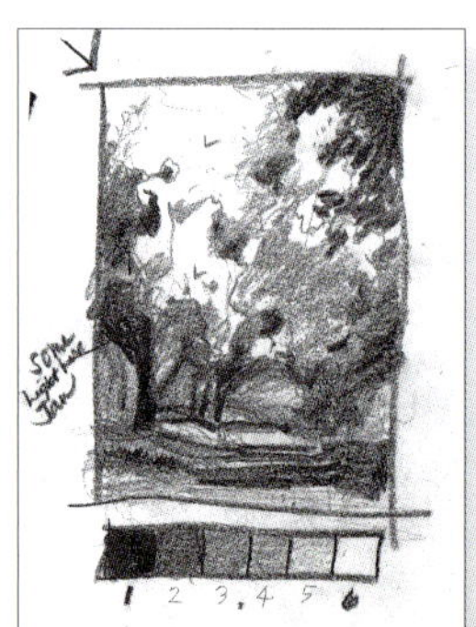

A pencil sketch of Fall Thunder (see opposite) with value scale underneath. The value scale establishes the value of the colors to be used in the painting, then the sketch applies this to the subject.

PIGMENT FAMILIES

The value of a pigment generally results from the amount of blue or yellow reflected in the pigment. Yellow-reflecting pigments are lighter, and blue-reflecting pigments are darker. Other groups of pigments have different values:

- Earth pigments are darker than their yellow hue suggests.
- Cobalts are lighter than their blue hue suggests.
- Phthalocyanines are darker than their hues suggest (and they are good for mixing dark darks).
- Quinacridones are lighter than their bluish hue suggests and are at the light end of the value scale.

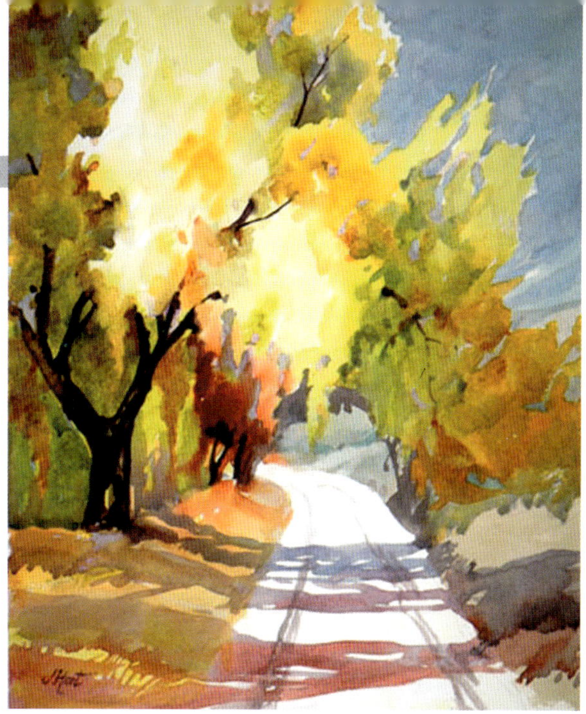

USING RED PLEXIGLAS

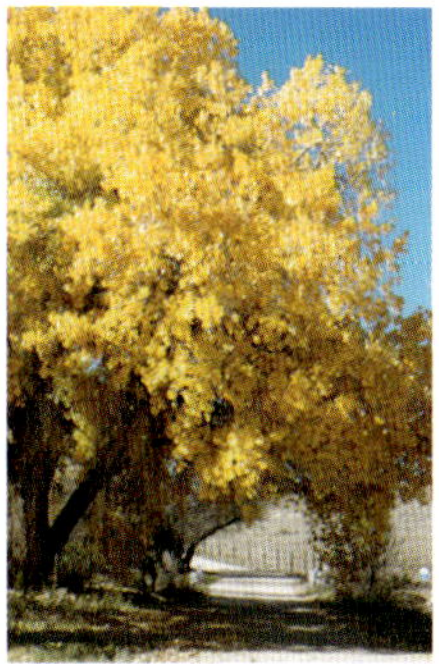

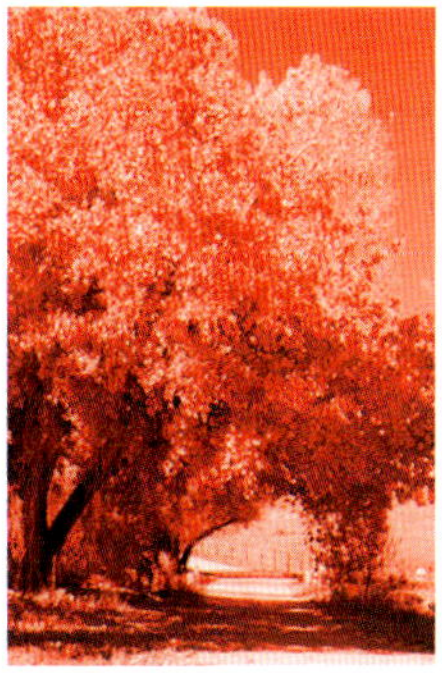

Fall Thunder The red-filtered photograph shows details about the relative values that may not be immediately apparent in the actual photograph: The sky and the yellow foliage are darker than they seem; the distant road is the lightest area of the photograph; the drooping branches are as dark as or darker than the highest sky area; and the lightest area of the tree is the upper branches against the contrasting sky.

A piece of red Plexiglas (you can probably order a piece from a local glass shop) will help you check values in your subject as well as in your painting. When you look through the red plastic, all the subject colors appear in shades of red—much like the black-and-white photocopy—and you can see the value differences. Of course, the only color you cannot see through the red Plexiglas is red. Red is fairly rare in the landscape, so red Plexiglas generally works best for value comparisons in the landscape. If you paint a lot of red subjects, it's best to get a green Plexiglas.

SOME THINGS TO CONSIDER

- Try squinting or looking through red Plexiglas to see value differences in colors. Bright, intense colors may appear lighter than they really are.
- Creating a value study in either black-to-white or monochrome before you paint helps to see values and to plan your painting.
- Adding a bright, light yellow never makes a painting lighter; it just adds another layer for the reflecting light to penetrate.
- The colors at the center of the spectrum—yellow, yellow-green, orange—appear the brightest because they reflect much more light.

MONOCHROMATIC OR VALUE PAINTING

These two monochromatic watercolor studies by John Deyloff demonstrate value differences between color choices of quinacridone gold and Prussian blue. It is easy to see the value differences between the two colors at full strength. The intensity of the quinacridone gold fools the eye into believing that there is more contrast than there actually is. There is another interesting lesson here. Note that the underwashes of each sketch are the same value, even though the blue underwash appears darker. Both cut out approximately the same amount of light reflected from the surface of the white paper. That is why applying more yellow to the paper or painted subject never helps brighten it. Even a faint yellow darkens by cutting out the light.

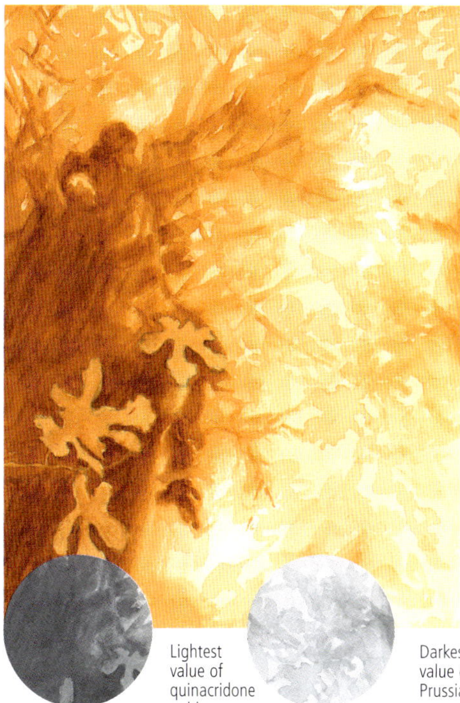

Darkest value of quinacridone gold

Lightest value of quinacridone gold

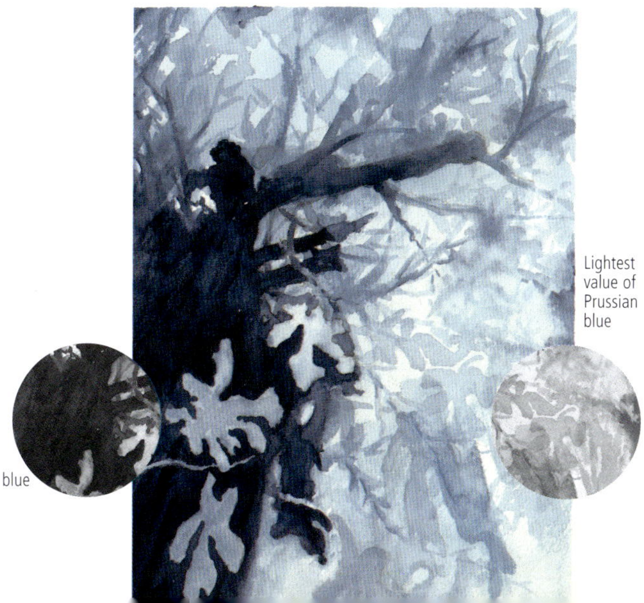

Darkest value of Prussian blue

Lightest value of Prussian blue

Color temperature

The concept of color temperature is of great importance to the artist—and is often misunderstood. Artists began referring to warm/cool contrast in the 18th century, when Moses Harris' book *Natural System of Colors* presented the first warm/cool color wheel diagram. Then, as now, both yellow and red were included in the warm side of the color wheel. Artists still disagree about the absolute warmest or coolest hues. Some cling steadfastly to yellow as the warmest, citing the sun in their defense. But most agree that red-orange is the warmest color and that its complement, blue-green, is the coolest.

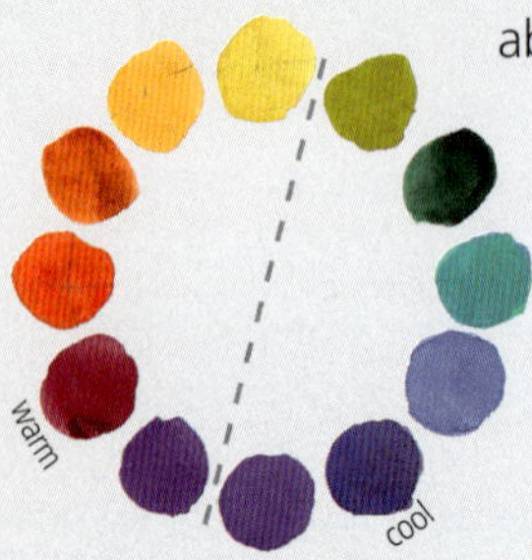

VISUAL EFFECTS OF WARM AND COOL COLORS

Each color temperature has inherent characteristics. It is generally best to create a painting that is predominantly warm or cool—not half and half. A cool painting may appear calm or somber while a warmer painting is livelier. Objects depicted in either warm or cool colors share certain general characteristics.

Cool	Warm
Appear to move back	Appear to move forward
Appear smaller in size	Appear larger in size
Produce a more somber/sad feeling	Produce excitement/energy
Exclusively seen at night	Seen along with cool colors in daylight

Warm and cool are relative temperature terms. By comparing one blue pigment to another blue pigment, you can determine which one is closer in color to blue-green and, therefore, cooler than the other. For example, ultramarine blue is warmer (contains more red) than cobalt blue, and alizarin crimson is cooler than cadmium red because it appears to contain more blue. (See "Split-primary six-color palette," page 50, for cool and warm examples of each primary color.) It is important to make sure that you are not confusing saturation or intensity with temperature.

Which is warmer?
Red is warmer than "hot pink," which is more intense but cooler in color temperature. The pink dot contains more blue than the red dot.

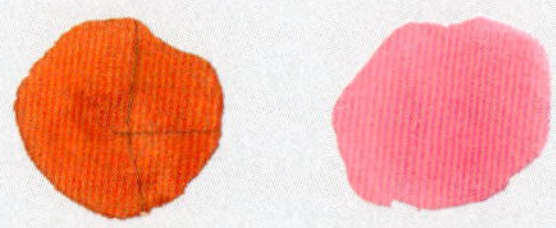

Which is cooler?
The green circle is closer to blue-green than the violet circle—and therefore it is cooler.

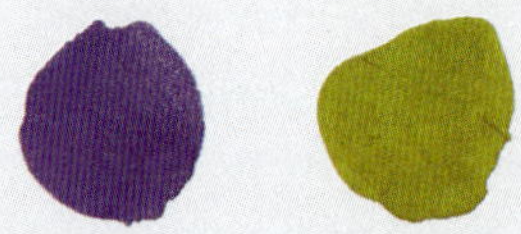

CHOOSING WARM AND COOL COLORS

Warm colors—especially hues from magenta through orange—tend to dominate a color mixture. This is partly because modern warm colors are nearly always synthetic pigments that have a high tinting strength. This also is because our eyes are more sensitive to the warm color ranges. There are several red-orange pigments to choose from:

- perinone orange
- cadmium red light
- vermilion
- pyrrole red
- quinacridone sienna

The coolest color is whatever hue provides the best visual contrast with the warm hue already selected. A red-orange hue's visual complement is a blue-green, which may include:

- phthalo blue
- peacock blue
- cerulean blue

COLOR TEMPERATURE AND DEPTH

These quick color studies by the author demonstrate the way cool and warm colors operate in a landscape. Cool colors recede, and warm colors advance.

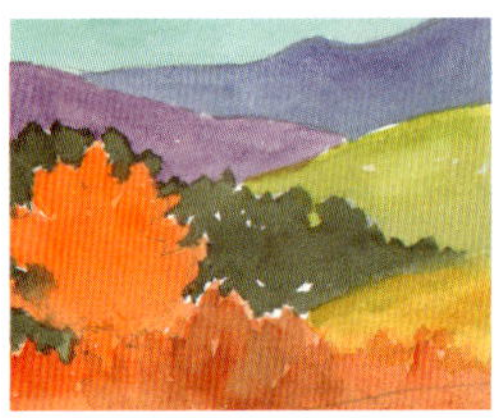

Study 1
The cool background colors appear to recede into the far distance, and the warm foreground colors appear very close. This exaggerates familiar landscape color relationships. Note that the middle neutral green is carried along by the more extreme color temperatures around it.

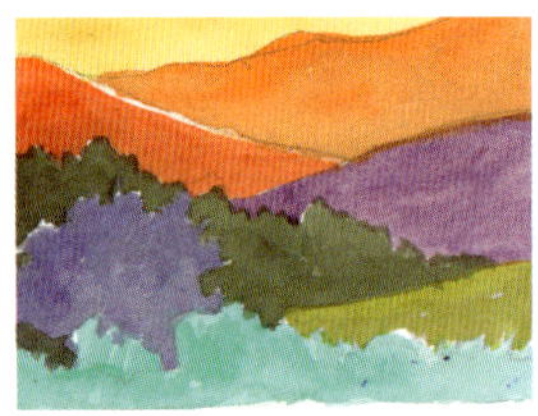

Study 2
Here color choices are reversed with cool foreground colors that want to recede and warm background colors that want to move forward. The effect is a sense of flatness. A viewer's mind may try to justify this less familiar color arrangement. Shade in the foreground and light in the background may be one way to "see" it.

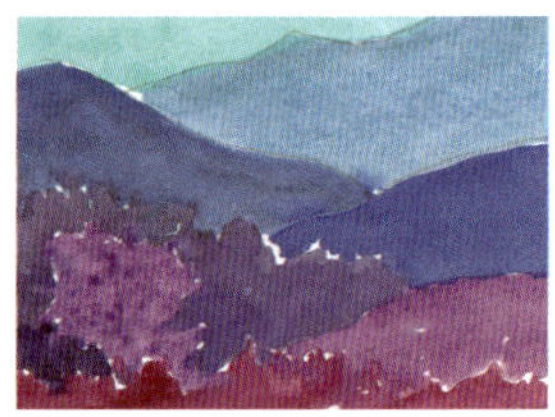

Study 3
This sketch offers a skewed view of color—from cool blue to cool red—roughly half of the color wheel. This analogous palette is capable of showing great depth.

COLOR TEMPERATURE AND FEELING

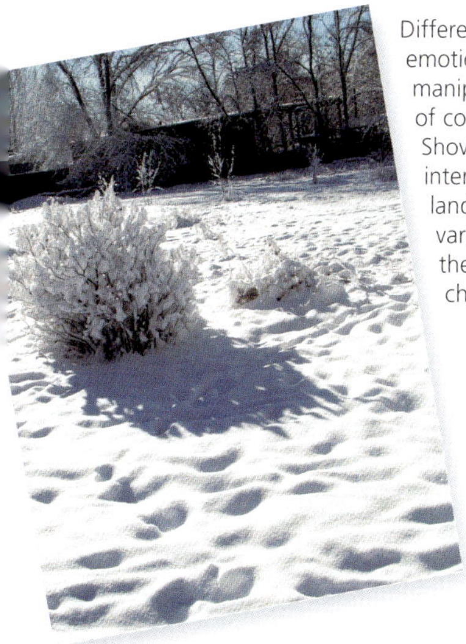

Different times of year and emotions can be created by manipulating the dynamic of cool and warm colors. Shown at right is how interpretations of one landscape can have varying feels according to the temperature of the chosen color palette.

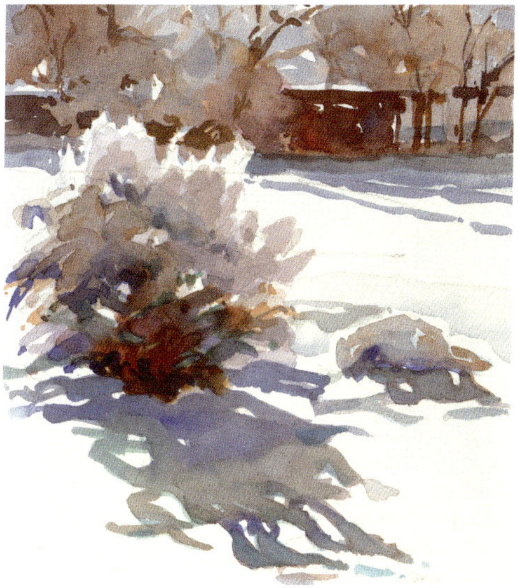

Winter Backyard
A cool underwash and other cool colors predominate in this winter snow scene. Cool reds provide some warmer accents. The feeling is calm and cold. The background recedes easily, allowing plenty of space between the background and the foreground bush.

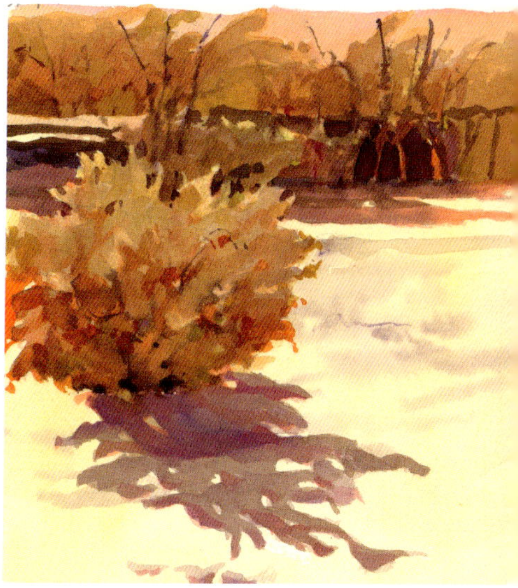

Sunshine Backyard
A yellow underwash immediately casts a sunshine glow upon the earth. Yellow is not the warmest color, but it leans warmly and is balanced by warm violet, a near complement.

COLOR TEMPERATURE AND GLAZES

Lake Superior and Gulls
Susan Wiig has chosen the same full palette of paints for both the winter and summer versions of her painting. Her choices in glazing, shade, and color highlights push each painting toward the desired color temperature—it is the color shades and glazes that make the difference.

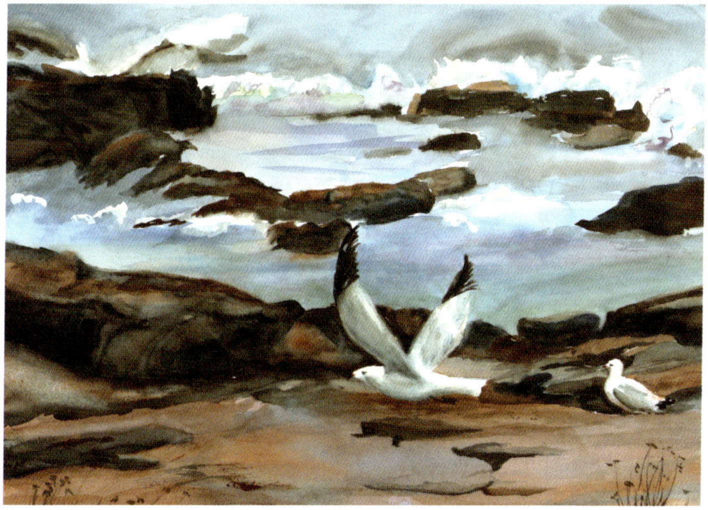

Winter
- Darker, cooler rocks
- Water grayish with pale blue shading
- A few somber red-brown and cool blue accents

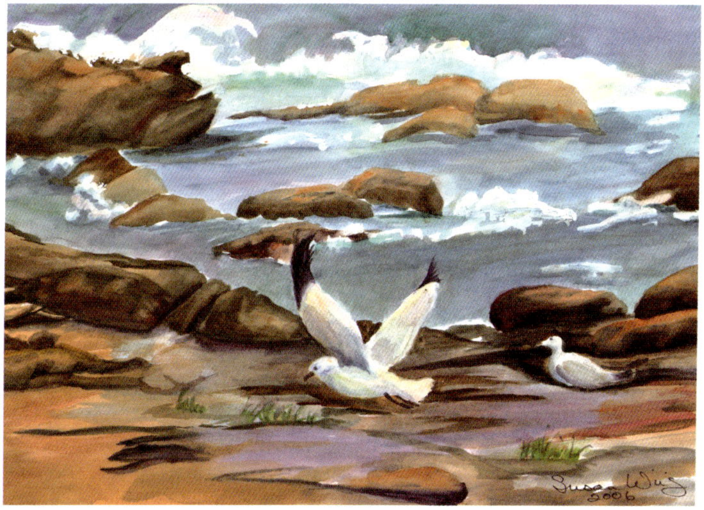

Summer
- Warm oranges and browns for rocks
- Water blue with lavender and cool blue glaze
- Gulls with pale lavender glazing
- A few lively red and orange color accents

Neutrals

Most paintings are composed mostly of neutrals—the subtle tones we often call browns or grays. These low-chroma hues, like actors in supporting roles, play alongside the starring colors. The somber yet glowing Dutch masters—and even the explosive, loosely painted watercolors of John Singer Sargent—underscore the importance of the muted hues. Their presence in a painting helps convey the mood and focus the attention on the nearby color accents.

MANUFACTURED NEUTRALS

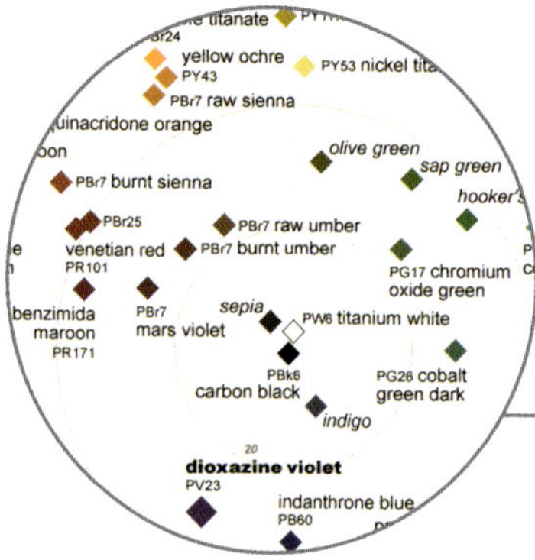

Traditionally, many unsaturated pigments were made from natural clays mined throughout Europe and the Middle East. Many were called earth pigments, and most were natural oxides. Some manufacturers still market them, but many have been replaced by synthetic, iron oxide paints, which are still referred to as "earths." The main characteristic of manufactured neutrals is that they are composed of low-chroma pigments.

Manufactured neutrals are located toward the center of the pigment map by Bruce MacEvoy, away from the high chroma edges. For the complete version of this pigment map, see "Color Wheels," page 14.

MANUFACTURED NEUTRALS WHEEL

The manufactured neutrals wheel is based on the same principles as Hart's color wheel (see page 15). It fits inside Hart's color wheel to show the low-chroma center.

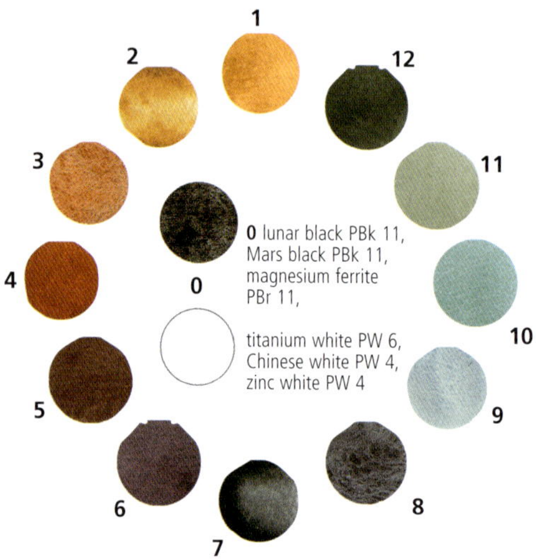

1 raw sienna PBr 7, buff titanium PW 6
2 yellow ochre PY 43, burnt umber PBr 7, transparent yellow oxide PY 42, Naples yellow PY 35, PR 101, PW 4 or PY 37, PY 42, PW 4, raw umber PBr 7
3 lunar earth PBr 11, burnt sienna PBr 7, Mars brown PR 101, lunar red rock PR 101
4 transparent red oxide PR 101 , Venetian red PR 101, Indian red PR 101, English red earth PR 101
5 Mars violet PR 101, PV 23, PBr 7, perylene maroon PR 179, napthamide maroon PR 171, caput mortuum violet PR 101, rose madder genuine NR 9
6 moonglow PG 18, PR 177, PB 29, potter's pink PR 233
7 indigo PB 15, PV 19, PBk 6
8 Payne's gray PBk 6, PB 29, neutral tint PR 23, PB 29, PBk 6
9 genuine azurite
10 natural sleeping beauty turquoise
11 Davy's gray PBk 19, PW 4, PBk 6
12 shadow green PBk 31, PBk 6

The first listed color is the one in the corresponding numbered position on the wheel.

HOW TO MIX NEUTRALS

Mixing neutrals from the colors selected for your painting provides guaranteed color harmony and unity. Often the beginner is more excited by colors than by neutrals—until shown what they can do in a painting.

1. Add a manufactured neutral to a higher chroma color Adding a gray, such as Davy's gray, or burnt sienna, or one of the natural mineral neutrals from Daniel Smith, such as tiger's eye genuine, to a complementary pure color creates magic. The new, subdued mix is a lively combination offering fresh excitement in neutrals. Often a shimmer is introduced because the pigments settle differently onto the paper. The selection of the added manufactured neutral is important. Begin with one of the starring colors for the painting. Choosing an analogous neutral offers similarity in color and color temperature. The choice of a complementary neutral can shine the spotlight onto the star color. A choice of a granulating neutral may work beautifully in a landscape but not so well in a delicate floral.

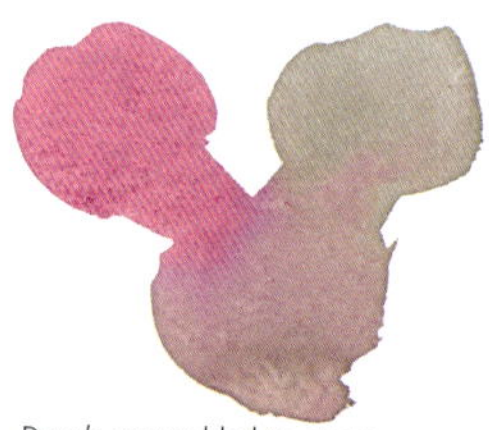

Davy's gray added to opera (Holbein)—a soft, pink gray

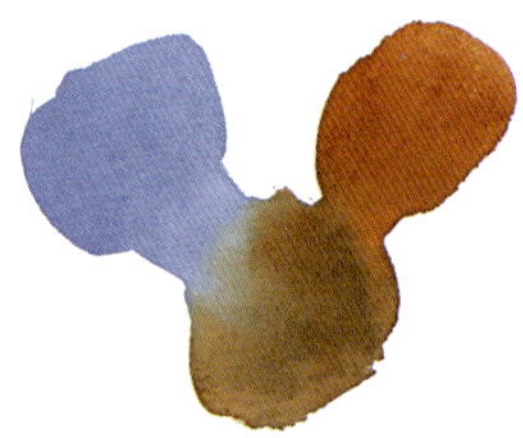

burnt sienna added to cobalt blue—cobalt blue's nongranulated complement, burnt sienna produces a smooth yet rich neutral that can be "pushed" to either color

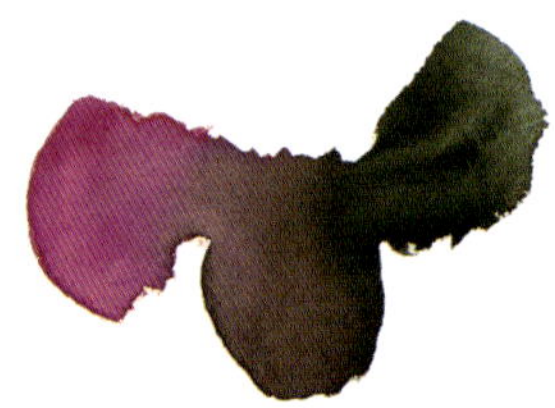

shadow green mixed with quinacridone magenta results in a atmospheric gray

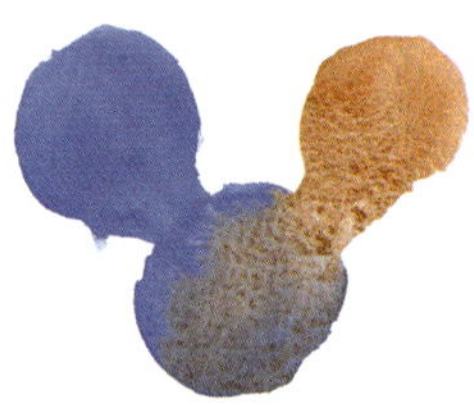

lunar earth (DS) added to cobalt blue—note the subtle granulation

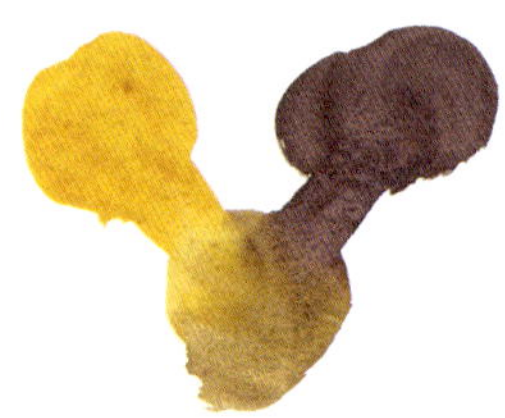

purpurite genuine (DS) added to aureolin yellow—the complementary purpurite genuine subdues the aureolin yellow creating a true neutral that can be "pushed" toward either hue. Slight granulation is added in the mix

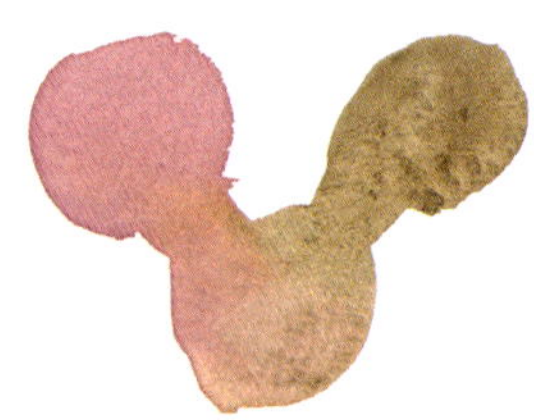

tiger's eye genuine (DS) added to rose madder genuine—a soft, earthy, granulated, warm neutral

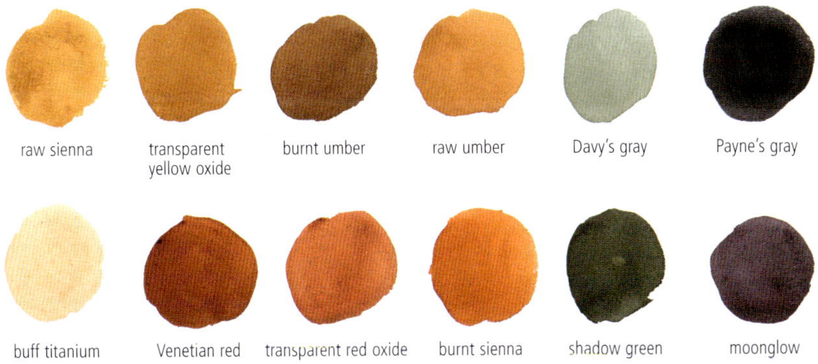

Also:
purpurite genuine
sodalite genuine
lunar black
Mars black
buff titanium titanium white
neutral tint
lunar earth
magnesium ferrite
moonglow
Mars violet
tiger's eye genuine
natural tiger's eye

IDENTIFICATION NUMBERS

Paint nomenclature can be confusing as very different pigments among the manufactured neutrals have the same chemical identification number. This is because a particular compound can undergo color changes in the laboratory. When natural hematite (iron oxide) is roasted (calcined), its color changes. As a result it may range in color from raw sienna and burnt sienna to Venetian red and vermilion, but manufacturers keep the basic chemical molecules within the same general chemical ID number.

2. Mix complements in the palette In theory, a neutral black or gray is the result of mixing two complementary colors on the color wheel, but it rarely works so cleanly. Very few pigment colors are exact opposites, so the artist mixes near complements to create the desired neutral, nudging the result toward either complement. Semineutrals are ready to play their supporting roles in the painting.

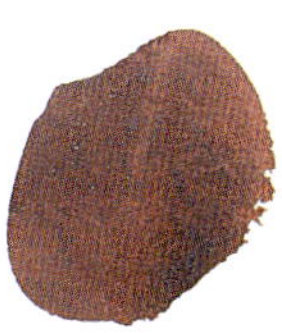
cerulean blue added to Winsor orange

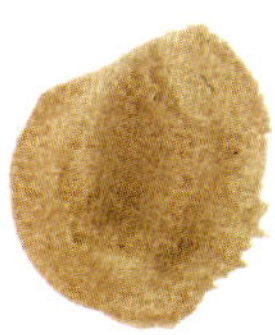
cobalt violet added to green gold

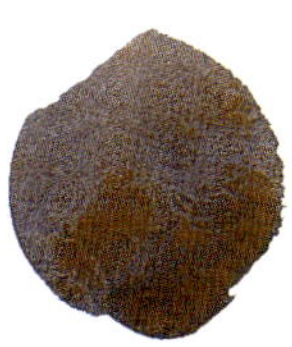
indanthrene blue added to lunar earth

napthamide maroon added to ultramarine turquoise

3. Mix complements directly on the paper Sometimes it is fun to apply complementary colors and allow them to mix where they meet, creating their own neutral. The pure colors remain as exciting nuances at the edges.

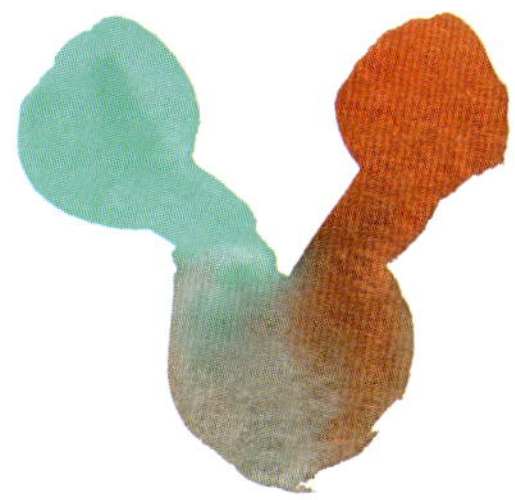
cobalt teal added to quinacridone sienna

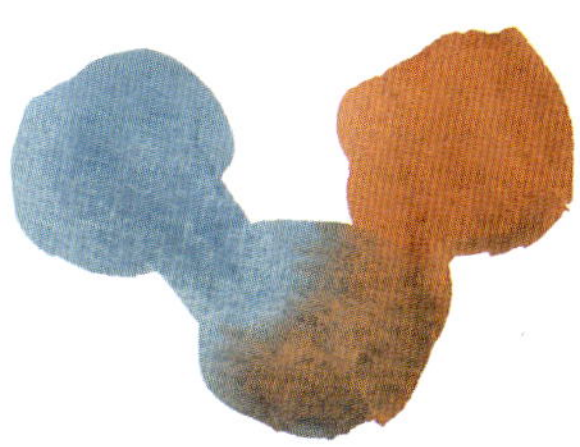
cerulean blue added to Venetian red

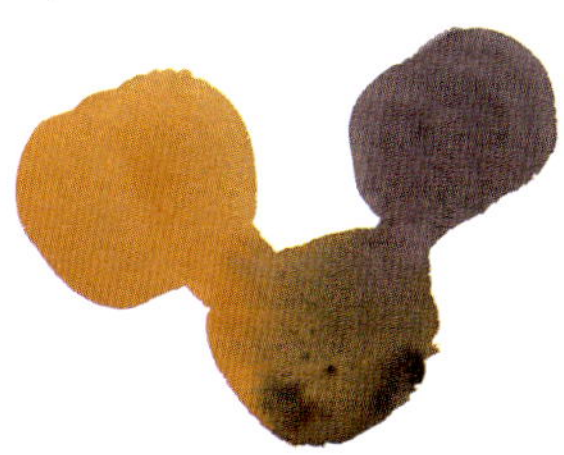
quinacridone gold added to moonglow (DS)

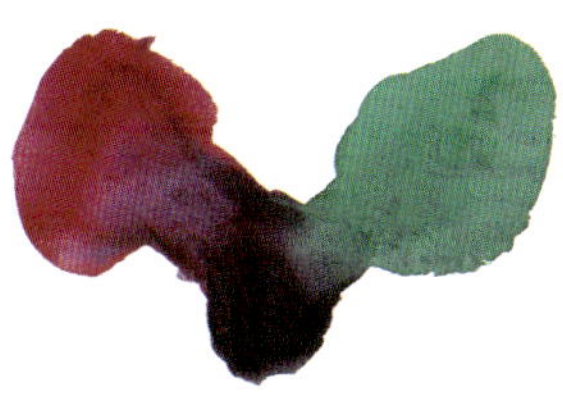
quinacridone magenta added to ultramarine turquoise

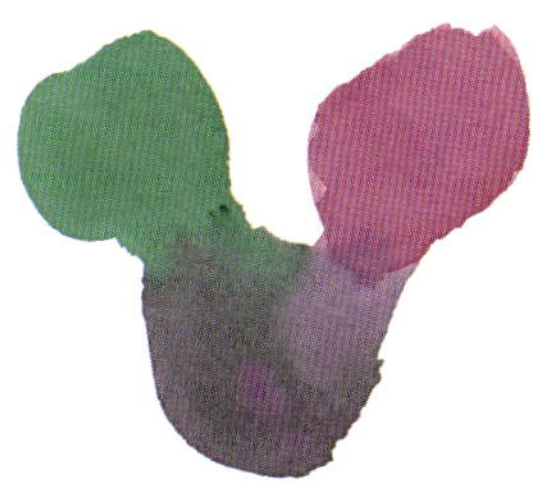
ultramarine turquoise added to rhodonite genuine

4. Mix three primaries Primary colors—magenta, cyan, and yellow—offer valuable lessons in color theory and practice. Mixing two of the primaries produces the secondary color; mixing three produces a gray/black. The qualities of the neutral are determined by the properties of the pigments.

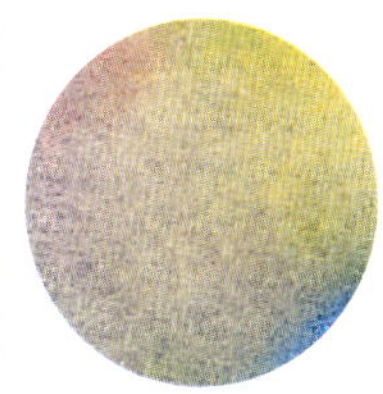
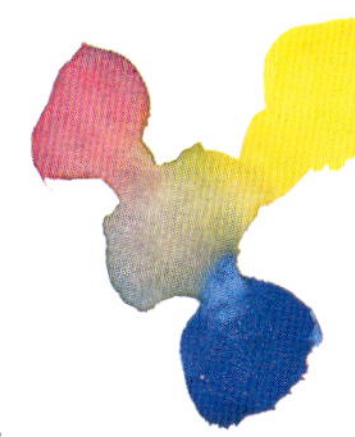

Cobalt blue, rose madder genuine, azo aureolin
These three non-staining transparents mix to a luminous gray reminiscent of coastal fogs and soft clouds.

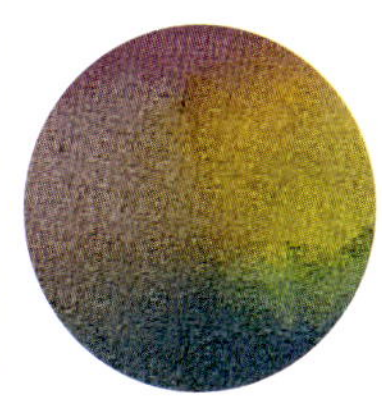
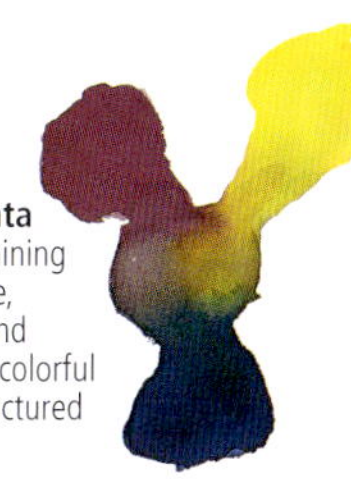

Phthalo blue, benzimida yellow (Winsor), quinacridone magenta
These three intense, staining paints produce indelible, mysterious soft grays and offer a more lively and colorful substitute for a manufactured black paint.

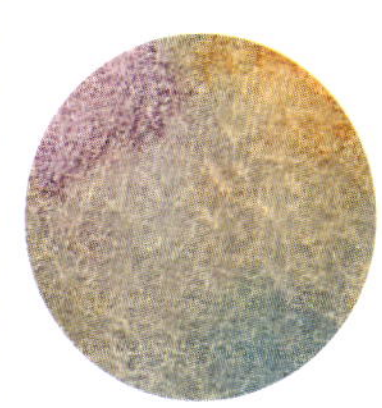
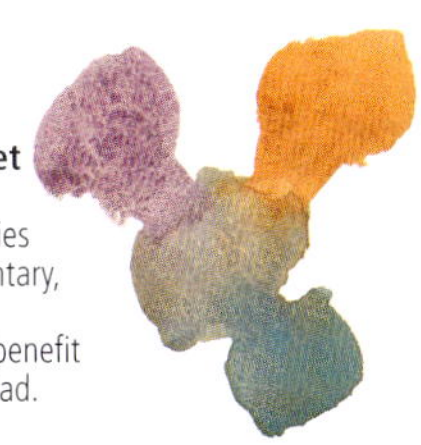

Cerulean blue, deep ochre, manganese violet
The mixture of these three primaries is opaque, sedimentary, and often soft. Landscapes often benefit from this earthy triad.

PAINTING A NEUTRAL SUBJECT

A common choice for a neutral tree trunk is "brown" or "gray." Instead of trying to mix one of these colors in the palette or preselecting a manufactured color, try mixing two complements on the paper. The resulting neutral is far more exciting than any flat brown or gray.

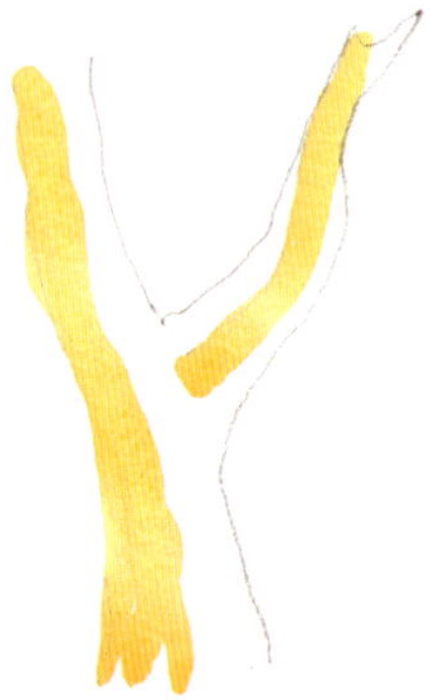

1. Consider a warm color for the sunlit side and a cool complement for the shaded side. With a round brush, apply aureolin yellow to the left side of the tree and branch, as if the sun is lighting this side of the tree.

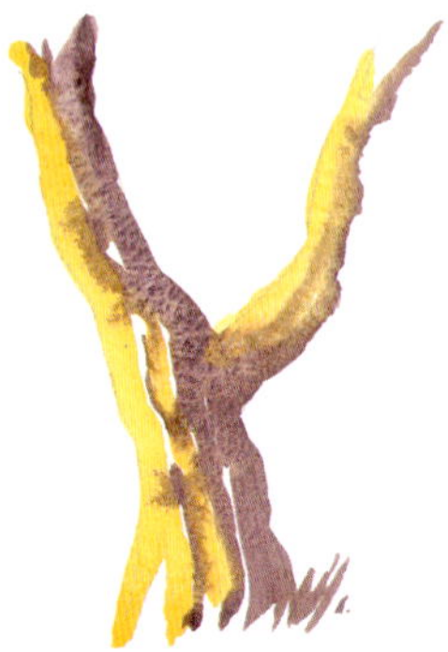

2. Immediately add purpurite genuine (DS) to the right, shaded sides, as well as some linear strokes into the yellow. Watch the two pigments meet and mix to create a granulated neutral.

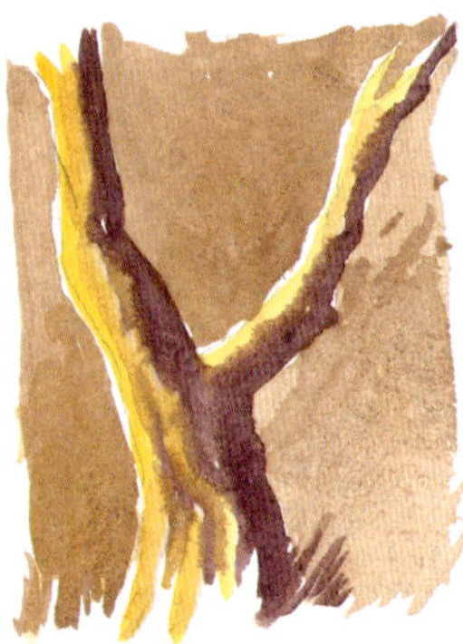

3. Add a neutral mix of aureolin yellow and purpurite, pushed toward the yellow, to the background next to the sunny side for contrast. Leave some of the white paper showing along the yellow edge to create strong contrast between the tree and background. You also can add a layer of drier, darker purpurite for more contrast on the right sides of the trunk and branch. Then add details, if desired.

ATMOSPHERIC EFFECTS

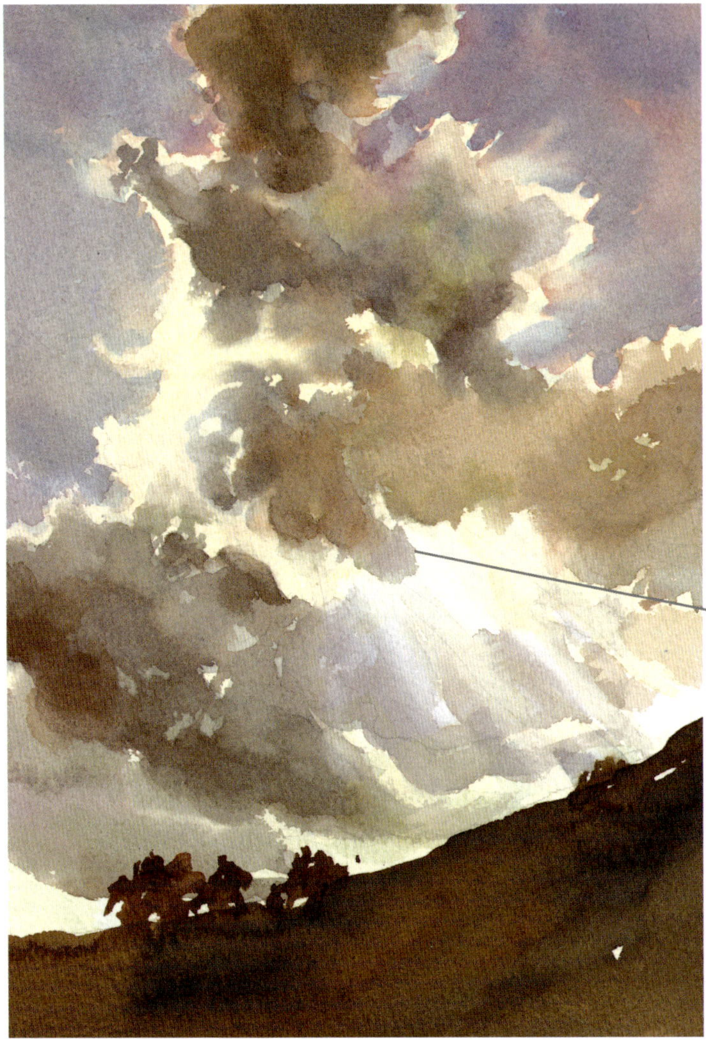

Clouds

The mixed neutrals in this painting include: cobalt blue, rose madder genuine, aureolin yellow (mixed triad); and ultramarine blue and burnt sienna (mixed complements). Limiting the palette to five pigments helps promote color balance. The transparent primary triad fills the sky with suggested soft clouds. The heavier, mixed complement provides the contrasting drama and cloud underbellies. Here and there splashes of transparent pigments play their soft color accents. Both ultramarine blue and burnt sienna add their sediment to the earth below.

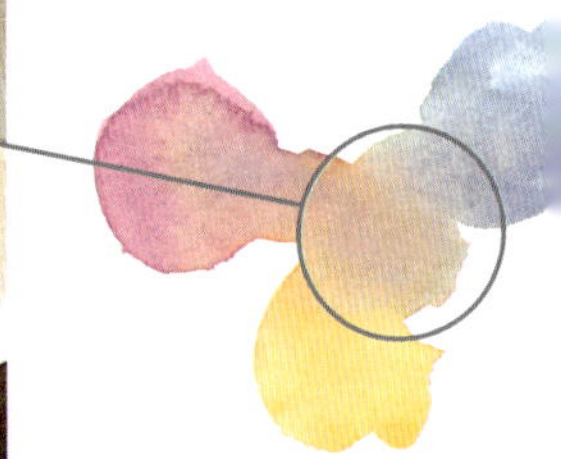

Cobalt blue, aureolin yellow, rose madder genuine

These three delicate, transparent, nonstaining pigments produce a translucent gray that glows in mountain fogs and coastal mists. In the white pigeon study (see opposite page, below left), the primaries have been mixed together unevenly. The resulting transparent glow on the white pigeon is especially notable near the darker semineutral and color-biased grays.

NEUTRAL STUDIES

White pigeon studies The complementary and triadic mixes are used to set the stage for a few "singing" colors. In each, only two complementary pigments were used. The beauty of the neutrals is that they do not compete with the pure colors; they enhance.

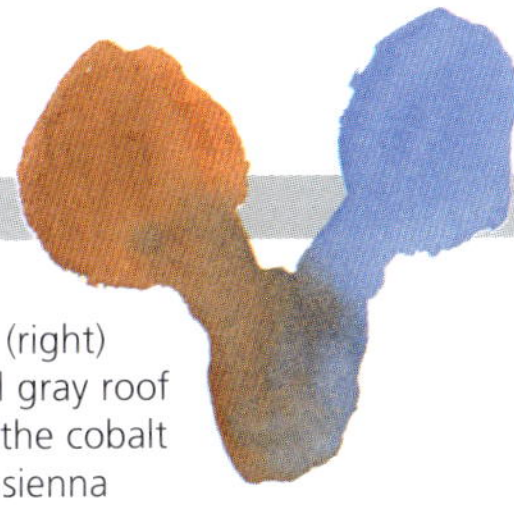

Note the glow of the bird's orange foot (right) against the semineutral gray roof made from combining the cobalt blue and quinacridone sienna

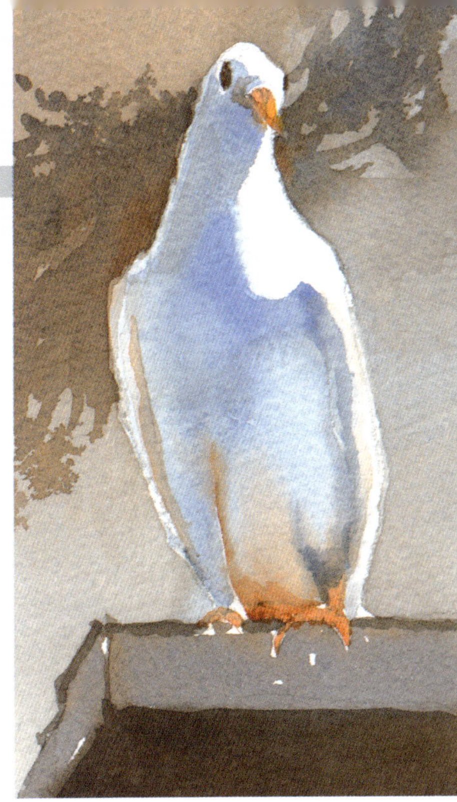

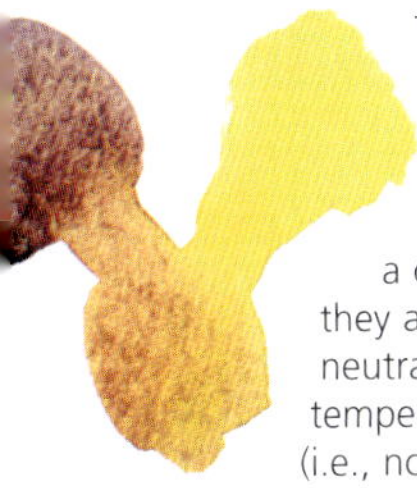

The choice of manganese violet and yellow-green (right) presents more of a challenge because they are both somewhat neutral in color temperature (i.e., not hot red or cool blue). Still, the semineutral background accentuates the violet.

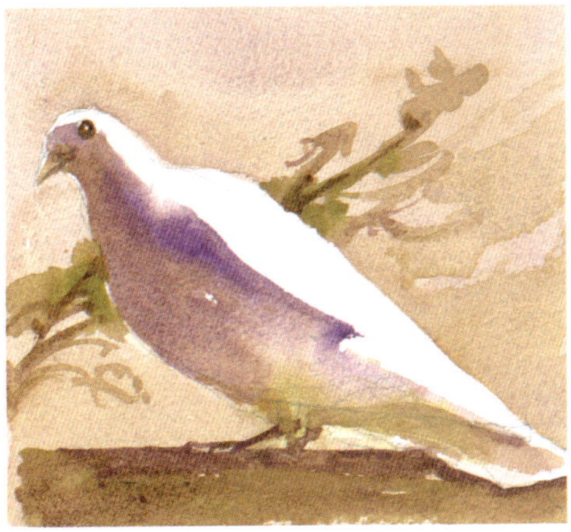

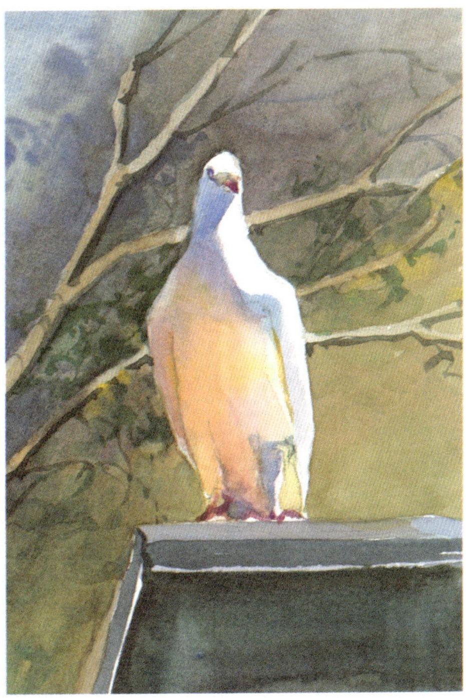

Selecting just the three transparent, nonstaining pigments of cobalt blue, aureolin yellow, and rose madder genuine (right), biased neutral mixes were used in the background to showcase the pure pigments on the white pigeon. Arraying the luminous pigments from light yellow through darker pink and lavender sets up the glow.

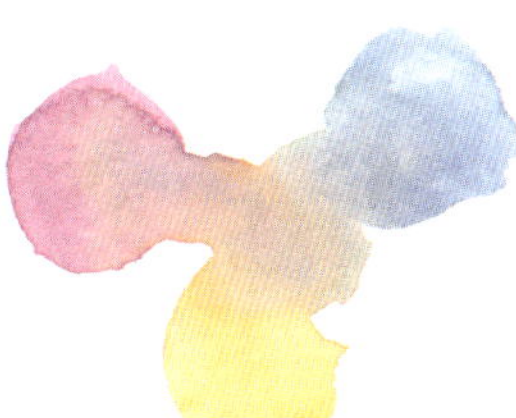

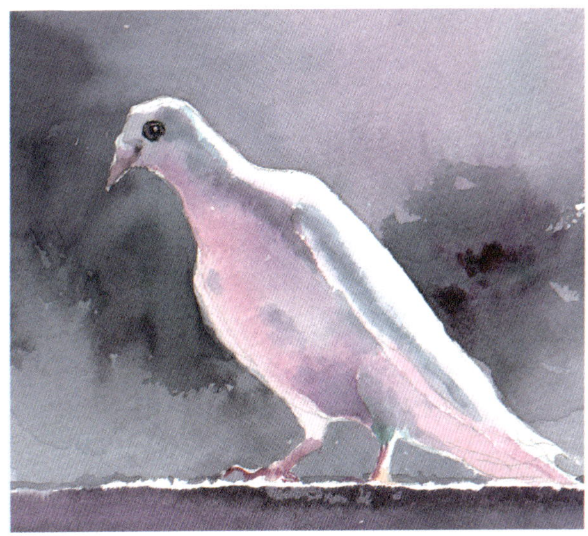

The combination of quinacridone magenta and ultramarine turquoise (above) produces some exciting dark grays that contrast with the pure magenta.

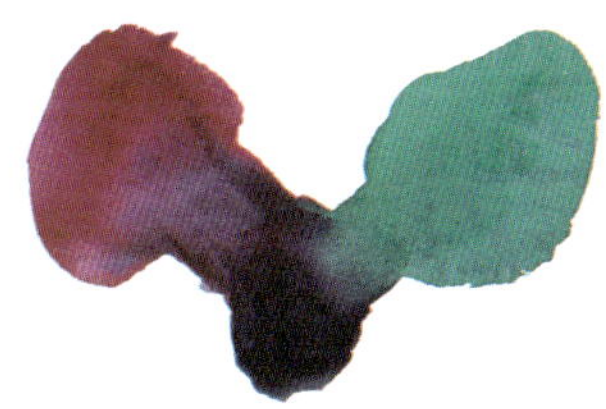

NEUTRAL COMPOSITION

Avalanche Lake This painting by the author provides an opportunity to create colorful neutrals through mixing triads and complements of various pigments that have been selected for what they do best.

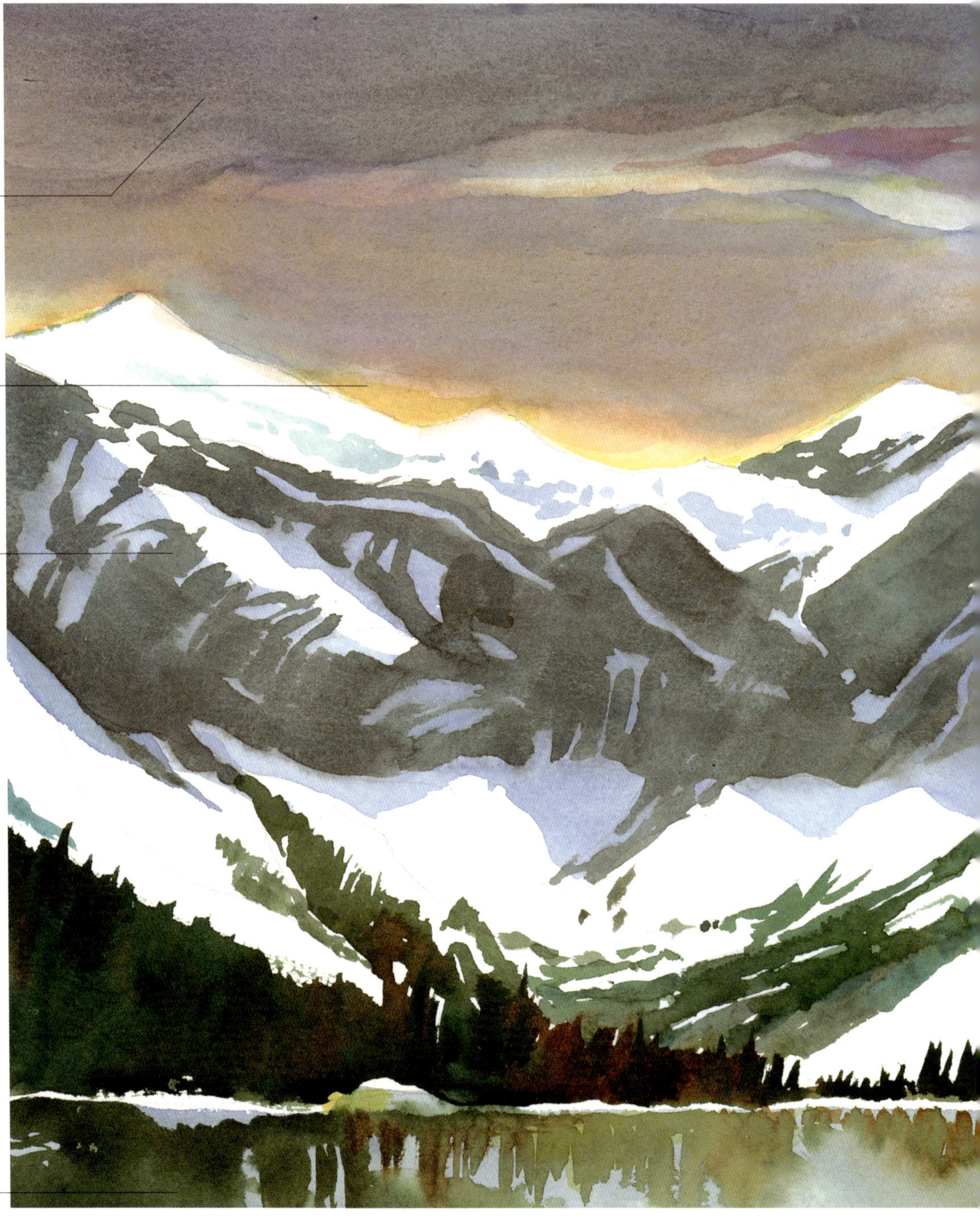

Sky The sky has been painted with three layers of the transparent, nonstaining primaries—aureolin yellow, cobalt blue, and rose madder genuine. A mix of cobalt blue and rose madder genuine was added to darken and accentuate the clouds and upper sky.

The yellow was left unglazed near the tops of the peaks. Mixing the three paints produced a translucent, gray lower sky.

Mountains The complementary opaque and sedimentary pigments cerulean blue and Venetian red seemed perfect for rock and soil. The neutral mountain material was mixed in the palette with a bias toward blue and then painted on the exposed cliffs, leaving the white of the paper to remain as snow. When the paint was dry, a glaze of pure cobalt blue established the shadowed areas of snow.

Lake The evergreen tree mix was added in vertical strokes to the still-wet cobalt blue wash of the lake. Leaving the lake edge white gives the impression of a snow bank.

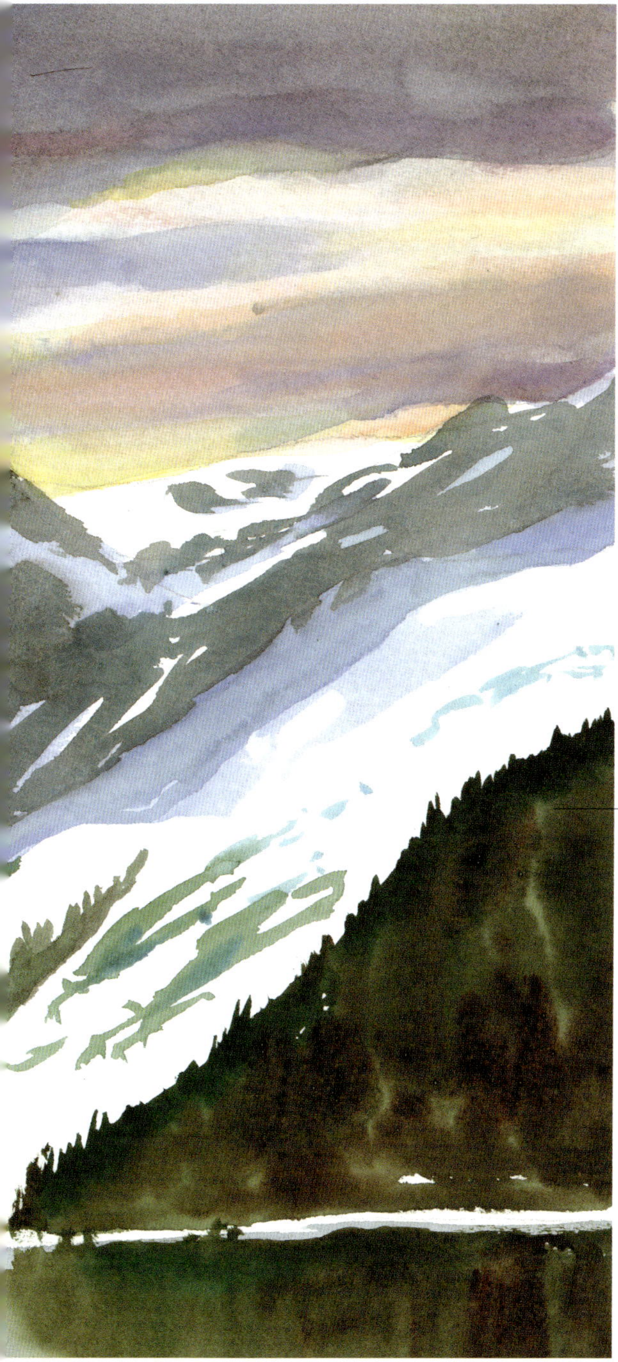

Evergreen trees Instead of a manufactured green, the mix of burnt sienna and ultramarine turquoise offered a more exciting way of varying the color temperature and adding variety to the dark trees. Spiky, vertical, and irregular brush strokes simulate the distant conifers. Some areas received the nuance of pure colors—and they stand out! Lighter washes of the same mix are used in the foothills with cerulean blue added to the areas farthest away.

MUD VERSUS NEUTRALS

One of the most frequent cries in a watercolor workshop is, "I've made mud!" Sometimes artists mistake "mud" for a semineutral color, which it is not. A true "mud" has a sludgelike quality, lacks liveliness, and is generally made up of three or more sedimentary pigments. It is usually the result of overmixing in the palette or on the paper (see page 26). When three or more sedimentary pigments are mixed together in the palette, the pigment particles become evenly distributed in the liquid. The pigments lose their individual identities, and, when painted onto paper, they result in a lifeless, flat wash.

Mixing mud

Mud was mixed using ultramarine blue, Venetian red, and cadmium yellow.

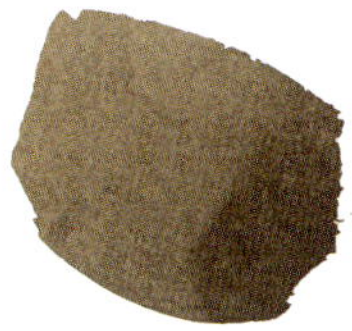

The three paints were mixed in the palette to produce a uniform, lifeless brown.

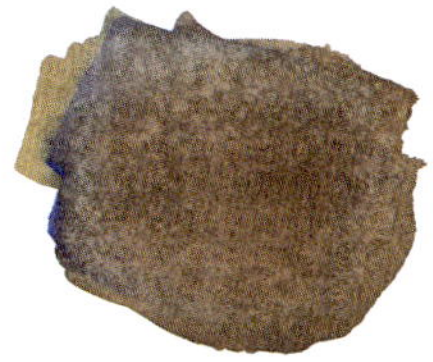

The paints were added on top of each other and over-mixed on the paper. Some of what appears to be sedimentation is actually pieces of sizing, washed up into the mix.

SOME THINGS TO CONSIDER

- For the best results, mix semineutrals from higher chroma paints. Many low-chroma paints are already combinations of two or more pigments. Mixing even two of these multi-pigment compounds together produces a mix of four or more pigments and can be an unwanted recipe for mud.
- When mixing neutrals, use only the colors that are already planned for the painting.
- Avoid adding in a new manufactured neutral at the last minute. It will throw off the entire color balance of the painting.
- Beware of manufactured grays or blacks. Neutrals you mix yourself are generally more lively and exciting.
- A mud-colored neutral is not the same as mixed mud. A neutral has life and lightness; a mixed mud is lifeless, dense, and sludgelike.
- Avoid mixing more than three sedimentary pigments. Too often the result is mixed mud.
- Experiment! Mix some pigments, and find the new mixes that work for you.

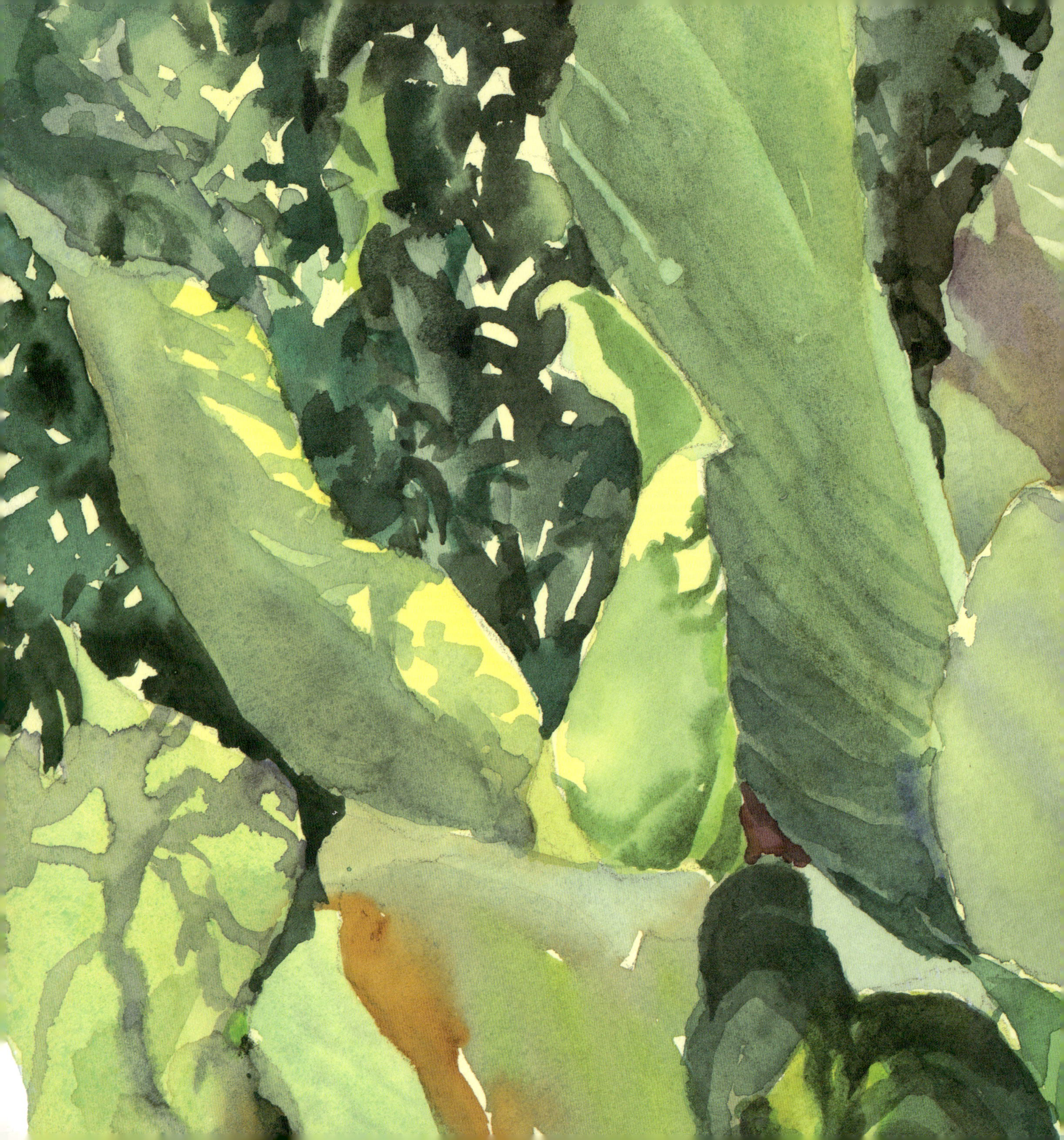

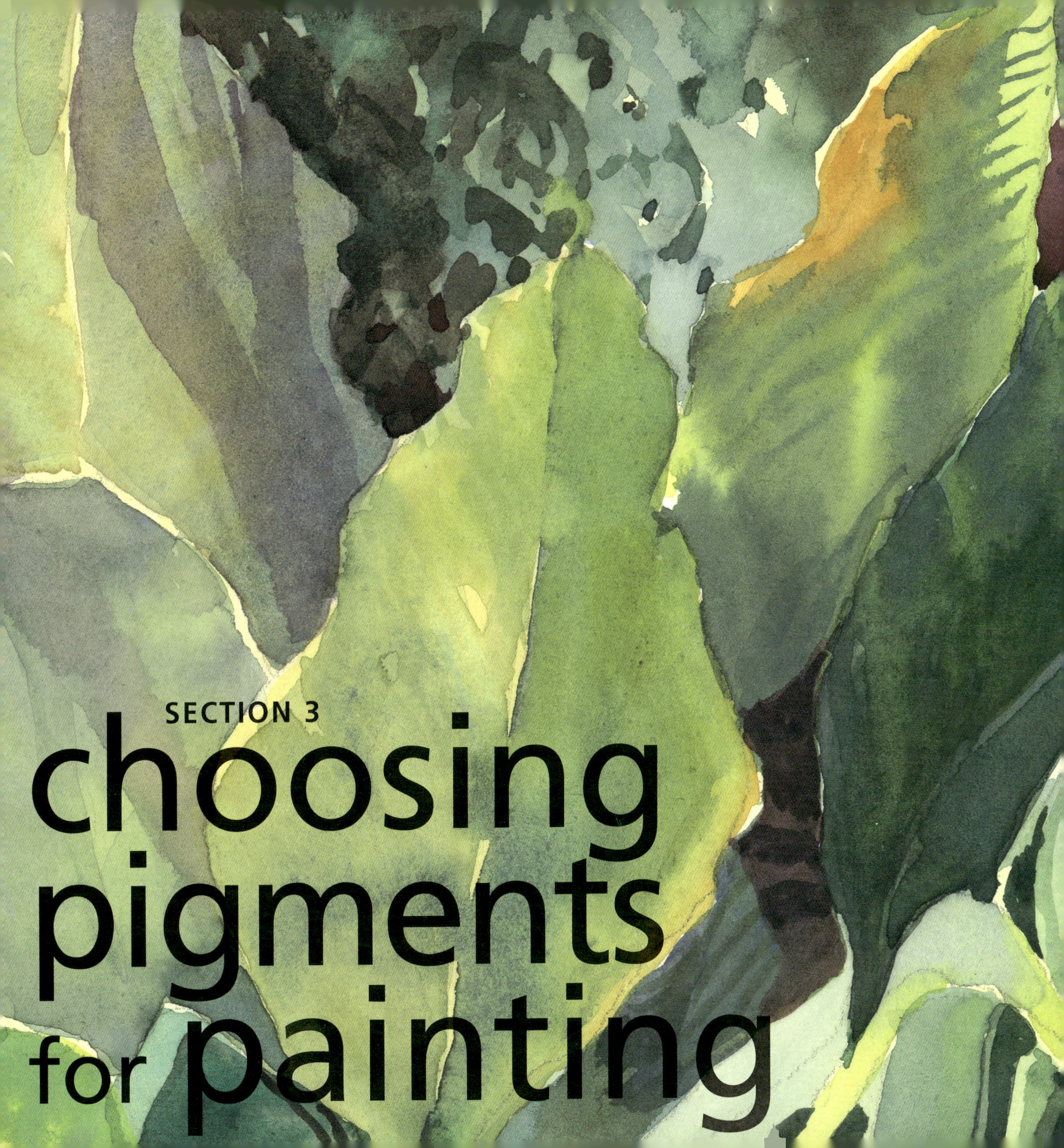

SECTION 3

choosing pigments for painting

Choosing and using a color scheme in a painting

From the mid-1800s, many artists—including the Impressionists—have stressed color over other elements such as values or line. Using color effectively is one of the most important aspects of good painting design. Painting begins with the selection of colors and pigments that will communicate the artist's feelings and intentions, and it continues until the last brushstroke. This example demonstrates how you apply this to your planning and painting process.

SELECTION METHOD

Two macaws Two scarlet macaws in a sea almond tree provide a colorful subject.

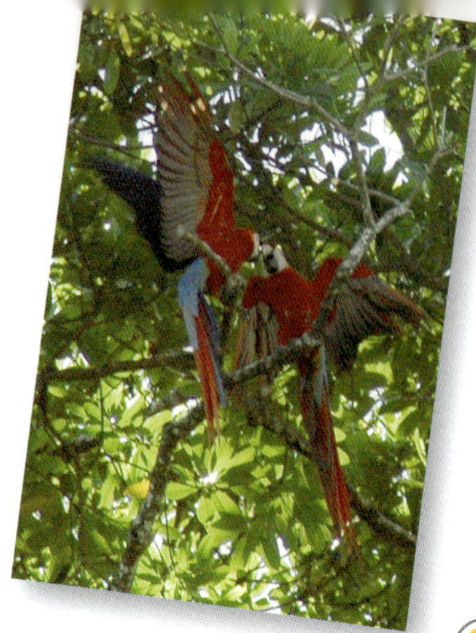

1. First select the one color that your painting cannot do without. Next decide on a color scheme that works for the subject. Although a selected scheme may seem to limit your hues, in fact it broadens your mixed colors, providing some exciting surprises along the way.

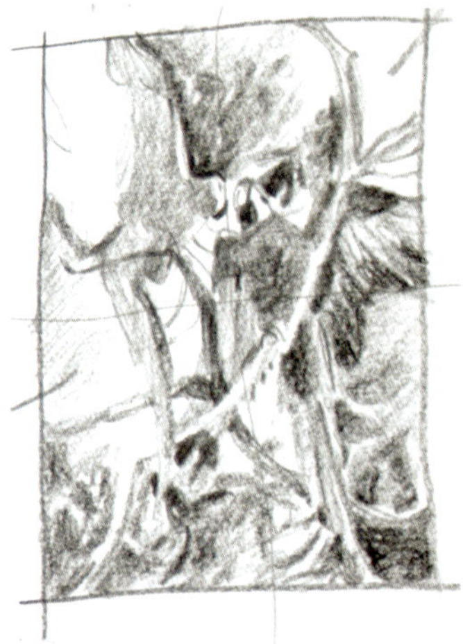

2. Study the design and values by making a sketch (see "Color value," page 66).

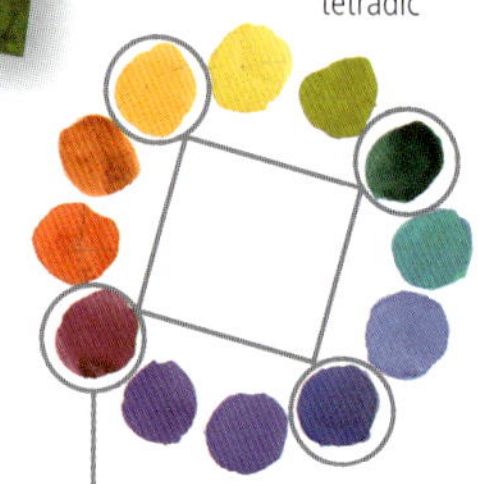

3. Use Hart's color wheel (see "Color wheels," page 14) to select the pigments that will work best for you. Quinacridone magenta was chosen as the first color for its intensity and because of the importance of the reds and magentas in the proposed subject. Because the other predominant colors are yellows and blues, the tetradic color scheme (see "Tetradic color scheme," page 58) came to mind. Ultramarine turquoise, quinacridone magenta's complement, was chosen for the greens and turquoises. Next came the two remaining complements, yellow-orange and

LEARNING TO SEE COLOR

Human vision has evolved to function best in the daytime when there is maximum color information available. Nocturnal animals appear to have lost some of their color vision because it is not needed at night. Others, such as many birds and honeybees, can see ultraviolet wavelengths, which are invisible to humans. As humans we each see color a little differently. Color perception is influenced by individual physiology, psychology, culture, and even by language. For this reason, it is impossible to identify an object's true color. We can predict how color is seen, but results are always subject to individual perceptions.

Light: Color originates in light Without light, you do not see color. If you look at a red tomato it is not emitting red light, but absorbing all the wavelengths of light around it, except for those that humans call "red." They are being reflected from the tomato to your eyes. You perceive the tomato as red because your eyes distinguish between all the different wavelengths.

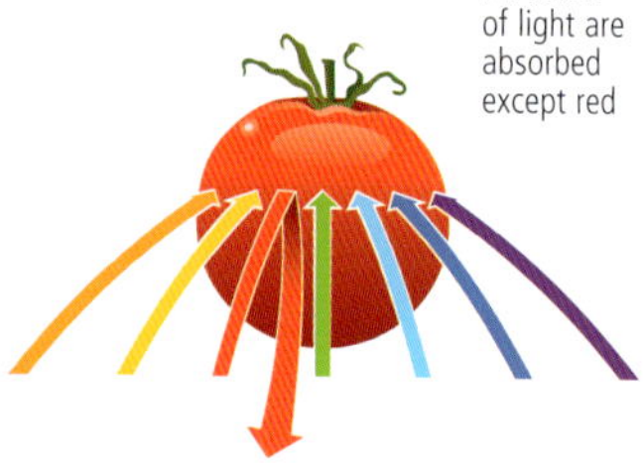

The eye: When light enters the eye, it is focused on an area at the back of the eye known as the retina. The retina is composed of millions of specialized photoreceptor cells called "rods" and "cones." They convert the light into electrical signals that will be sent to the brain. The cones near the center of the retina are responsible for color vision. You see the tomato's color most strongly when you look directly at it. Humans have between six and seven million cones. There are three types—red (64%), green (32%), and blue (4%)—that operate together to produce color vision. In addition, there are two opponent processes that contribute to color vision. They produce the afterimage that is created when you stare at a color, close your eyes, and see the complement of that color.

The brain: The brain interprets the information that is sent to it by the eyes. By comparing a patch of color to the surrounding colored region, the brain is able to reconstruct a stable visual representation of reality. The brain also can add in memories, associations, and other factors. This complex process enables artists to represent objects in a way that is different from the way they see them. They may also charge an object with greater emotional or expressive power by accentuating or changing color.

middle blue. Ultramarine blue with cobalt blue and nickel azo were selected.

4. Test some mixes and apply them to paper.

5. Use accents of color to direct the eye around the painting and to suggest atmosphere. Subdued quinacridone magenta was used throughout to help direct the viewer's eye from the parrots into the foliage and back. Small, dancing strokes of bright yellows, yellow-greens, and magenta were deliberately placed near the parrots' heads to suggest excitement and interaction. With the intention of creating a "path of light" through the painting, the corners were darkened. Note that some interference pigment (see page 125) was added to the shadowed wings to simulate the shimmer of feathers.

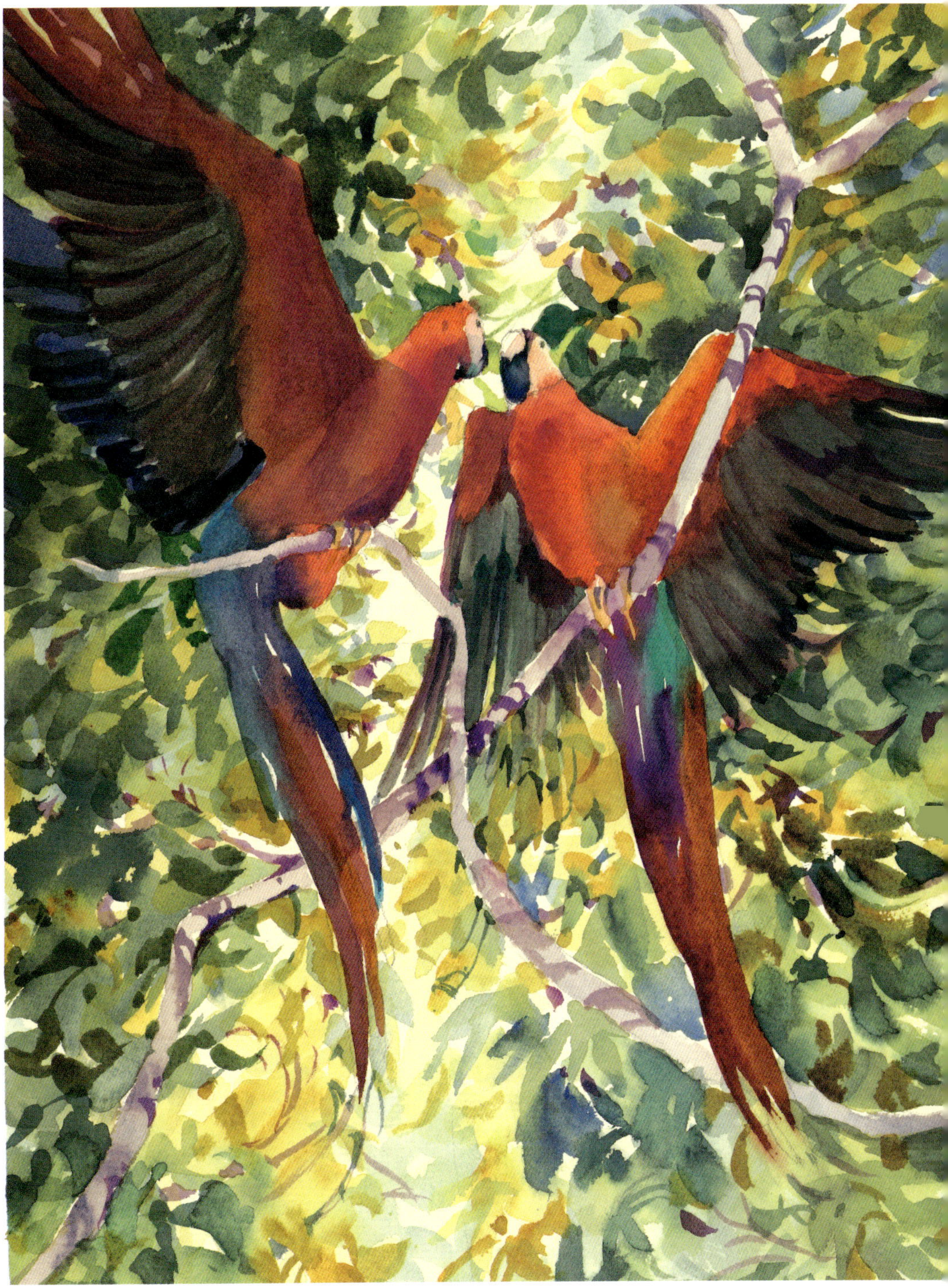

SOME THINGS TO CONSIDER

- The best way to train your color vision is first to study it and then to use it. As you learn about the composition of shadows, complementary colors, and simultaneous contrast, you begin to see examples all around you.
- Remember that you, as the artist, make the selection of colors for your paintings. Do not allow the photograph or the subject to take control. They can suggest, but you decide.
- Color and pigment selection are two of the most important decisions a watercolor artist can make before beginning a painting, so spend time planning and thinking about how the colors will work together.

ASSESSING PROGRESS IN A PAINTING

While painting, you may suddenly reach a point where you do not know what to do next. Stop. Know that the painting is not yet completed, and you need to decide how to finish it. This is the perfect time to stand back and look at it from a distance. First ask yourself what is working well. You could be happy with the color and the composition, but you need to ask yourself, "What needs work now?" Perhaps shaded areas need to be darkened and enriched, or the darks need to be more connected. Maybe cast shadows need more definition. By taking yourself out of the painting process and looking at your painting anew, you may find the best way to move forward.

Light, shade, and shadow

Through light we understand form, texture, and color. Manipulation of the overall lighting in a painting affects mood and feeling, so it is no wonder this subject is one of the most essential in painting. One of the best-known movements demonstrating this is French Impressionism. The Impressionists were known for capturing the transient effects of atmosphere and light, painting outdoors in the French countryside with its clear air and warm light. There they expressed what they saw—the incredible colors of light, shade, and shadow. Creating shadow and light in watercolor is notoriously difficult but can be made easier by understanding the theory behind it.

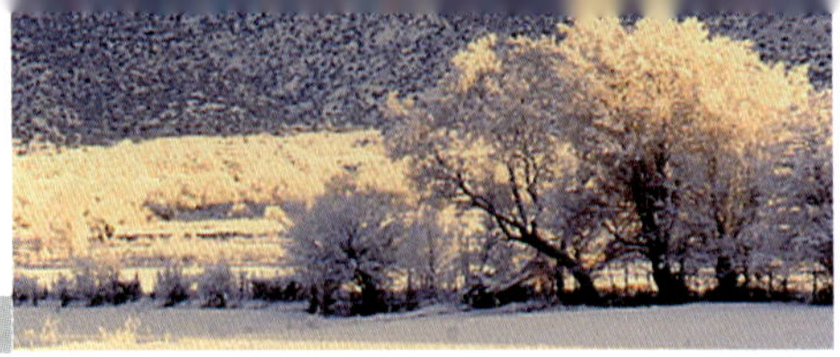

THE BASICS

Natural light The color of the light from the sun depends on the time of day. Sunlight in early morning and late afternoon is warmer (more yellow or orange) than direct light at noon.

Shade and reflected color Conventional wisdom suggests that the color of shade (the part of the object turned away from the sun) is a darker shade of the object's local color, however, colors from the surroundings are also reflected in. There are a few general points to take on board which will help you to paint shadows correctly.

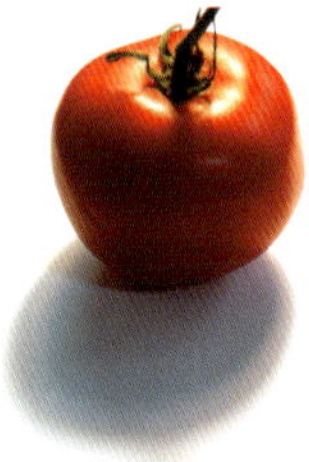

Tomato experiment Under warm incandescent light, a tomato was placed on three different colored surfaces—pure white, dark green, and yellow-gold. The direct yellow-orange light produces a blue cast shadow, which appears to our eyes as a combination of the shadow color, surface color, and any reflected color. The shadow variable edge is due to other sources of light in the room.

Tomato on white
The cast shadow is blue and appears as it is on a pure white surface. Within the cast shadow, closest to the base of the tomato, is some red reflected from the tomato creating some appearance of violet (red + blue). Note the band of reflected light from the white surface back onto the middle area of the tomato.

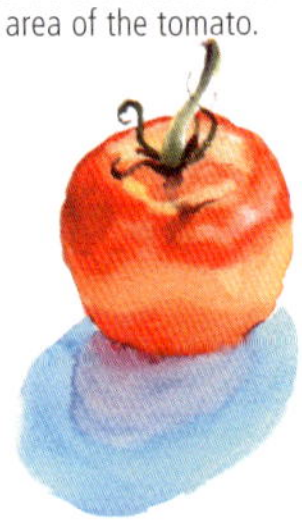

Tomato on dark green
The color of the cast shadow is still blue but it appears darker on the dark green surface color. As the surface color is reflected back onto the tomato, the combination is a dark neutral of (red + green).

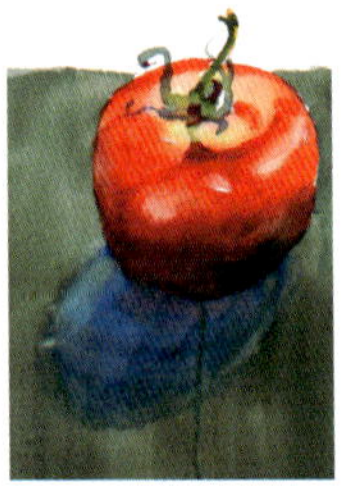

Cast shadow A cast shadow is the dark area that falls behind an object when a light source is in front. When asked the color of shadows, most people reply, "gray." This is because they are not searching for the nuances of color. The base color of the cast shadow is the complement of the light source; in the above case the shadows are violet with the complementary yellow light source.

Shade and reflected light When a light ray bounces, its light waves become longer and the color of the light becomes warmer. The shaded area receiving bounced light grows warm.

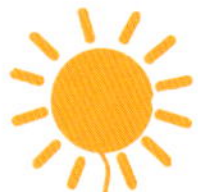

This concept helps to explain why in bright sunlight we see orange in the shaded side of a building.

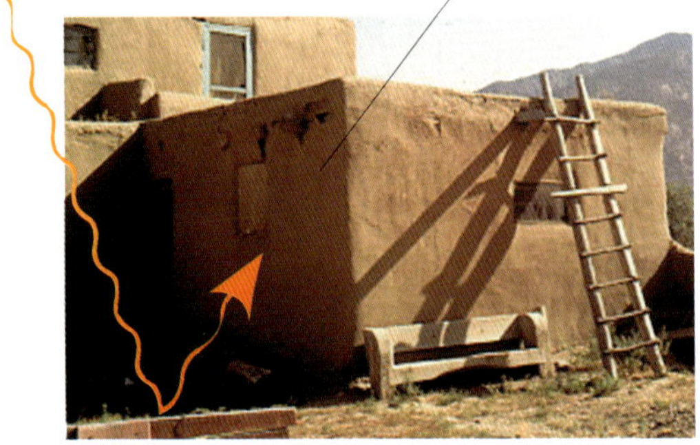

Tomato on yellow-gold
The cast shadow is the same blue—but now its visible color is a mix of the blue and the yellow gold surface—a pale greenish gold. Because the shadow is light enough, some of the reflected tomato red can be seen in the shadow. Yellow color from the surface reflects back onto the tomato to create orange (red + yellow).

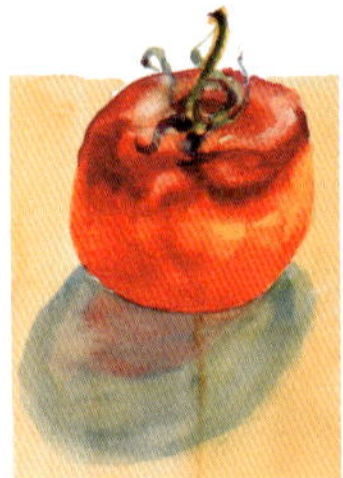

EIGHT POINTS ABOUT CAST SHADOWS

1 Cast shadows of trees that extend horizontally across the ground are linear and generally appear longer than they are wide. If you paint them very wide, they won't appear to be lying flat on the ground. The shadows closest to the viewer are widest, warmest, and darkest. Those farther away become progressively thinner and cooler.

2 Cast shadows of foliage often produce "sun pictures" on the ground. The sun filters through the numerous openings of foliage to create irregular patterns of light. This is what we call "dappled light."

3 A cast shadow is darkest, sharpest, and coolest at its origin. It is always attached to the object that is casting it unless that object is in the air.

4 Cast shadows of near or hard-edged objects have hard edges. Shadows of distant or fuzzy objects have soft edges.

5 Cast shadows change as they pass over different surfaces. They may change in color, direction, and shape. For example, when the cast shadow of a roof overhang passes over a recessed area, such as a doorway or window frame, the shadow changes, usually jogging downward.

6 In northern climates, it is possible to experience cool light that produces a complementary, warm shadow. Northern climates are generally cloudier than southern climates, and since clouds contain water droplets that scatter light rays penetrating them, the light becomes bluer. If the resulting cool blue light is strong and direct enough to produce a shadow, the color of that shadow is the complementary orange.

7 Cast shadows are always transparent, allowing the underlying subject to show through.

8 Within a cast shadow, you may find colors of adjacent objects and even light reflected from another surface.

SHADOW EXAMPLES

These photographs and accompanying studies demonstrate choices in painting cast shadows.

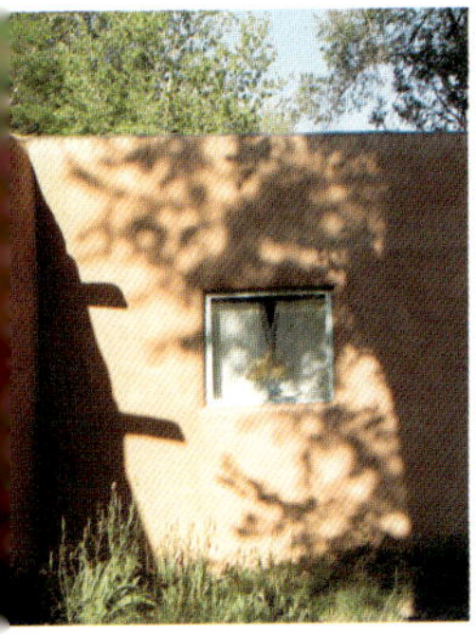

Photograph The sun (which is behind and to the left of the viewer) casts solid, hard-edged shadows of the rain spout and beam end (not shown) onto the sunny wall. Note the reflected light glow on the shaded left wall. A tree also casts its shadow onto the sunny wall in softened linear shapes and dappled sun pictures. The shadows change in color as they fall over the white window curtains.

Painting An overall underwash of aureolin yellow anticipates the sunshine. The window is left as it is. Beginning with the shaded left wall, brush a bright mix of rose madder genuine and aureolin yellow into the reflected light corner and pull it across to the left edge. While it is still wet, blend in a darker mix of rose madder genuine and napthamide maroon, leaving the upper corner alone. On the sunny wall, rose madder genuine over the aureolin yellow is the perfect base for a darker and drier shadow mix applied with a round brush. The area can be rewashed and more soft shadows added. Apply pure cobalt blue to the water-dampened window area using similar soft strokes for the cast shadow. Finally apply the harder-edged cast shadow from the left wall using cobalt blue-violet, taking care to paint the negative space around the sunlit grasses in the foreground.

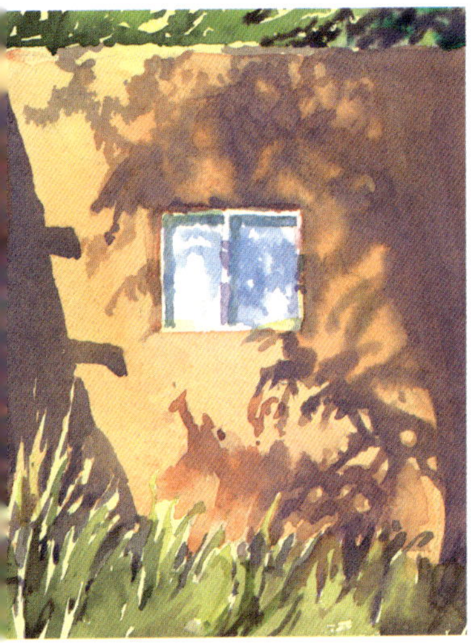

Photograph The shadow tapestry cast on the paved walkway by a tree demonstrates a wide variety of shapes and values. The farthest leaf branches cast soft shapes, which are covered by the stronger, sharper shapes of the closer branches. Sun pictures are scattered here and there, some soft-edged, some hard-edged.

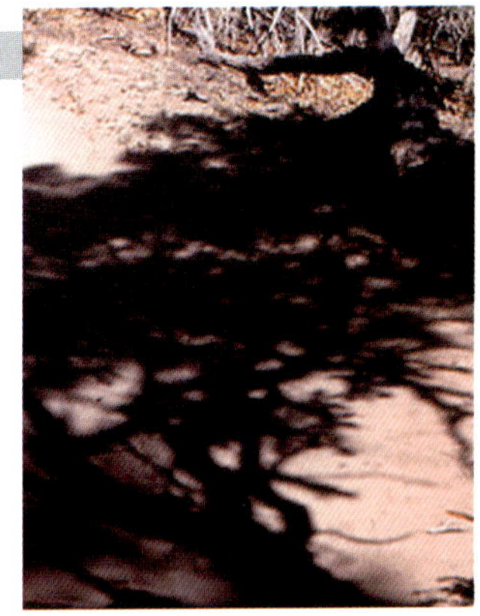

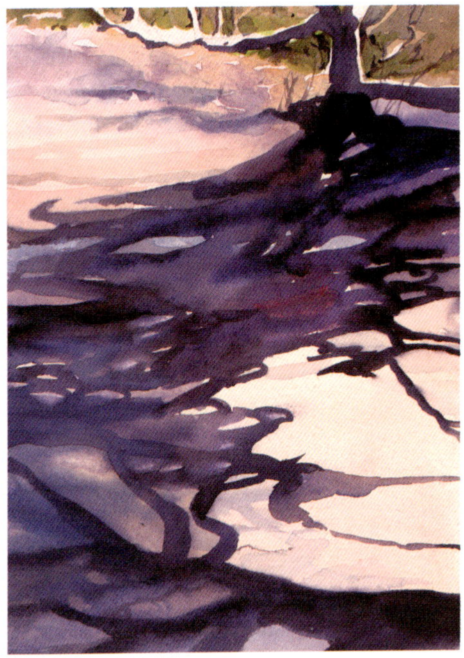

Painting The dark, undulating, cast shadows demand stronger pigments than the customary, transparent cobalt blue and rose madder genuine. They are based in ultramarine blue and carbazole violet (dioxazine violet), which are warmed with quinacridone magenta and napthamide maroon. The mixes are applied directly onto a rose madder genuine underwashed paper. Before painting the shadows, dampen the paper in some areas and leave dry in others so that, as you paint, both hard- and soft-edged shadows are created.

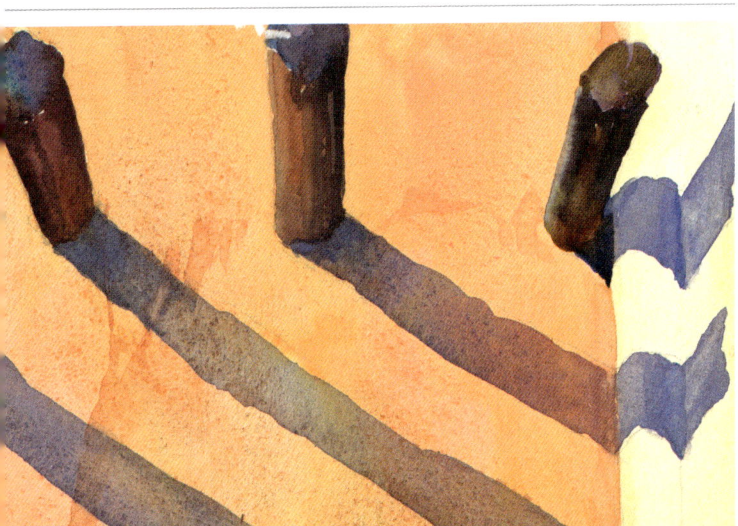

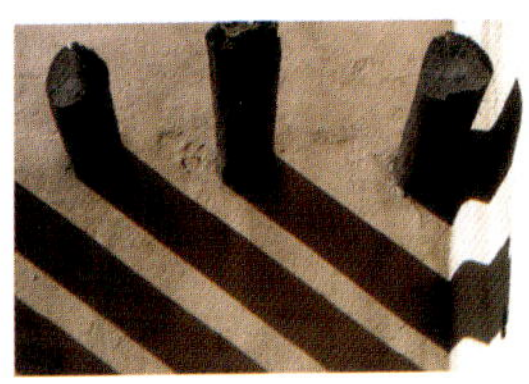

Photograph The sun shining from the upper left makes parallel beam shadows across the mud surface of the building. When they reach the perpendicular light-colored wall, the shadows change direction and color. Note that the darkest, sharpest, and coolest part of the shadow is at its origin—the base of the protruding beam.

Painting The texture of the dried mud wall is achieved with granulating pigments such as lunar earth, hemetite violet, cobalt violet, and zoisite. Add them directly into a still-wet base of rose madder genuine. Paint the undersides of the projecting beams warm and lighter, assuming reflected light. The shadows are transparent cobalt blue, which thin and warm up with rose madder genuine as they move away from the beams. To assure convincing transparency in the cast shadow, add a surface detail (surface irregularity) that extends across the shadow after everything is dry.

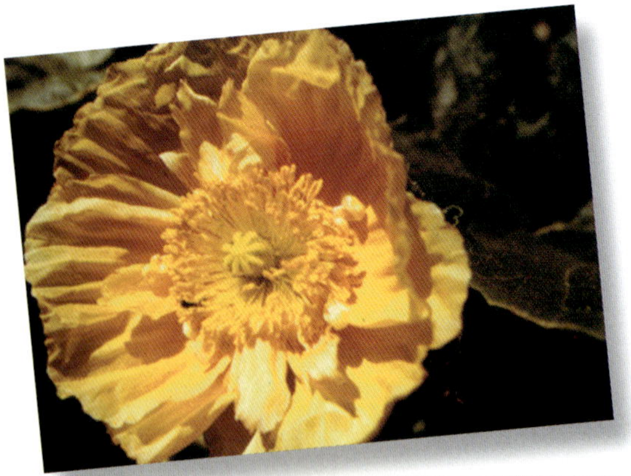

POPPY WITH LIGHT AND SHADE

Understand the values An object in direct light has at least five, and often more, value changes from direct light to cast shadow details.

Color/paint considerations The strong yellows, oranges, and greens suggest a "loose" split-complemetary color scheme with the loosely analogous colors of red-orange, yellow, and green-blue played against the complementary blue-violet color position on Hart's color wheel (see page 15). The paints can include several from each color position including the luminous trio of aureolin yellow, rose madder genuine, and cobalt blue.

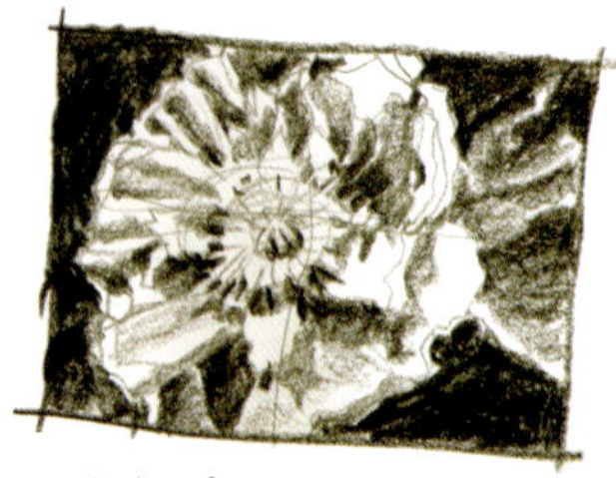

Value/composition study A black non-graphite colored pencil is perfect for creating the entire range from 1 to 6. The study also enables you to make reminders for the painting.

Direct perpendicular light—highest value **6**
Direct light—next highest value **5**
Shade **4**
Reflected light in shade—mid-value **3**
Cast shadow **2**
Crevices within the cast shadow—darkest dark **1**

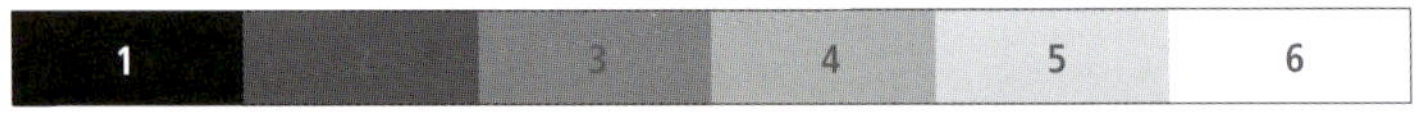

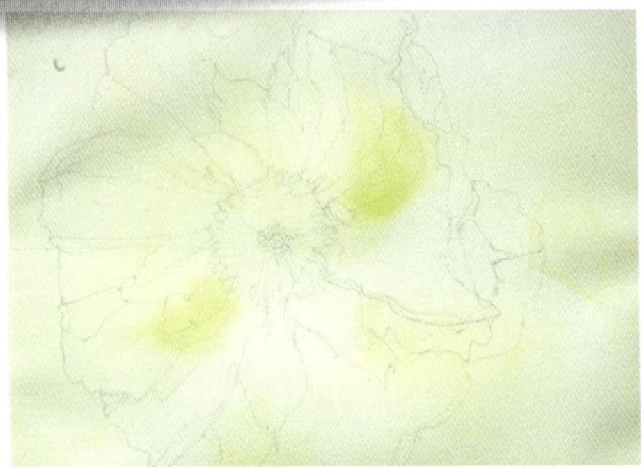

1 Outlines Subject outlines are drawn onto the watercolor paper and followed by an underwash of aureolin yellow to enhance the sunlight and unify the warm color temperature. A few areas receive a little extra pigment where it could be useful later on.

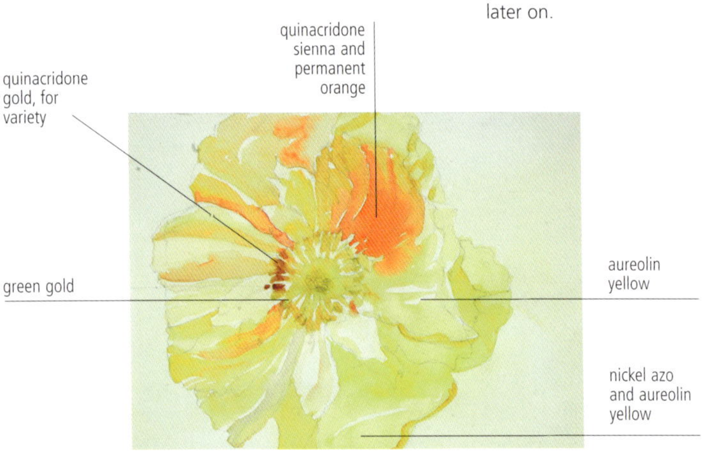

2 Local color and shade with reflected light Brush in color quickly and loosely using several yellows and oranges, such as nickel azo, aureolin yellow, quinacridone gold, green gold, permanent orange, along with new gamboge and quinacridone sienna, to show the hot reflected light in some of the shaded petal upturns and curves. Take care at the base of a petal—especially the shaded petal—to paint carefully around the stamens to achieve depth and focus.

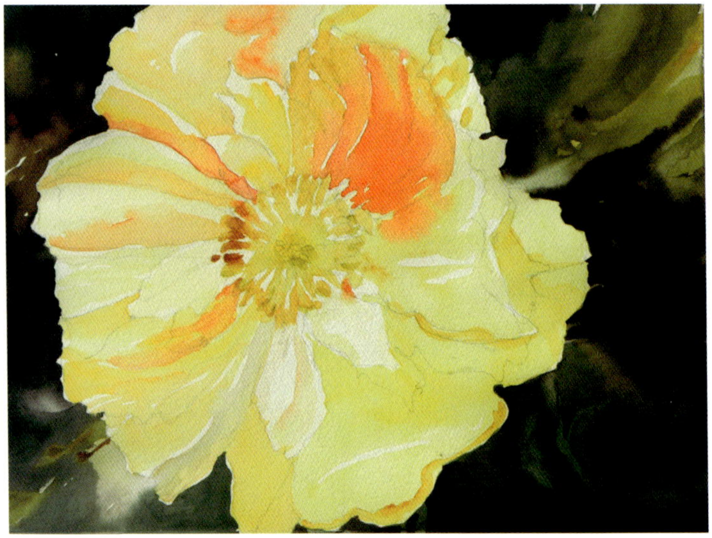

3 Background Lay this in quickly, loosely, and darkly. In such a light, bright painting subject, it is a good idea to put in your darkest darks early so that your eye can register the complete value range. Dark greens with maroon and yellows are selected. Add a sprinkle of turquoise to play against the orange. Mix ultramarine turquoise and napthamide maroon in the palette. Paint onto a dry area, and then add other pigments directly onto the now-wet surface in directional strokes suggesting leaves. This is the place to experiment. Stroke in some nickel azo and watch the explosion. Add in some buff titanium to lighten and highlight. Avoid making too many strokes or painting as the surface dries. The idea is to blend and push the paint, not to make the background too busy.

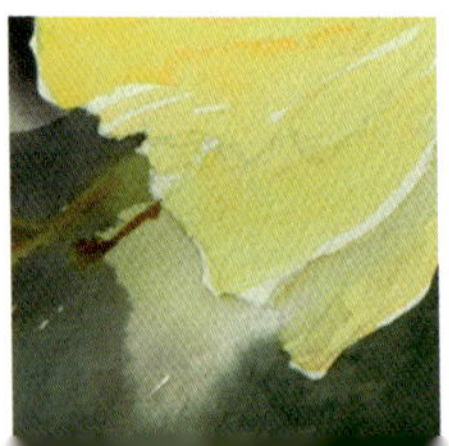

Note that the edge of the flower is broken in a few places in an effort to combine the dark negative shapes with the bright and light positive shapes. These will be useful later on. Don't paint over the "lost edges" of the flower.

SHADOW MIXES

Always think before you paint. Ask yourself questions. For example, "If I place a cobalt blue shadow over a bright yellow petal, what will I get?" Answer: green. If green is not desired, change the shadow mix. "If I place the lavender mix over a bright yellow petal, what will I get?" Answer: gray. Try a spot of nickel azo to move the paint; a bit of opera for surprise; a touch of cobalt blue for a dark corner; or a spot of permanent orange for fun. On the yellow poppy, a pale lavender glaze was applied to the upper left, just to slightly tone down the yellow so that the right side could sing louder.

When any two of the three transparent, nonstaining pigments are mixed together, they create colors. When all three of them are mixed together they create gray.

rose madder genuine and aureolin yellow

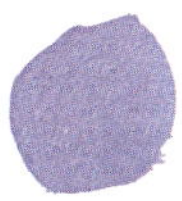

cobalt blue and rose madder genuine

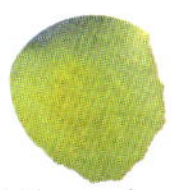

cobalt blue and aureolin yellow

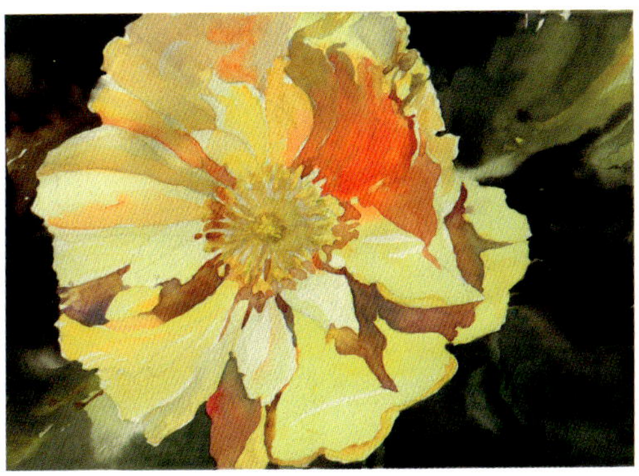

4 Cast shadows Carefully apply the cast shadows, one by one, to create beautiful and varied shapes. The transparent, nonstaining pigments are best for showing the shadow transparency. But glazing over bright yellow requires some thought before painting (see shadow mixes, above).

Mixes of cobalt blue, aureolin yellow, and rose madder genuine glazed over yellow.

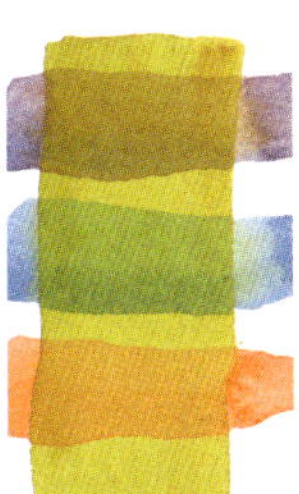

SOME THINGS TO CONSIDER

- A transparent shadow mix can be the wetting agent for your next wet-into-wet exploration.
- Show transparency in a cast shadow by adding a wrinkle or blemish that crosses from the sunlit area into the cast shadow.
- "Tuck in" the cast shadow at its origin by applying a drier dark into the still-damp shadow.
- For soft-edged cast shadows, keep the paper surface wet. For crisper edges, apply shadows to a completely dry surface.

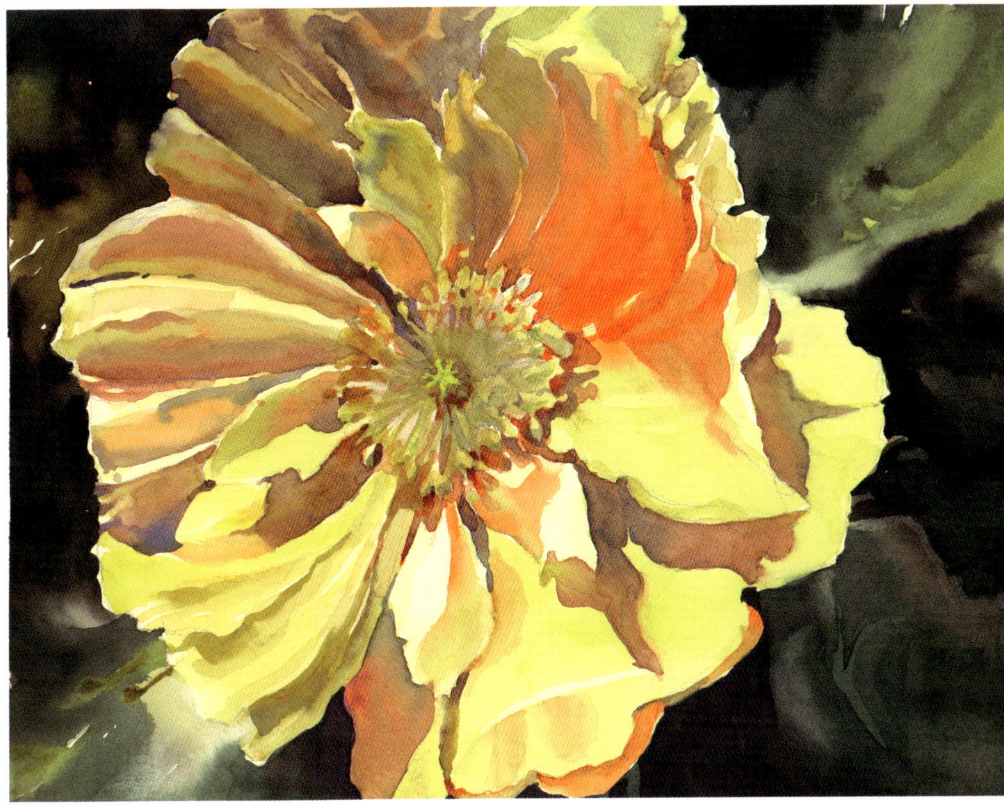

5 Review So far so good, but the left side is still too light. Now is the time for some accents and finishing. Apply more lavender and orange to a few undulating, upper left petals. Be careful to create a soft edge on one side (top) where it curves and a hard edge on the other (bottom). This creates the illusion of a ripple or undulation. Place accents of orange, using quinacridone sienna for its transparency, near and around the center for reflected light. Also add accents along the upturned petal at the very bottom.

Quinacridone gold added to the top creates an illusion of undulation.

6 Finishing touches The finished painting shows a few tucks and hue exaggerations.

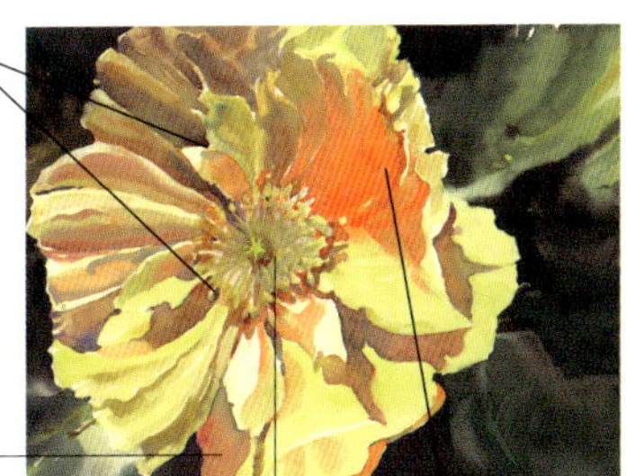

Backgrounds

Many a student has voiced the plaintive cry, "What am I going to do with the background?" A compelling subject, such as a flower, can sweep the artist into action and remembered advice comes too late: make background decisions early. A number of options can be considered when faced with empty white surrounding the painted subject.

CHOOSING A BACKGROUND

1 Apply an analogous color scheme (see "Analogous color palette," page 52) using a warm, neutral dark. This will create analogous harmony.
2 Apply a contrasting dark. A flat, cool blue, for example, would complement and spotlight a dark flower.
3 Apply a "black" background. This will feature the subject prominently but add little else.
4 Apply a hazy, soft, washy background using analogous and contrasting hues. Although this is a widely used solution, all too often it creates further disharmony between the subject and the background.
5 Apply shapes that are reminiscent of the subject's natural background, such as a floral habitat. This will integrate the background and foreground subjects.
6 Leave the background paper white. A painting or drawing that has no border but is gradually faded into its background at the edges is called a "vignette."

Each of the options above is viable, but for the demonstration below, option 5 has been chosen.

PAINTING THE BACKGROUND

Several ideas spring from the reference photograph. By combining the white iris shapes in the background, a diagonal stem shape to help balance the subject flower, and the layering linear leaf shapes, the background content begins to come together.

The choice of colors will augment the original analogous reds, oranges, and magentas. This creates a color scheme that is nearly tetradic (see "Tetradic color scheme," page 58), plus yellow.

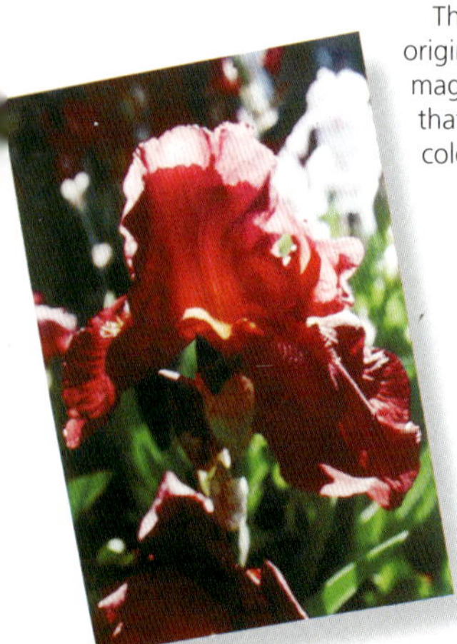

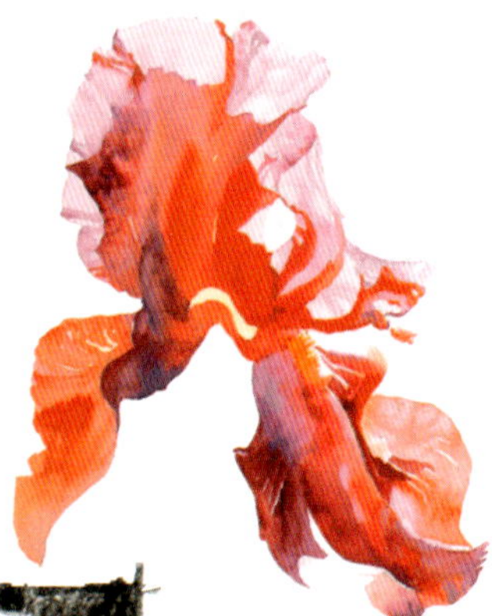

For a painting demonstration of the iris, see page 98.

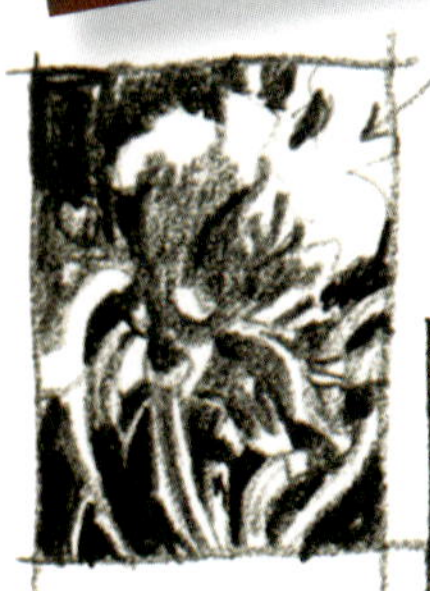

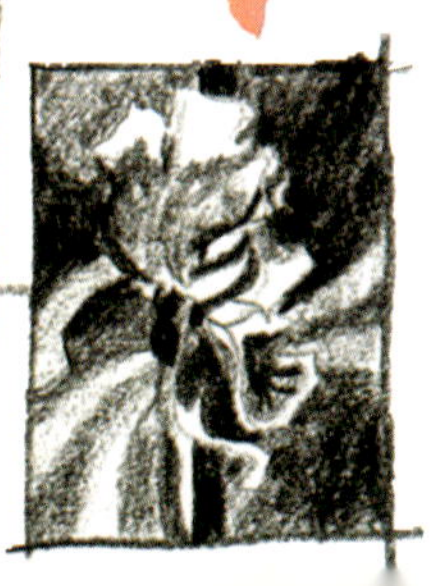

Value sketches of the iris and background

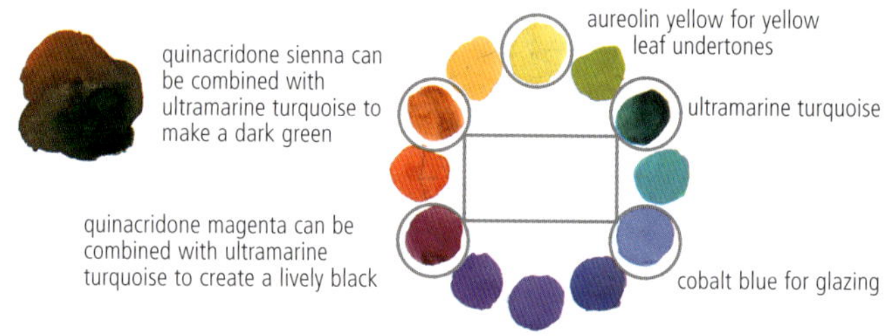

1 Starting loose The start is loose and experimental, using each of the tetradic paints to play against the dominant reds of the iris. Thinking in terms of complements helps as blues are placed near the warm reds and yellow greens next to the violets. Linear diagonal swoops of yellow-green (cobalt blue and aureolin yellow) are applied from the base of the flower to the lower right. A stem is captured with an application of the mixed green over the dried yellow base. Next the shapes are defined by negatively painting a dark green mix of ultramarine turquoise and quinacridone sienna. The soft iris shapes in the upper right are painted wet into wet.

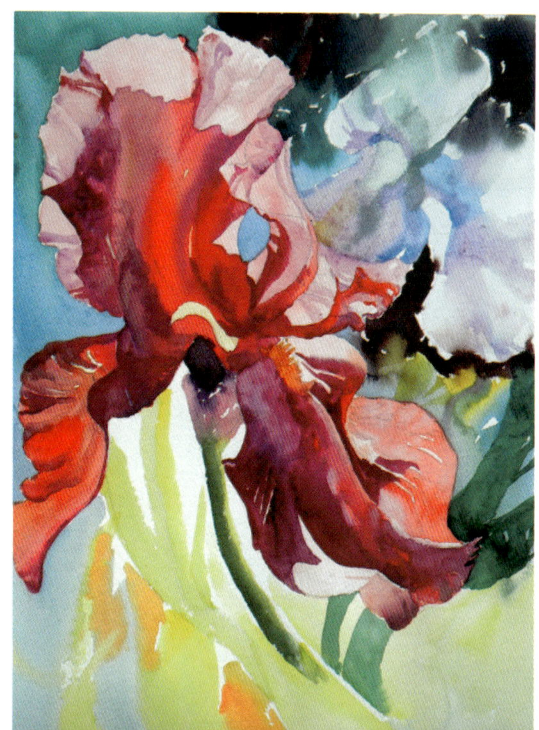

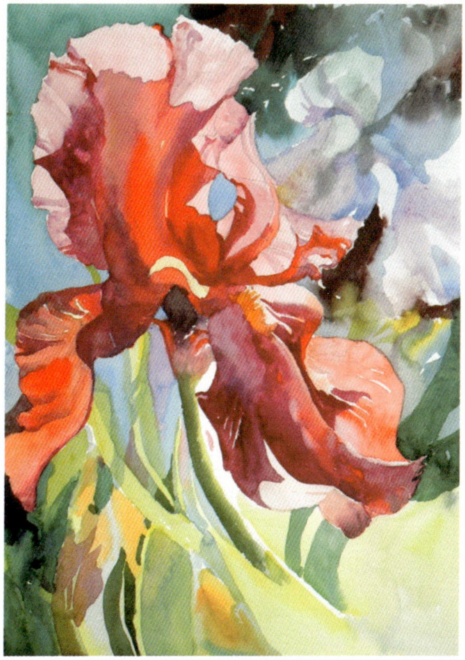

2 Emphasizing More dark green is added over the yellow base in the lower left to balance the darks in the upper right, and to counterbalance the diagonal design. Repeating shapes and iris colors continue into the vegetation. Adding shades of red is especially important to harmonize and integrate the background with the dominant iris. The painting continues to evolve as it suggests new responses. Note that the white iris was reglazed and some edges were deiliberately lifted for better connection.

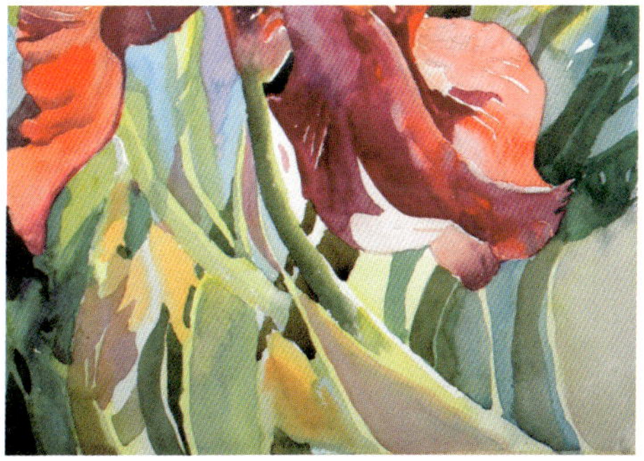

3 Defining Suggested leaf shapes are defined while adding more reds and continuing to darken, solidify, and detail. Be careful not to cover up all of the delicious yellow-green undercolor.

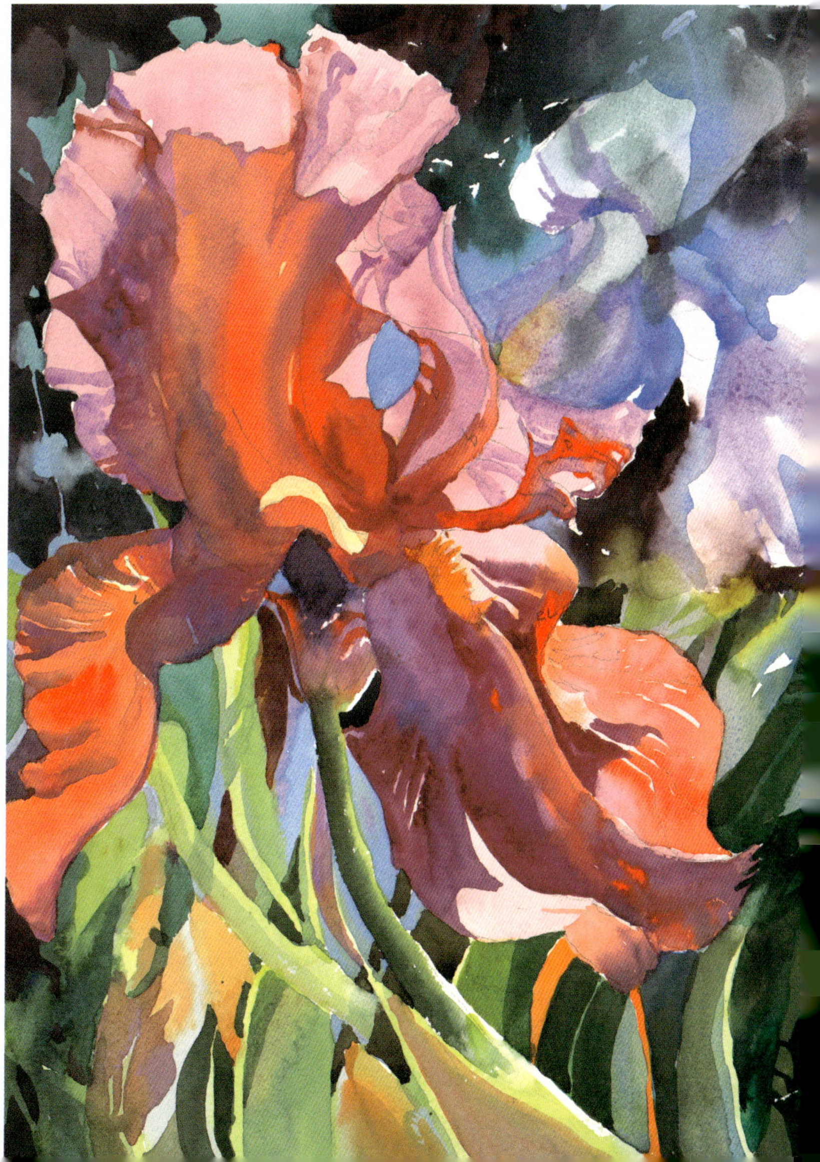

4 Finishing touches Step back to the other side of your painting space and study the painting before adding the finishing touches. Darken all corners except for the upper right. Paint mixed dark green and glaze with cobalt blue to suggest depth in the foliage. Add some bright orange color accents to the abstract foliage shapes to help the eye move through the painting. The painting could be simplified further with more glazing if desired. Sometimes it is best to stop and look at the painting for some time before deciding.

SOME THINGS TO CONSIDER

- Plan your painting as a whole—the background and foreground are equal partners. A value/composition study helps.
- The gestures and shapes used in the subject suggest the gestures and shapes for the background.
- Find ways to integrate the foreground with the background: A lost edge in the foreground subject can encourage the eye to move into the adjacent background; subject color notes can be used to accent areas of the background; the overall movement of the background should work with the foreground, either continuing or contradicting; shapes in the background can repeat those of the subject, but in a softer, lighter way so that they do not compete with the subject.
- Always look for the undercolor first. And then be sure to leave some of it unpainted so that it shows through.

Skies and clouds

Skies can pose a daunting challenge to an artist, but they also offer great excitement—strong colors, transparency, and an overwhelming freedom, as well as clouds and rain. Should you paint the sky first or last? If the painting is primarily about the sky, then paint it first. When the sky is right, go on to the rest of the painting. If the subject is the land, paint the sky last. The sky may help you resolve problems. For instance, a very dark sky may be the solution to a painting with too much light. The sky, with its infinite variety of value and color, can give life to a landscape and transform an ordinary painting into something special.

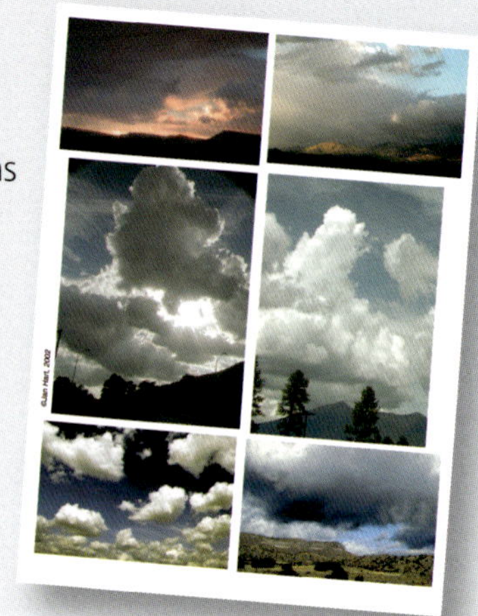

SOME THINGS TO CONSIDER

- Paint the sky first in a skyscape but last in a landscape or cityscape.
- Clouds are elements of the sky that continually move and change in a dramatic, improvisational dance. The artist can direct the dance.
- Consider that a cloud has dimension and size. It is much like a floating box, with an underside, sides, and an out-of-view topside.
- When lifting out sunrays, less is best. Lightly suggest some of the rays, and allow the viewer to fill in the rest.
- Keep a file of sky photography for reference and inspiration.

Clear sky A primary color scheme featuring cobalt blue, rose madder genuine, and aureolin yellow are the perfect choice for a transparent sunset sky. Painting in layers and drying in between enables the glow of optical mixes. Here evening sunlight plays magically on the west-facing Sangre de Cristo Mountains near Santa Fe, New Mexico. Begin with a graded wash of aureolin that is strongest at the mountain edge. Instead of glazing the entire paper with yellow, stop at the mountain edge in order to catch the slightly orange mountaintop. When the glaze is completely dry, carefully apply a graded layer of cobalt blue over the yellow. The darkest part should be at the top of the painting where the sky is darkest.

For the land, you can play a fairly dense mix of cerulean blue, rose madder genuine, and some hemetite violet (for sediment and neutrality) over the mountain surface. Later add more rose madder genuine so that the foothills glow pink. A bit of drier cobalt blue will suggest soft cast shadows. Finally, apply a single glaze of rose madder genuine over the entire painting.

Three colors used in both paintings

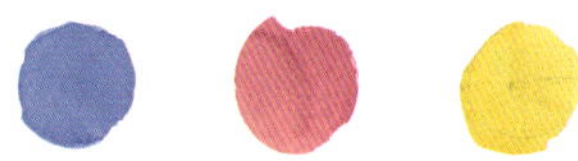

cobalt blue rose madder genuine aureolin yellow

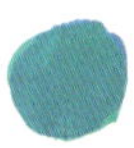

cerulean blue

hemetite violet

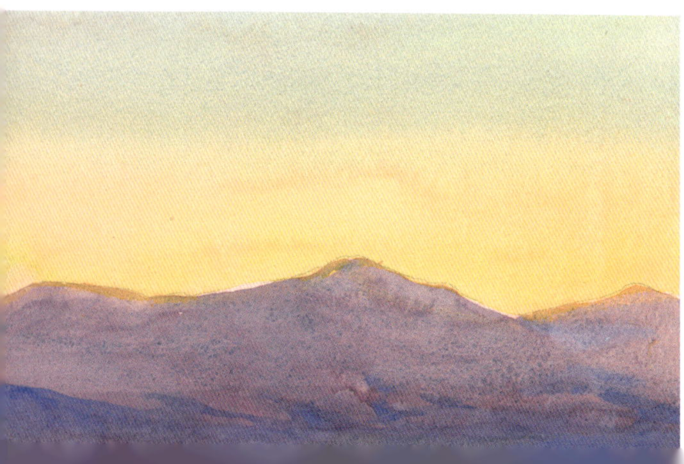

Misty northern fog This scene suggests a cool palette of analogous soft violets to blue-greens. It is easier than you think to use watercolor to paint a beach scene with distant mountains partially obscured by soft, coastal fog. The key is to wet the paper and then delicately find the mountains behind the wisps of fog while the paper is still wet. Getting the right dampness is always a challenge, but if you start wet and then add in the mountains with a drier and deeper color mix, the added color will stay where you put it and create soft fog edges. It is negative painting at its loosest. You can keep working "drier in wet" as long as the soft edges prevail. If you see streaks or hard edges, stop. Wait for the paper to dry fully, and then rewet and continue.

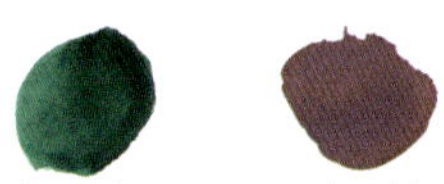

ultramarine turquoise napthamide maroon

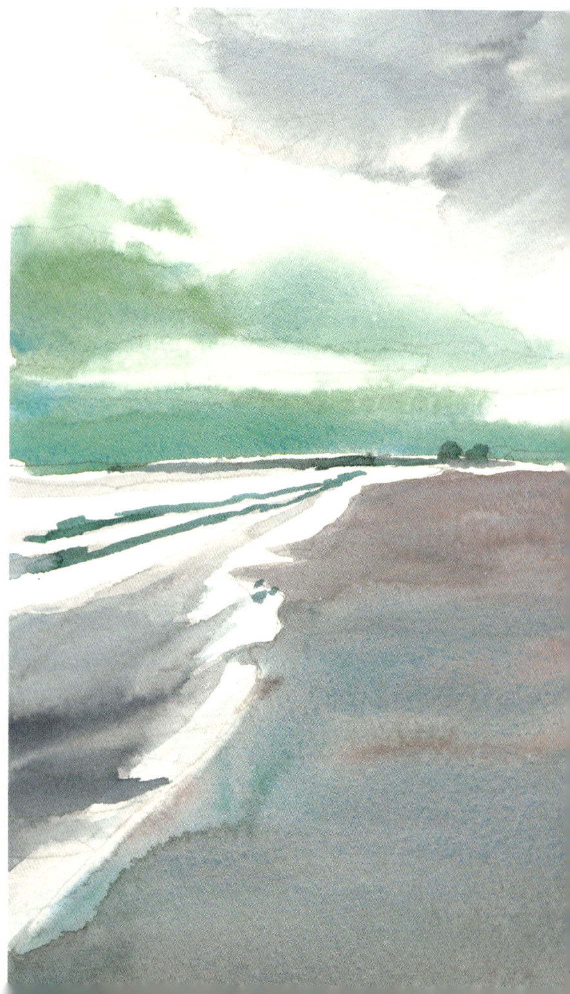

Four colors used above and below

cobalt blue

rose madder genuine

aureolin yellow

ultramarine blue

Cloud patterns Clouds in the sky are like trees in a landscape—except that clouds dance more freely. The artist can give them directionality, flow, and gesture even if these qualities are not immediately obvious. Notice that the sky at its zenith is a warmer and darker blue (ultramarine blue). The clouds are larger and more separate with definite undersides. At the horizon, the clouds are thinner and closer together in a cooler sky (light blue-green).

quinacridone gold

Cumulus and thunderheads Dramatic thunderheads and cumulous clouds demand to be the focus in a painting. Consider the sky around the cloud as the negative shapes, and start by carving out the cloud with the blue of the sky. For variety, create a few soft edges while the paint is still wet. If the underside of the cloud is below the sun, add color into the shade to reveal reflected light from the earth.

buff titanium

cobalt violet

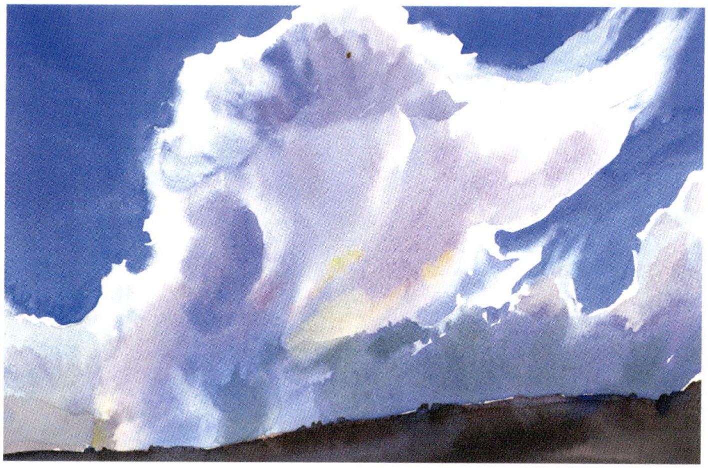

Wispy clouds The easiest clouds to paint are probably wispy ones. Quickly paint a clear, cobalt blue upper sky. Add aureolin yellow for a cooler horizon. Before it has a chance to dry, knot a clean white paper towel and gently pull it across, lifting paint off in a directional fashion. You can lift several clouds to create a soft sky texture.

cobalt blue

aureolin yellow

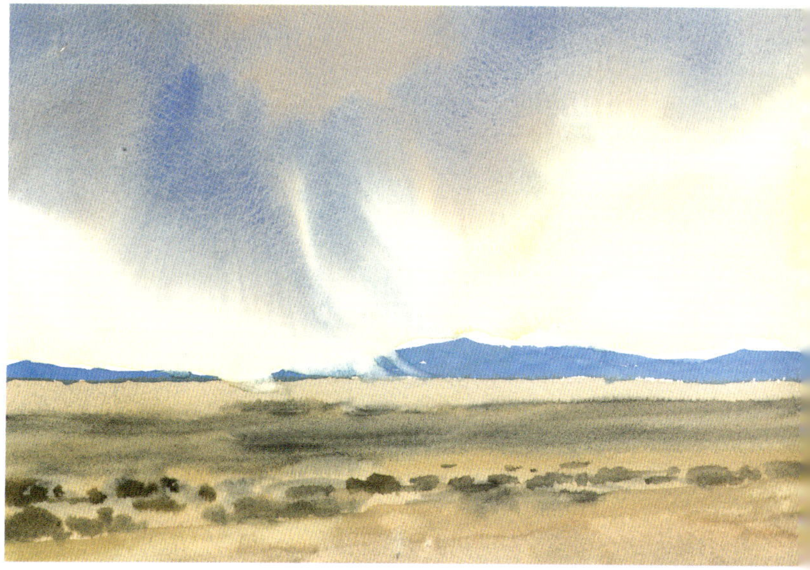

Rain clouds A rain cloud is generally darker and more neutral in color. Here cobalt blue is mixed with some quinacridone sienna and added at the top of a still-damp aureolin yellow sky on a slanted surface. As the paint begins to run, a small round brush gently suggests the direction and flow. A continuation of the rain past the distant mountains can be suggested by a gestured lifting. The earth is painted in with a mix of aureolin yellow and quinacridone sienna, with a drier mix of ultramarine blue and burnt sienna dotted in for suggestions of vegetation.

cobalt blue

ultramarine blue

aureolin yellow

quinacridone sienna

burnt sienna

Skies and clouds

Skies and clouds provide endless color opportunities as well as some interesting pigment choices, as shown here in the gallery. While a blue sky's horizon is generally cooler than its zenith, a setting or rising sun can change everything. And while the clear sky is transparent, clouds can be dense, opaque, and granular.

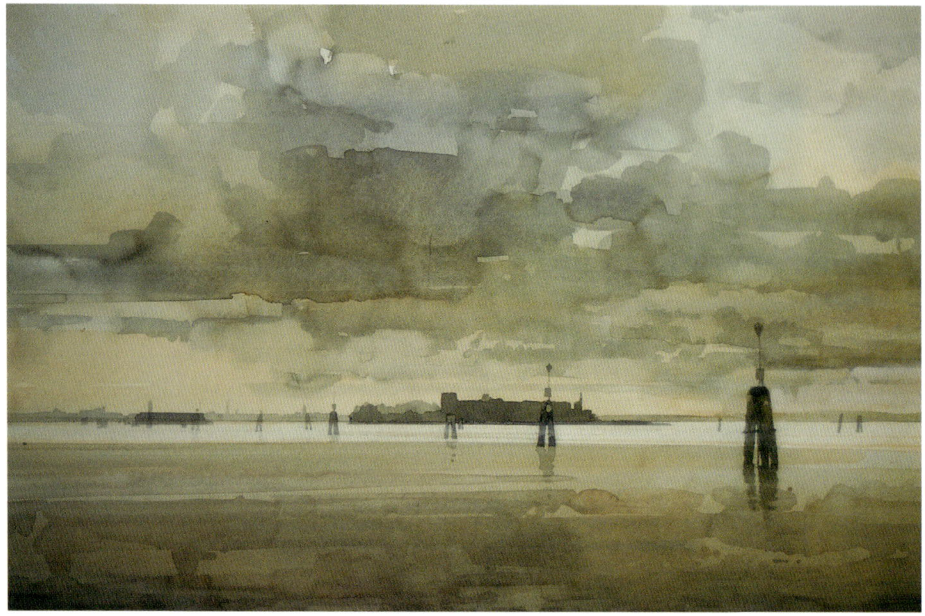

▲ ***Storm Clouds over Lagoon*** PETER KELLY
The underlying and very subtle use of viridian green in this painting provides a sense of expectation—the calm before the storm, which is amplified by the horizontal band of quiet reflection in the water.

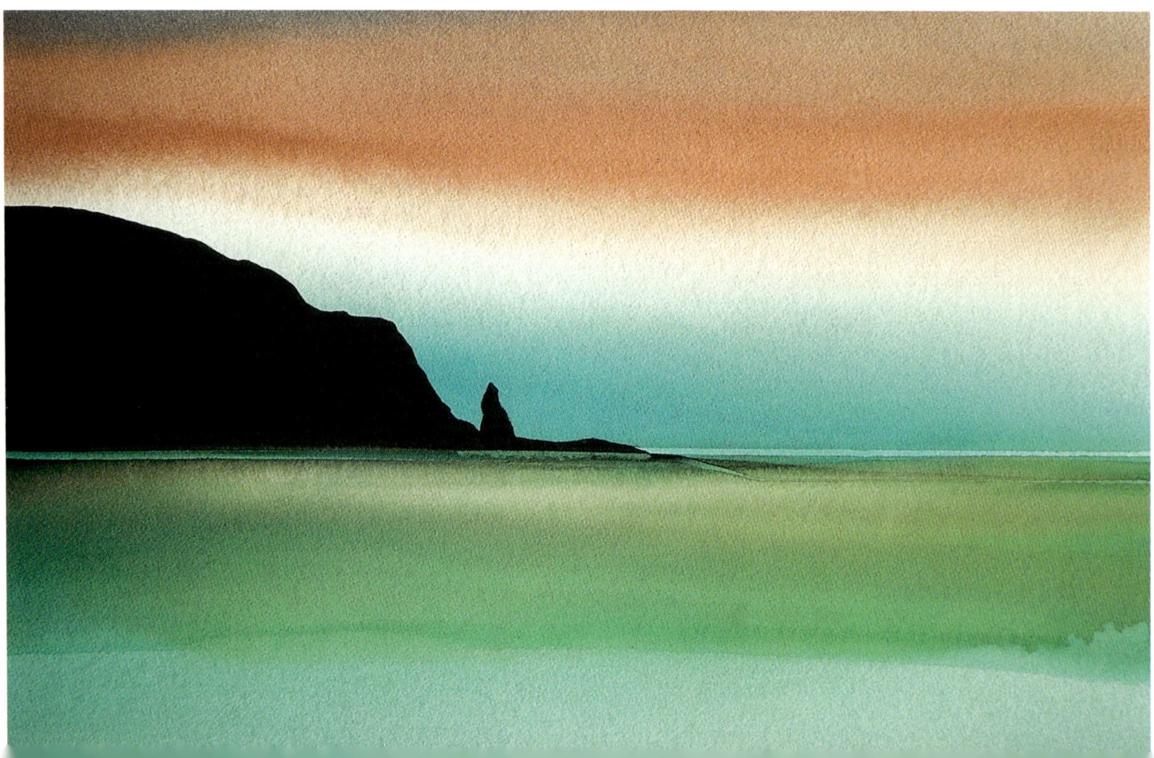

◀ ***Low Tide, Plemont, Jersey*** ROBERT TILLING
The artist uses a highly controlled wet-into-wet technique for his evocative and unusual paintings (see also page 19). This was begun with a pale wash of cerulean blue, which was allowed to dry before being rewet, left to dry just a little, and then propped up at an angle to encourage each band of color to flow slightly into the one below with no hard edges. When all the color had been applied and the painting was nearly dry, he scratched the horizon line with a piece of card.

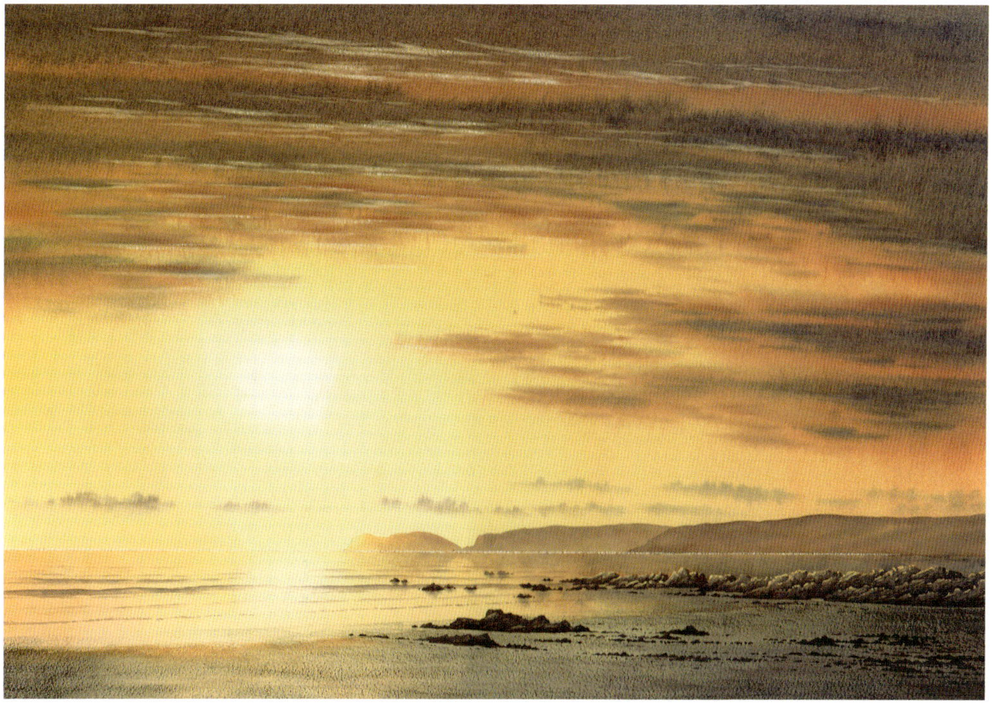

◀ *Freshwater West*
ADRIAN JAMES
The artist uses a limited primary palette of French ultramarine blue, cadmium yellow, and alizarin crimson. He achieves a six-color palette by adding cadmium red, a mixed purple, and a mixed orange with a bare whisper of mixed green. The sky is painted wet into wet, leaving the sun area dry.

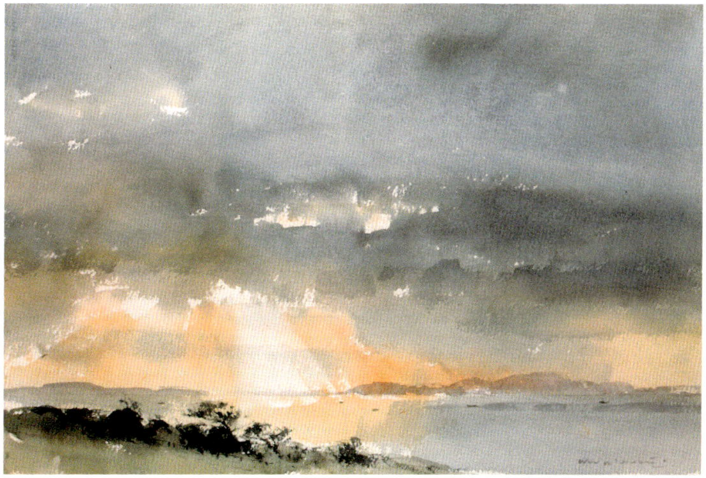

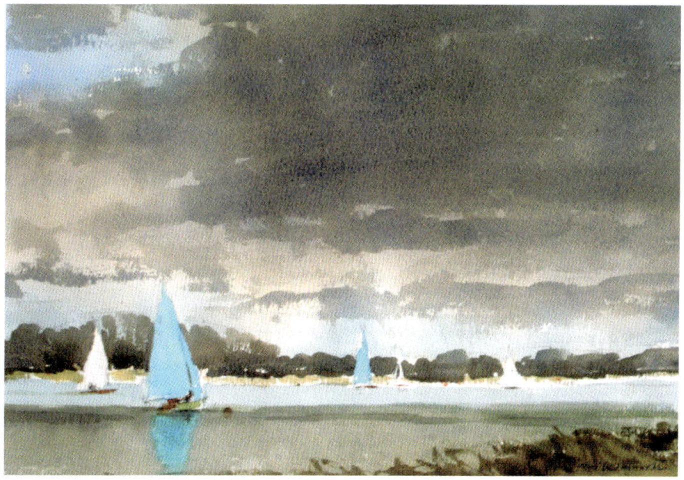

▲ *Evening Light at Culzean*
MICHAEL WRIGGLESWORTH
The artist uses an interesting limited palette of two adjacent complementary blues and oranges—cobalt blue/cadmium orange and French ultramarine blue/raw sienna. The greens and grays are easy mixes.

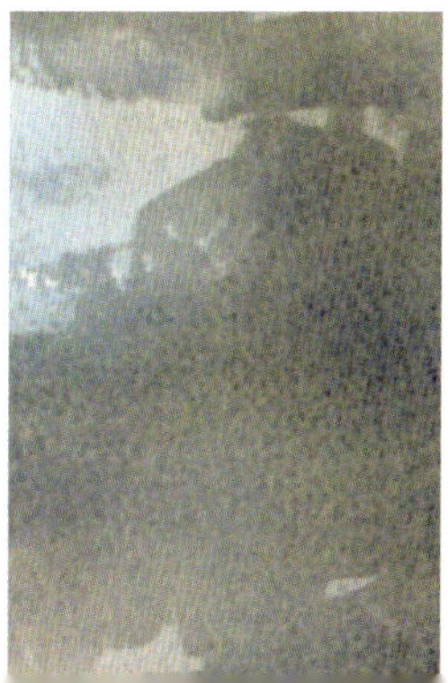

▲ *Blue Sails* MICHAEL WRIGGLESWORTH
The artist used a process of underpainting and overpainting and a limited palette of adjacent complementary pairs (ultramarine blue/raw sienna and cobalt blue/cadmium orange), plus burnt sienna. The sky, water, and background trees were first painted with a thin wash of burnt sienna. The overpainting consists of mixes of cobalt blue, ultramarine blue, and burnt sienna.

Waterscapes

Still water, like a mirror, reflects the colors and shapes on and beyond the water. The reflected sky adds subtle nuances, creating reflected colors that are either darker or lighter than the actual colors—seldom the same. Moving water, on the other hand, reflects parts of everything around it—sky, trees, rocks, clouds, a bit of shore edge, and maybe even a bird. In order to paint the slivered, wavy slices of color in continual motion, you need to understand what you are looking at.

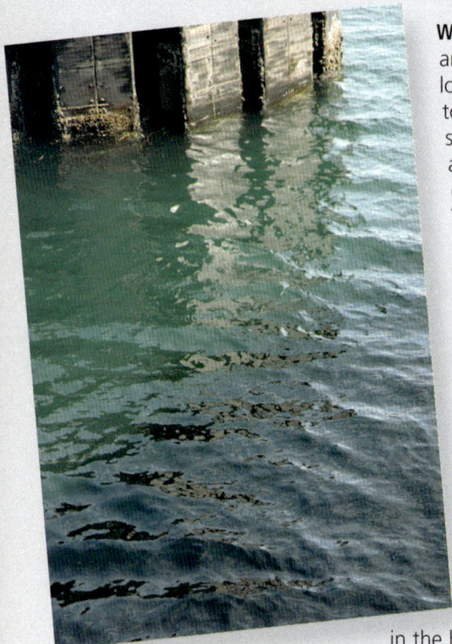

Water reflection Imagine you are standing on a boardwalk looking over the rippling water to a pier beyond. The reflections show a dazzling array of shapes and colors from white through greens and blues to near black. The only way to freeze the hard- and soft-edged shapes is to take a photograph. The diagram below shows that reflected scenery varies according to the continually changing orientation of the water surface. Also, at some viewing angles, the undersurface of the water is visible. As the viewer, you affect how the water reflections appear. You are the point of origin in a reflected one-point perspective. From a boat in the harbor at night, distant, lit-up, high-rise building reflections will all appear to converge toward you. And all the ripples or swells on the water surface will appear generally horizontal—to your eyes.

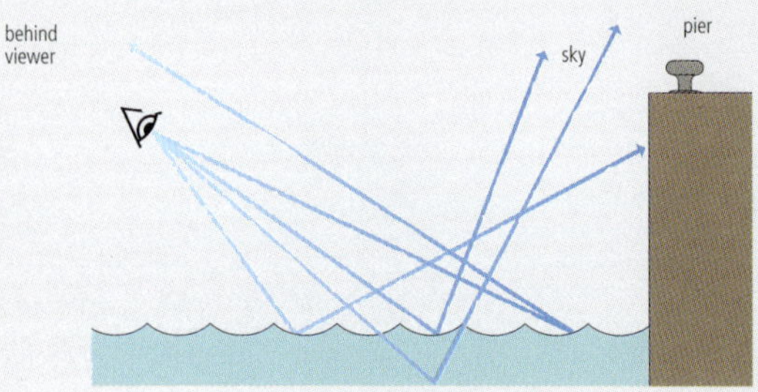

PORT TOWNSEND PIER

Moving water The rippling water under the pier is mesmerizing. At least six different values of linear shape continually undulate, stretch out, disappear, and reappear. A photograph stops the motion for study (shown at left). Each shape is part of a reflection from something in the surroundings—the sky, the pier, and the barnacles—all arranged in horizontal slivers and dots.

Color value/shape study Your study of the colors and shapes in the water will help you prepare for the painting process, build your confidence, and provide a map. Sometimes the study process is more important than the actual painting.

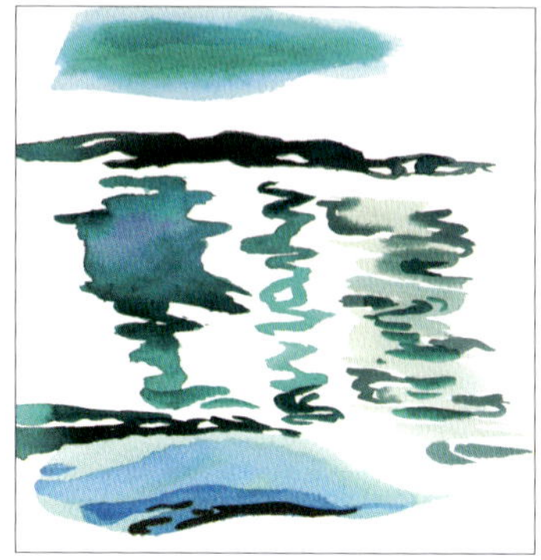

Count the variations in color and values. Begin with the lightest blue reflection of sky. Narrow it down to about six different color values, and then study the shapes. Shapes with soft edges can be painted wet into wet, and those with hard edges should be painted in when the underlying paper is dry. The shapes in the closest waves are larger than those in the distance, and the close-up dark shapes are warmer (redder) than the distant dark shapes. The distant shapes also are lighter in value.

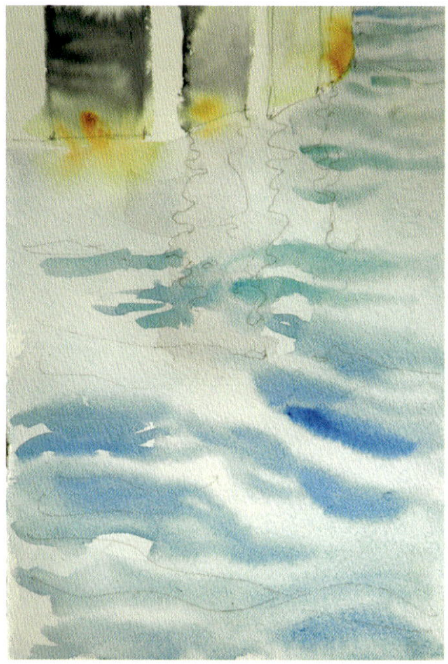

1 Underwash Begin with an underwash of the lightest color—the pale blue. Let it dry so that you can decide where to work next—the water or the pier—without fear that either will run. First paint distant reflections in the water with soft shapes. Note that the horizontal shapes painted on the right side are closer together and cooler than those painted in the middle and foreground areas. If the paint mix on your brush is drier than the dampened paper, the applied soft shape will stay where you put it. Some of the soft, underlying, larger shapes in front can be laid in using warmer cobalt blue and French ultramarine blue.

Color considerations A modified rectangular tetradic palette will work well with both cobalt blue and ultramarine blue for the middle-blue position on Hart's color wheel (see page 15), and cerulean blue tossed in just because we need it!

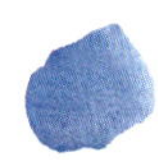

cobalt blue for transparency and color

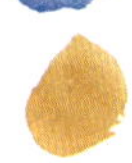

nickel azo yellow to add accents

ultramarine blue as a warm blue for close-up water colorations and accents

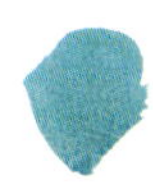

cerulean blue as a cool blue for distant, dark horizontals

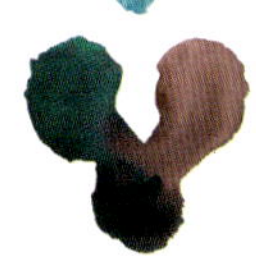

ultramarine turquoise for strong blue-green color and ability to mix with napthamide maroon to make a lively black

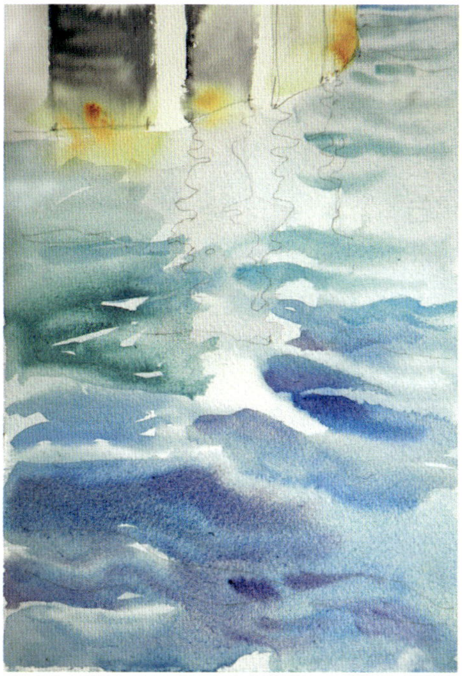

2 Continue the soft shapes Once the area you are painting begins to dry, stop and wait for the entire paper to dry fully before rewetting. Painting on paper that is almost dry but still damp is unpredictable. If your brush is too wet, you'll get blossoms and runs. If your brush is too dry, you may get streaks where the underwash is lifted off. So, to be safe, stop and wait. Take a break. Then rewet and continue. You can add more soft shapes or accentuate some of the former shapes. Remember to keep the color closest to the viewer the warmest. Add ultramarine blue to the foreground with some cobalt violet. In the middle area, restate cooler blues such as cerulean blue and ultramarine turquoise.

3 Hard shapes When the paper is completely dry, add some hard, definite shapes to the top of the softly rolling washes below. Now is the time to play with some dark mixes of napthamide maroon mixed with ultramarine turquoise. Push the mix toward red as well as toward green. Add darks to the middle ground in zigzag patterns.

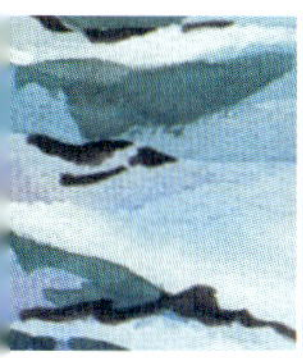

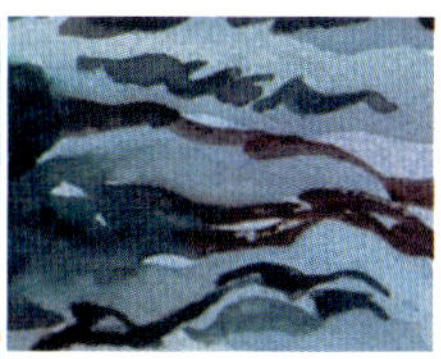

4 Finishing After a good look from across the room, add the final touches. Look twice and paint once. Glazing the foreground with cobalt blue can help focus the attention more on the middle water shapes and cut down the "whites." Make sure your foreground shapes are larger and more dominant. Connect a few of your dark shapes. Always refer back to your reference photograph for new ideas and fresh confidence. The idea is to create variety and portray the dance of shapes in the water.

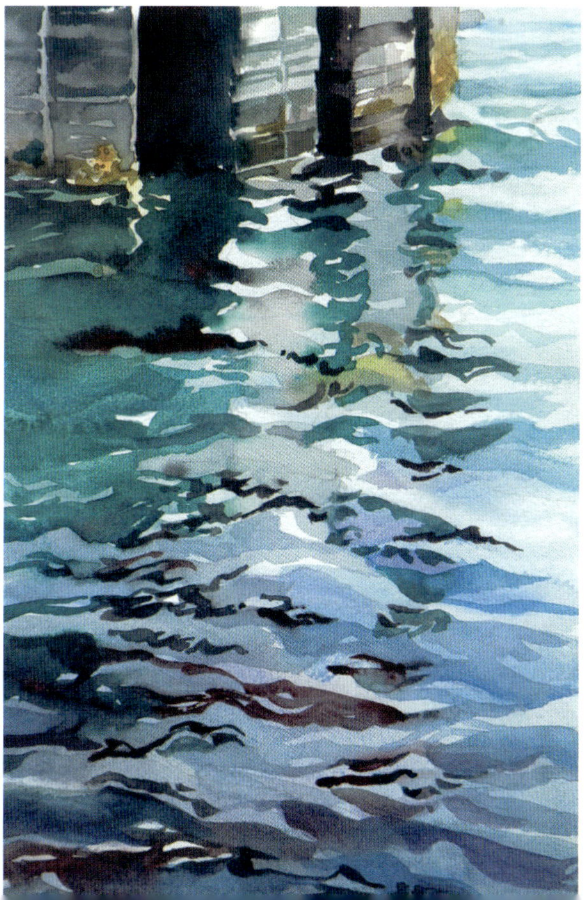

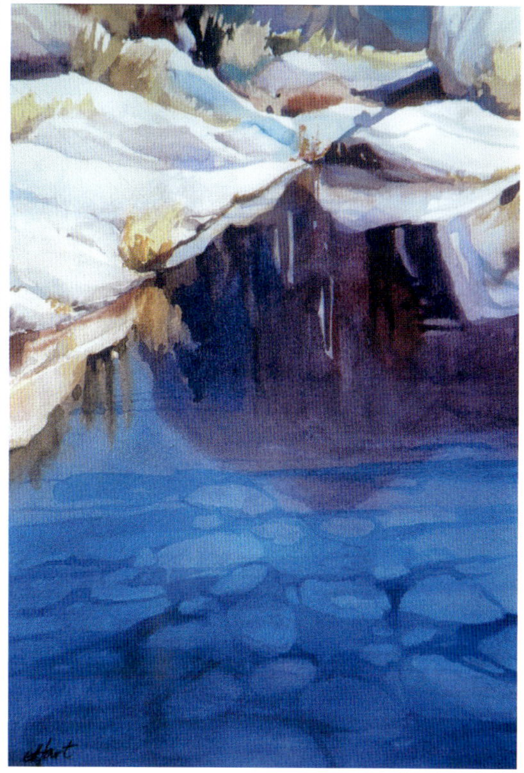

Reflections

Reflections in still water begin at the base of the object. Trees and bushes that are farther from the shore appear abbreviated or shorter. Note that the reflection here is darker than the actual object, and the disturbance in the water creates some distortion.

SOME THINGS TO CONSIDER

- When nearing the end of the painting, consider connecting the darks to help move the eye through the painting.
- Paint vertical reflections with horizontal strokes.
- Distant water shapes are lighter, cooler, smaller, and closer together than the dominant water shapes in the foreground.
- Study the water before you paint it. Notice the irregular, horizontal shapes and the incredible variety of shapes in the foreground versus those in the distance.

Waterscapes

The continually changing, reflective surface of water presents both opportunities and challenges to the artist. While a watercolorist may have the advantage in using a water-based medium, it is the choices of colors, shapes, and gestures that combine to create a convincing illusion of water. The reflected sky blue is an obvious color choice, but it often is the other color notes that star.

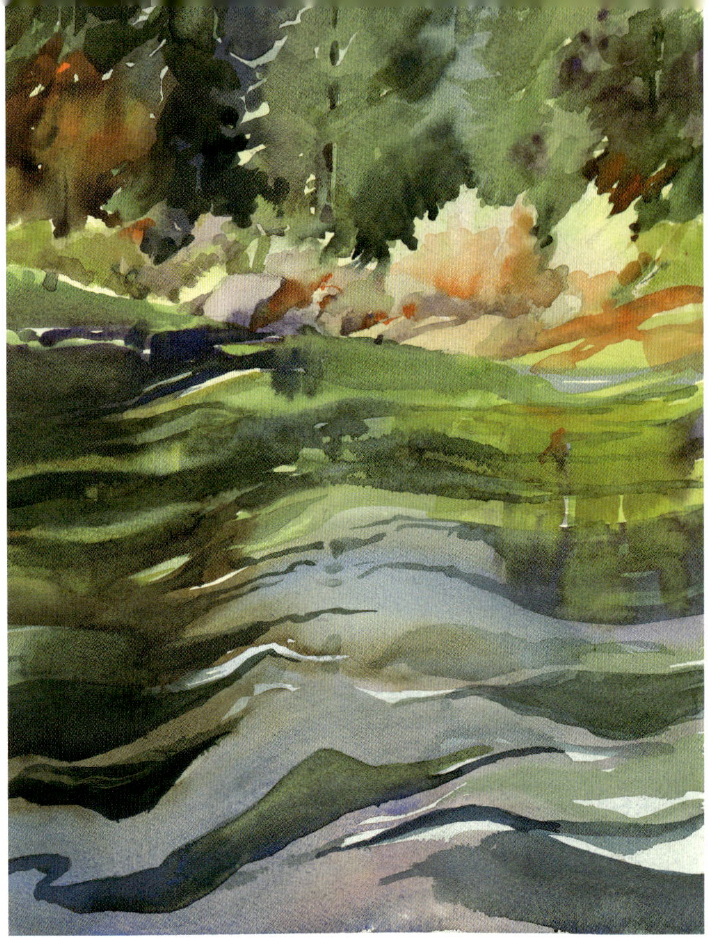

▶ ***The River*** JAN HART
The author's intention of immersing the viewer in the river is achieved by accentuating the sizes of the reflected forest green and sky blue shapes in the foreground. Additionally, the occasional wet-into-wet verticals in the distant water suggest the forest trees, whereas the crisper edges of the foreground shapes suggest proximity.

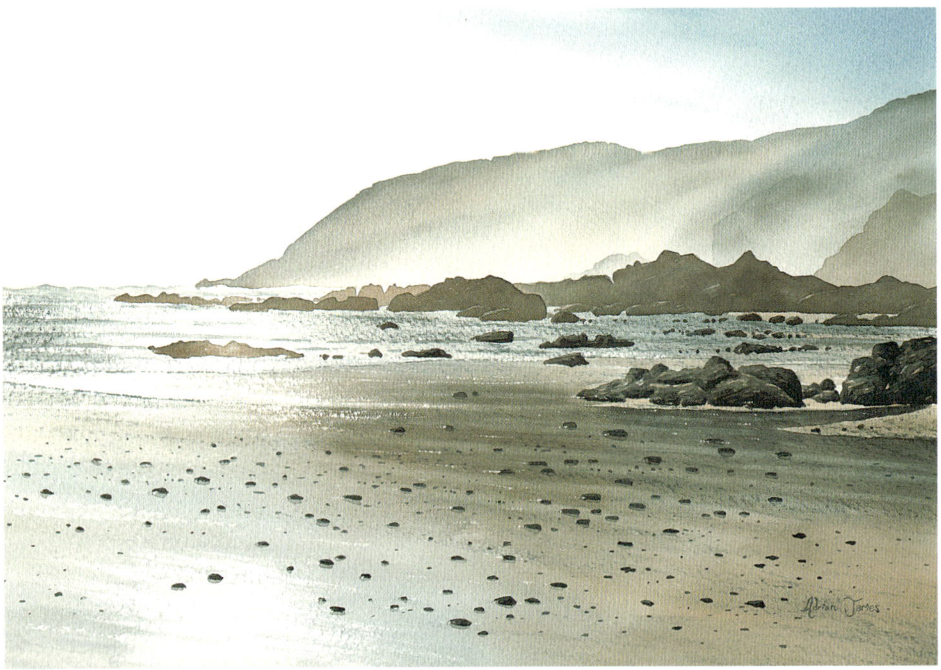

◀ ***Summer Sand***
ADRIAN JAMES
The artist, wanting to portray the impression of sun glare on the water and shore, deliberately downplayed color intensity in selecting a complementary palette of two low-chroma paints—Venetian red and Prussian blue. By pushing mixes toward red for brown tones and blue for gray tones, the relative dampness of the sand is suggested.

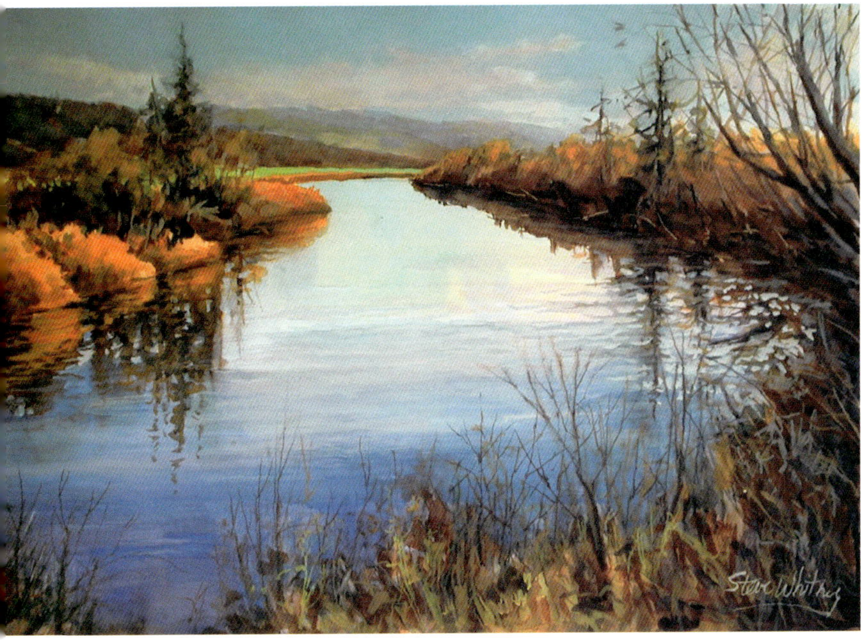

▲ *Snoqualmie River in Autumn*
Steve Whitney
The artist's predominant choices of blue and orange suggest a complementary color scheme. A skillful stretch has been made to include yellow-greens, a few subtle magentas, and many colorful neutrals to balance the bright oranges and blues. Perspective is aided by fading the color of the water from nearby warm, intense blue to distant cool blue-green.

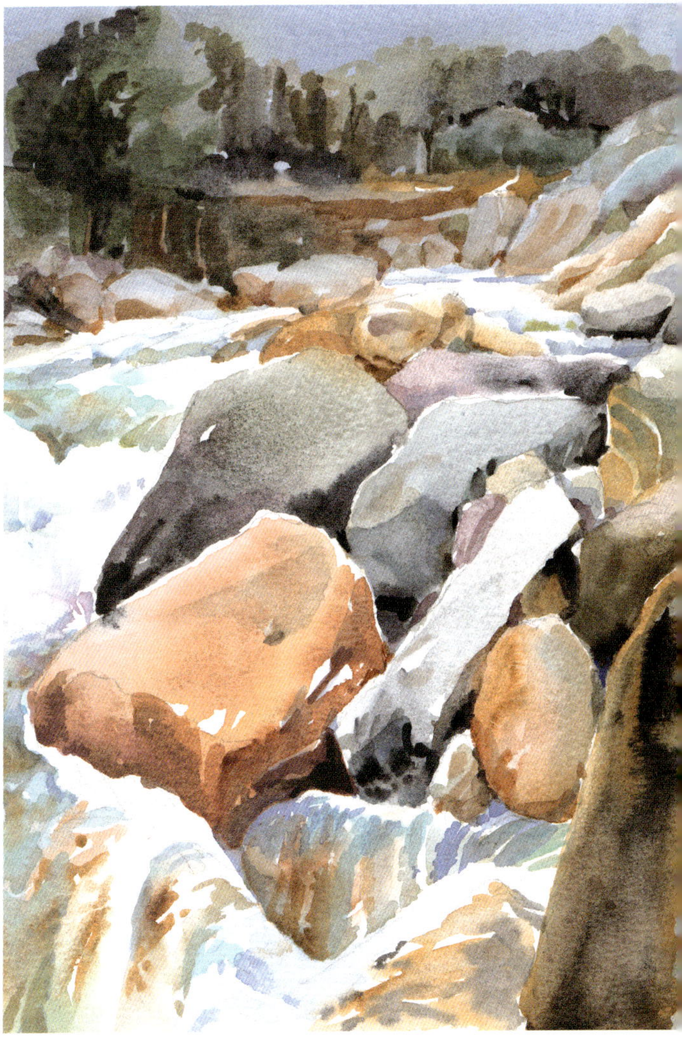

▶ *River Run* Jan Hart
Though most of this piece was painted with granulating PrimaTek pigments for texture, transparent cobalt blue was used to "push back" the distant elements and suggest falling water, white water details, and shade. Note that some PrimaTek pigments added into the still-wet foreground cobalt glaze gives the impression of rocks beneath the moving water.

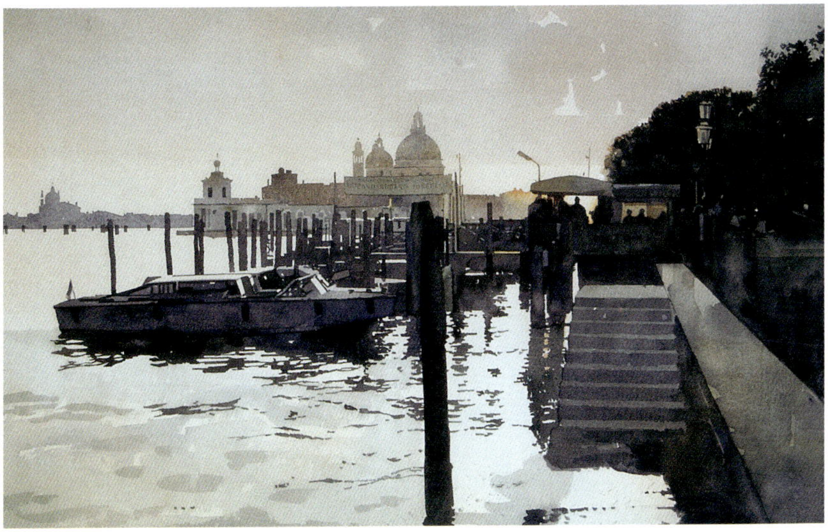

◀ *Santa Maria della Salute* Peter Kelly
An overall wash of cerulean blue sets the stage for this painting that stars the distant cathedral accented with pale cadmium orange. The split-complement scheme includes cobalt blue and Payne's gray foreground details. Note the pale use of neutralized cerulean in the sky and water, letting the pure cerulean shine.

Buildings

Painting a house, a barn, or a cabin involves far more than accurately describing windows or rooflines. To create a memorable painting of a building, you must convey its sense of place. Color selection is a crucial aspect of sense of place. Note the paintings of Edward Hopper to better understand. His paintings of buildings may surprise you with a novel way of experiencing them—from exaggeration of color complements or a different perspective to a change of time. A night view may evoke a sense of security and warmth inside the building, while the outside is darkness and the unknown.

Below are the initial colors used on the two paintings on these pages, the mixes are shown opposite.

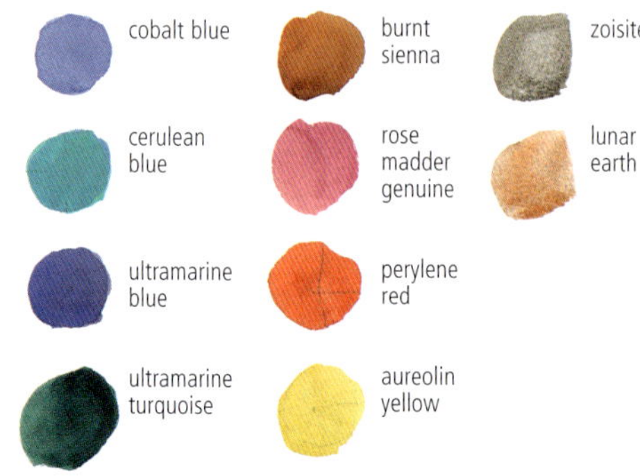

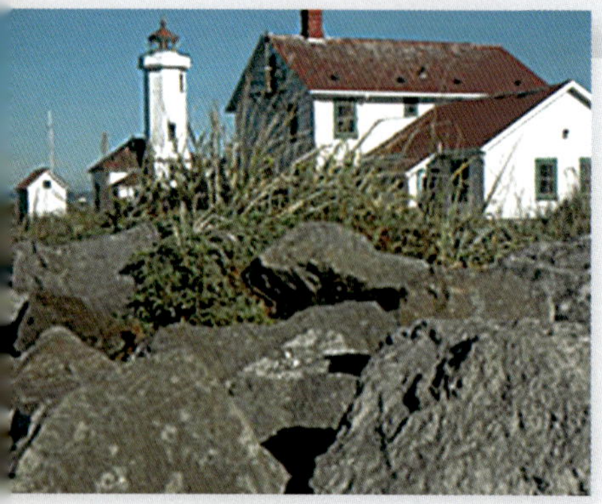

PORT TOWNSEND LIGHTHOUSE

The lighthouse is on a rocky spit, surrounded by sea grasses, rocks, and concrete. The lighthouse is sentinel, with the blues of sky, shadows, and sea above and below surrounding it, the red roofed buildings, scattered about beginning the visual descent to the sea. The idea of applying rosy tones to the rocks to continue the downward red flow ignited the color considerations for the palette. The greens of the beach grasses completed the planning. The full primary palette would include all the blues plus yellow and yellow-green opposed by red. In addition, granulating paints such as zoisite and lunar earth add texture to the dominant rocks.

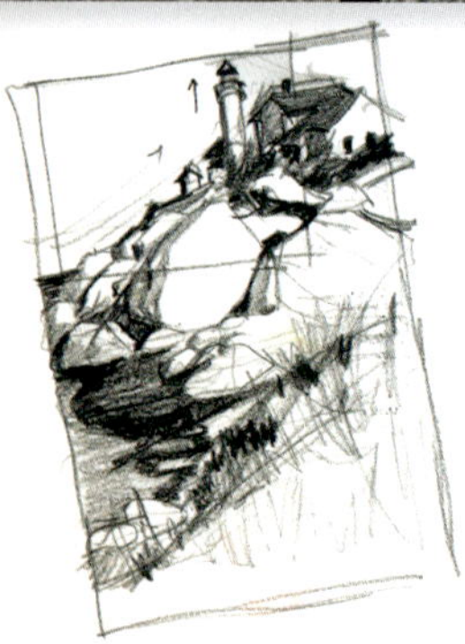

1 The sketch Your initial sketch can be very rough. Its purpose is to record your thoughts and work out proportion and perspective. As soon as the pencil touches paper, it is apparent that the lighthouse is the most important element and that the other features will be supporting players.

2 The "adolescent" phase A vertical format suits the verticality of the lighthouse. Start by sketching in the basic shapes. The basic colors are painted in loosely, taking care that each primary color group is used throughout the painting. The shading and shadows will come later. The idea is to cover the paper with paint—usually only an hour's worth. Don't worry about details, blossoms, or "mistakes." Take a break before you look at it again. A loose approach helps encourage the magical "accidents" that watercolor does so well.

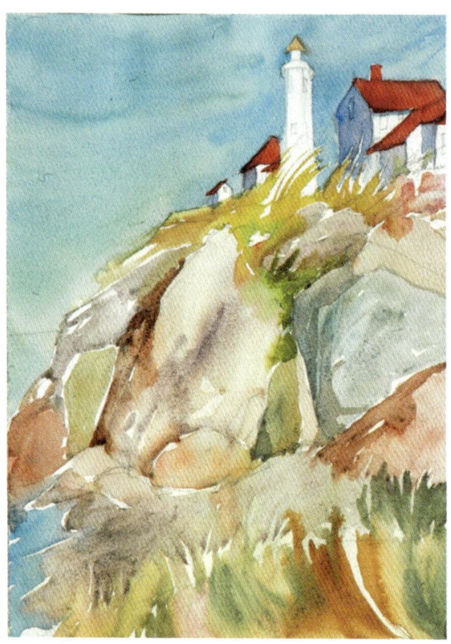

3 Final touches Yesterday's "adolescent" can be approached with fresh eyes in the morning. Add shade and shadows to the rocks and buildings, taking care to use transparent mixes of cobalt blue and rose madder genuine so that the individuality of the rocks shows through. The strong diagonal sweep of the cliff and shadows is resolved with strong verticals and horizontals. Because the diagonal points right to the vertical lighthouse, it is useful but mustn't overwhelm the composition. The grassy foreground is suggested using negative and positive painting, carefully placed red color notes helping to guide the viewer's eye through the painting.

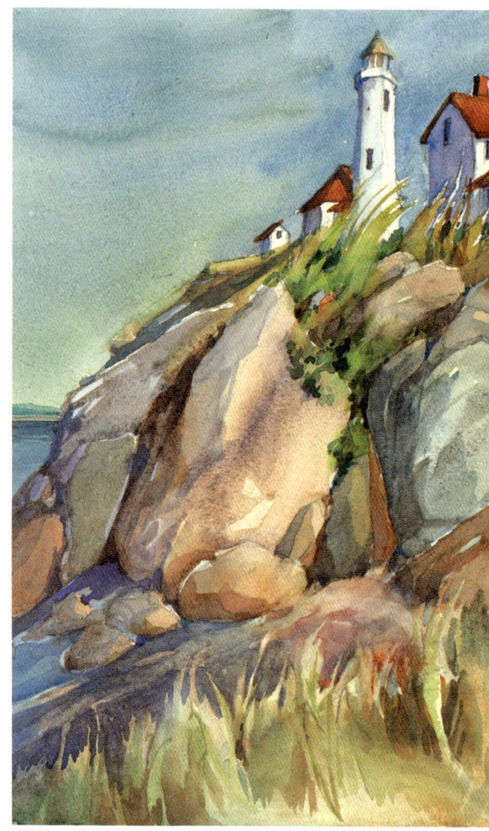

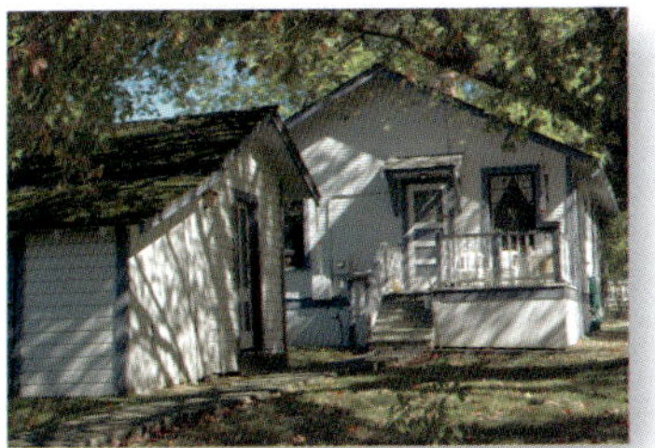

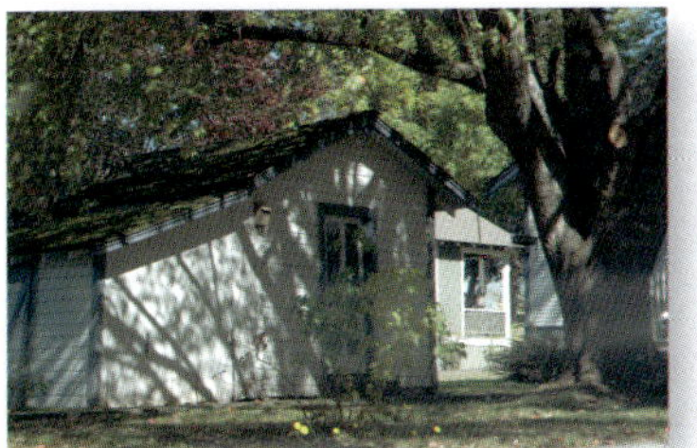

PORT GAMBLE HOUSE

Port Gamble, on Puget Sound, looks much like an old postcard. Shadows flicker on the white clapboard siding, creating a sense of motion and activity around the still house. The first leaves of autumn on the ground mark the calendar. There is a sense of nostalgia that suddenly brings the tertiary color scheme to mind. Substituting in some essential paints for the tertiary colors (see page 60) creates an exciting palette of green gold, ultramarine turquoise, cobalt blue-violet, cobalt blue, napthamide maroon, rose madder genuine (which suffices for the middle red color and is needed for glazing), quinacridone gold, aureolin yellow, and burnt sienna.

The glazes and mixes

The cobalt blue shadow must be strong enough or the yellow underwash weak enough to not make green.

Quinacridone gold is glazed over the lavender shadow of the upper eve to add the reflected light that is evident there.

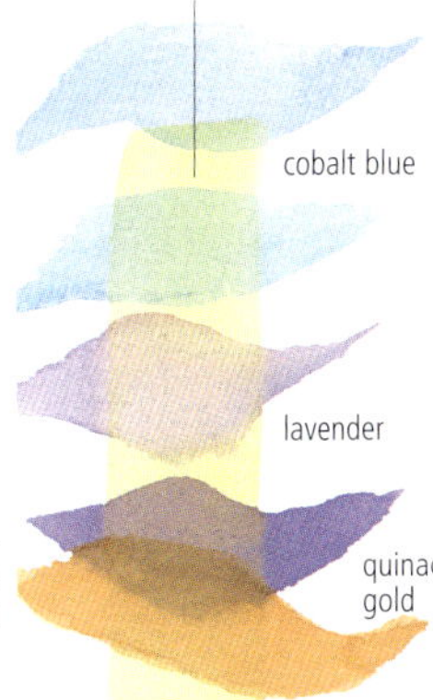

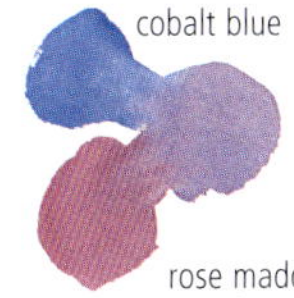

cobalt blue violet, mixed with some gold for the grayish trim

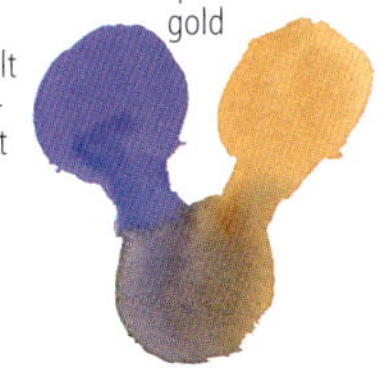

The four colors here can be used to mix browns and grays for the tree and roof, as well as dark greens for the leaves and grass shadows.

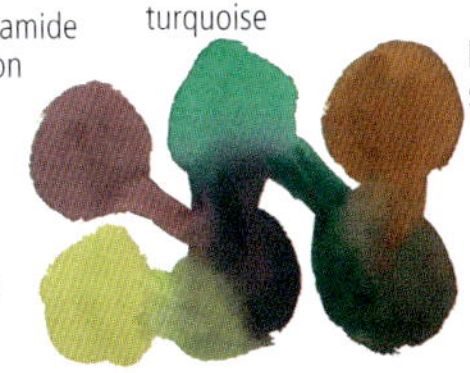

The sketch These two sketches help work out some of the issues. The sketch on the left deals with the whole composition, whereas the sketch on the right works out the pattern of the cast shadows, which are a major feature. The author has identified the horizon line (HL) and right vanishing point (VP) in order to draw the angles for the west-facing horizontal features. The low HL helps create the sense of walking up to the house. Note that the cast shadows from the tree must respond to different surfaces with different color values.

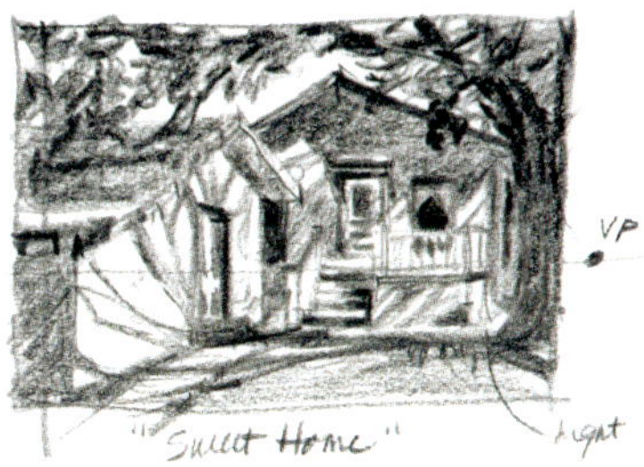

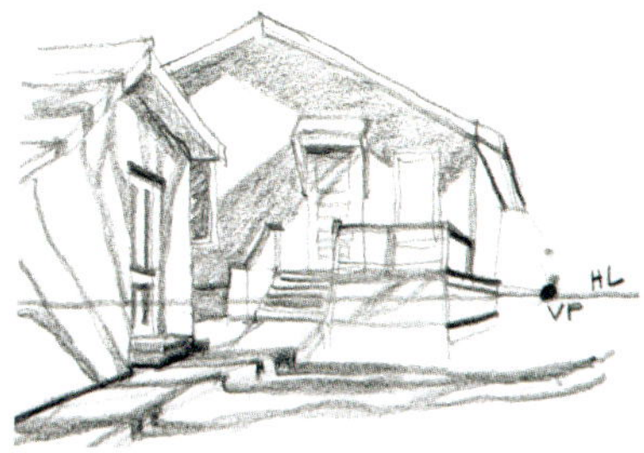

The painting Although the site is located in a northern latitude, the late afternoon light suggests an underwash of aureolin yellow. The west-facing garage is given a heavier application because of the direct, warm sunlight. The photograph offers the artist an opportunity to play with shadow colors that range from cobalt blue to lavender. Shadow glazes of cobalt blue are house shadows, while the lavender ones are garage shadows. The shadows that flicker over the west-facing garage appear more neutral, suggesting a complementary relationship of lavender shadows on the yellow wall.

Value adjacencies As the painting proceeds, continually compare value adjacencies to achieve contrasts that appear realistic. Some shadows need several layers. Note that it takes two or more value steps of difference to create effective separation between two adjacent shapes; through juxtaposition of lights and darks, separation is achieved between the side of the garage and the house (see detail at left). In comparison, when two shapes of different color but the same value are adjacent, they form one shape visually, for example, the shadow on the garage is made up of patches of different colors that are tonally similar.

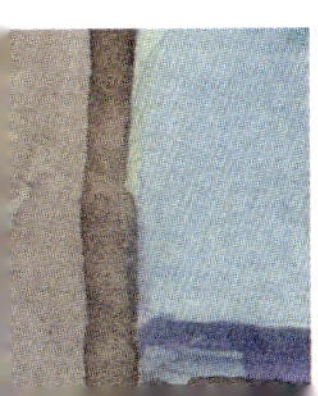

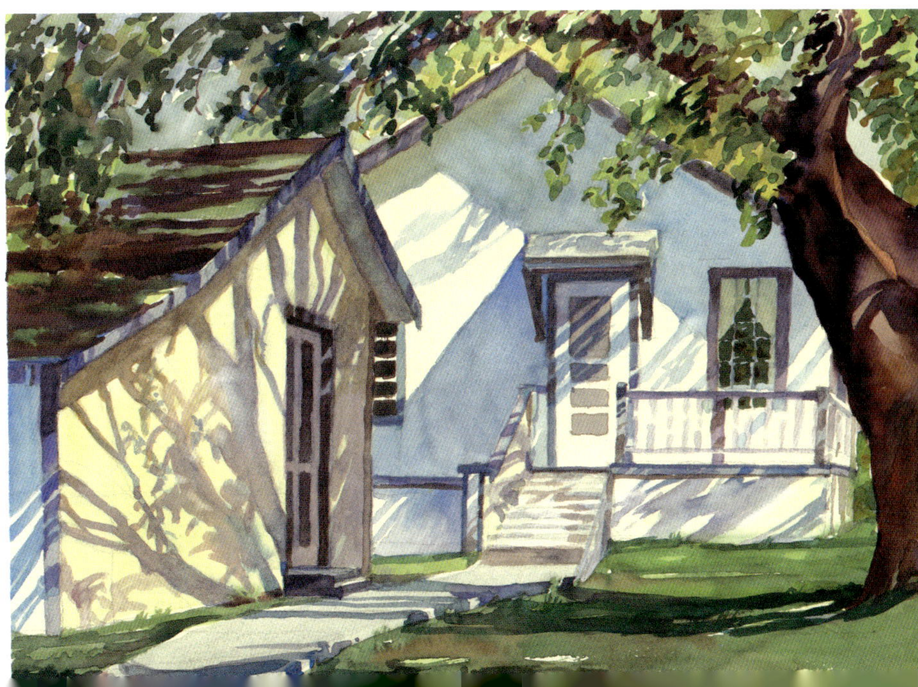

Buildings

A painting of a building is not intended to be an architectural rendering. A structure's character and sense of place in time must be communicated to produce a successful painting. On their own, buildings can be inorganic, stiff, and geometrically repetitive, but artists can use color and value to present buildings in new and exciting ways.

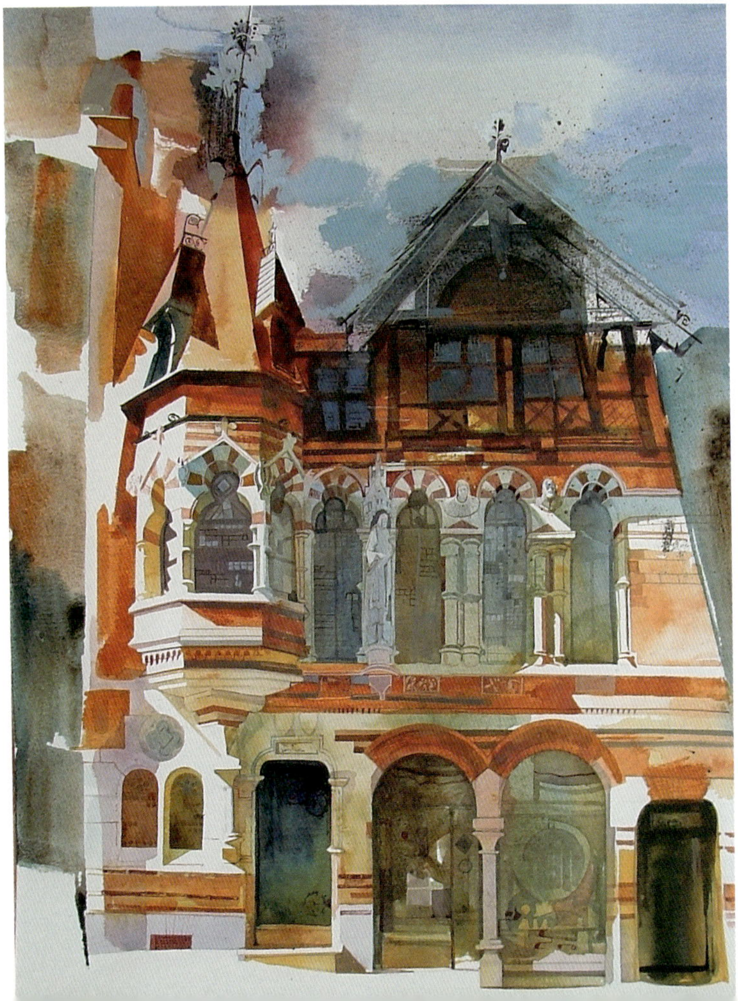

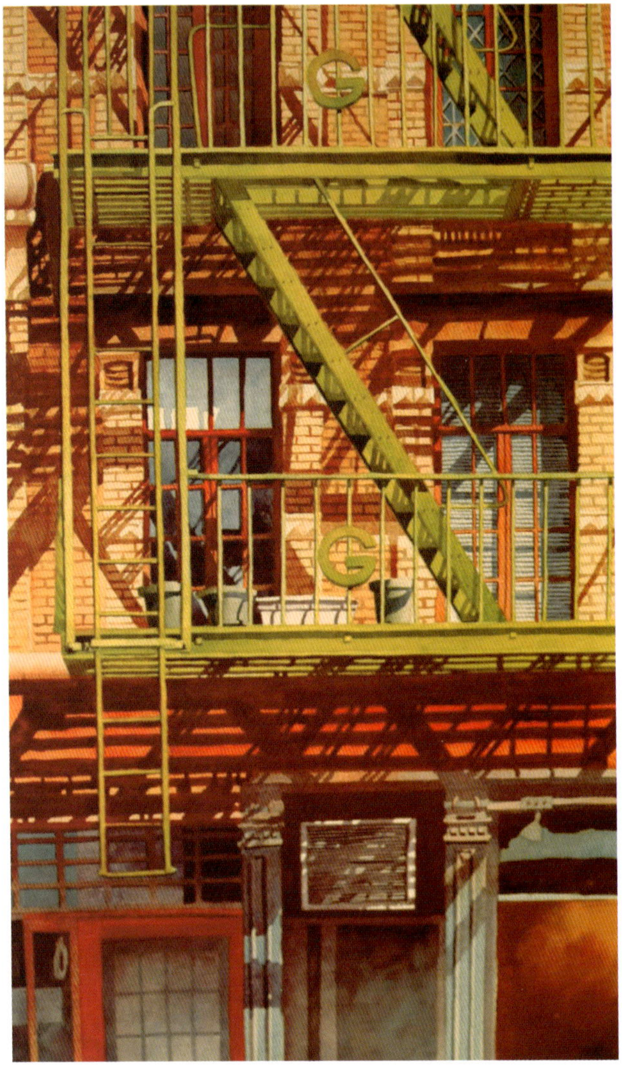

◀ *Splendid Mr. Fothergill* JULIAN BRAY
The artist's goal was to create an image that shows the precise architectural style of the building, but at the same time to contrast this precision with looser areas of color. This gives a sense of movement in what might otherwise have been quite a static composition. The key colors are burnt sienna complemented by Prussian blue. Areas of the paper have been left untouched to provide brilliant whites.

▲ *The G* DANA BROWN
This very complex painting relies heavily on a limited palette of aureolin yellow, French ultramarine blue, and Winsor red with a few "wild card" paints thrown in for some exciting accents. The artist uses many glazes of transparent paints that are allowed to dry overnight to achieve the strong, clear colors. Note how skillfully she has woven together the building elements and shadows.

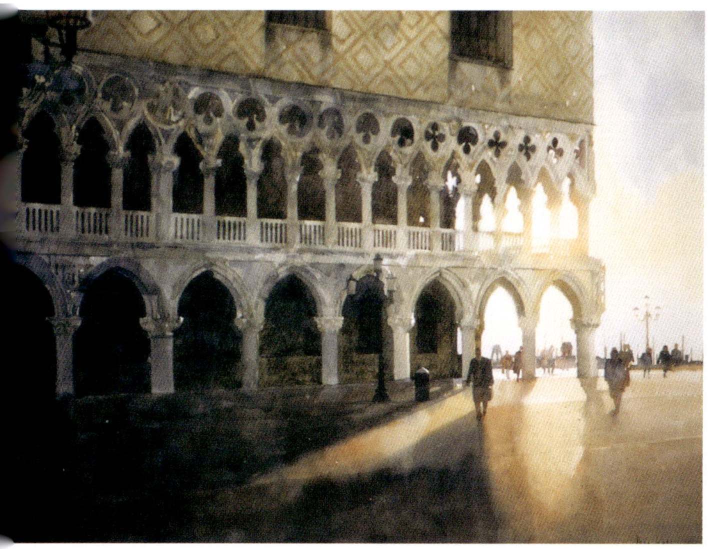

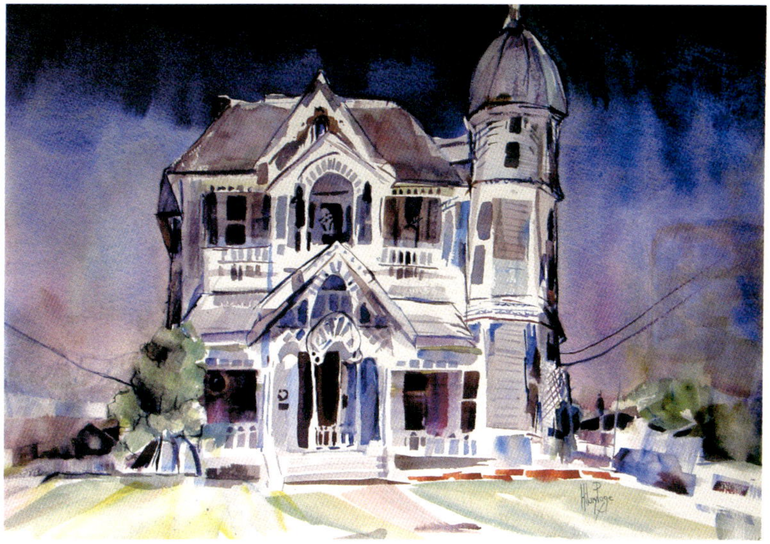

▲ *Early Morning, Venice*
Peter Kelly
Peter Kelly uses a traditional palette of low-chroma paints including yellow ochre, raw umber, Payne's gray, and viridian green along with some opaque black and white to achieve a moody early morning at the Doges Palace. The skillful backlit sun glare, the strong shadow darks, and the near complementary color scheme of yellow and blue-violet combine for high drama.

▲ *Old House Nacogdoches*
Hilary Page
Using a primary palette of magenta, cyan, and yellow, the artist uses a strong, regal violet and purple atmosphere to showcase the magestic white Victorian house. She uses glazes of quinacridone magenta and cobalt blue as effective transitions from the loosely painted house to the less obvious surrounding.

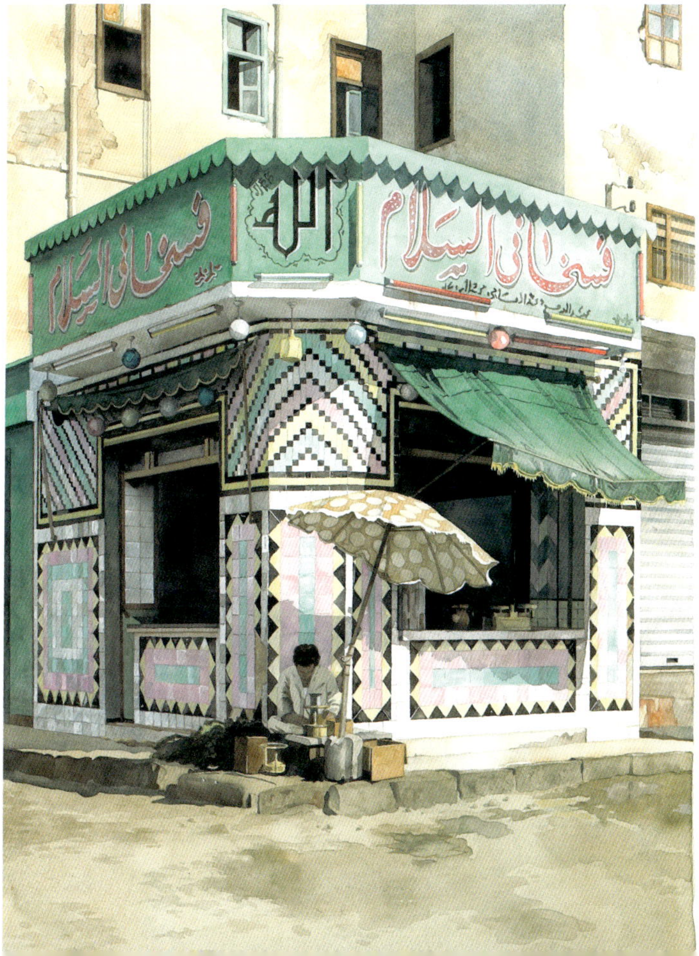

▶ *Tiled Shop* Moira Clinch
The pastel tile work on the shop provided a high-key subject, contrasting with the dark shadow work. In this piece the artist laid down the light shadow work first using a neutral tint with mixed washes of ultramarine violet and ultramarine blue. Then all the detail tile work and facade were painted over the dark underwash in the shadows and onto white paper in the sunlit areas. Subsequent layers of shadow work were then added to achieve the desired depth.

Flowers and plants

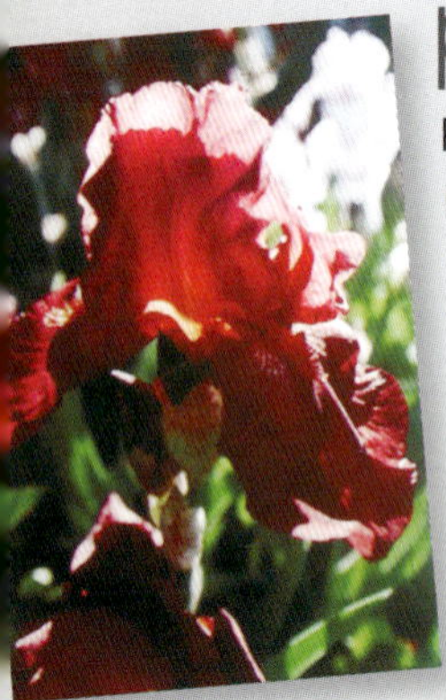

Painting a flower is like painting a single, brief moment in time. There it is—in all its exuberant color, perfume, and brilliance. And yet, in the next moment, it is wilting and fading. If you are painting from life, paint quickly and do not overwork. Keep your work as fresh as the flower itself. A good photograph in pure sunlight works well for a more detailed study, but remember that the objective is to catch the freshness, so let accidents happen!

Study the subject You must understand a flower before you can paint it. How do the petals work? How many petals are there? Take a few moments to examine the flower and immerse yourself in it. The folds and swoops of the petals offer wonderful gestures for the artist.

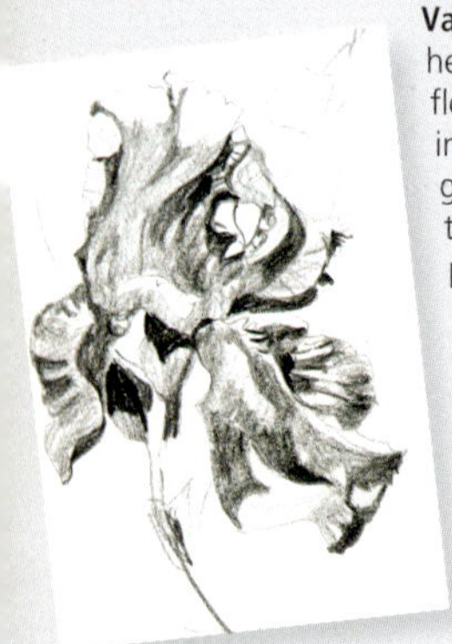

Value/composition study This can help you get acquainted with the flower. It can be small and done in black pencil. Put down the gestures you see, and then add the shapes of the values in each petal of your flower. In this way, you are preparing yourself for the actual painting process—feeling the curves, punctuating the darks, and noticing the lights. Do not worry about proportion and tiny details, but look for the curves, swoops, gestures, and flows. Ask yourself a series of questions. Where are the darkest darks? Where are the lightest lights?

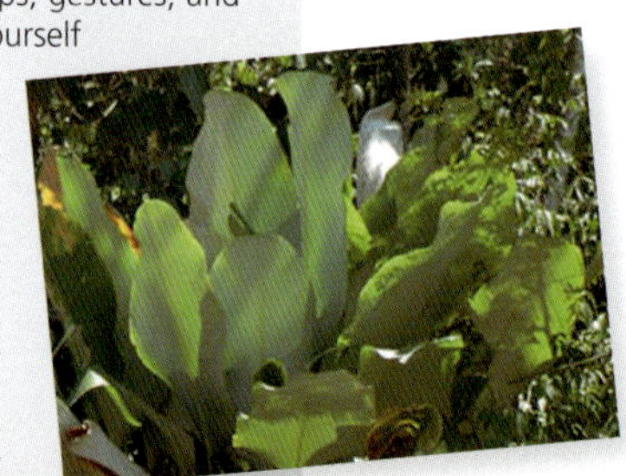

RED IRIS

Select the subject Select a favorite flower. Set it up under a light or next to a window for natural light. If you are photographing a flower to paint, be sure it is under direct natural light from one side to illuminate the forms.

Color considerations The red iris glows in backlight. The front petals reveal delicate veins and subtle details. The color range is wide and mostly warm—from pale pinks and yellows through bright red-orange to cooler depths of maroons and purples. An analogous palette (see "Analogous color palette," page 52) will extend from yellow to violet with the majority of the painting in warm and cool reds.

1 Sketch on paper You can grid off your study and copy it onto your paper, or just do it freehand, expecting that some things will change in the process. Remember that you are after the essence of the flower, not its exact portrait. You may mark some areas with a letter, such as "L" for light and "D" for dark. A letter reminds you not to go over a light area. Erase the letters just before you paint as the eraser does not work through your painted surface.

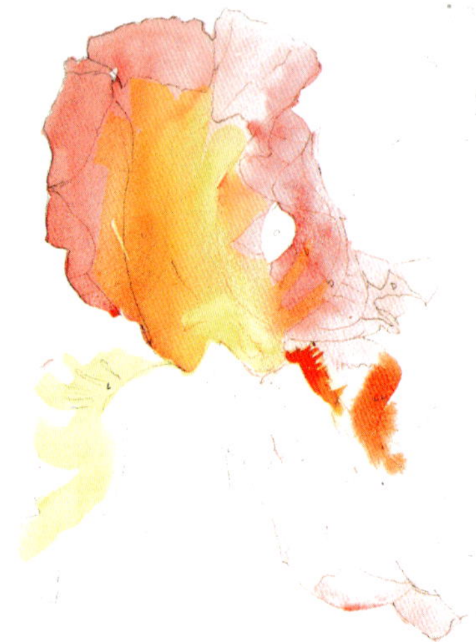

2 Painting the lighter areas "Lightest, brightest, or scariest first!" If you wait until the end to do the scariest part, and everything is working well up to that moment, you'll really understand fear. The lightest and most delicate areas of the petal are the backlit, pale pink parts. Paint these first. Rose madder genuine floats effortlessly and can be painted over all the light petal areas. You also can add the bright yellow light feature at the base of the main petal, which will be left glowing through when the red is added. Add yellow under much of the main petal to enhance the red-orange, then paint the bright orange-yellow "tongue."

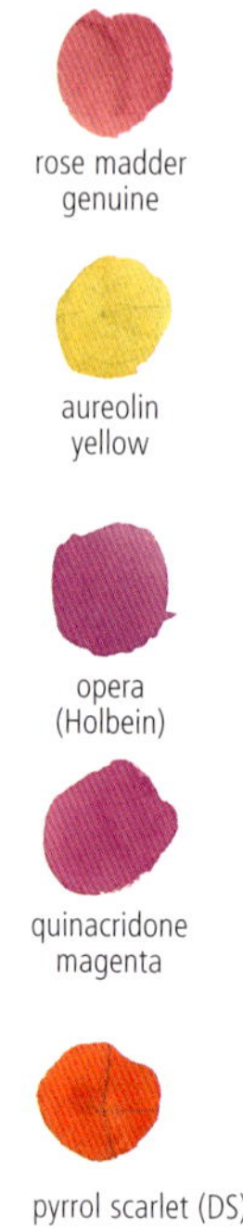

JUNGLE PLANT

Study the subject In the midst of the jungle greens of Central America, the author spotted a beautifully lit plant with large, wide leaves surrounded by the glitter of lacy layers of foliage. Here were nearly all the colors of the rainbow in one plant—lavenders, reds, oranges, yellows, yellow-greens, and blue-greens. Dark maroons were tucked into the deepest shadows. Both sunlight and shadows are at play among these leaves. An underpainting of yellow for the sun-bathed areas and blue for the shadows and shade will suit this subject well.

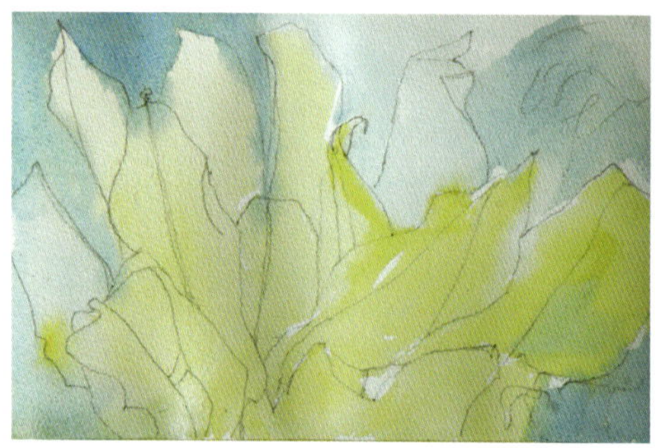

1 Painting undercolors Most of the plant is painted in cobalt blue and aureolin yellow, wet into wet. Start loose and wet. Then paint the leaves one by one in sequence. Decide the undercolor of the leaf. Paint onto the still-damp or dry undercolor, leaving "whites" for the center vein, which may be colored differently later on if you choose. Paint a yellow undercolor with any yellow, and then immediately add a soft blue wet in wet–for fun and variety.

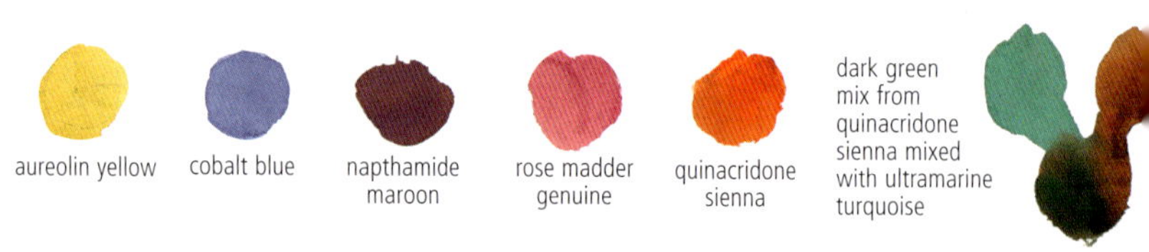

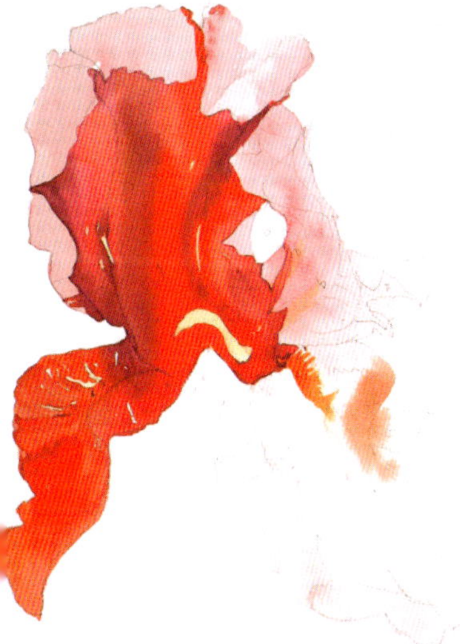

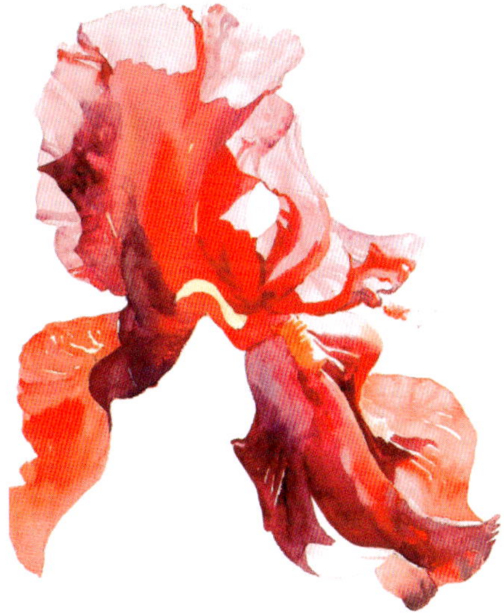

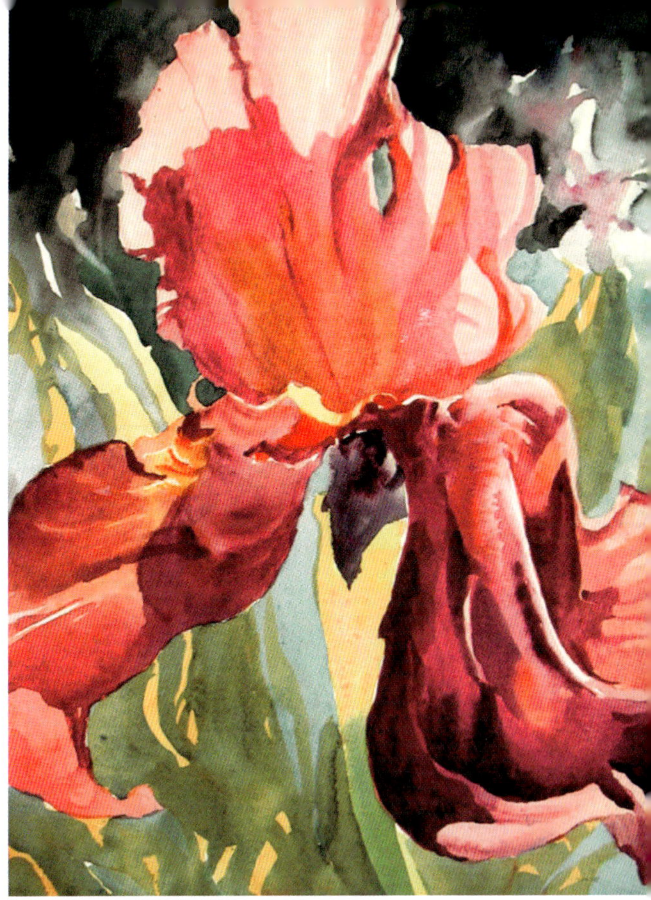

3 Painting the brighter areas Allow it all to dry and get ready to paint the brightest red-oranges and cool reds. Vermillion, quinacridone magenta, opera (Holbein), rhodonite genuine (DS), and pyrrol scarlet (DS) work well here. Begin at the top and apply the reds, playing in a long flow with pyrrol scarlet, opera (Holbein), and quinacridone magenta. Use your loaded brush as if you are describing the flower's shapes with your hand. Do not worry about the darkest darks yet.

4 Painting the lower petals Paint the lower petal in the same way, playing with the variety of reds over the soft rose madder genuine base. Use the cobalt blue-violet for a few of the shadow areas as it is transparent enough to allow the underlying color to glow through. Cobalt violet also is used to create some surprise in the wet paint. (For the completion of the flower, see "Backgrounds" page 84.)

5 Final touches This background for a different version of the red iris uses a complementary scheme with the variety of blue-greens to yellow-greens playing against the wide analogous warm hues of the flower.

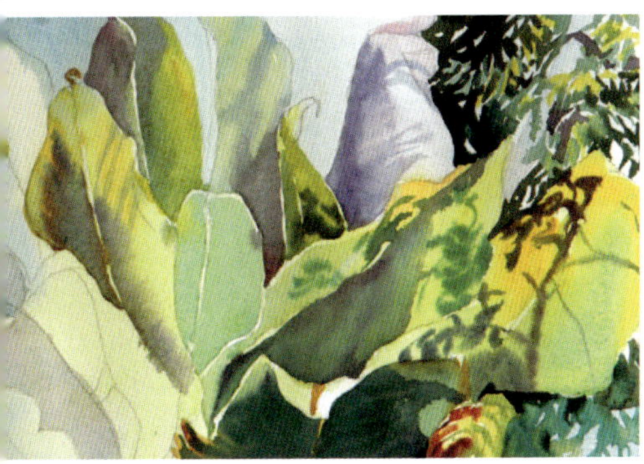

2 Darker greens Brush on the darker, soft blue-greens and lavender shadows using more mixed greens and mixed lavenders, such as cerulean blue and opera (Holbein) or cobalt blue and rose madder genuine. Keep the accidents, and then figure out how to weave them in. Add in some dark darks. Jump into some of the darkest darks in order to begin to see your complete value range. A favorite darkest dark green is ultramarine turquoise and burnt sienna. The darks can be painted negatively using a dancing brushstroke to create leaf shapes over the blues.

3 Keep on painting Complete all the negative spaces and the leaves. Pay attention to each leaf, enjoying the process of adding shadows and other details as you go. Be sure to enjoy the dancing strokes of greens for the background—and take care not to cover it all. The colors underneath will provide the illusion of dappled light. Continue painting leaf-by-leaf with surrounding background darks. A predominantly green painting begs for some deep reds. Napthamide maroon is a superb deep maroon for that almost unseen imperative burgundy. The deep reds in the lower part of the painting are asking for more in the upper areas. To help balance the yellows, more lavender glazes are needed. The curved branch in the upper right needs to be partly covered, shaded, and finished. Cobalt blue can be glazed over the upper left for depth. Some shapes need to be lifted out of the lower left, which feels too dark and flat.

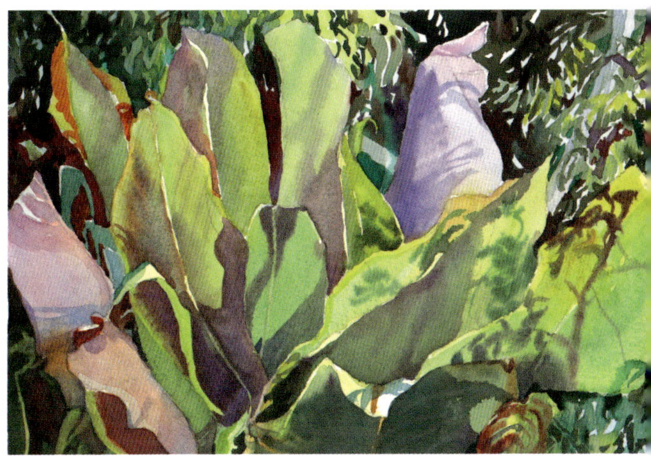

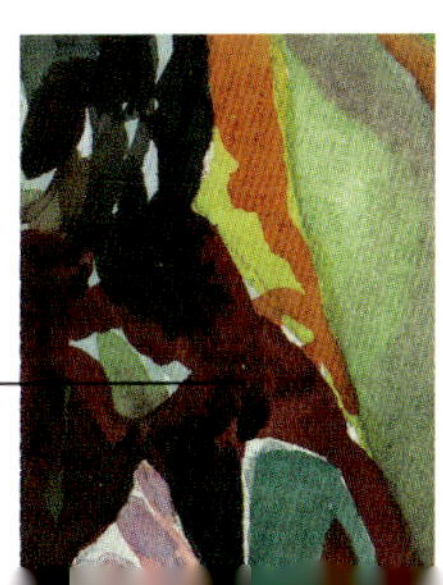

Napthamide maroon lowlights create a feeling of jungle humidity.

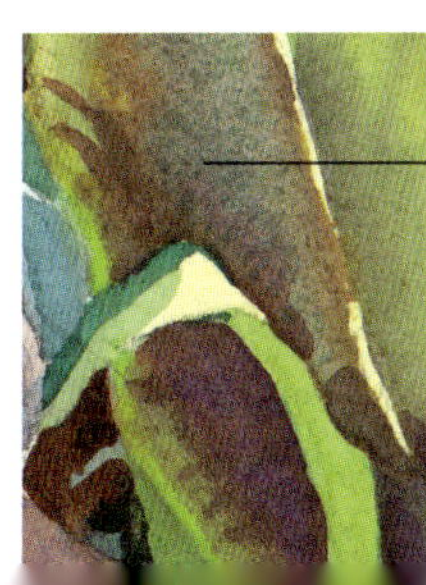

A lavender glaze applied over an existing wash with cobalt violet added to cobalt blue and rose madder genuine.

Flowers and plants

There are few things in nature more flamboyantly colored than a flower in bloom. Color relationships found within the blossom can determine the color scheme and painting mood.

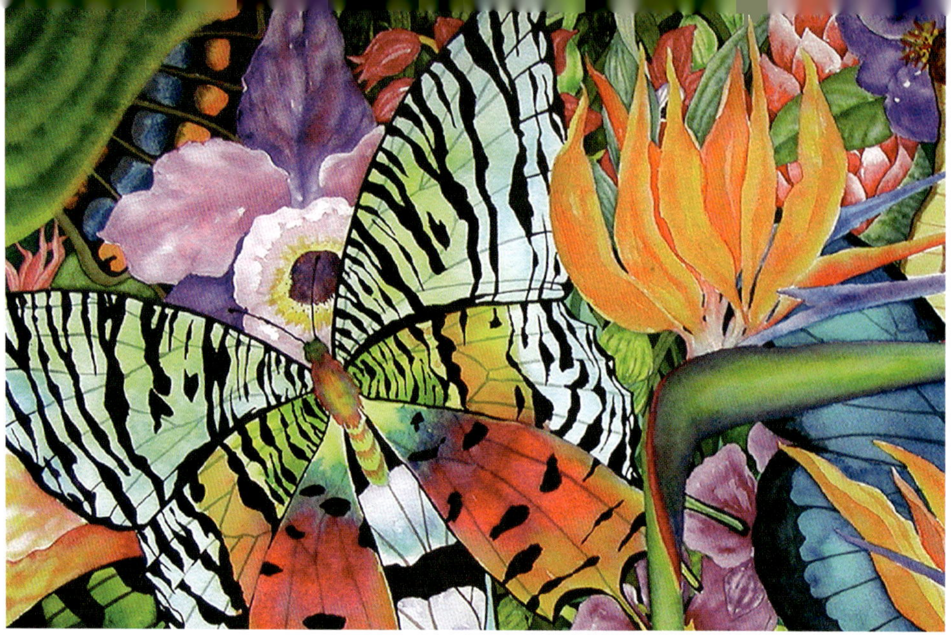

▲ *Paradise* Lucy Arnold
Lucy Arnold's palette is full of color and so is her painting! Bringing together a full palette of high-chroma colors involves careful design and a complete understanding of color relationships. Notice how the artist plays analogous and complementary colors against one another and how she uses colors and shapes to guide your eye around the painting.

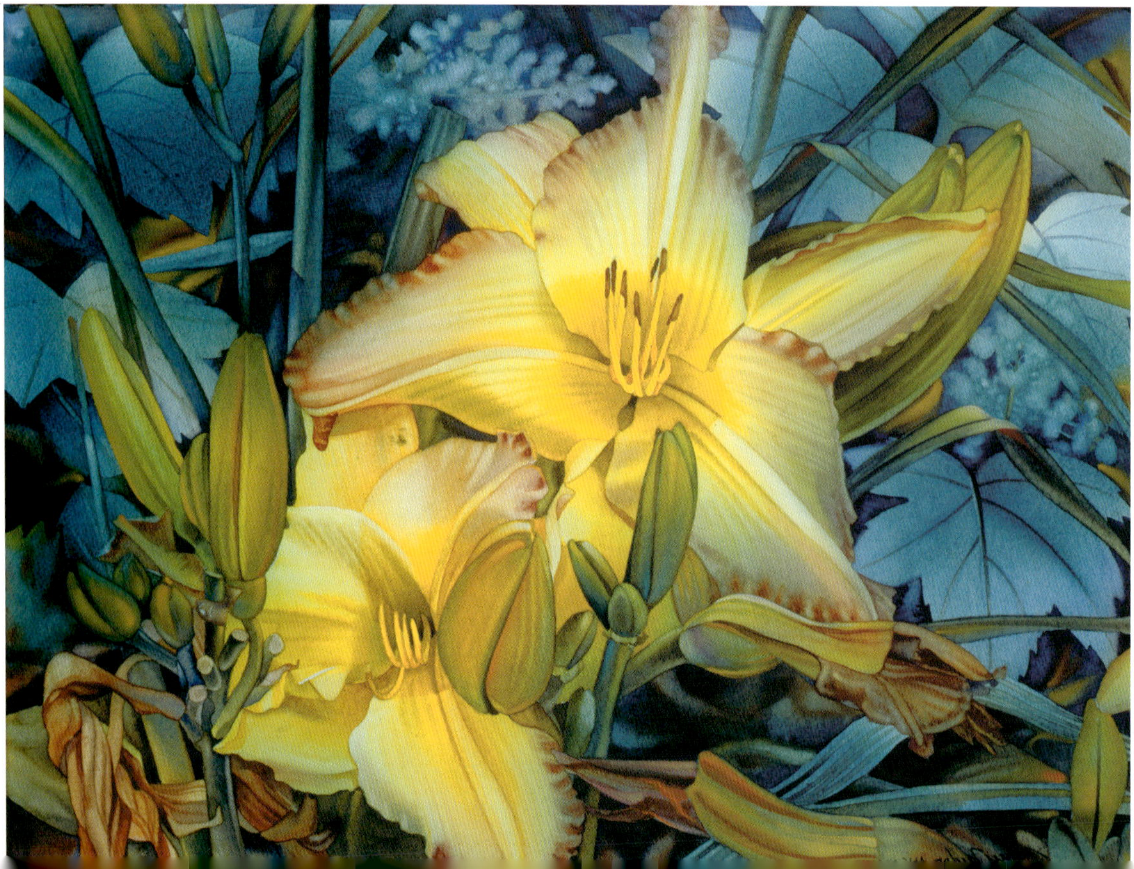

◀ *Adagio*
Nancy Meadows Taylor
This painting was begun with an underpainted layer, in which warm and cool transparent colors were poured onto a wet surface and allowed to mingle in some places while preserving the lightness of the paper in others. More opaque colors were used for the second layer, which established the dark values while leaving the light ones open.

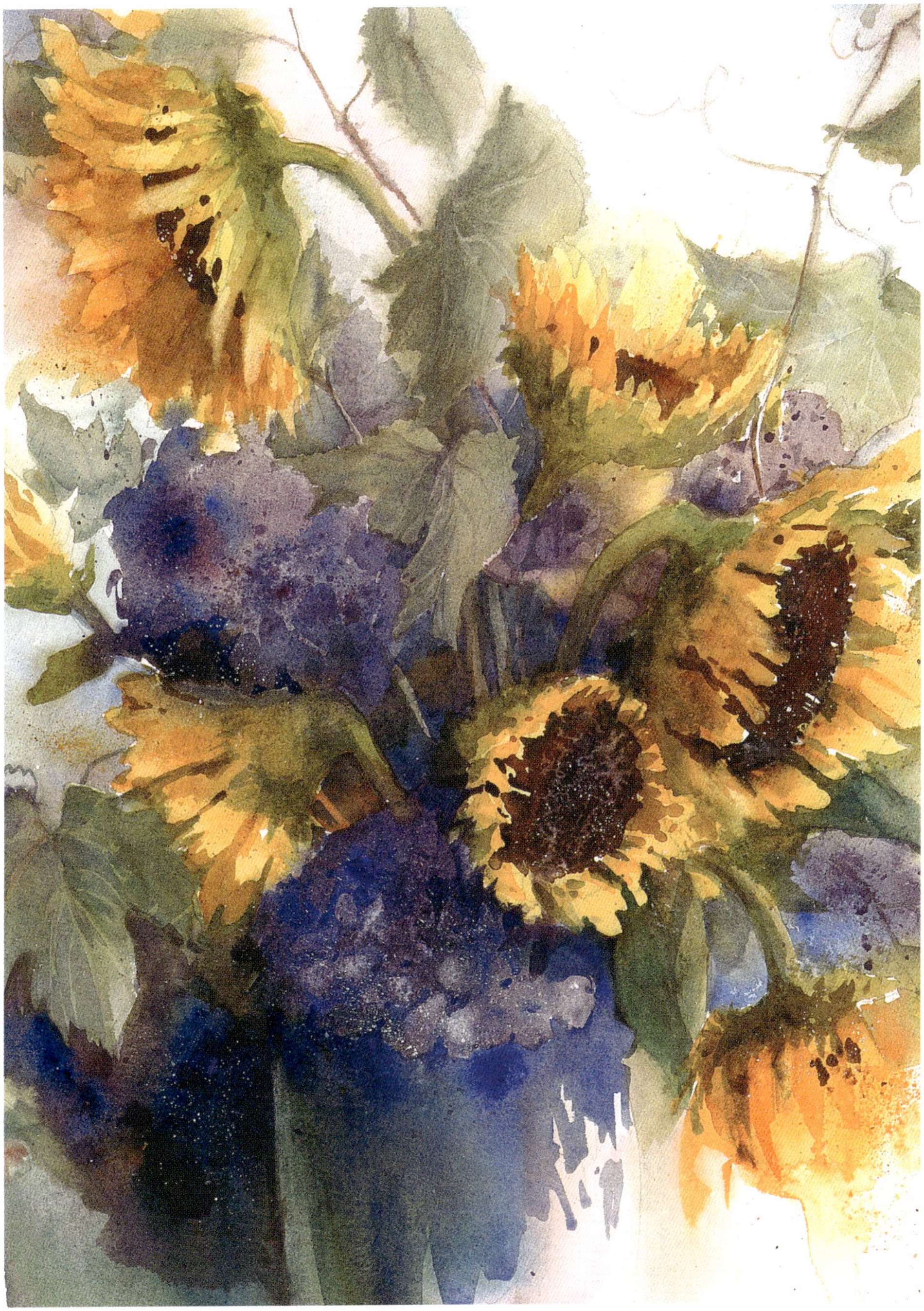

◀ ***Sunflowers and Hydrangeas*** JENNIFER BOWMAN
The success of this painting stems from the composition and the use of edges. The two flowers on the right and the large one at the top form an elongated, tilted triangle, anchored by the central pillar of the vase. These three flowers are picked out with crisp edges, while the central mass of leaves and flowers is soft-edged. Cleverly, the artist has defined the left edge of the vase with a soft band of highlight, while leaving the edge on the right to merge into the flowers, suggesting a reflection.

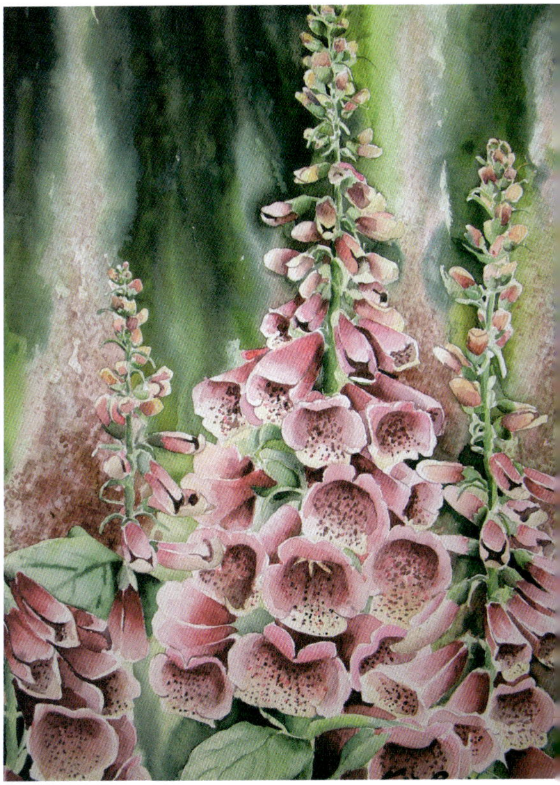

▲ ***Foxgloves*** KIM RICHARDSON-MEYRICK
The artist has used a combination of complementary and split-complementary colors—reds, greens, yellow, and pinks, most of which have a blue bias so that they create harmonies rather than contrasts. She masked out the flowers before applying color, which allowed her to paint the background very freely and loosely. The background foxgloves were formed by using a sponge to create the darker areas.

Animals

Painting an animal is far more than painting feathers or fur. If you do it well you engage the animal's character—and the entry point is through the eyes. A digital image or photograph taken in natural light will help define an animal's anatomy, as well as its fur or feather color and texture. If fur or feathers shade the animal's eyes, try lightening a digital photograph to see the eye details. Paint the eye before applying shade over it. Start with a value/composition sketch (see "Color value," page 66). This will identify the areas you still need to study. If the animal is black, the value study definitely should show several separate values. Now decide on your color palette and try it out. If the animal is light colored or mostly white, the three glazing primaries will create a harmonious result. A black subject will show many other colors—some reflected and sometimes iridescent. Reflecting blue from the sky is most common.

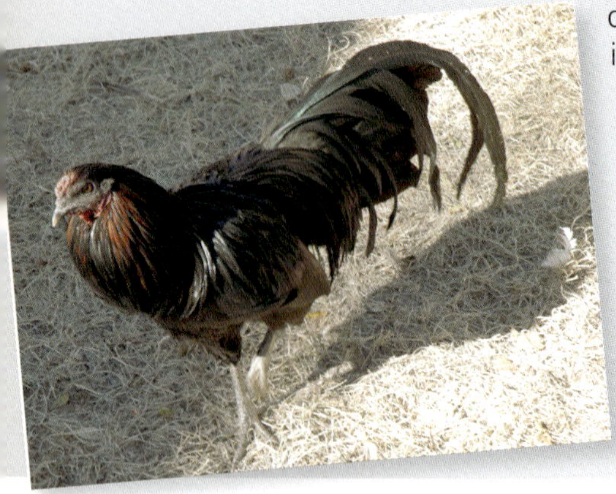

SOME THINGS TO CONSIDER

- Take care when painting an animal's eyes. It is essential to get the color right and to place the highlight in the right spot.
- Most Western people read a painting, as they do text, from left to right, so try to locate your light source 45 degrees to the left and 45 degrees up from the subject. Direct sunlight is best.
- When looking at an animal's legs, think about what you are seeing. Is it an ankle, a knee, or a hip? For example, in dogs, the knee is high and the ankle is where you'd expect a knee.
- Paint in the direction that the fur, the feathers, or the fins lie.
- Don't use a flash to take a reference photograph. A flash fills in the shaded and shadowed areas, creating a flat version of the animal.
- A few well-placed, negatively painted hairs give the impression of fur.
- The tapered tip of a round brush makes it perfect for creating feathers.
- Feathers often have their own shadows, which can be added carefully.

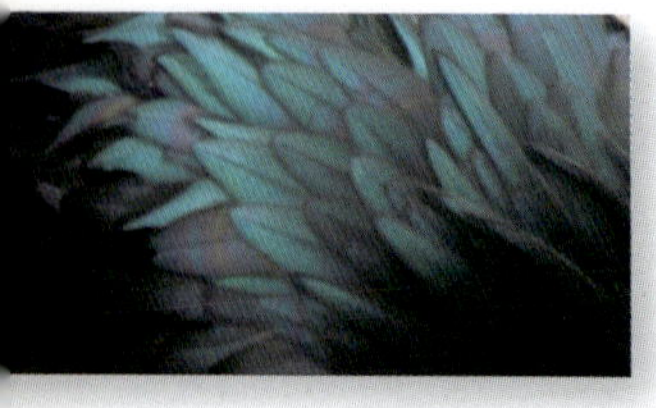

Capturing iridescent features This Sumatran rooster, has wonderfully varied feathers. Lightened digital closeups provide references for his shaded eyes and feather patterns. Because his glossy feathers reflect the sky, he is entirely underpainted in cobalt blue violet and cobalt blue.

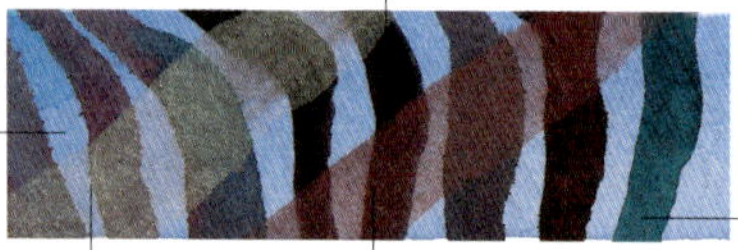

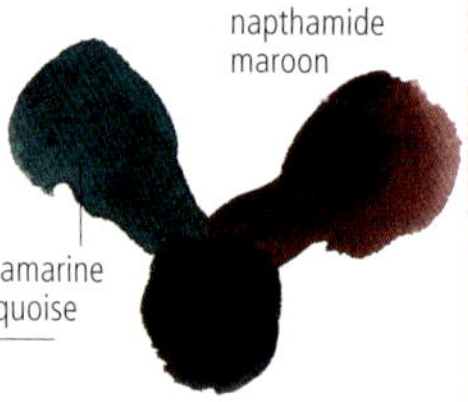

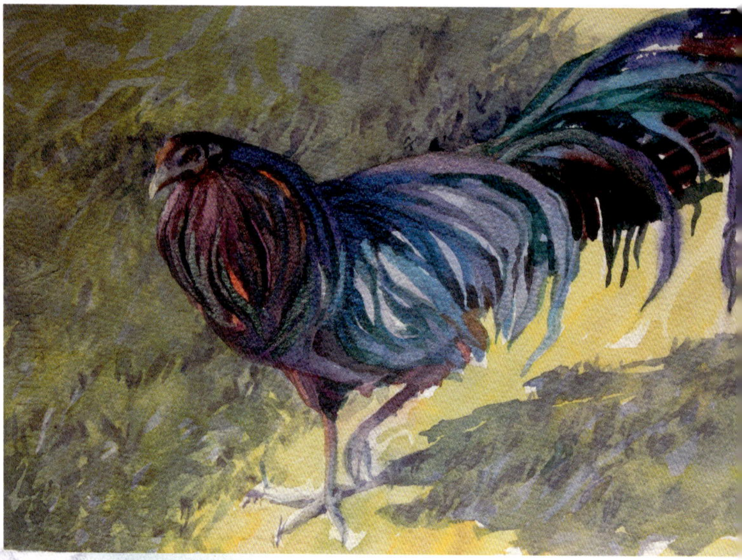

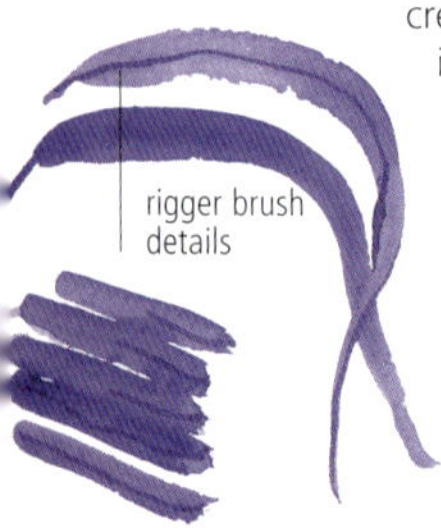

Feathers An ultramarine turquoise and napthamide maroon mix creates lively darks for the shaded feathers. A 1" flat brush is useful for the first layers, a smaller (6–8) round brush is ideal for individual wing, neck, and tail feathers, and a rigger is useful for feather quills and details. Shade and shadow are crucial for both the bird and the background of dry grass. Cobalt blue and Iridescent indigo are useful for cast shadows. Iridescent pigments (green and blue) are used over the dark feathers for effect.

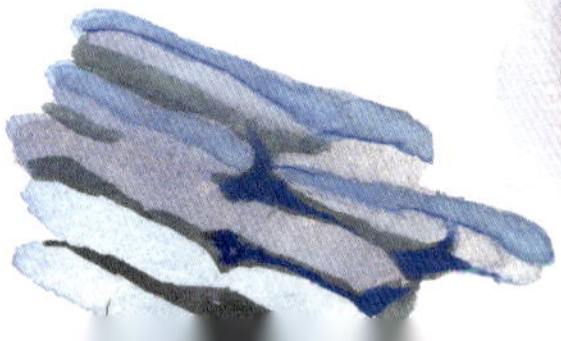

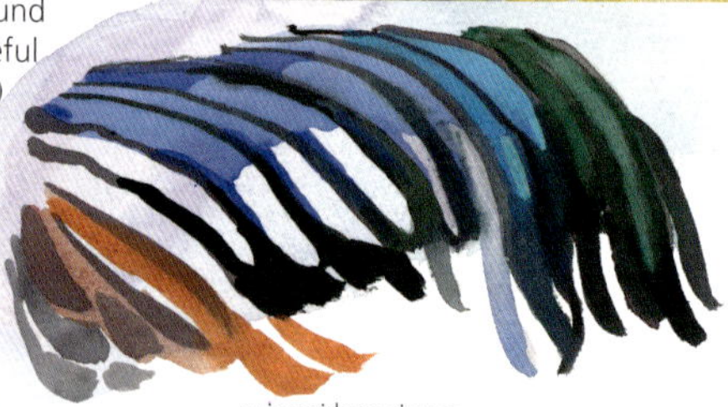

Grass After an initial painting of grass shapes in Indian yellow, some buff titanium creates soft contrasts and suggests the varied shapes. When the background is dry, add a glaze of cobalt blue mixed with rose madder genuine over the shaded grass and the cast shadow of the rooster.

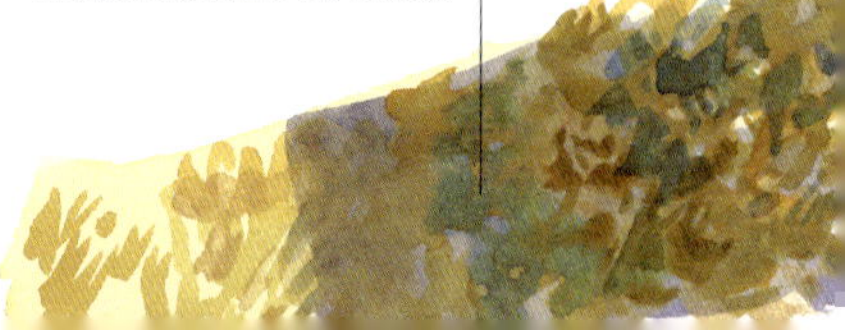

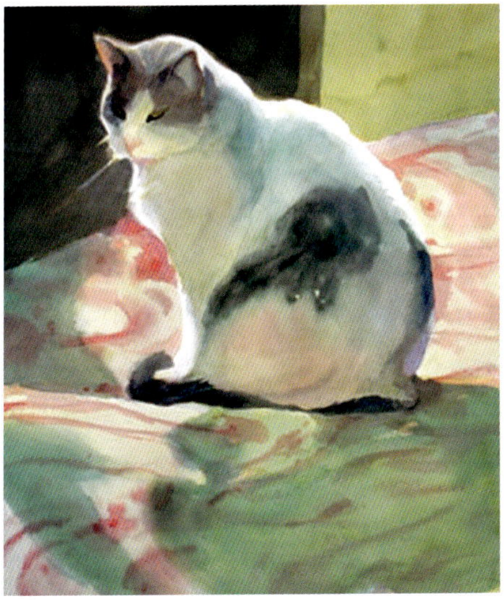

Painting a back-lit subject This painting shows that an unseen light source, such as a window, can provide a perfect back light. Use three transparent, nonstaining pigments—cobalt blue, rose madder genuine, and aureolin yellow—for the entire painting. Glaze the cat's shaded side several times with individual glazes, keeping these edges soft and away from the white edges. Let brushstrokes suggest her whiskers and allow the viewer to interpret the rest. The fur is mostly suggested by soft glazing in the direction of the hair growth. Soften the edges of the darker markings. Take care to darken the areas on the neck and side where the fur follows her curves.

Layers and details Immediately after an overall wash of aureolin yellow, apply the head markings with quinacridone sienna. Carefully sculpt the body with successive layers of transparent, nonstaining glazes. Simulate the shaded fur with brushstrokes. Painting in layers involves the excitement of optical mixing (see page 36). When you have laid down all three layers, add the details, with particular attention to the shape, color, and surrounding of the eyes. For uniformity, paint the background in a physical mix of the three nonstaining transparent pigments. Prewetting the paper where the gray fades to "white" produces a soft transition. Losing the sunlit edge of the head adds interest.

Painting fur textures Several digital shots are taken of the dog lying in the morning sun. The low backlight brushes over her ears, chest, and back and helps guide the contrast decisions for the value/composition study. The shaded eyes are made visible by brightening one of the photos, so they can be painted before the shade is added. The value study guides the decision to bring the light from the upper right down over her sunlit side to define the shapes of the cast shadows.

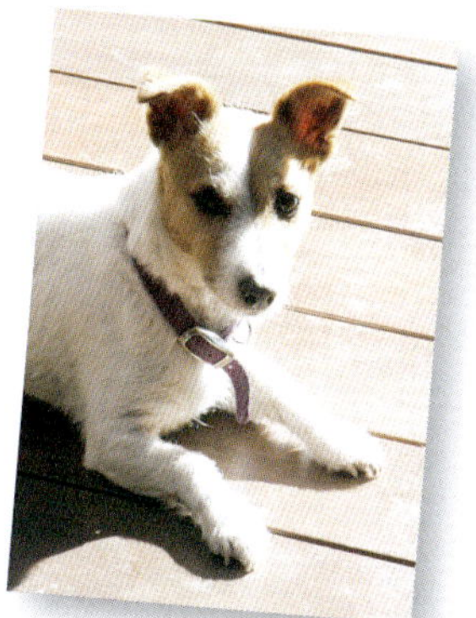

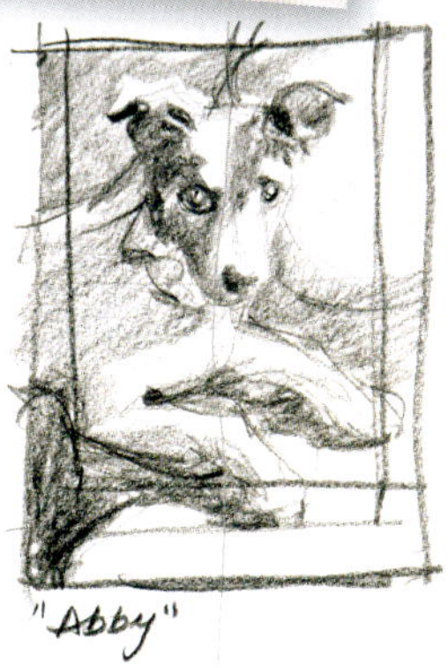

quinacridone sienna applied over washes defines the head markings

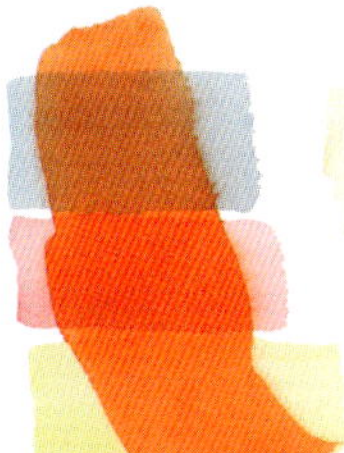

Optical mix
Layers of transparent, nonstaining washes create shadow and texture on the fur.

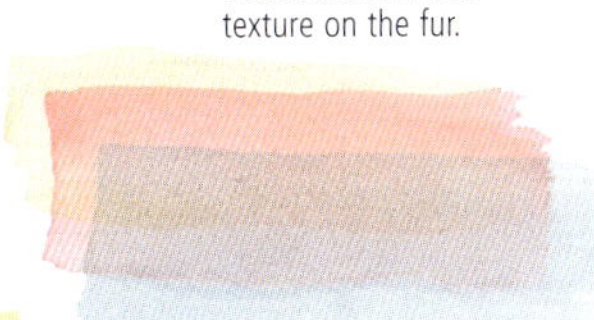

Physical mix
Mix of the three transparent pigments in the palette to make gray.

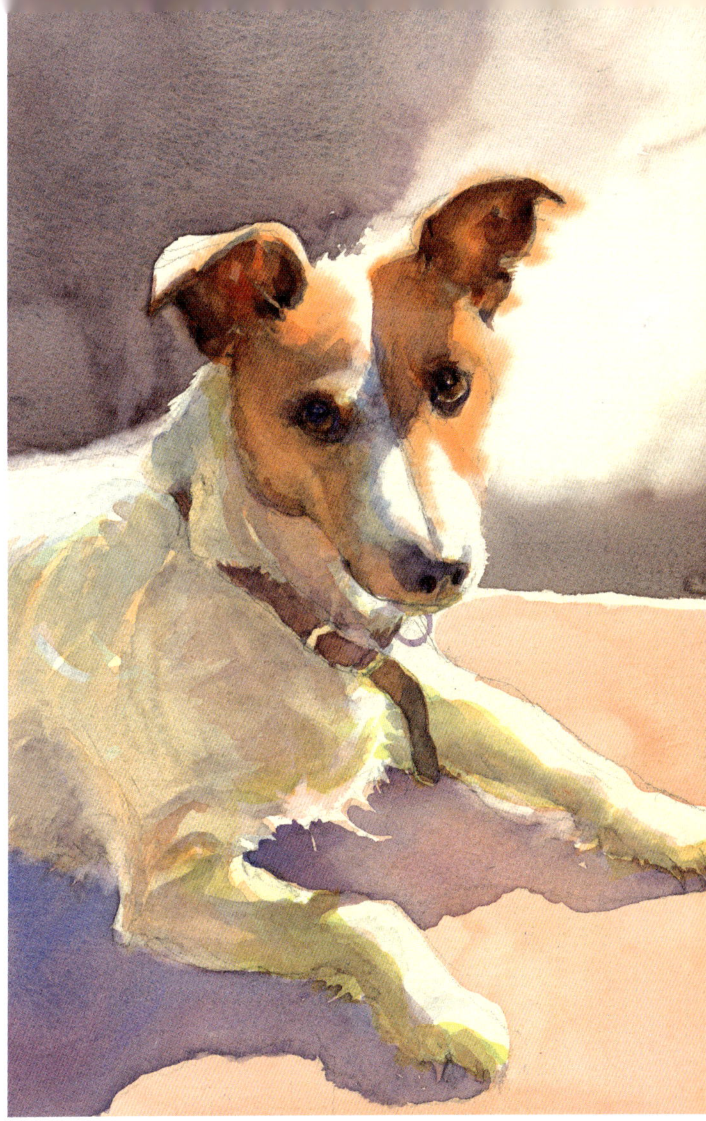

Hair Apply small strokes of transparent, nonstaining pigments—aureolin yellow, rose madder genuine, cobalt blue—to create an optically mixed gray. Use a small round brush to indicate the direction of the hair. Leave undercolor to show through in directional marks that simulate the hair directions. Some dog hair edges are negatively painted. Some edges of the chest and underpaw are softened to convey the softness of the coat. Softening can be done while wet or dry. Use a drier brush to soften if the edge is still wet. If dry, dampen the edge with clean water and use clean paper towel to make a single, gentle lift. Always lift toward the darker area, away from the light.

directional brushstrokes to indicate the hair

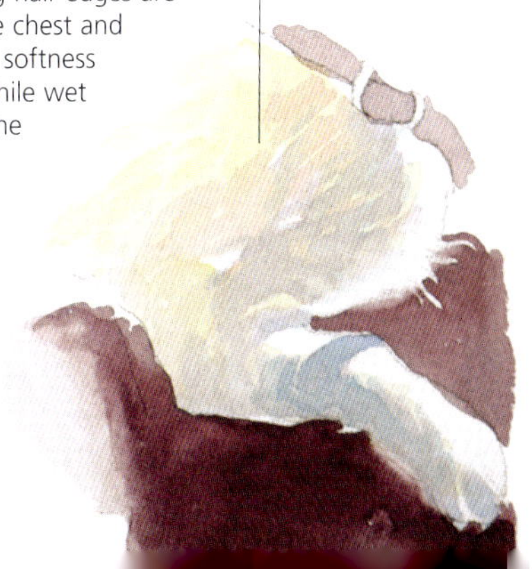

Animals

Painting an animal is about painting from the heart as well as the mind. It is important to somehow express the animal's character—and there are many ways to do that, as shown in this gallery. Some of the best animal paintings are as much about the animal's habitat as the animal itself. Since the subject rarely stays still, working from photographs is ideal.

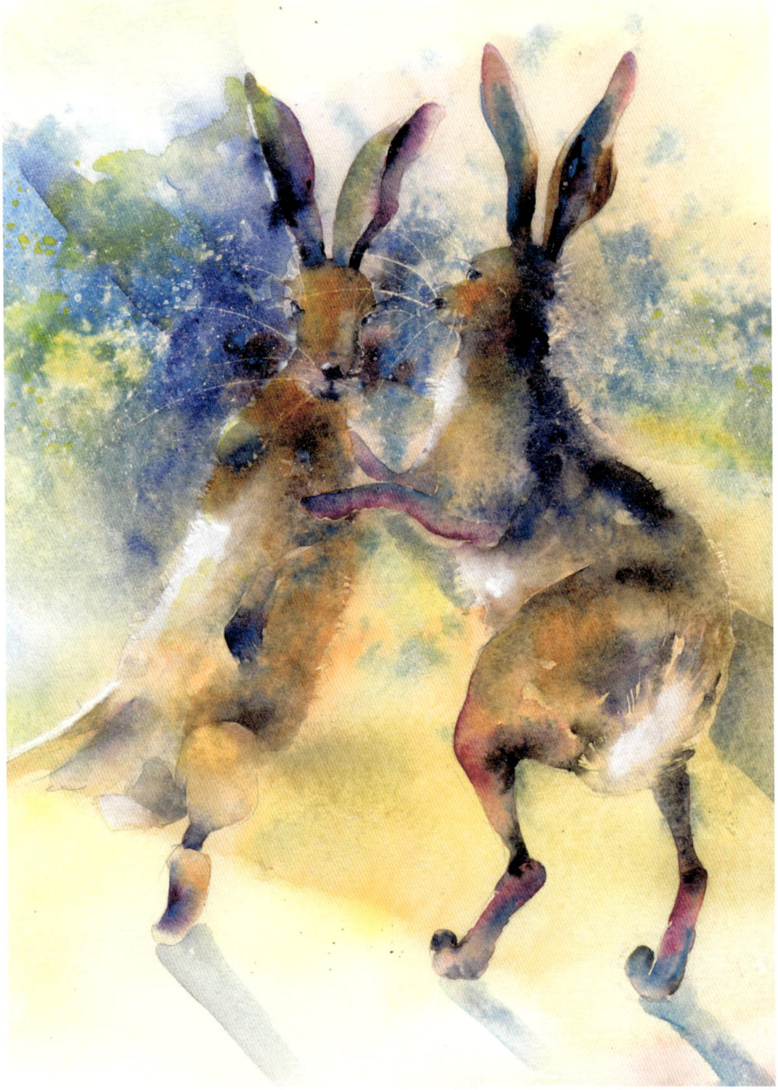

▲ *The Main Event* Sheila Gill
The lovely blending of blues, magenta, and pink was achieved through the carefully controlled use of wet-into-wet methods, and a sharp knife was used to scratch into dry paint for the whiskers. Before painting, the artist draws until she feels the tightness is out of her system; then she feels she can enjoy herself.

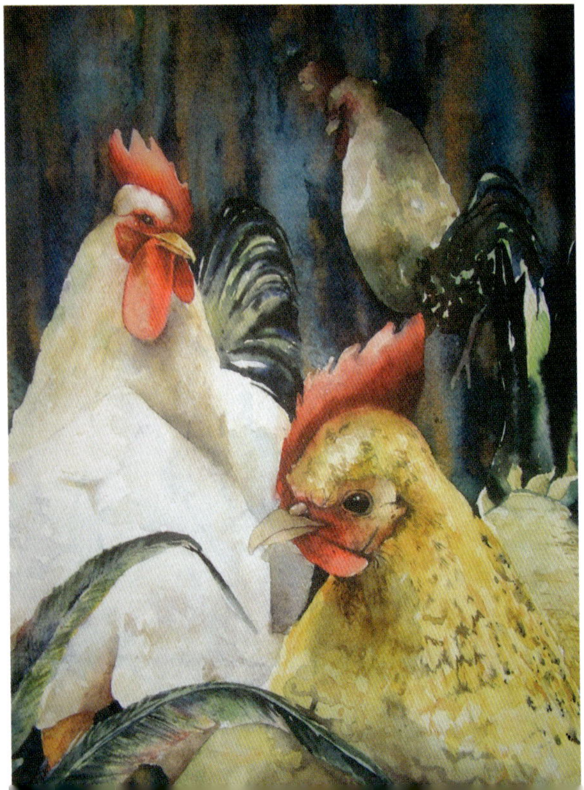

◀ *Chickens*
Kim Richardson-Meyrick
Both strong tonal contrasts and the use of the orange/blue complementary pair give vibrancy to this image. The background was painted wet into wet, with water dribbled into the paint to create runs, and the chickens were built up wet on dry, with an addition of copper powder mixed with water for the final coat.

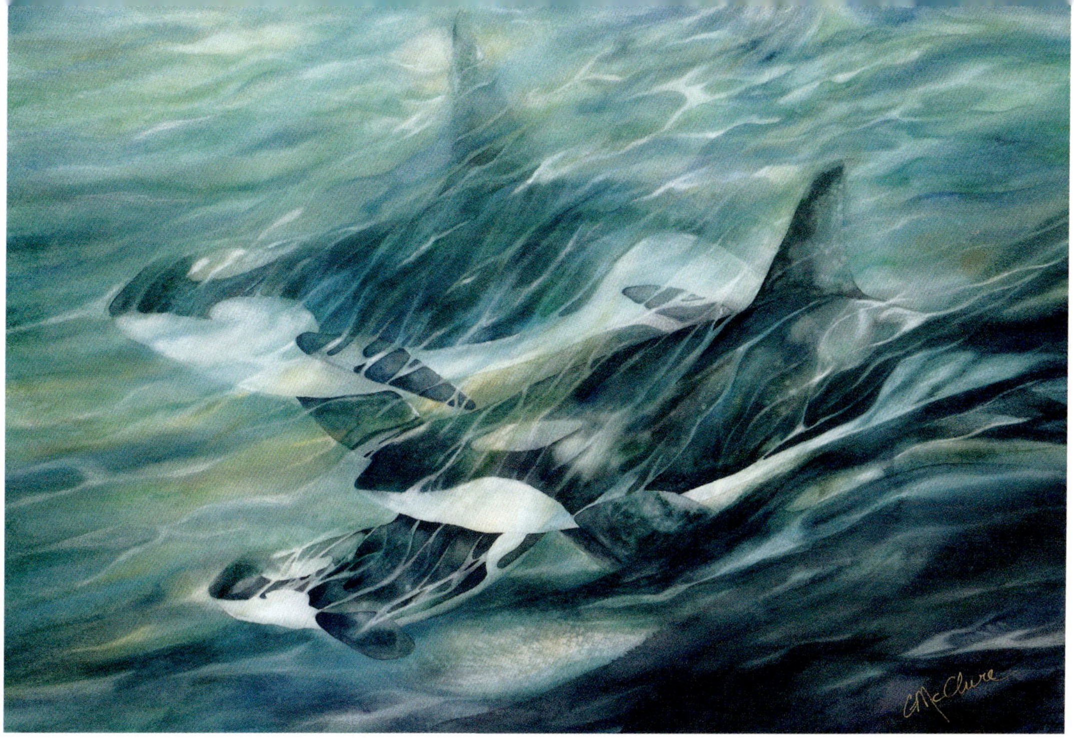

◀ ***Going Home*** Connie McClure
Using mostly transparent staining and non-staining paints, Connie McClure blends her colors with successive glazes on wet paper while lifting some areas to keep them light. The glazed layers make her subjects appear underwater and help communicate movement. Using a full color palette, her blues (cobalt, Prussian, and ultramarine) and greens (phthalo and viridian) dominate with aureolin yellow and cadmium orange for sparkle and alizarin for darks.

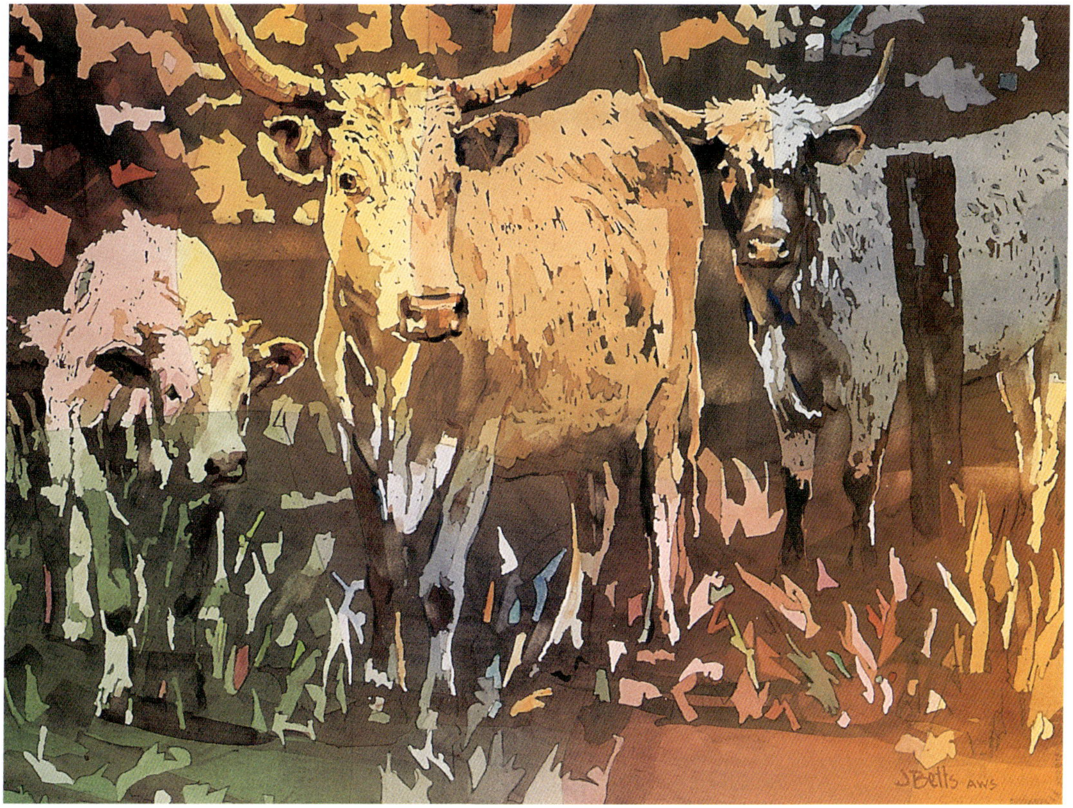

◀ ***Trumpet Voluntary*** Judi Betts
Judi Betts creates vibrant color paintings of familiar animals through her unique process. First she underpaints a grid of four or more rectangles of flat color in light values. Her subject matter is added later using complementary colors to each undercolor. The juxtaposed complements create both vibrancy and neutrality!

Landscapes and trees

When you encounter a forest landscape, often your first impression is that it is entirely green. But if you immerse yourself in that landscape and really *see* it, you will find that it contains many other color jewels hidden within the leafy foliage.

FIND OTHER COLORS AMONG THE GREENS

Study these photographs of verdant landscapes to see if you can spot all the colors in them.

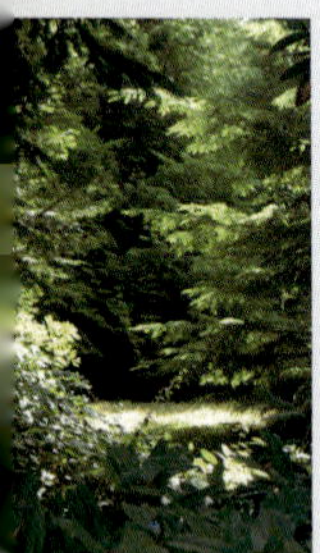

Blue and yellow
On a sunny day in the evergreen forest of the Olympic Peninsula National Park, Washington, the yellows of the afternoon sun reflect on some of the extended leaves and grass. And the shiny rhododendron leaves that face the sky reflect the blue.

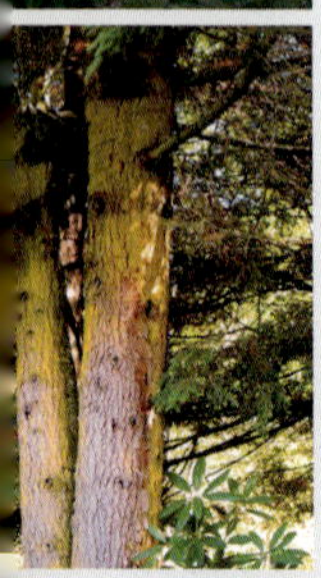

Lavender
On the bases of these two Douglas firs, with their characteristic mantle of yellow-green moss, you can see the startling lavender bark of the trees' bases. Why? Gaze directly at the greens and yellows, and then turn your gaze to the relatively neutral tree bark. You will see their complementary colors—red and purple—as a warm lavender. This optical illusion is called "afterimage."

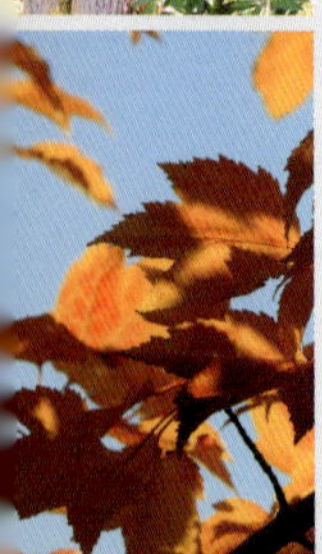

Oranges
When leaves begin to lose their chlorophyll, the color of the leaf changes. When the drooping, lower leaves are backlit by the sun, the oranges and orange-golds begin to glow. Similarly, the trunks of desert trees glow orange when warm light bounces off the surrounding landscape to become warmer reflected light in the shaded trunks.

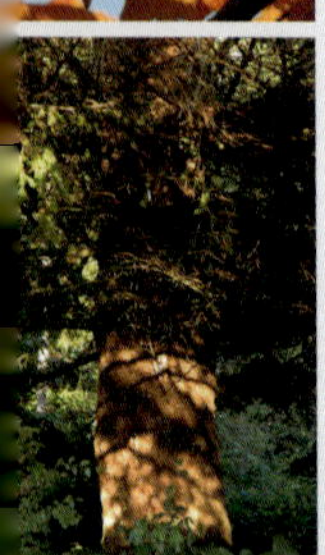

Reds
When you walk through a forest of varied greens and blue-greens, deep reds begin to creep into the shadows and darks. The bark on the trees begins to look red-orange. Keeping the phenomenon of afterimage in mind, remember to drop in the red while painting mostly greens.

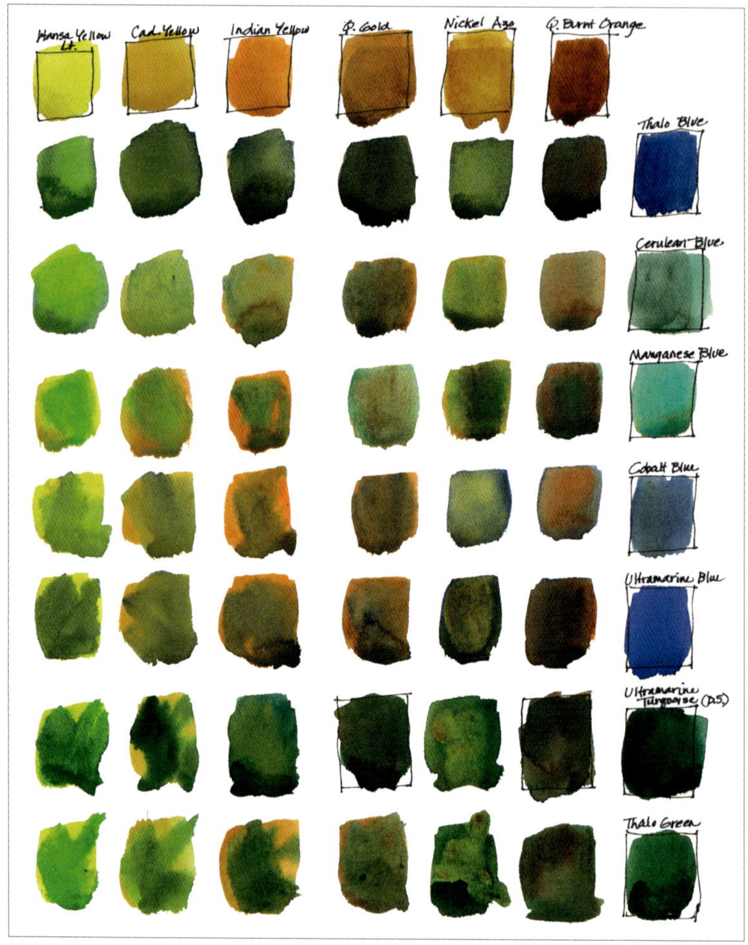

Green exercise Green is basically a secondary color made up of blue and yellow. These two colors can dance together in the greens and are the reason why many artists prefer to mix their greens rather than use manufactured greens. This exercise shows you how to mix a variety of greens.

SOME THINGS TO CONSIDER

- Avoid thinking about or painting individual leaves unless they are large. The gesture of branches and clusters of leaves are much more effective. Allow the gesture (the swoop or the droop) of the branches to inform your brushstroke.
- You can best see the variation in values by squinting at the photograph or the scene.
- Doing a green exercise will acquaint you with the wonderful variety of greens that you have in your palette—ready to mix and use!

Mixing greens for foliage The startling lavender and the yellow-greens are perfect complements. The greens that surround the trunk are neutral mixes of blues and yellows. Use these pigments to mix the greens and supporting colors.

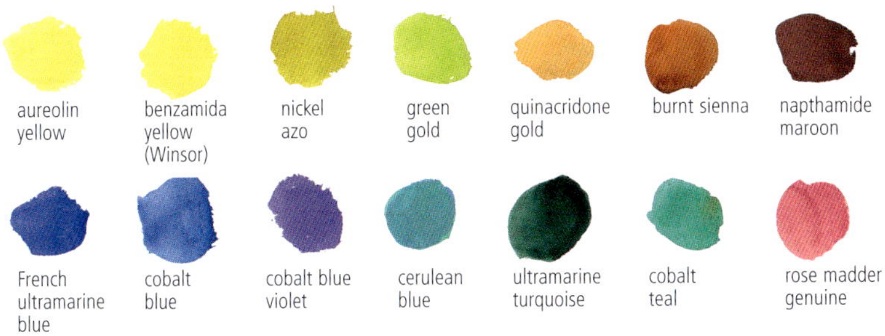

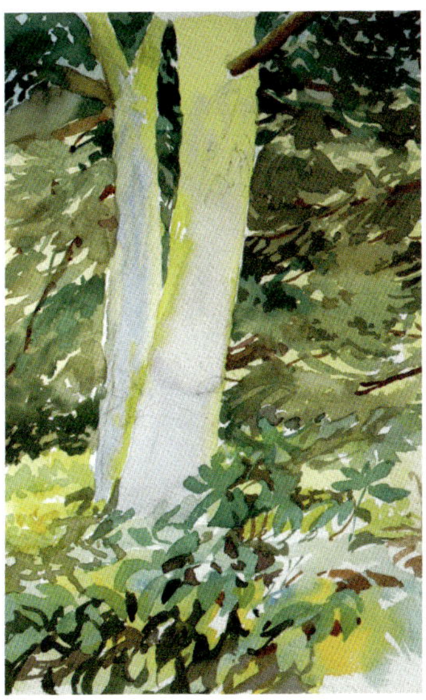

1 First stages Paint in the yellow-green and lavender bases of the two trunks, wet into wet, by first applying the lavender (cobalt blue and rose madder genuine) and then allowing the green gold to run along edges and into the lavender. Apply yellow sporadically into the areas around the tree trunks as an underwash. Apply the greens in dancing strokes—some wet into wet, some dry—with the corner of a 1″ wash brush. Paint the rhododendron leaves positively and negatively. Use the underwash to express an occasional gesture by painting around it.

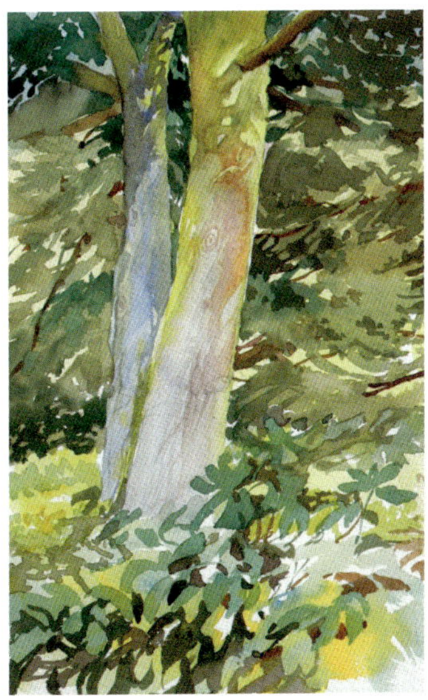

2 Building the values Cobalt blue is an ideal glaze to darken areas in the lower front, as well as to push back some of the area behind the trunks. Use cobalt blue alone and mixed with green-gold to darken the upper trunks. Look carefully at the gestures of the branches, as well as at the colors and leaf type.

3 Finishing touches The finishing touches include glazing with cobalt blue, adding more darks, and connecting the darks in interesting ways to encourage the eye to move around the painting. You can use small, repeating strokes to emphasize directionality and suggest movement.

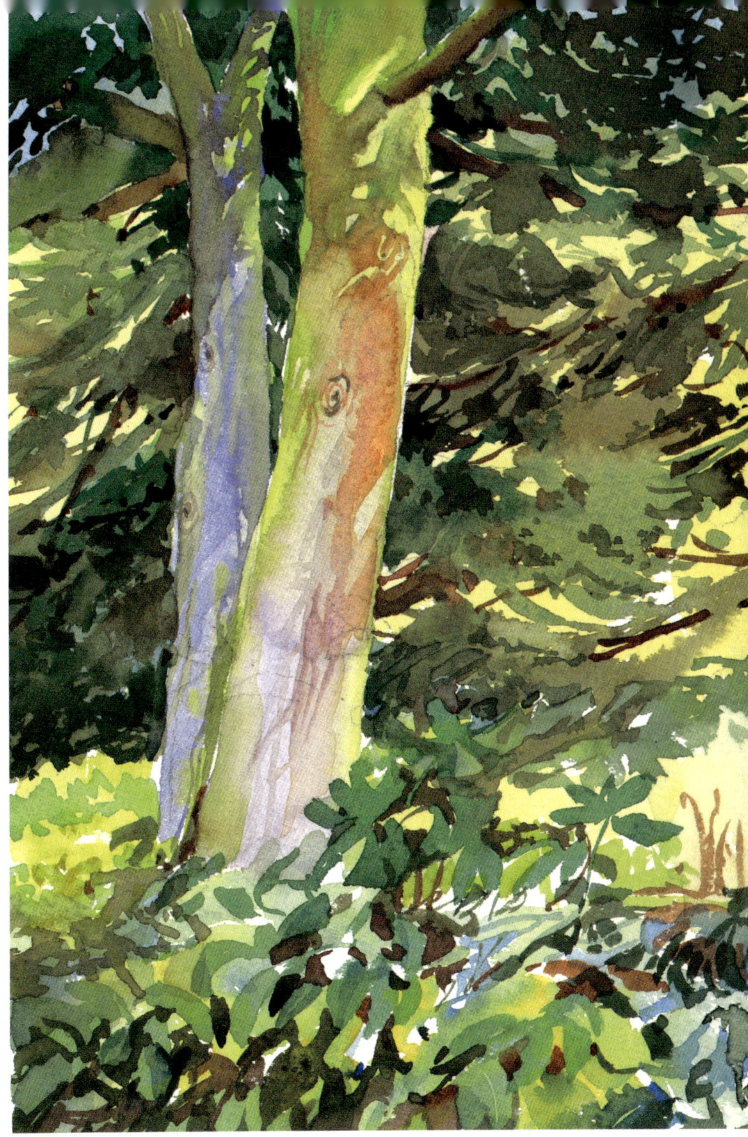

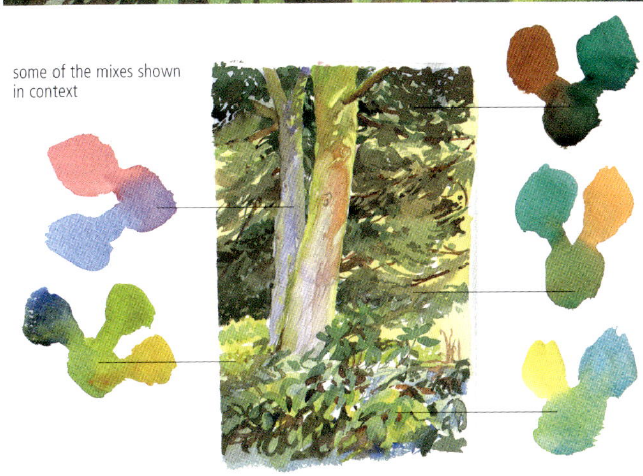

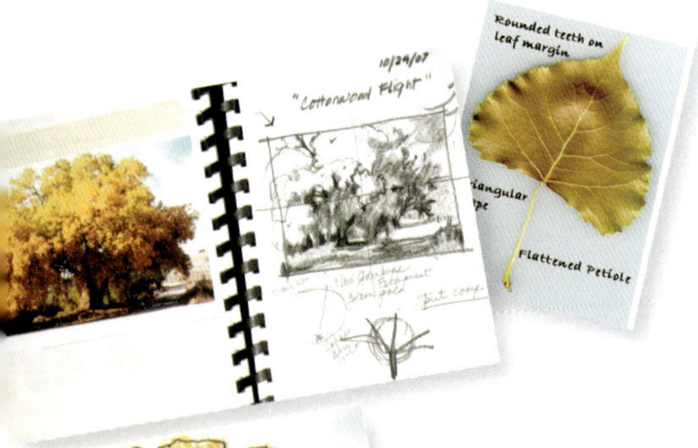

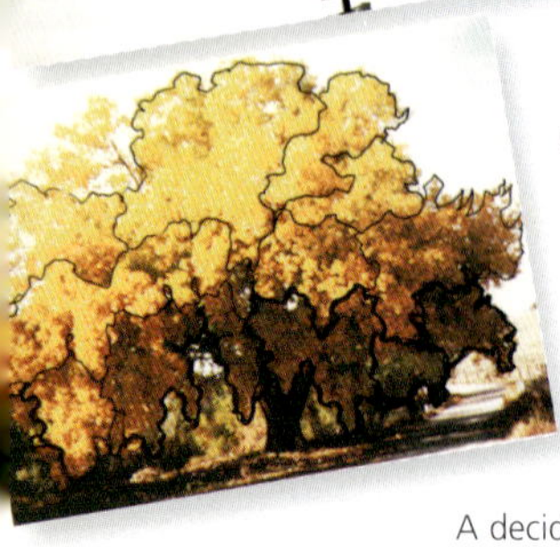

Creating fall foliage Fall colors jolt us out of our familiarity with the greens and blues of summer. Every year, almost overnight, there is an explosion of warm, analogous colors—the reds, oranges, and yellows of the fall foliage. A deciduous tree makes a great subject to experiment with fall foliage colors. It's important to understand the tree before you paint it. If you can, make studies of the individual leaves, the structure of the foliage, and the light and dark values.

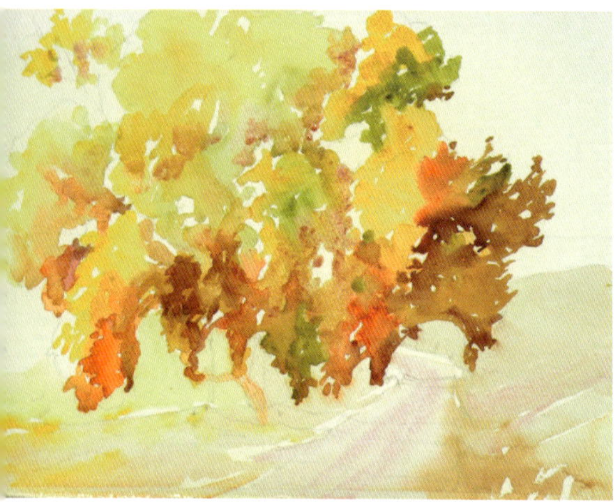

2 Darks The dark trunk can help the eye see the entire value range. A warm dark for the trunk will refer to the presence of reflected light. Napthamide maroon is perfect, while a vertical daub of ultramarine blue can suggest cast shadows. Paint shadows on the ground in ultramarine blue, cobalt blue, and quinacridone magenta. When adding cast shadow colors, take care to keep the strokes horizontal with occasional brush flips to suggest grass. Take care also to make sure the shadows change at each change in landscape surface.

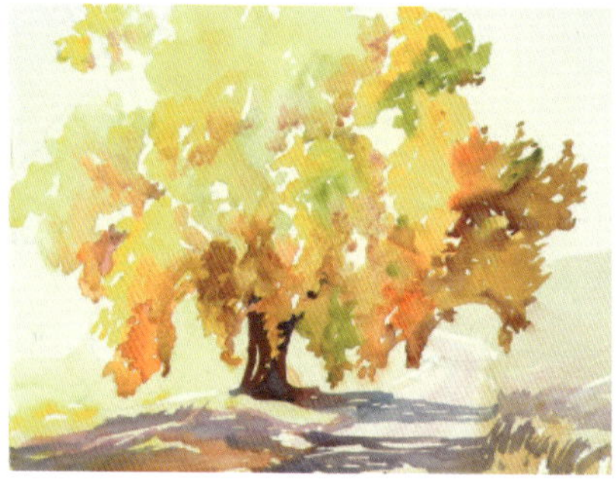

3 More darks Add more warm darks to the background at left, using napthamide maroon, quinacridone gold, and quinacridone magenta. Where the dark left shape approaches the hanging leaf clump, take care to leave a bit of white paper beside the painted leaf clump. Negatively paint the edge in a jagged, varied manner.

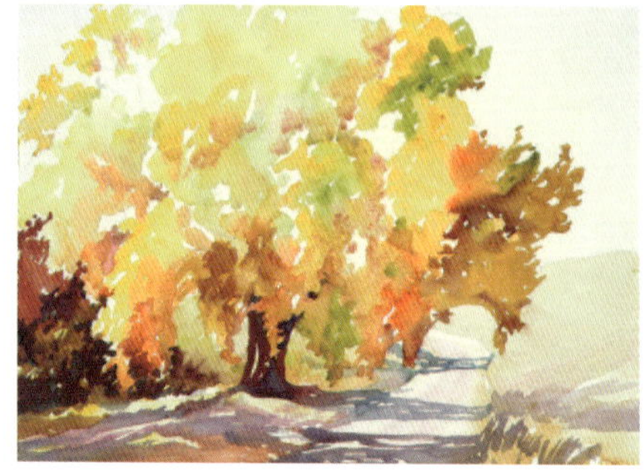

aureolin yellow | ultramarine blue | cobalt blue | green gold | napthamide maroon

The sharply pointed leaves suggest an upwardly dancing brushstroke.

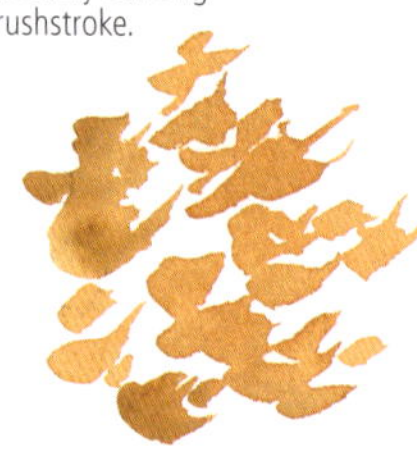

1 Underpainting, form, and ground A full underpainting of aureolin yellow establishes the sun-drenched setting. Beginning from the left, paint each clump of leaves with a 1" flat brush. Remember that the left side receives sun, and the right can be a bit darker and brighter, out of the sunlight. Try different pigments such as cobalt blue or green-gold in your mixes. The underside of the foliage is painted in darker, more orange pigments, as is the right, shaded side. Use only warm paint colors to communicate the intense yellows and oranges, warmed with reflected light. Some cooler tones can be added much later. Dancing brushstrokes and flips help show the tree's canopy. The ground is painted loosely, using directional strokes to show the terrain. The ground usually is the lightest area as it receives more direct light.

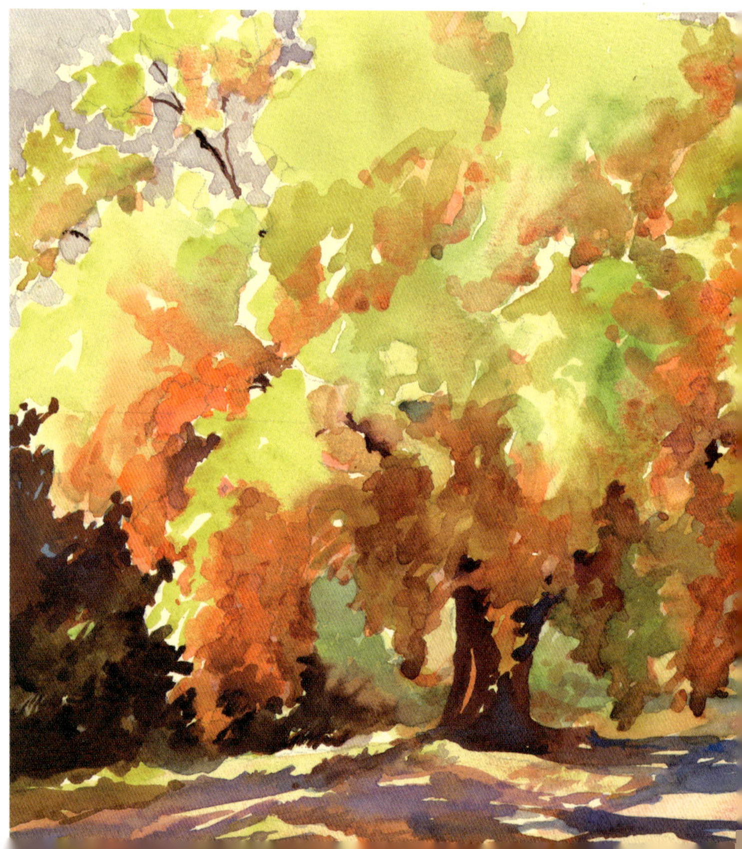

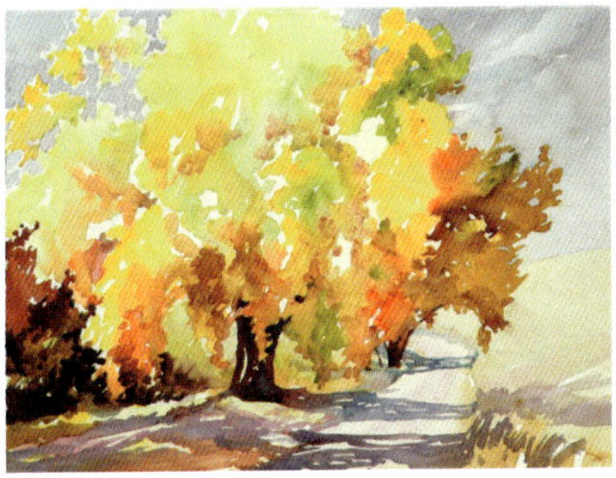

4 Sky Use a mix of cobalt blue and rose madder genuine for the sky, making strokes that continue the upward gesture of the leaves. Paint a bit of a darker mix (using less water) negatively around the darker left branch, taking care not to go into the upper left branch, taking care not to go into the upper left branch, taking care not to go into the yellow. Painting over the yellow produces a darker edge, which is not desirable on the lightest side of the tree.

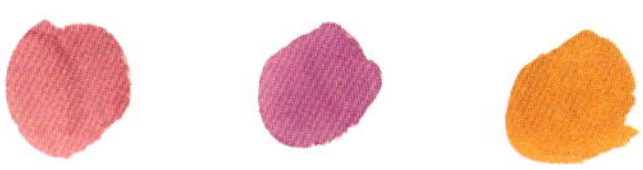

rose madder genuine

quinacridone magenta

quinacridone gold

With a rigger, apply napthamide maroon to suggest branches. Dampen the base of the upper leaf clump, and then paint the branch, beginning at the hard edge of the lower clump and moving up to the wet area. This allows the added branch color to spread naturally.

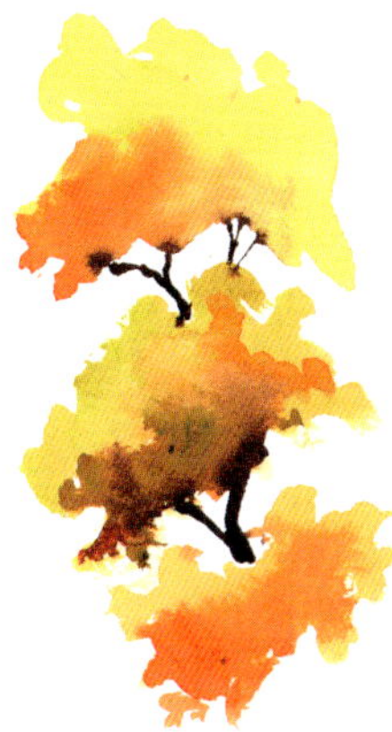

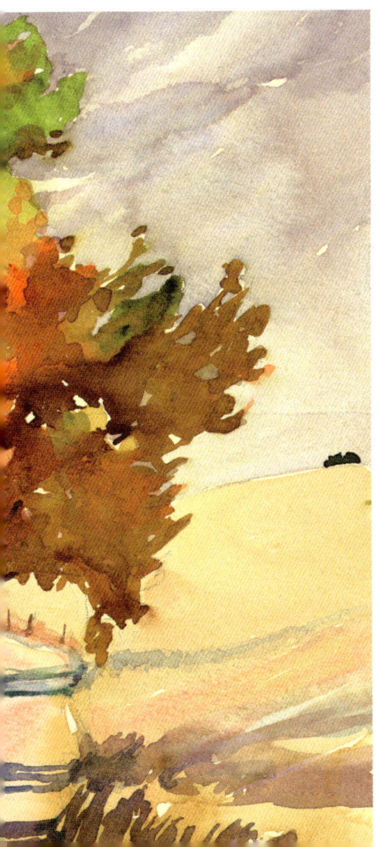

5 Glazing and finishing Stand back to assess the overall impact of the painting. Glazing the shaded areas with variations of the nonstaining, transparent trio (cobalt blue, rose madder genuine, aureolin yellow) is a perfect way to increase the color and value contrast without losing the beauty of the underlying mixes. Beginning at the left lower branches, apply a mix of rose madder genuine and aureolin yellow to the shaded areas. When applying glazes, use the tip of a flat brush to make zigzag strokes along with some flat, smooth washes. Care must be taken to avoid disturbing the dried pigments below. Notice how the areas brighten and darken. Cobalt blue is useful where there is no concern about turning the area too neutral; e.g., blue over orange, or too cool. The cast shadows on the ground can take the cool blues and lavenders. After a few more touches to the sky and distant hill, and some playful punches of cobalt blue, the painting feels finished.

Sweet gum tree This beautiful sweet gum tree has upwardly arcing branches and deep, multi-tiered, maplelike leaves that droop slightly toward the ground.

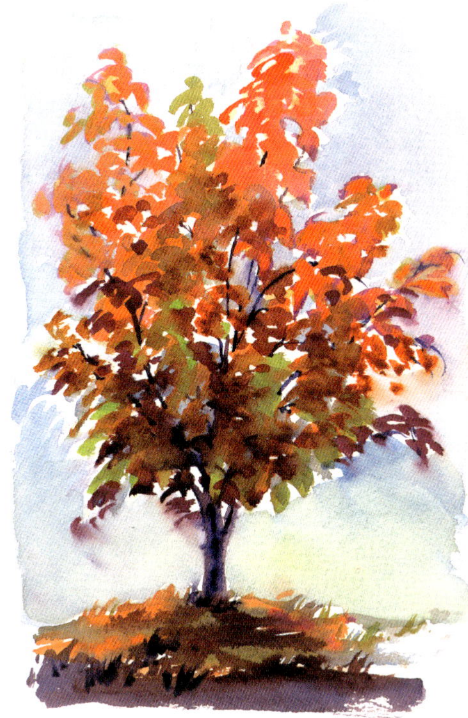

A dancing brushstroke with a downward lilt will work for the leaf shapes.

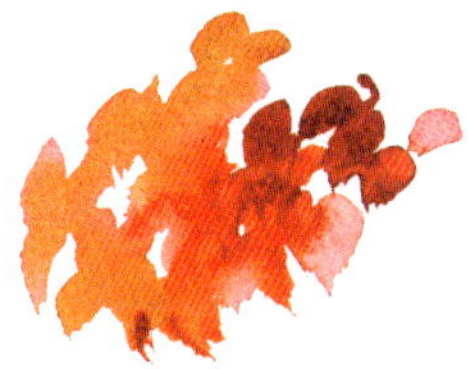

Modifications to the square tetradic color scheme can create an interesting palette variation.

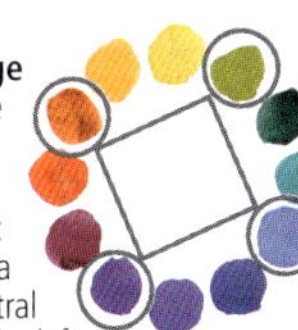

red-orange
1. cadmium orange
2. quinacridone sienna

yellow-green
1. green gold
2. azo yellow (aureolin), shifted

red-violet
1. napthamide maroon—a near semineutral
2. carbazole violet (dioxazine) shifted to the left
3. opera (Holbein), shifted to the right to allow the mix with quinacridone sienna

cyan
cobalt blue

SOME THINGS TO CONSIDER

- Bright, high-chroma hues of yellow to red are the primary hallmarks of the fall foliage—and a good origin for deciding on color scheme.
- Fall foliage in full, side sunlight offers the best opportunities to view and paint strong contrasts and form.
- Close examination of the tree's structure provides clues for painting gesture, stroke, and brush type.
- Always look for the undercolor first. Be sure to leave some of it unpainted.
- Gestures and confident brushstrokes are more important than detail in communicating foliage.
- Backlighting offers a wonderful opportunity to illustrate the subtle veining of a leaf.
- Look for the dark and deep red within the mass of green.
- In a warm subject like fall foliage, areas to be in shade can be painted darker and warmer right from the start in anticipation of later glazes. These colors will glow through the shade as the reflected light warms their tones.
- When painting leaves against the sky, leave some white edges outside the leaf shapes for better contrast with the sky, and an effect of light glitter.

Landscapes and trees

From small, tightly enclosed gardens to vast, open wildernesses, a wide variety of landscapes are available for painting. Regardless of their scale, these richly colored scenes offer exciting opportunities for working on the portrayal of space and depth. This illusion can be achieved through a variety of techniques illustrated and explained on the following pages.

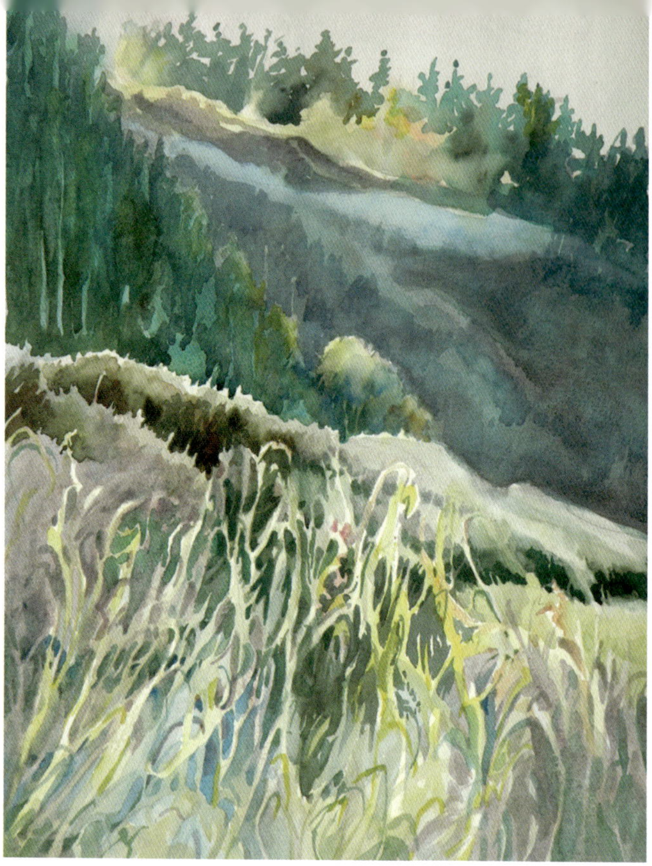

▶ *Pacific Shoals*
JAN HART
There are several ways to achieve the impression of great distance. In this painting, the author uses color, size relationships, and detail. The foreground foliage is larger and more detailed, and it contains greens that are warmer (mixed with more red and orange). The distant evergreens are cooler (more blue in the mix), smaller, and painted without detail. Overlapping shapes contribute to the sense of depth as well.

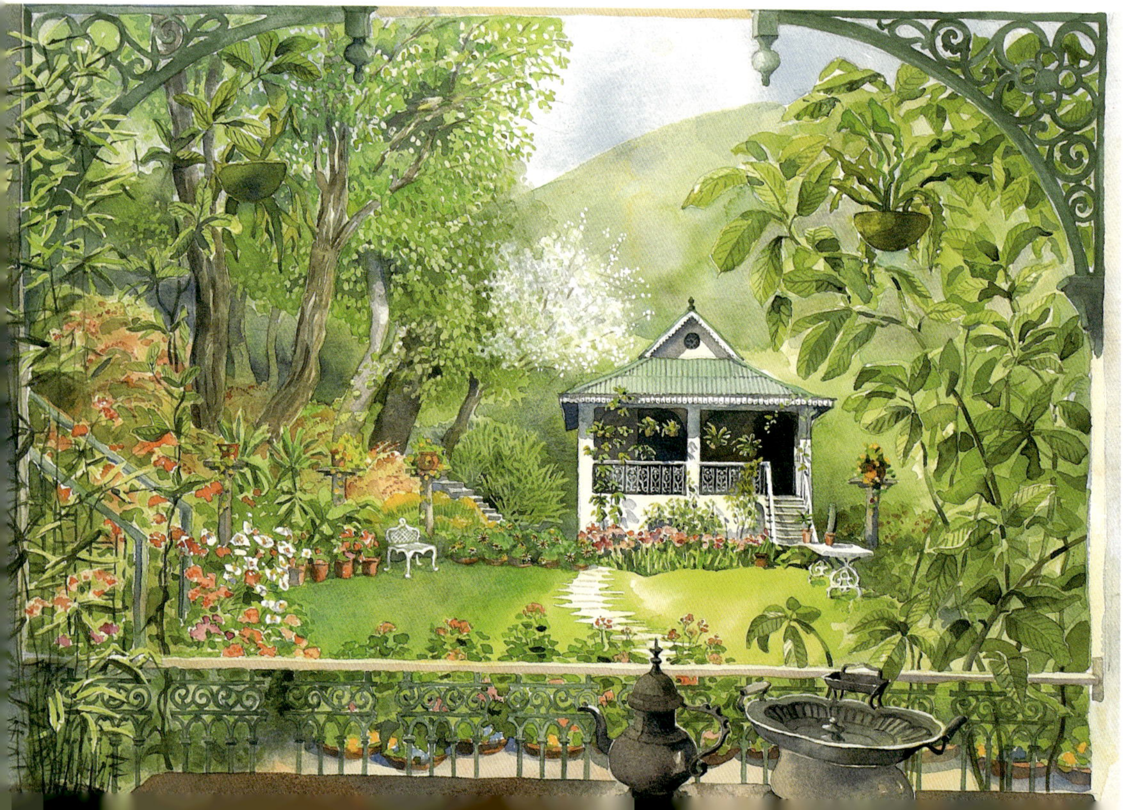

◀ *Indian Paradise* MOIRA CLINCH
Over a lemon yellow underwash, the artist chose to use primarily phthalo green mixed with cobalt or ultramarine blue for a uniform bright green color palette that plays against the red and magenta flowers. Distance was achieved through overlapping shapes. Note how the warm neutrals in the foreground help to accentuate the greens.

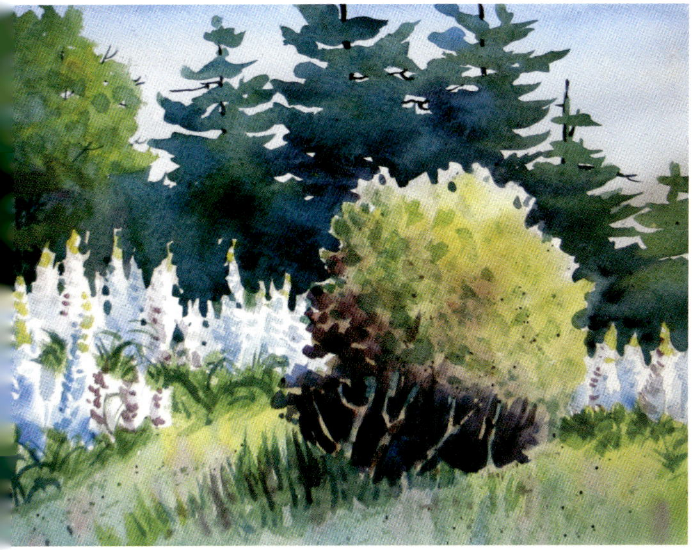

▲ *Backyard in June* Joan Gregory
Overlapping shapes, different degrees of detail, and changing color values and chromas accentuate the illusion of great distance in this three-color split-complementary painting. Using just aureolin yellow, permanent magenta, and ultramarine blue, the artist has created a lively foreground against a darker, cooler background. Note the very effective use of permanent magenta in the foreground bush.

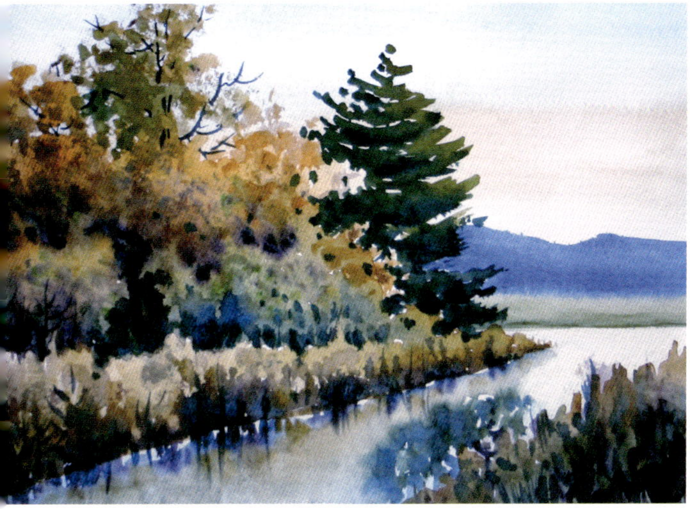

▲ *Mary's Point III* Joan Gregory
The artist uses a four-color tetrad for this lush fall painting. A skillful combination of sap green, cadmium orange, permanent magenta, and cobalt blue creates harmony and unity. Note how warm magenta and orange enliven the foreground to contrast with the quiet, cool background.

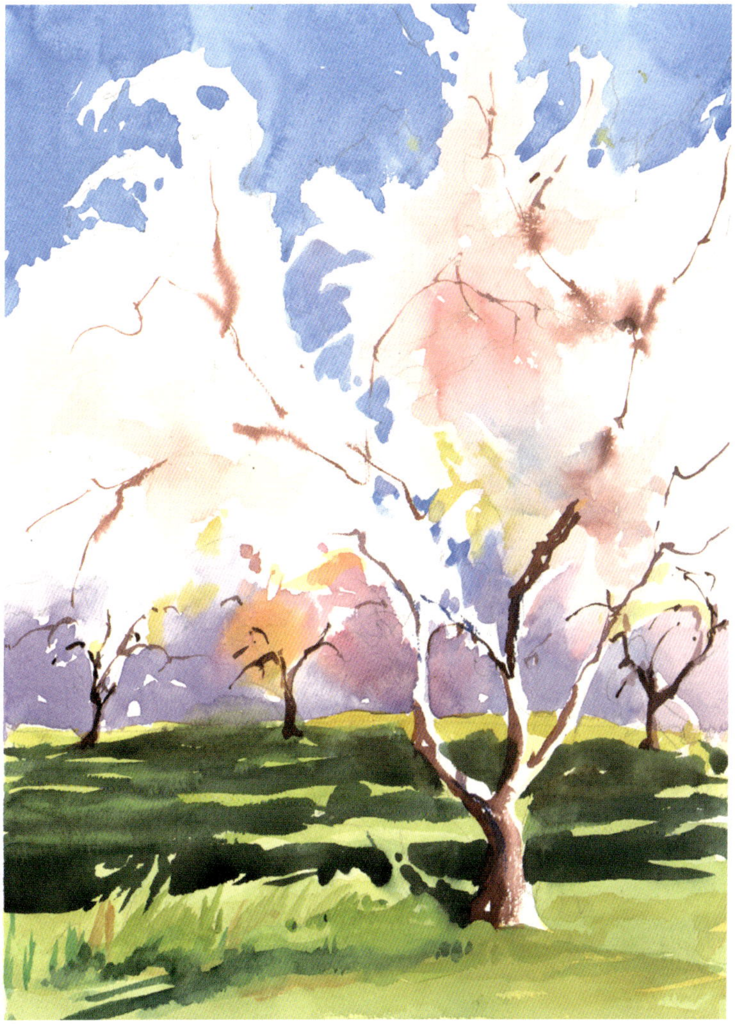

▲ *Spring Ballet* Jan Hart
Spring offers a wonderful opportunity to paint white apple blossoms against the blue of the sky, Here the foreground tree takes center stage with suggestions of other trees in the background. The four-color square tetrad comprises ultramarine turquoise, cobalt blue, quinacridone magenta, and azo yellow (aureolin) brought this painting to life. Note that some napthamide maroon also was added in the tree limbs and trunks.

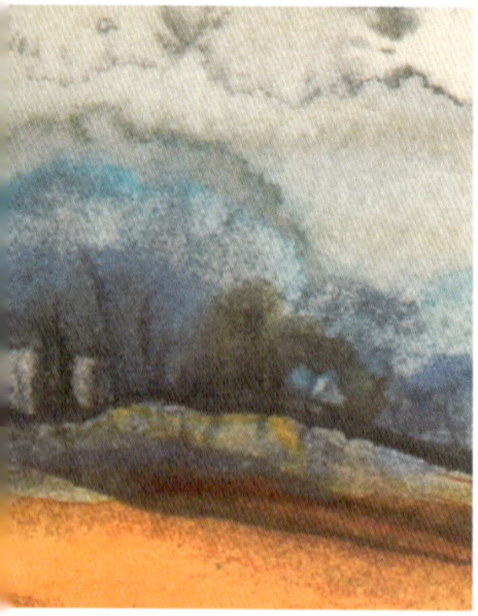

▼ ***Golden Field*** Judy Linnell
As in her painting on page 18, the artist works wet into wet, in this case using washes of quinacridone gold, brown madder, indigo, and cerulean blue. She takes advantage of the direct, immediate approach and exploits the semi-abstract effects. Notice the hard edges at the bottom of the clouds, where clean water has been dropped onto dry washes to create backruns. She describes her method as one that relies on "happy accident" suggestion rather than literal description.

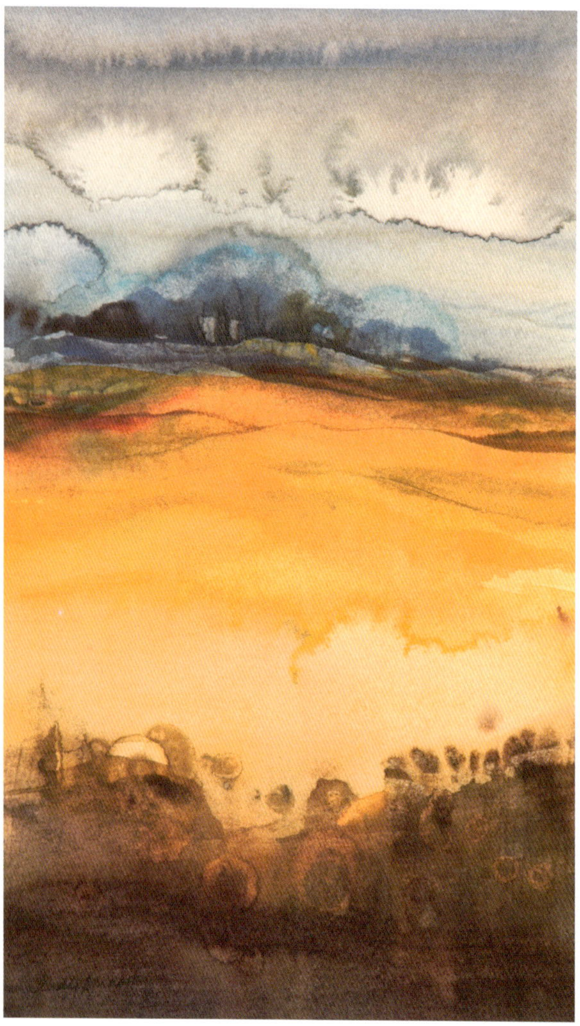

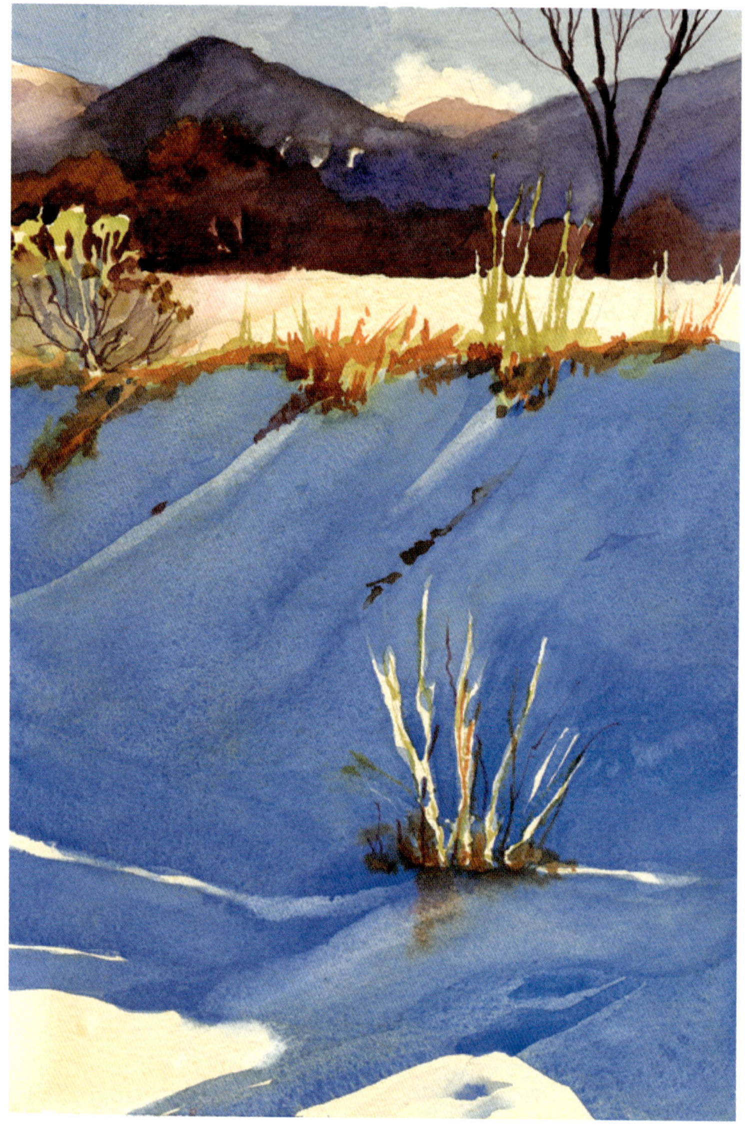

▲ ***Taos Snowbank*** Jan Hart
Using a "loose" split-complement of magenta, red-orange, and yellow opposed by cobalt blue, the author focuses attention on the brilliant cobalt blue-shadowed snowbank, accentuating it with aureolin yellow and quinacridone sienna accents. The warmer, darker background appears distant because of the lighter overlapping foreground vegetation.

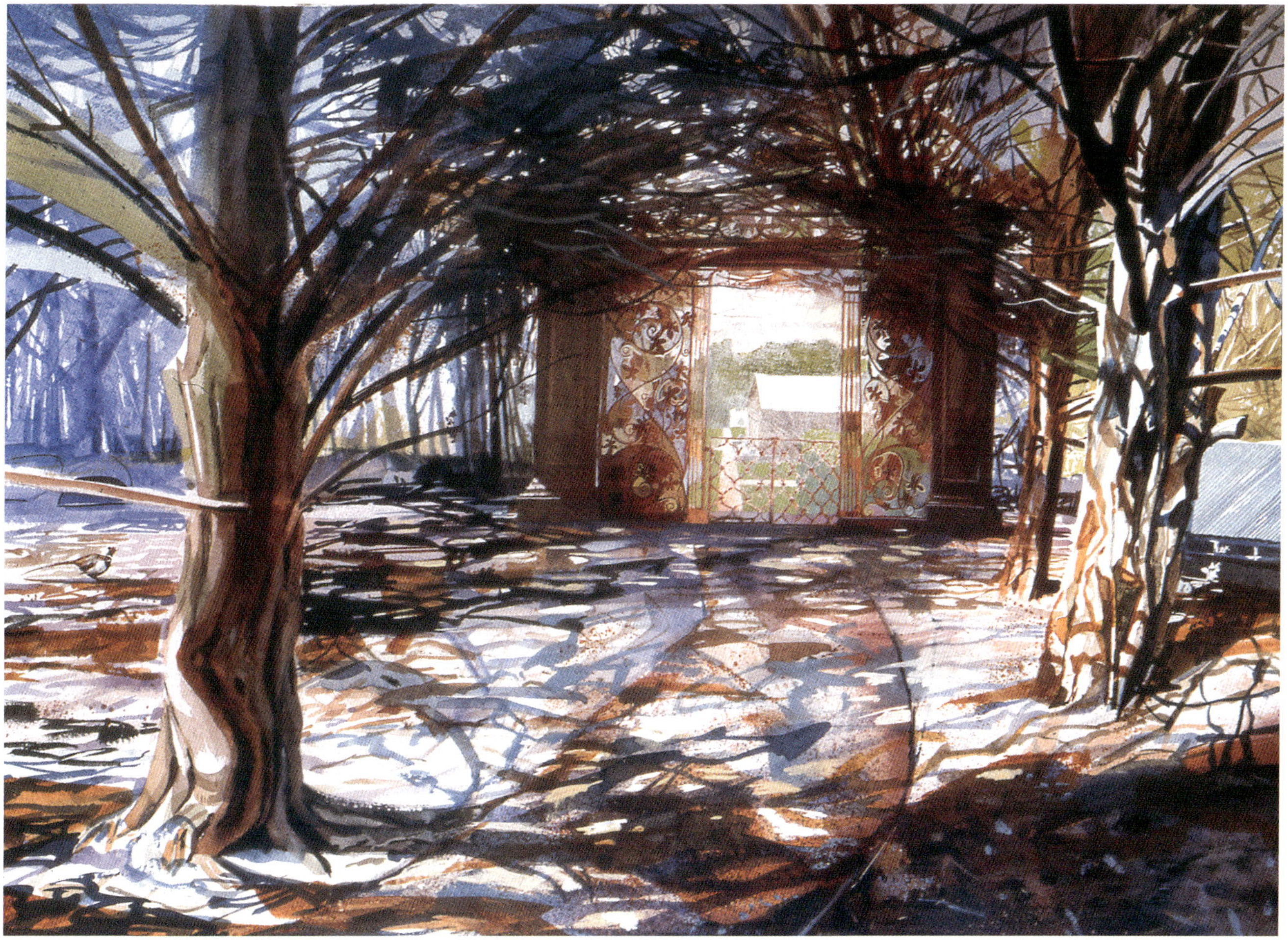

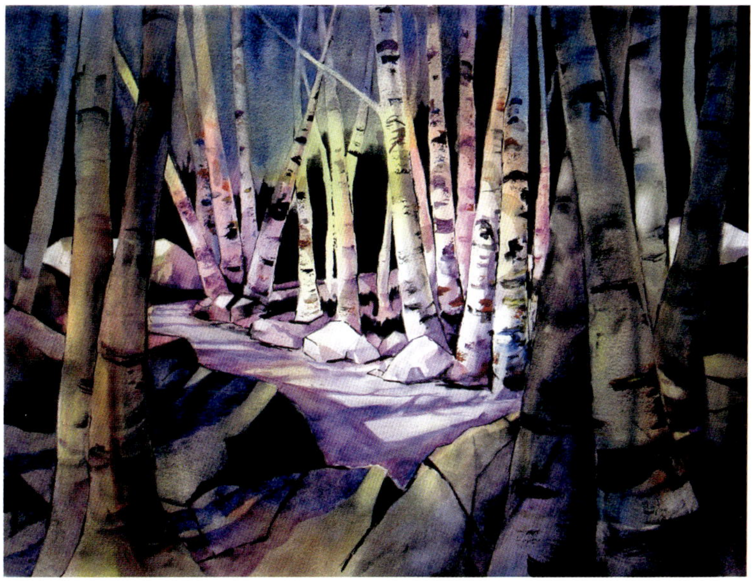

▲ *Through Trees* JULIAN BRAY
Most painters have their own personal palettes. As in many of Bray's paintings, this palette relies on the contrast of Prussian blue and burnt sienna. In terms of composition, he wanted to create a sense of deep perspective, so he used the receding scale of trees leading to an off-center gate opening, which, when viewed closely, is full of rich decoration.

◀ *Aspens 4* HILARY PAGE
In a theme of sunlight in the deep forest, the artist uses bright magentas, violets, and blues opposed by yellow-green in the focal area, with darkly glazed trees providing strong contrasts. Note the extensive use of texture attained by lunar black, lunar earth, cobalt violet deep, and cobalt violet.

Portraits and figures

Painting a human figure involves an intimacy with the subject like no other which makes it especially difficult to paint a figure or portrait that meets our own expectations. Taking it in steps helps. When someone complains that the only figure he or she can do is a stick figure—good! That's a great start! Beginning with a stick figure that represents the skeleton is a perfect way to initiate a drawing. The same is true for a portrait. The first step is to draw the skull and work out from there. Musculature, skin, and features all come later.

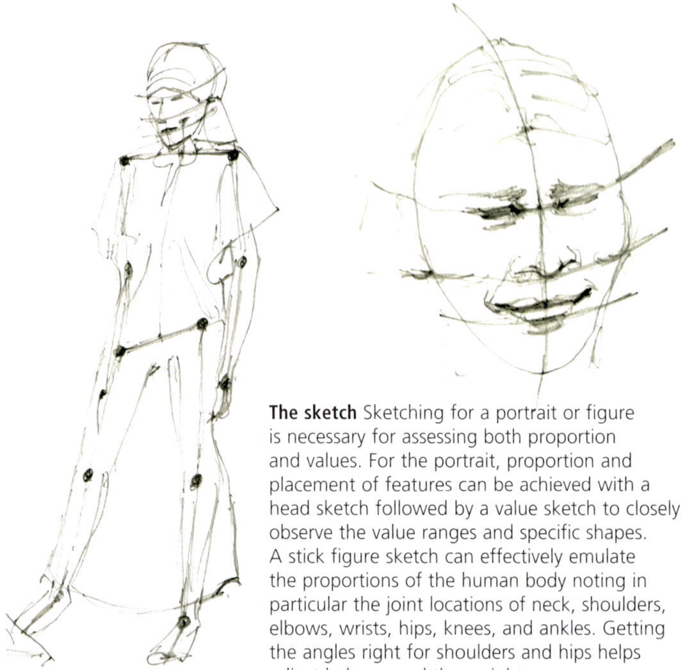

The sketch Sketching for a portrait or figure is necessary for assessing both proportion and values. For the portrait, proportion and placement of features can be achieved with a head sketch followed by a value sketch to closely observe the value ranges and specific shapes. A stick figure sketch can effectively emulate the proportions of the human body noting in particular the joint locations of neck, shoulders, elbows, wrists, hips, knees, and ankles. Getting the angles right for shoulders and hips helps adjust balance and the weight.

CHOOSING A SKIN TONE PALETTE

A near-primary palette is a favorite for the portrait painter, using warmer colors for the lit areas and cooler hues for the shade. The paint choices depend upon the skin color. Note the importance of the relationships of the reds to blues in each portrait. Avoid mixing together complementary colors or you'll create gray, lifeless skin.

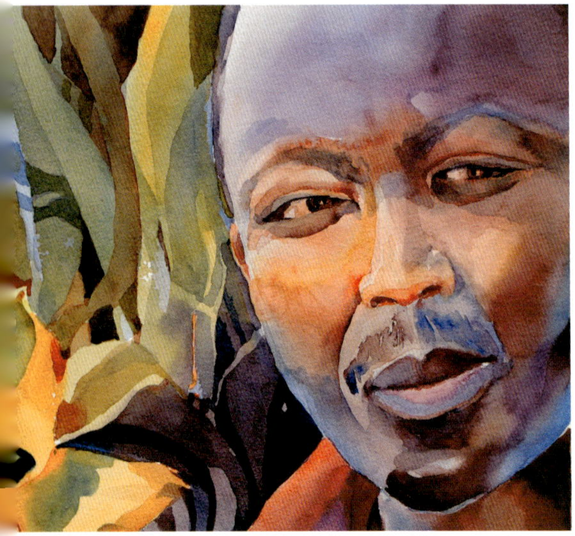

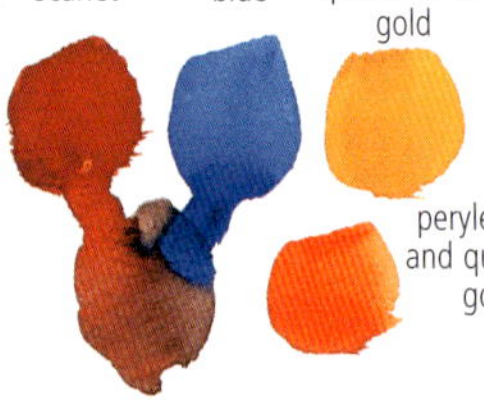

African skin tones A primary palette that combines cool red with warm blue works well for dark skin. The cool red and warm blue mix to a nice purple. An ideal palette would be perelene scarlet or alizarin crimson, ultramarine blue, and quinacridone gold.

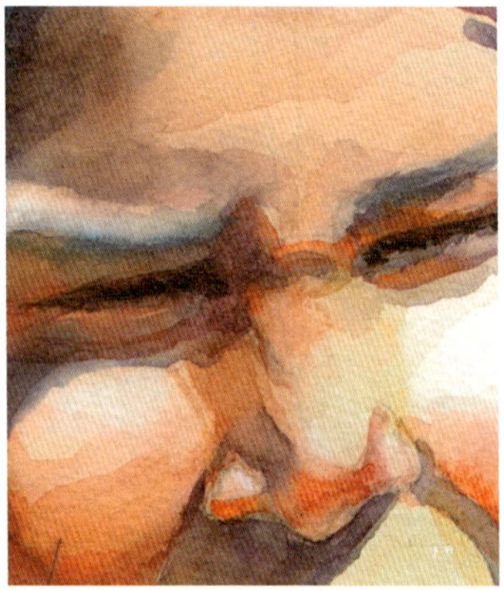

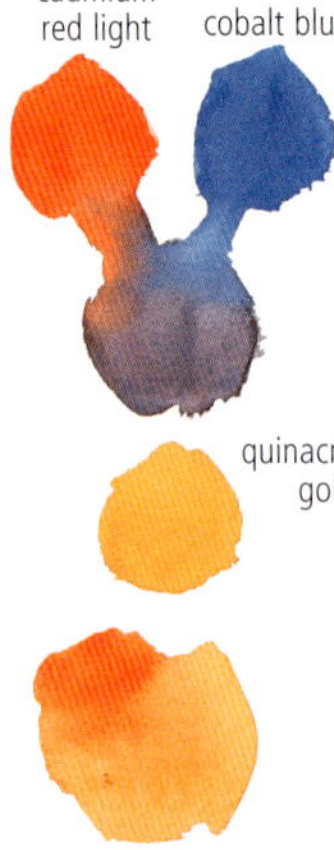

Indian, Hispanic, and Asian skin tones The warmer tones of mid-brown skin can be especially receptive to warm red and mid blue, such as cadmium red, cobalt blue, quinacridone gold, or raw sienna.

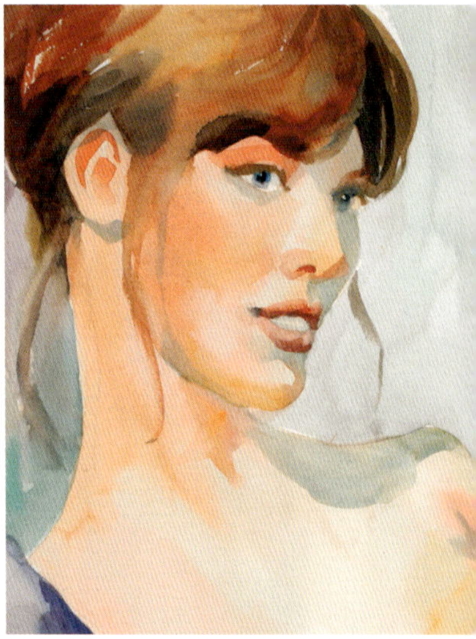

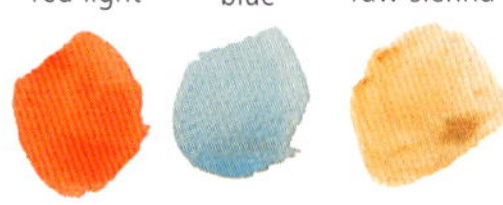

Caucasian skin tones A quick study of a young woman offered an opportunity to use a split-complementary color scheme featuring cerulean blue and raw sienna played against hot cadmium red light, which was carried into all of her features. Note the effective use of cerulean blue for the shadows and shading.

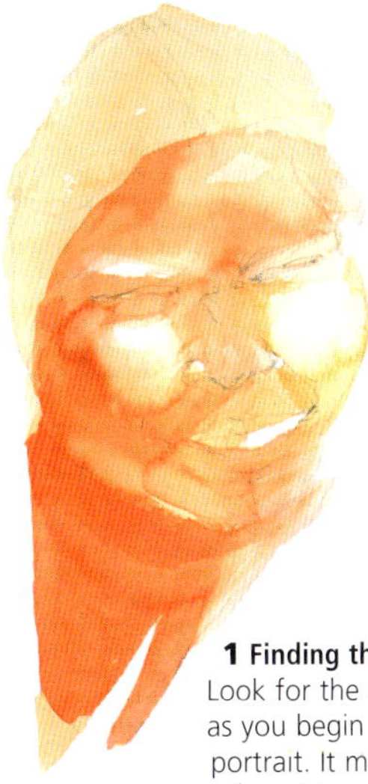

1 Finding the undercolor Look for the undercolor as you begin your portrait. It may be a yellow, blue, or even green—a glimmer of reflection from the sky or a strong golden hue from warm sunlight. Often darker skin colors have a cool undercolor, whereas lighter skins may contain warmer hues. The selected undercolor can be painted over the entire head and neck, including the hair.

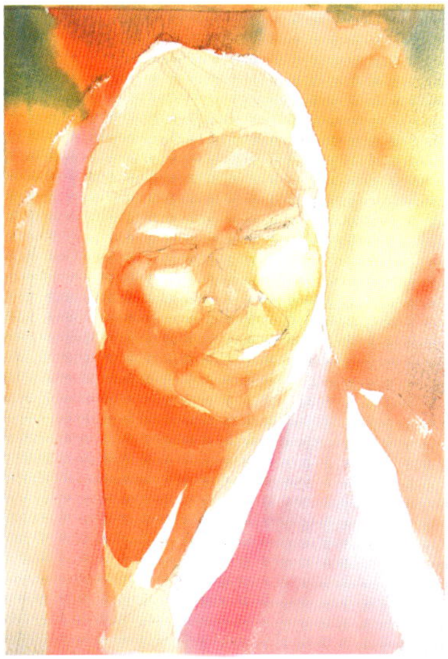

2 Study the planes Before you study, add some rough colors into the background so your eye can see the entire value range without the distracting whites of the paper. All the planes of the face are directed upward toward the sky or downward toward the ground, or in between. The upward-facing planes may reflect the sky or sunlight (forehead, cheek bones, and nose), whereas the downward-facing areas may be shaded and also receiving reflected light to become even warmer (under the nose, jaw, and brow). Depending upon the lighting, some features may cast shadows, which will appear cooler.

SOME THINGS TO CONSIDER

- It is more important to get the shadow patterns right than details such as eye color.
- A value/composition study can help acquaint the artist to the subject and prepare the mind for how to paint it.
- When you paint a portrait or a figure, think about shapes—not about features.
- A hand gesture used to describe the flow of flesh can be the basis of your brushstrokes.
- Paint portraits or figures in angled sunlight to see the forms and contrasts.
- Always look for the undercolor first. And then, when painting over it, be sure to leave some of it unpainted.
- When adding a figure to the landscape, take care that your figure's size, shading, and shadows fit correctly with the landscape.

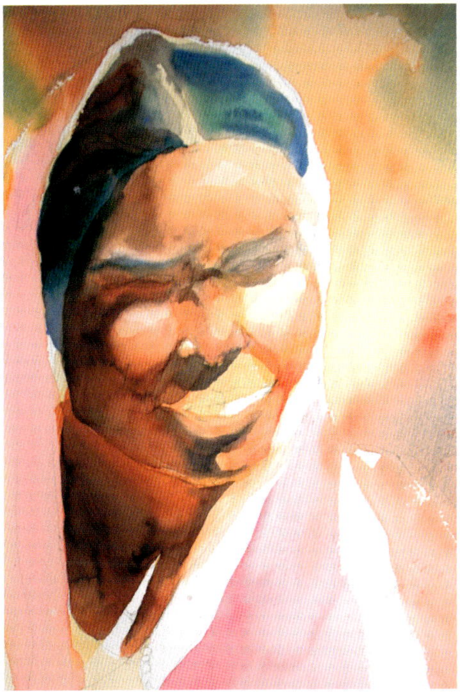

3 Creating shadow Selecting an appropriate color for the lighted side of the face, the application can now begin with the lightest upward-facing area—typically cheeks, above brows, upper nose, upper lip, and upper chin. After the washes are dry, the shaded side of the face can be painted and molded with darker tones—mixes of the red and blue). The planes that have actual cast shadows get the darkest wash, with attention given to their exact shapes.

4 Finishing touches The finishing touches are often the most fun. Using primarily the transparent non-staining paints, small corrections, alterations, and details are added. More definition is added to the background and then it is glazed to create depth.

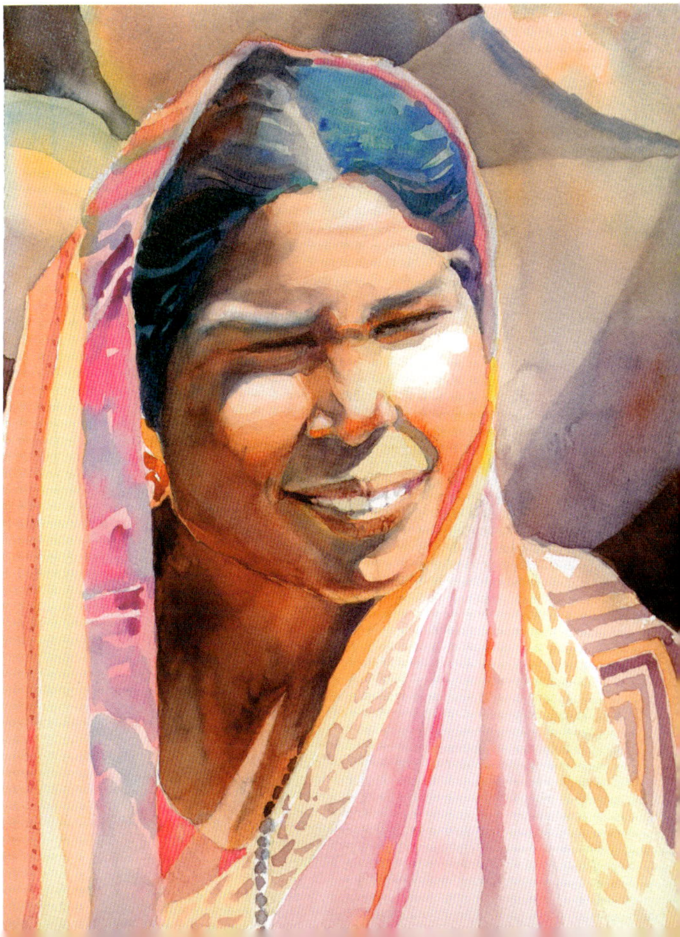

Portraits and figures

The figure is always the center of interest in a painting. We cannot avoid it. We relate to each other through eyes, which can be emphasized or not, depending upon the artist's intention. When painting portraits and figures, color, values, and lighting must be carefully considered. From cool or quiet neutral passages to pounding rhythms and hot, sultry darks the spaces beyond and around the figure tell the story.

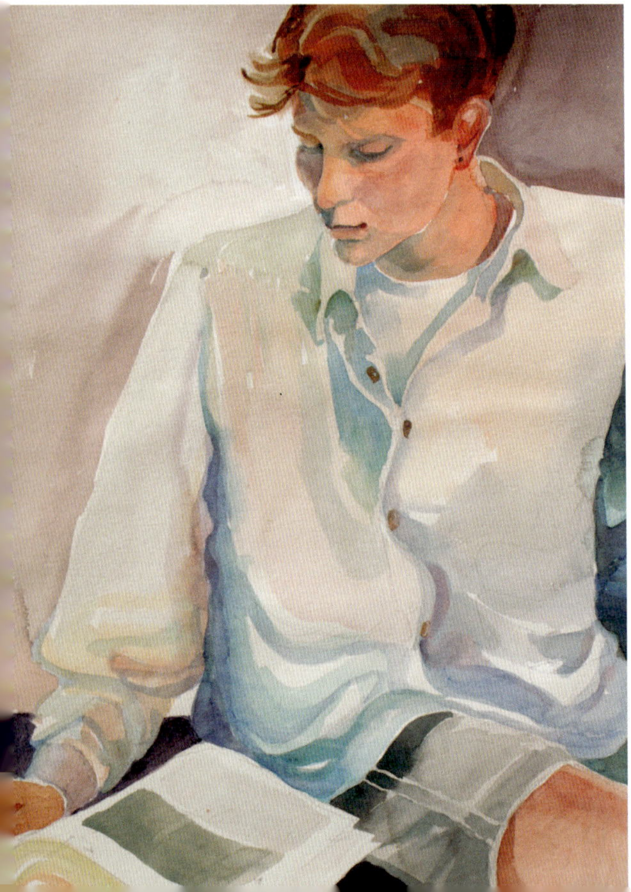

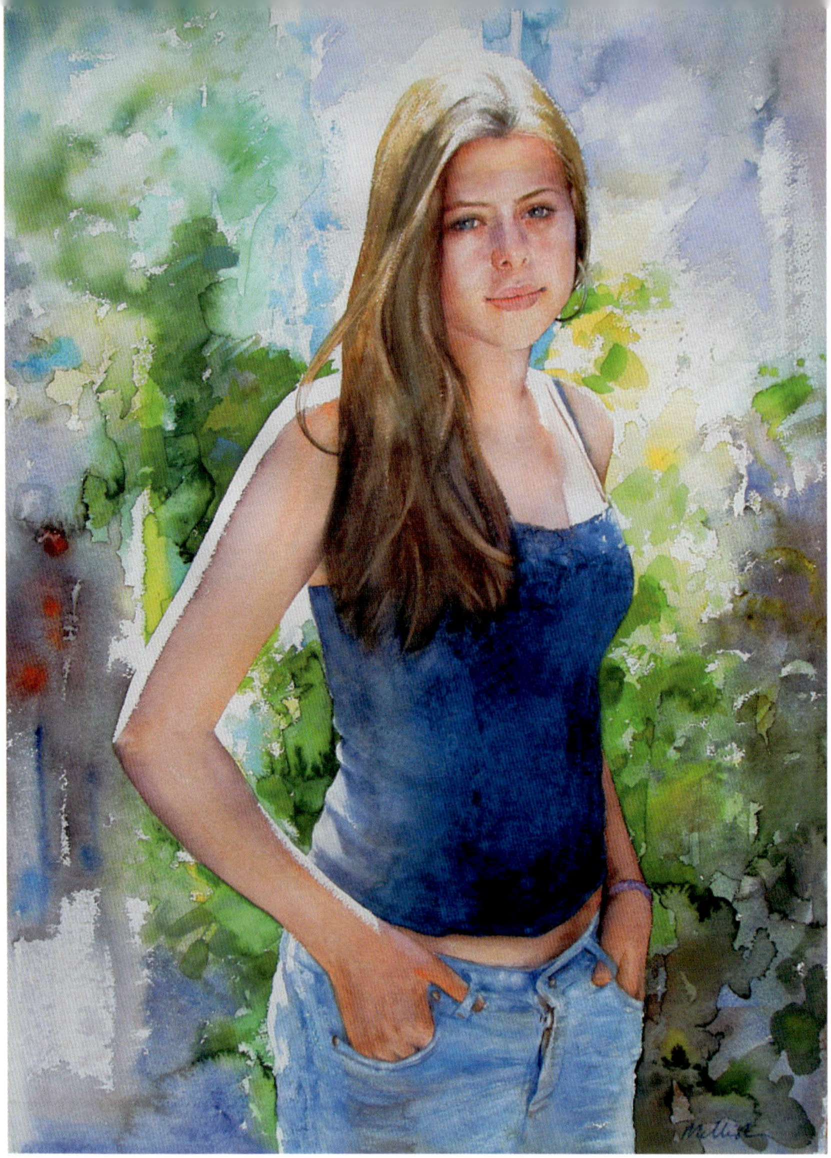

◀ *Jonathan* JAN HART
The author's son posed for this figurative study that portrays his quiet and contemplative demeanor. The diagonal composition plays the book against his attentive concentration. The cool and neutral colors help to convey calm and play against the warm reds and oranges that guide the viewer's eye around the painting.

▲ *Lauren* GLYNIS BARNES-MELLISH
Lauren stands still and calm in the moment while loosely analogous colors ranging from bright yellow to cyan play around her, suggesting sunlight, youth, and activity. Note how the artist plays the warm skin tones against turquoise and cerulean at her thumbs, chin, and eyes. The wet-into-wet background contributes life and vibrancy, while suggestions of red bring the viewer's eye back to Lauren's eyes.

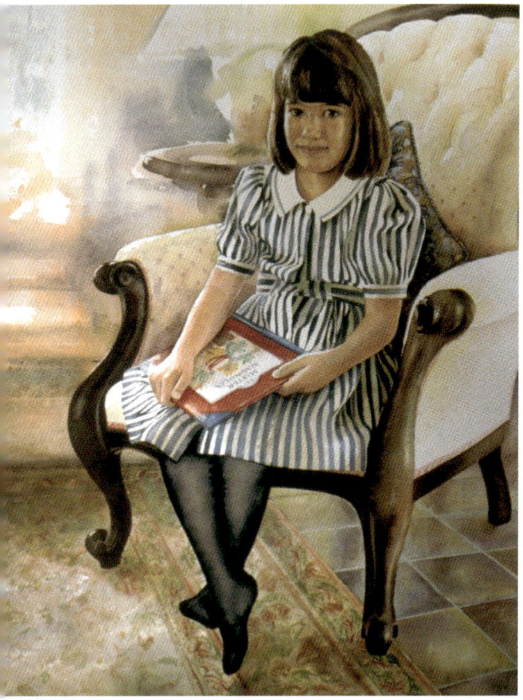

◀ *Lucy*
GLYNIS BARNES-MELLISH
The formal setting and quiet colors suggest the calmness of Lucy's personality. Using mostly neutrals and cool colors, the artist further communicates the girl's demeanor with the red book, noting importance and relevance.

▶ *Cassie*
GLYNIS BARNES-MELLISH
Bathing a subject in strong light is an effective portrait technique. Here the large mass of Cassie's hair, painted in multiple glazes of color that have been built up after each layer has completely dried, plays actively against the contrasting subtle tones of her face. The almost whispered use of warm yellows and oranges helps attract the viewer's interest to her quiet features.

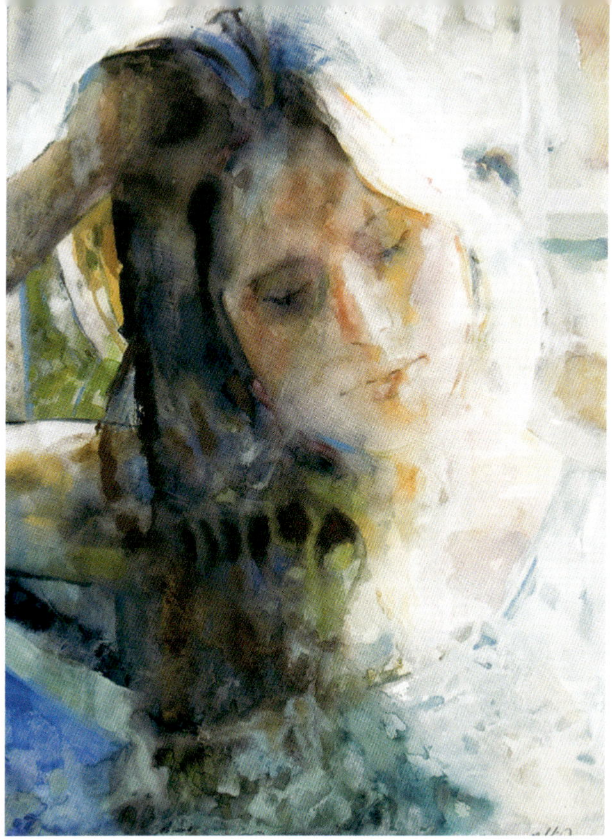

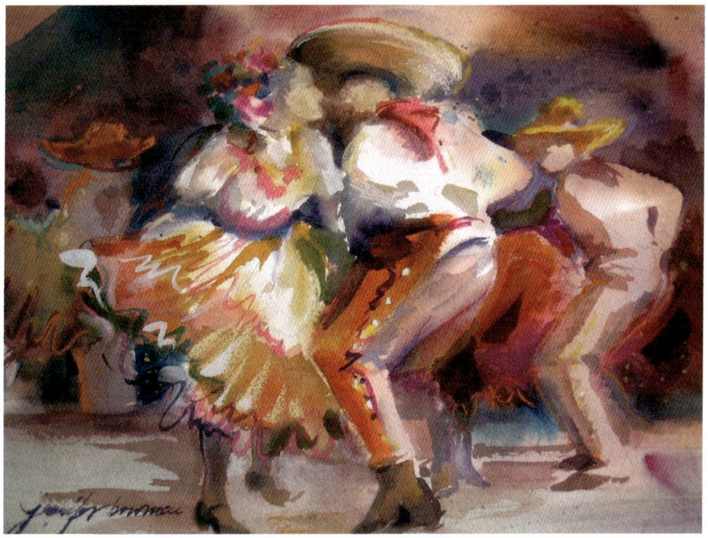

▲ *Ballet Dancers* JENNIFER BOWMAN
Selecting hot, bright analogous colors and repeating shape rhythms, make this study appear to pulse. Note how the path of cooler blue helps unite the dancers. The sharper gestures of pastel add their shimmer and punch to this painting in motion. See the placement of hot red-orange next to cool blue-green for complementary sizzle!

▶ *Tangoheat* GARTH ALLAN
A loose analogous color scheme is perfect for this sultry figurative painting featuring the hottest reds along with color wheel neighbors yellow and red-violet. The low color key also contributes to the darkly erotic mood. Note the punctuation of skin lights that carry the eye diagonally to be resolved with rectilinear elements in opposite corners.

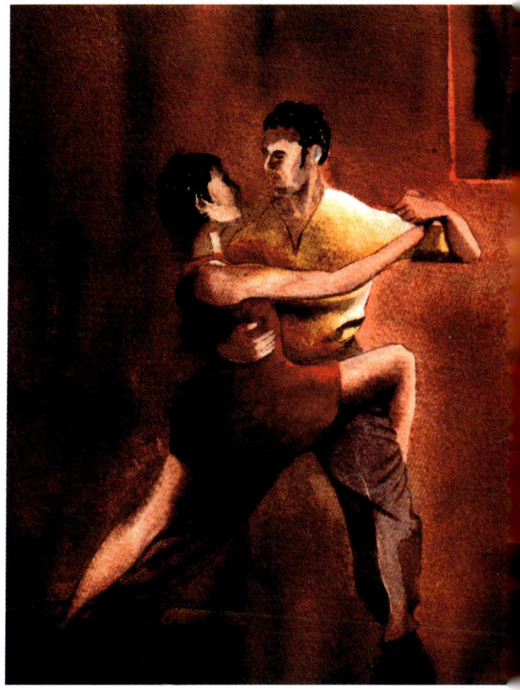

Paints, brushes, and other equipment

Over the next few pages, you'll find information about tools and equipment that will help you make the most of your colors. The tools and accoutrements used by artists are as individual and varied as the artists themselves. It is important to find what suits you best, but do try new things occasionally to keep growing as an artist. The basics for watercolor painting are paints, brushes, paper, and water. Beyond these, you will discover your individual preferences.

PALETTES AND WATER CONTAINERS

There are all kinds of palettes available online and through art supply stores. If you use a lot of different pigments for different uses, try a palette that contains at least 30 wells, along with an extra color palette that has another 15 wells for less frequently used and specialty paints. If you are preparing a large quanitity of a mix or need to keep it for a little while, then you can keep the mix in a small, screw-top jar.

Always have clean water jars so that you mix with clean water. Clean, recycled plastic containers work well in the studio. If you have two containers, you can use one to clean brushes after a wash and the other to wet the brush for the next stroke. There are collapsible containers available for plein-air painting.

TUBES OR PANS?

Tube paints Paint straight from the tube is highly concentrated and produces the most vibrant washes and mixes. When the paint hardens it can be revitalized with a quick spritz of water a few minutes before painting. Some artists feel happier approaching a painting with the feeling that they have plenty of paint to use and play with, so they squeeze the entire tube into its place in their palette and let it dry. Others prefer to squeeze only a little of each color at a time. Some paints contain a honey binder that does not dry out as much as gum arabic but will dry completely with time.

Some artists like to keep their paints moist by covering the palette box after use or by using closeable plastic containers for individual paints. If mold develops on the paint, wash it off thoroughly or replace the paint. You also can lightly rub the paper surface with denatured alcohol before painting to kill the mold spores.

Until you know your paints by sight, it is best to identify them by name and index number on your palette. A permanent fine point marker works well on plastic.

Dry pan paints Most of us begin painting with pan paints. You just open the manufacturer's box and wet the paint! Pans are great for painting while traveling, and they are easy to clean up, but they do require a bit more fussing to moisten and mix. The earth pigments and viridian, for example, form hard cakes that are difficult to work with. Some manufacturers are creating prefilled pans that you can drop into your paint box, or you can make your own selections and dry them out for easy transport.

ORGANIZING YOUR PALETTE

There are many ways of organizing your palettes and keeping track of your colors. You can place your paints in color families—reds, yellows, and blues—keeping extra spaces for special paints like neutrals. The landscape artist may include granulating paints to help dramatize textures. The colorist may use only the high-chroma synthetics.

Separate palettes Some artists prefer separate palettes for separate "types" of paint, for example, staining/permanent paints and sedimentary/opaque paints.

One palette Other artists prefer to keep their paints all together in one palette, using various means to keep track of them. A letter, or identifier, next to the color index name and number can indicate its main attribute, e.g., ST for staining. A separate list can identify the paint well location, color index name and number, and the paint's main attribute. A separate color wheel for each attribute can provide a painted example, relative complements, and color index name and number. Creating these color wheels can offer the greatest lesson (see "Color Wheels," page 14).

tubes full pans half pans boxed sets of pans

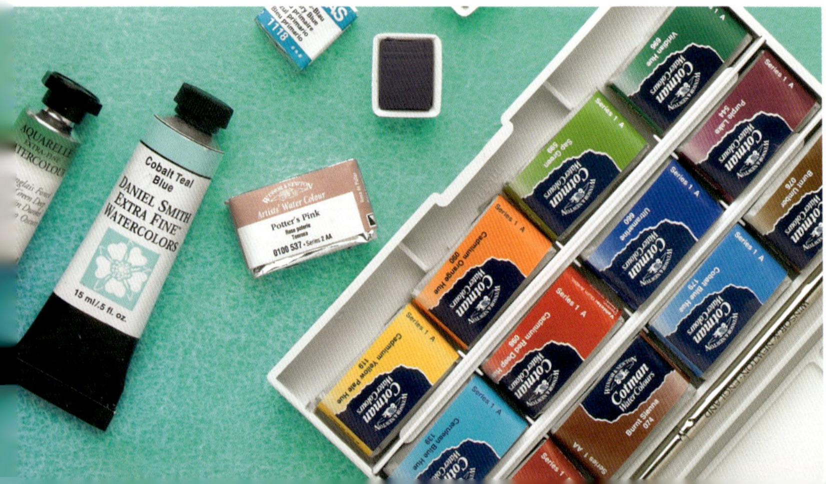

screw-top jar clean water jar plastic palettes

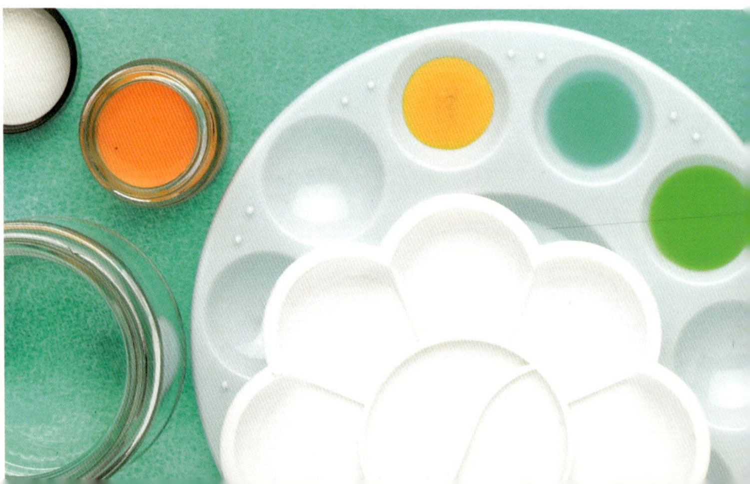

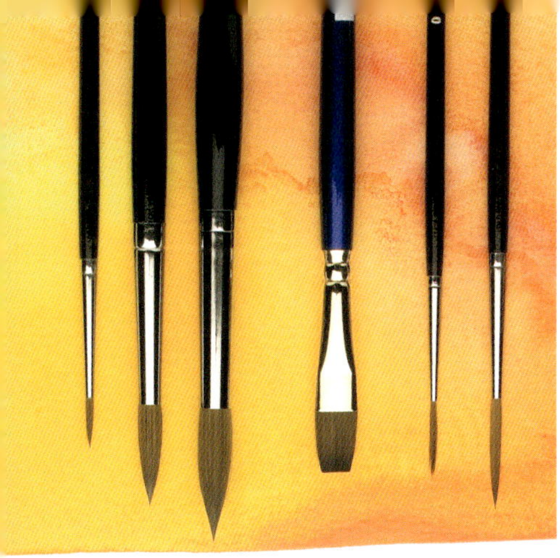

round brushes flat brush rigger brushes

BRUSHES

A watercolor brush is an artist's connection to the paper, and it hardly has changed since the first brushes originated centuries ago in Egypt and China. The most important thing to consider in your selection of a brush is how it fits with you and your painting style. There is a lot of marketing emphasis on Kolinsky sables. They used to be made from the tail of the male sable in winter and were reputed to hold the most water or paint. Mass production has confused the issue so that some "kolinsky" brushes are now made from the pelts of very different animals, both male and female. There also are brushes available that are a mix of synthetic and natural hairs. The synthetic hairs stand up to abuse and the natural hairs hold the water. Such brushes generally are inexpensive and durable—the kind that can be lost or replaced without traumatic concern. There are two basic types of watercolor brush that can do nearly all of your painting: flat and round. Others are designed for special applications.

Flat Flat brushes, also called "wash brushes," are chisel-shaped brushes with a straight edge that first became popular among Impressionist painters in the late 19th century. Because the edge is straight, this brush can provide a large variety of brushstrokes, lay down washes evenly, and even perform details with its sharp edge. Its rectangular shape and soft hairs that hold plenty of water also suit longer strokes and a more calligraphic range of brush marks.

Round With hairs that taper to a rounded point when wet, the round brush is the classic watercolor brush and is very useful for "gestural" painting. Because the water and paint are released unevenly at the point, these brushes are less useful than flat ones for laying down smooth washes over larger areas.

Special brushes A small round detail brush is useful for details; a rigger is good for small tree branches; a small flat wash brush can be used for small windows; a stiff scrubbing brush is great for lifting; and a small round brush for is perfect for your signature.

BRUSHWORK

Flat brushwork

Flat wash on dry paper The flat brush is made for flat washes. Apply consecutive horizontal strokes on a tilted surface. A good brush will cover a large area without running out of mix.

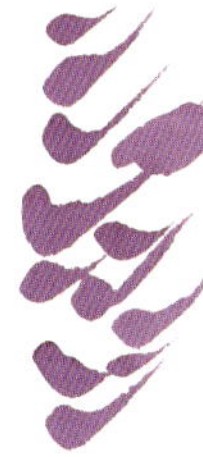

Dancing brushstroke Apply the loaded brush edge to the paper and sweep either up or downward to create interesing effects. Useful for trees and vegetation.

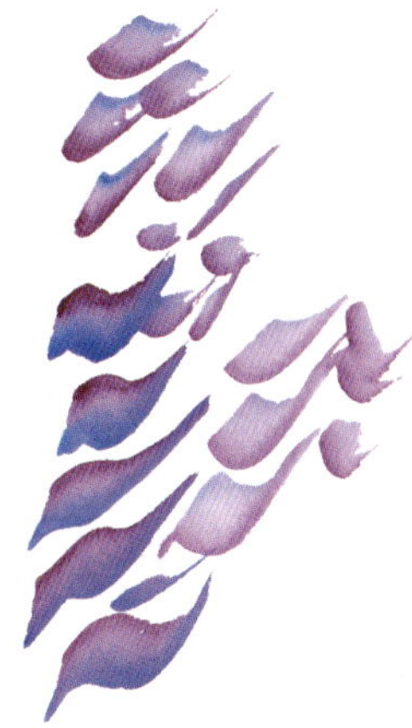

Two-color strokes Load one edge of a flat brush with one color, and then load the other edge with a different color, and make dancing brushstrokes.

Graded wash on dry paper Begin with a fully loaded brush on a tilted surface. After each brushstroke, dip the brush into water to dilute the mix, remove excess water by wiping over the container edge, and apply the next brushstroke.

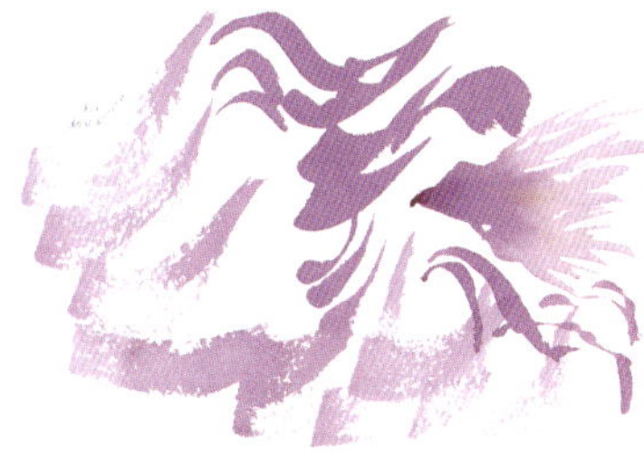

Drybrush Hold the very lightly loaded brush nearly parallel to the surface and move it quickly across the paper. Some paint is released onto the raised areas, creating a scumbled effect that is useful for depicting textured surfaces of wood and rocks.

Round brushwork

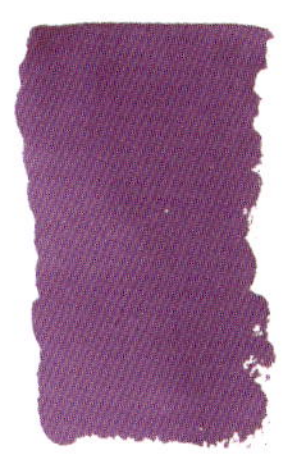

Flat wash A round brush tends to produce more irregularities in a flat wash because it concentrates the application toward the point.

Graded wash This fully loaded round brush creates a fine gradation.

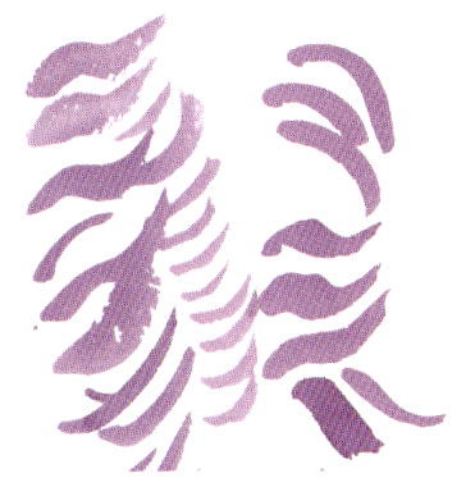

Dancing brushstroke Though the brushstrokes are not as varied in width, the round brush makes very consistent, narrow, pointed linework.

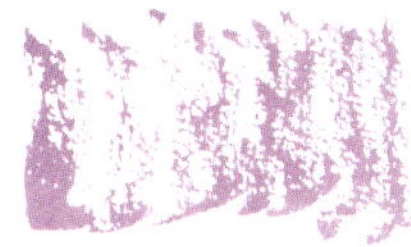

Drybrush A round brush works as well as a flat one.

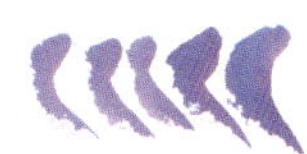

Two-color stroke Difficult, if not impossible, with a round brush.

Rigger brushwork

A rigger brush with a long ferrule is a wonderful addition to a painter's supplies. The artist can drag the loaded rigger across dry paper in a stop-start fashion for believable branches. The loaded rigger also can be used over a wet/damp wash to simulate branching in a shrub. The rigger also can be very useful for the drybrush technique.

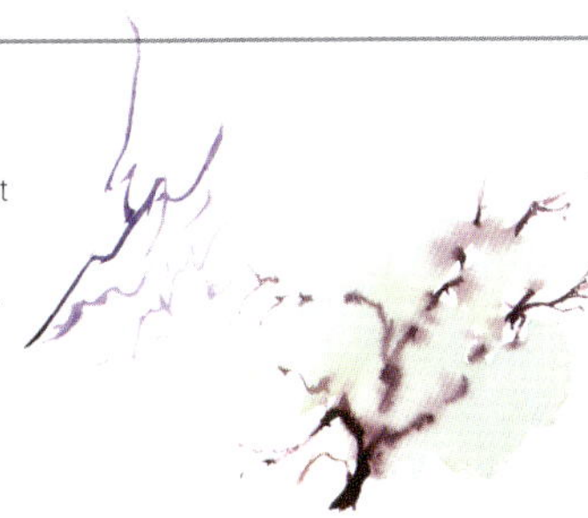

SOME THINGS TO CONSIDER

- Sometimes pigments and their vehicle have separated when you open a new tube, or the paint squirts out. Try unrolling the bottom of the tube as much as you can before you unscrew the cap to give the paint just a bit more room.
- If your tube paints become moldy in the palette, wipe them off, expose them to the air, and let them dry. You also can wipe your paper gently with diluted denatured alcohol before painting to make sure that the mold spores die.
- Loosen stuck caps on tubes by heating the area with warm water. Never use a flame, as the tube may be flammable.

OTHER USEFUL EQUIPMENT

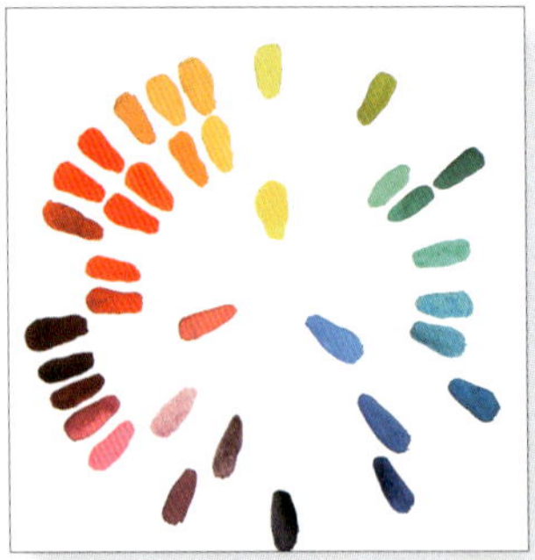

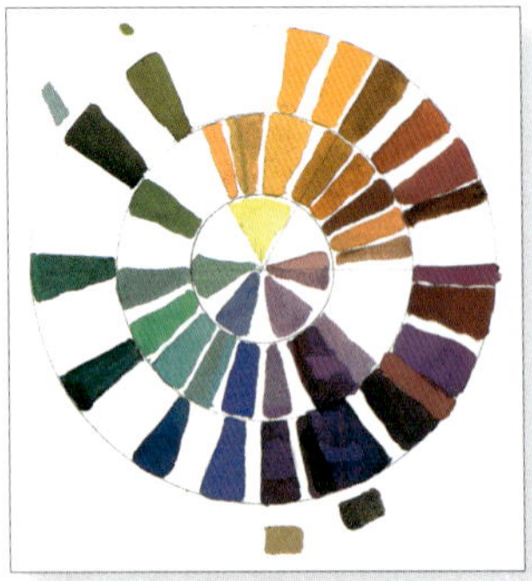

Color wheel Take your color wheel(s) with you when you paint. It is a good idea to keep any visual color wheels that you create very simple. There should be a lot of room for individual interpretation and substitution of pigments when something new and exciting comes out. When a new pigment comes out, add it to your existing color wheel or do a new color wheel—just to find out what your current thinking is.

Support boards Masonite, foam-core, and basswood boards are available in various sizes from most art supply stores. If traveling, try using a 16" x 20" (41cm x 51cm) piece of foam-core board that is cut in half on the 20" (51cm) side and then duct-taped back together (to create a hinge.) Tape your watercolor paper to the inside of one of the foam boards; the lightweight yet rigid foam-core is easy to travel with and keeps your watercolor paper flat.

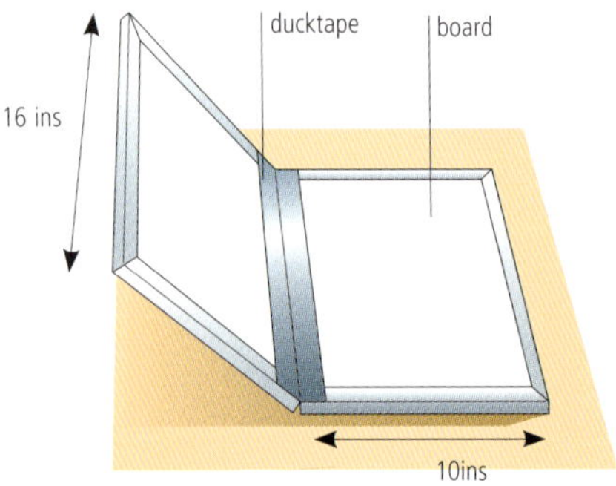

Red value square Color can confuse your perception of values. An intense color can appear lighter in value than it really is. Because value variation is one of the most important means of creating good design, artists must be able to see values as well as colors. A red, transparent Plexiglas square can help. You can order some pieces cut to 3" x 3" (7.5cm x 7.5cm) through your local glass shop. Or you can attach a small piece of red plastic to a blank slide mount. When you look through the red plastic, all colors are visible as values of light red to dark red. Why red? Red is the least likely color to appear in a landscape, so it is the best color to use as red objects will disappear when viewed through the filter.

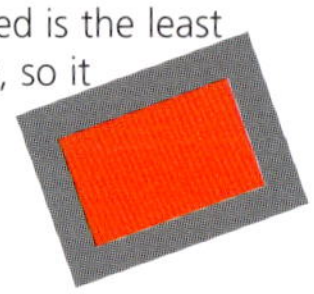

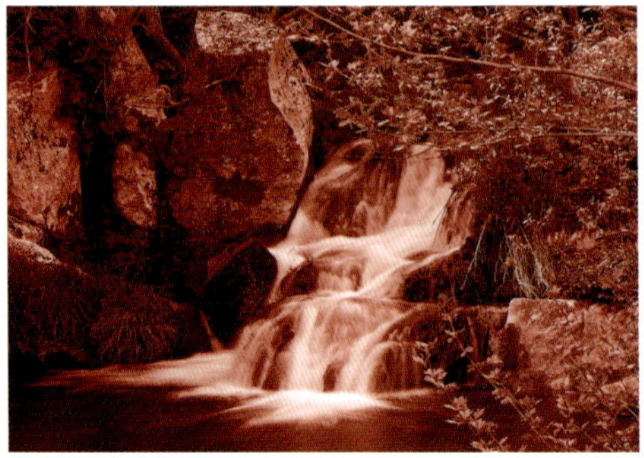

Note how the red filter enables you to see the darks and lights without the distraction of different color intensities.

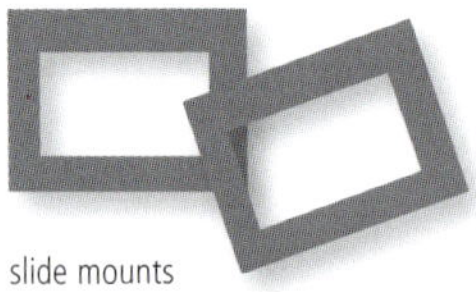

slide mounts

Viewfinder This is one of the artist's most important composition tools. Just throw a few empty slide mounts into your paint bag or make two L-shaped cardboard pieces. You can use them vertically or horizontally. When you are outdoors and tempted to paint everything you see, ask yourself what the most important thing is that you want to paint. Then crop everything else out by extending your arm and viewfinder toward the landscape. Look only at what is inside the viewfinder. Now draw and paint it. A camera can work the same way, but a viewfinder is lighter and easier to hold while you draw your value/composition sketch.

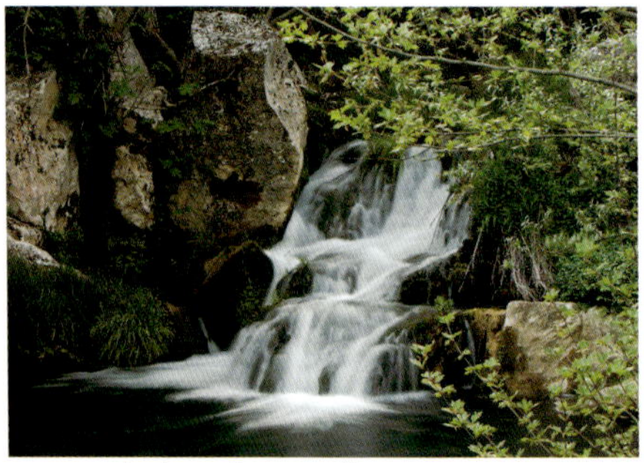

landscape "uncropped"

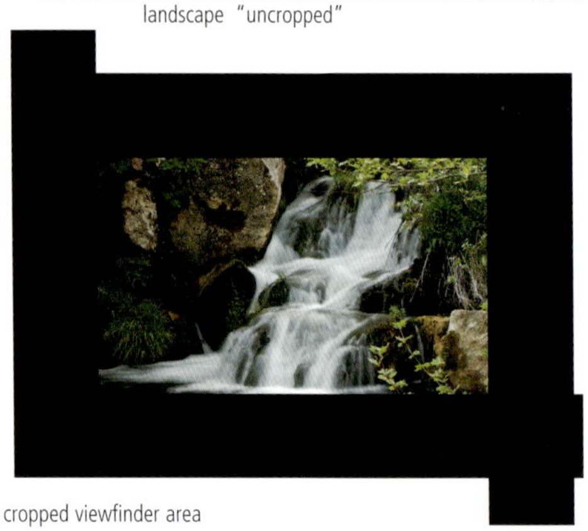

cropped viewfinder area

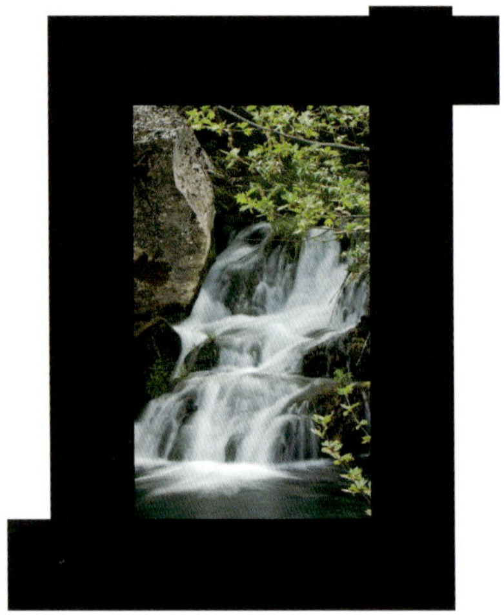

landscape with viewfinder, vertically oriented

WATERCOLOR MEDIUMS AND ADDITIVES

A watercolor medium is a substance that the artist can add to paint in order to achieve effects beyond those of pure transparent watercolor. Some mediums, like gum arabic and ox gall, already may be present in the paint, but if you add more, it will change the paint still more. Some watercolor artists prefer not to add anything to their paints, whereas others enjoy experimenting with mediums and additives. As always, you must decide for yourself.

Gum arabic Gum arabic is a water-soluble gum taken from Arabian acacia trees and used as a binder in watercolor and gouache paints. In the 20th century, synthetic glycol was developed and is used in some brands. You can add gum arabic to paint to increase the gloss and transparency, as well as to slow down the drying time. Keep in mind that it cannot change an opaque color into a transparent color.

Honey Honey is another traditional binder still used by some paint manufacturers that enables paints to dissolve rapidly in water, allowing for strong, vibrant washes.

Ox gall Ox gall is a liquid extracted from the gallbladder of a cow. It is used to reduce surface tension in paints, enabling them to spread out, or diffuse, more easily. Ox gall is especially useful for synthetic pigments that repel water. Some say that it also helps remove greasy spots from clothing. It is the presence of ox gall, or some other dispersant, that may make the paint diffuse aggressively or shoot outward when applied wet into wet. Ox gall or glycerin can be added to paints in very dry or hot weather to delay drying time.

Glycerin Glycerin is added to paints to soften the dried gum arabic and help it dissolve. It also can be added to water to slow drying time in hot climates.

Extender or filler Dextrin is a filler that often is used to thicken paint. To cut costs, some student-grade paints contain more filler than other grades.

Blending medium Blending medium slows the drying time of paints, which is particularly useful in hot or dry climates.

Masking fluid Masking fluid (also called "frisket," "Maskoid®," and "Miskit®") is similar to rubber cement. When applied to paper, it "masks" that area, enabling you to paint washes over it, secure in the knowledge that the masked area will remain untouched by pigment. Some artists employ masking fluid liberally, whereas others avoid it because of the hard edges left when the dried masking fluid is removed.

Lifting paint medium This medium primes the paper, enabling easier lifting of washes that have dried. It may prove useful for lifting clouds out of the sky, for example.

Granulation or texture medium This medium adds fine particles that give a mottled appearance to paints. It does not affect granulating pigments but adds granulation to normally transparent, nongranulating pigments.

Iridescent medium When mixed with paints, this medium adds a pearlescent or glitter effect.

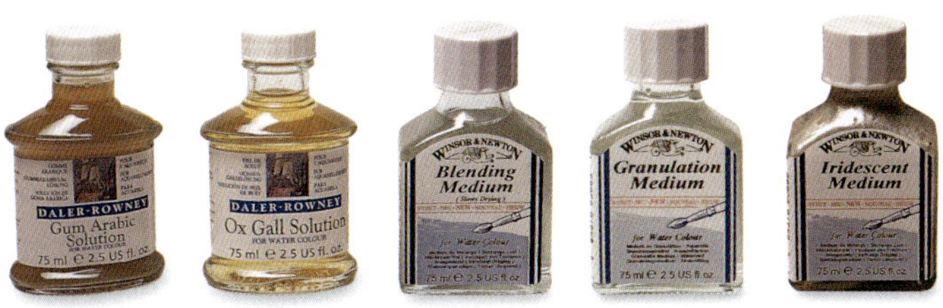

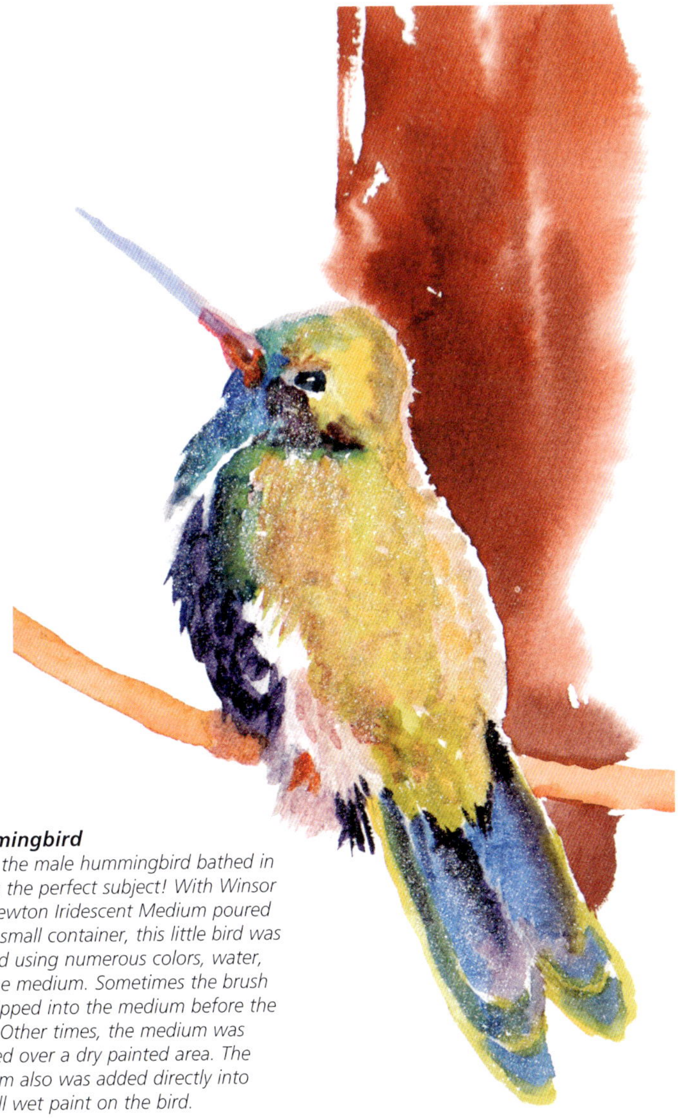

Hummingbird
Surely the male hummingbird bathed in light is the perfect subject! With Winsor and Newton Iridescent Medium poured into a small container, this little bird was painted using numerous colors, water, and the medium. Sometimes the brush was dipped into the medium before the paint. Other times, the medium was brushed over a dry painted area. The medium also was added directly into the still wet paint on the bird.

SOME THINGS TO CONSIDER

- Watercolor mediums can refer to anything that you add to your paints or painting process to facilitate desired effects.
- Experiment with various mediums and additives to find effects that please you.
- The medium should not make more of an impression than the painting itself.

Papers

Paper is probably the most important item on a watercolorist's supply list. You can use average brushes and student-grade paint and produce good work—but only if you are working on good-quality paper. After all, the paper is not only the surface upon which you apply paint, it also is your source of light. The choice of paper affects the clarity of your applied paint. Fortunately there are many good choices available.

TYPES OF PAPER

The first watercolor paper was made in the 13th century. Paper manufacturers produce paper that is 100 percent cotton and pH neutral. External sizing provides various finishes in warm to cool whites. Some manufacturers also add internal sizing. There are two main categories of paper: moldmade and handmade. Both types can take days or even weeks to dry.

Moldmade paper is manufactured by pouring paper pulp onto a cylinder mold machine. Rollers (felts) process the pulp, producing about 200 sheets per hour.

Handmade paper is pounded and mixed by hand before being poured into a rectangular, framed screen mold. It is possible to make about 80 sheets per hour. A handmade paper has four deckled edges, created when small amounts of pulp flow between the mold and the deckle (a second frame placed over the first).

PAPER FINISHES

Watercolor paper finishes are created by the weave of the wire screen in the mold. The sides of a piece of paper often have different textures, depending on the type of papermaking machine, the quality of the pulp, and the drying process. At the corner of the sheet there often is a watermark—usually the name or symbol of the paper manufacturer—that is formed by fixing a small copper wire image to the wire screen of the mold. You can paint on both sides of the paper, so choose the texture you like best.

Rough (R) papers are dried as they are taken from the mold. Handmade papers are dried without pressing; the rough texture results from the shrinking of the paper around the natural irregularities in the pulp. Rough sheets are usually the most absorbent of the papers.

Cold-pressed (CP) paper (called "NOT" in the UK) is made by hanging the sheets in clusters in a drying loft or by lightly pressing stacked sheets with felt-covered metal rollers. This cold pressing gives the sheet a subdued texture that is less absorbent than rough papers, relatively easy to use, tolerates some correction or lifting, and suits any style of painting.

Hot-pressed (HP) papers are pressed between heated glazing rollers, creating a smooth, almost polished finish. These sheets show a high degree of brush detail. They also tend to show pigment colors more brightly than other papers because the paint stays more on the surface. HP papers are especially suited to styles of painting that accent the watery irregularities of the paint. Lifting is easiest with HP paper.

Soft-pressed (SP) has a finish somewhere between CP and HP.

TRY SOMETHING DIFFERENT

Laminated rice papers Donna Caulton laminates traditional textured oriental papers, such as unryu white, tosa uzumaki, kinwashi and ohgoshi squares, to 140lb Arches watercolor paper. She uses acrylic medium, which both sizes and binds. Donna then applies layers of watery traditional watercolor. The textural variations in the rice papers create subtle and beautiful variations, allowing more depth and layers of interest in the finished piece. The textural interest of the paper predominates the fine line detail on papers such as these. If you are working with these papers, you need to experiment to find the right absorbency and textural properties for your working style.

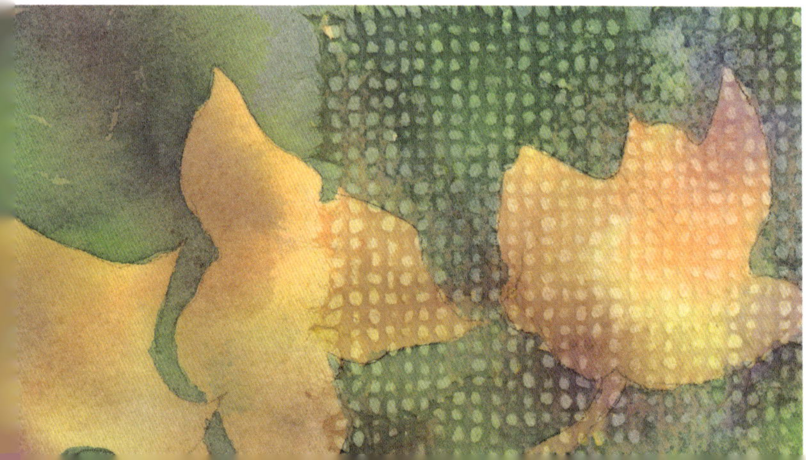

Yupo paper A recent arrival in the watercolor market, Yupo is not a paper and was not designed for watercolor painting; it is a plastic material that is primarily used for ink. But it offers some interesting challenges and results, and it can be purchased at most art supply stores. Because you are painting on plastic, there is no absorption. All of the paint stays on top of the surface, so it takes considerably longer to dry. It may be a good idea to do a first layer, allow it to dry, and then follow up with a second layer. Minimal glazing is possible, but the first layer comes up quite easily into the second application, so take care not to overwork. Yupo allows you to experiment with shapes and brushstrokes because each one shows immediately.

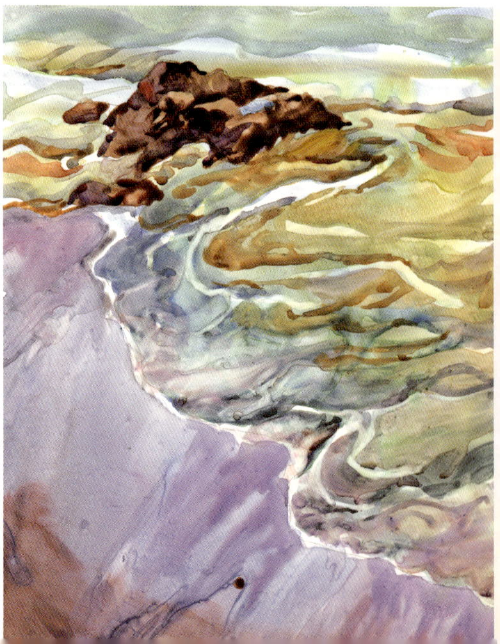

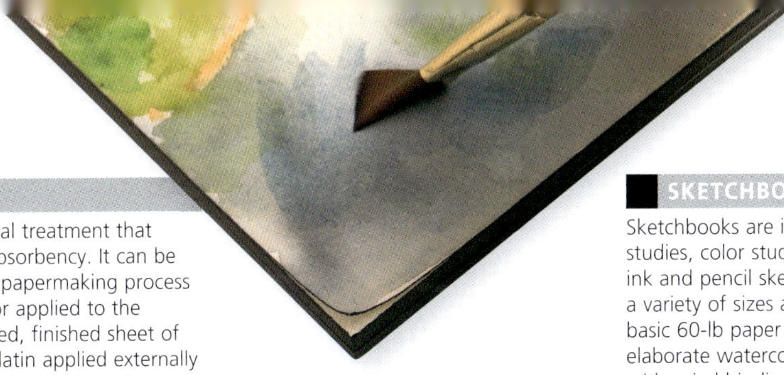

SIZING

Sizing is a chemical treatment that alters a paper's absorbency. It can be done early in the papermaking process (internal sizing), or applied to the surface of the dried, finished sheet of paper. Animal gelatin applied externally creates a hard surface that can be scraped or sponged without damaging the paper itself. Suspect improper sizing if you find a piece of paper that absorbs paint too quickly, leaving some darker, wet areas behind. Most paper suppliers will replace defective paper if asked.

WATERCOLOR BLOCKS

A watercolor block is a stack of 20 sheets (usually 300lb) that have been glued together on all four sides and then stuck to a backing board. Blocks are made for paper sizes ranging from 18" x 24" (46cm x 61cm) down to postcard size. You paint while the paper is still on the block. When the painting is finished, insert a blade under the top sheet at an ungummed edge area to remove the sheet. The texture of blocks is generally smoother than individual sheets.

SKETCHBOOKS

Sketchbooks are ideal for composition studies, color studies, diary notes, and ink and pencil sketches. They come in a variety of sizes and formats from very basic 60-lb paper sketchbooks to more elaborate watercolor paper sketchbooks with spiral bindings. Browse a good art store to choose what is best for you. It's a good idea to tape a photo reference on the open left side and create a value/composition sketch and/or color sketch and notes on the right.

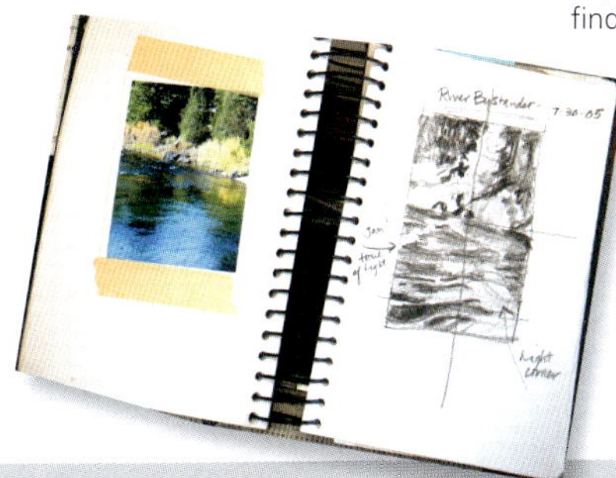

STRETCHING PAPER

Any watercolor paper that is less than 300lbs is bound to warp a little as you paint. Warping may affect your wash results, particularly if you use a lot of water on a full sheet, as some of the paint may pool or run differently. To keep watercolor paper flat while you paint on it, stretch the paper first. Some artists do not at all mind painting on warped paper. If you are experimental and get excited by surprises as you paint, a gently warping paper just adds to the fun and you'll find it sufficient just to tape the edges of your paper to a board.

Artists who prefer more control over their paintings and washes will find that stretching the paper is the safest way to go. There are numerous ways to stretch paper, so look online or consult a how-to painting book.

Colored paper The author used two different colored papers and a tetradic color scheme (see "Tetradic Color Scheme," page 58). On the right is a tan, off-white paper and on the left a gray, off-white paper. The pigments are cobalt blue, ultramarine violet, azo yellow (aureolin), and Winsor orange. Both papers create a nostalgic feel. The cooler off-white blends well with the cool ocean tones, whereas the warmer tan adds warmth to the sand and rocks.

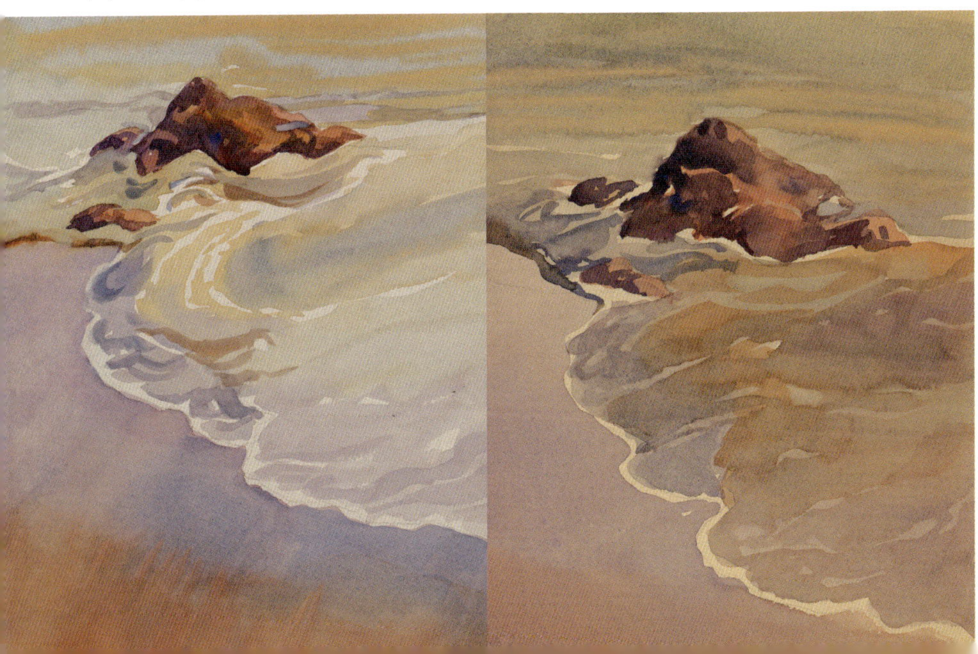

Watercolor canvas
Kathleen Murray demonstrates the drama and excitement of painting on watercolor canvas with her painting *Garden Gate*. The acid-free canvas offers great durability, nice tooth, and a hard surface upon which the artist can play—bold brushstrokes, easy lifting, scraping, scratching, and other techniques best used on HP papers. This canvas base encourages direct painting and provides a good opportunity to practice your brushstrokes. However, glazing and layering may be difficult unless you use a fixative to seal each layer.

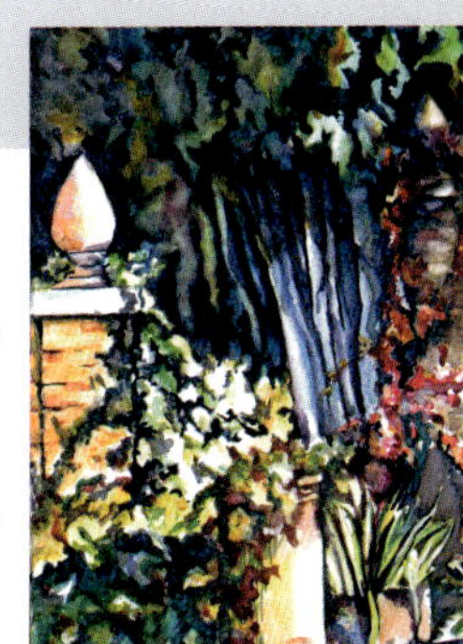

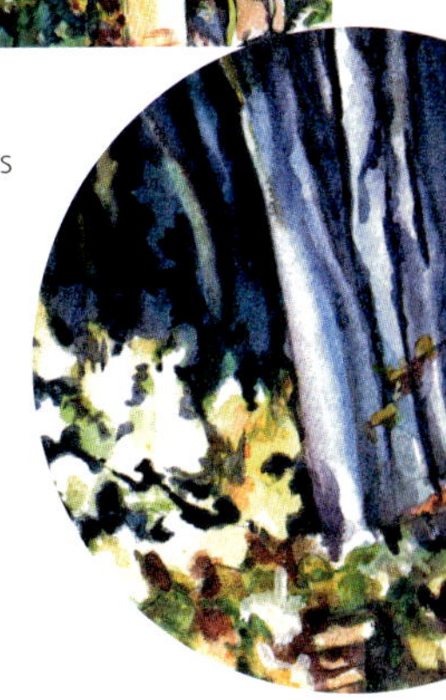

New developments

Until fairly recently, the artist had few choices with regard to metallic and luminescent effects beyond conventional pigment color. Then, in the 1960s, the automotive industry began developing various mineral-based, interference, and iridescent pigments of great durability.

Now, artists' paint manufacturers use this technology to create new colors—every year new colors are released and others discontinued. This page provides a survey of the exciting new developments within the industry, but you should also regularly check the catalogs and websites of all the manufacturers available to you for their latest launches.

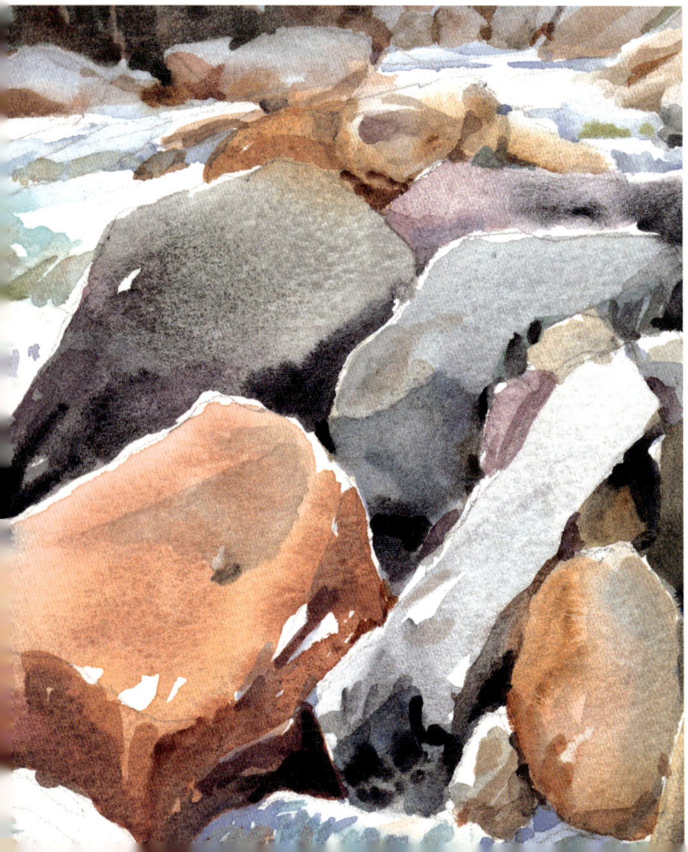

NATURAL MINERAL PIGMENTS

Natural mineral pigments

A natural, inorganic pigment is derived from a mineral compound occurring in nature that have been modified only by grinding, washing, filtering, or heating. Naturally occurring pigments such as ochres and iron oxides has been used since prehistoric times, notably in ancient caves. With the industrial revolution, less expensive synthetic pigments replaced many of the natural mineral pigments. Recently there has been renewed interest in natural minerals as pigments. For example, the PrimaTek series of watercolors are made with authentic mineral pigments often with names hinting at their mined location. The series includes the following paints:

Note that doing a color swatch study enables one to see the color, intensity, color value, transparency, and degree of granulation. It also allows the artist to experience the feel of the paint on the brush.

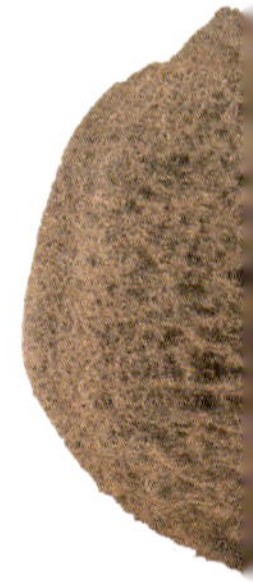

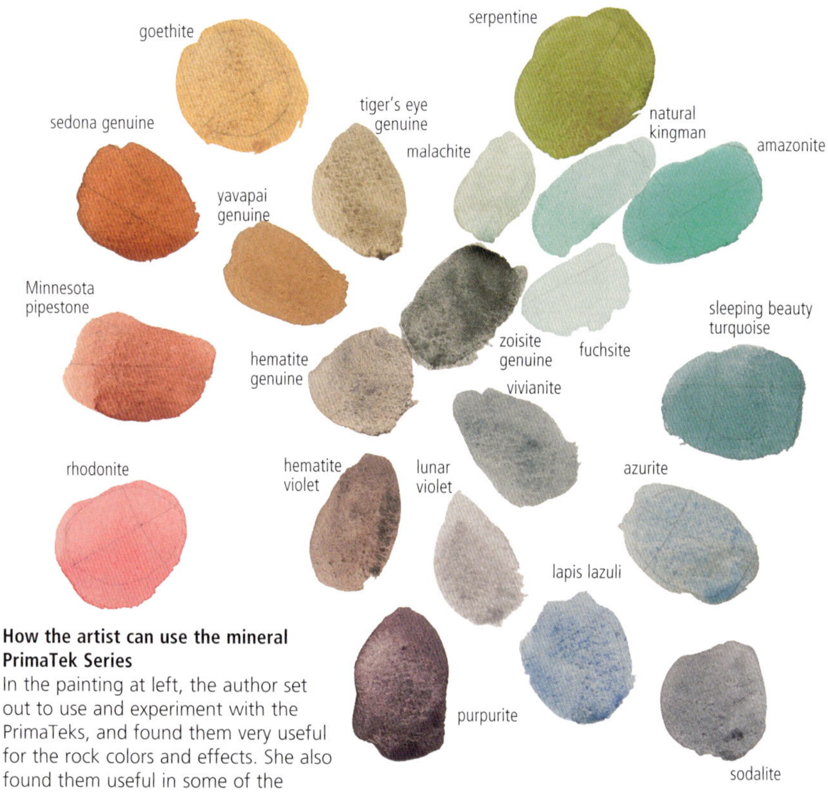

How the artist can use the mineral PrimaTek Series

In the painting at left, the author set out to use and experiment with the PrimaTeks, and found them very useful for the rock colors and effects. She also found them useful in some of the water areas to describe rocks beneath the water. Goethite worked very well for this. Sodalite worked quite well for the darks, and purpurite, Minnesota pipestone, and goethite were the main threads of the composition along with the granulating textures of zoisite, natural tiger's eye, and the hemetites. Transparent cobalt blue was used for water effects and background glazes. A few strokes of interference silver were applied in the foreground water—for an extra splash!

All paints featured on pages 124 and 125 are from the Daniel Smith range.

LUMINESCENT IRIDESCENT PAINT

Iridescent
Paints that contain coated mineral particles as well as a tinting pigment are called "Iridescent." The optical phenomenon of a change in hue occurs according to the angle of observation.

The example at right shows Iridescent paints applied over both a dark band of ultramarine turquoise and napthamide maroon (top) and white paper (bottom). Notice how some Iridescents fail to cover the dark, whereas others create a gauze-like sheen and nearly disappear over white paper.

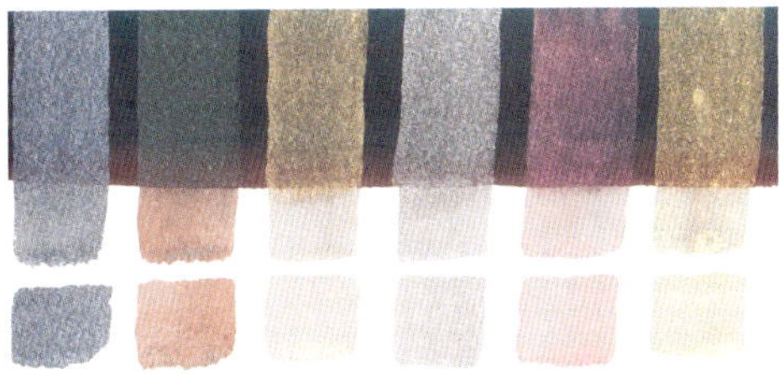

blue silver scarab red sunstone moonstone russet topaz

Winsor & Newton Iridescent Medium Another method of achieving iridescent effects is to use Winsor & Newton Iridescent Medium, which produces a striking glitter effect when mixed with paint (see "Hummingbird," page 121).

Interference and Pearlescent
Transparent paints that contain uncoated mica particles and are not mixed with another pigment are nearly invisible on white paper. The optical phenomenon of color is visible only when painted over a dark undercolor.

Nine Interference and Pearlescent paints applied over both dark undercolor and white paper (see right). Notice that all are very nearly invisible over the white paper and only appear when painted over the dark.

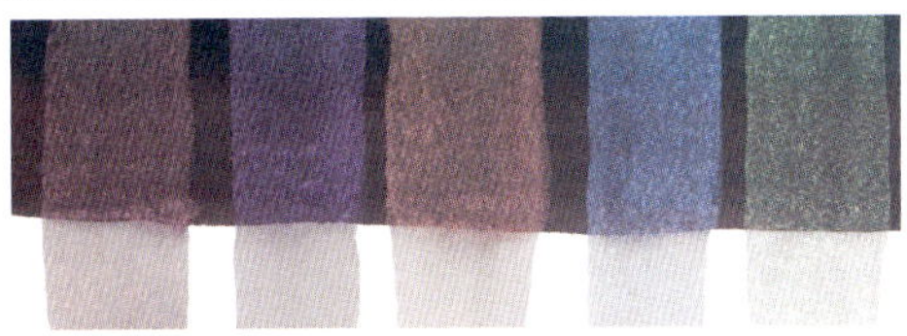

red lilac copper blue green

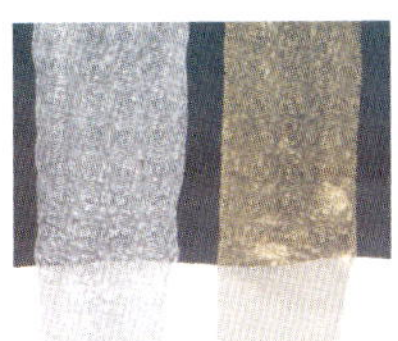

silver gold

Pearlescent shimmer Pearlescent white

Duochrome With the combination of Iridescent and Interference pigments, reflected light rays change from a predominant color to another color depending upon the angle of observation. In Iridescent scarab red (see above), the change is from an earthy red to an Iridescent green and is effective when painting predominantly green vegetation.

Duochrome paints applied over a dark band as well as white paper (see above right). Notice the change from one color on white to another over dark.

Note how Duochrome adobe reacts when mixed into a still damp analogous adobe, rock, and earth mix and the complementary foliage mix (see right). You can see that the Duochrome mixes in as well as sits on top when added over a drier base.

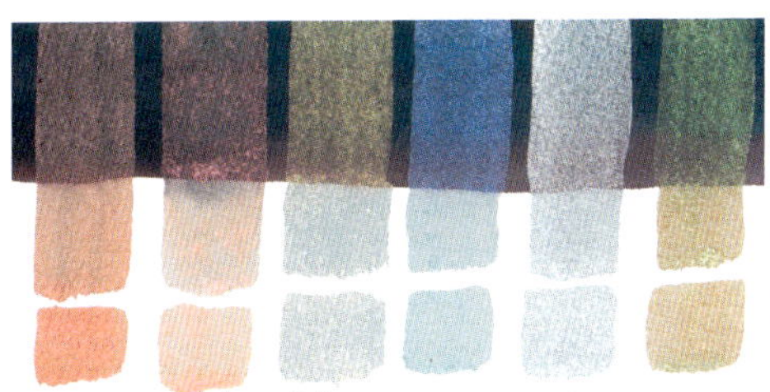

autumn mystery adobe Cabo blue agua marine blue pearl saguaro green

adobe, rock, and earth mix

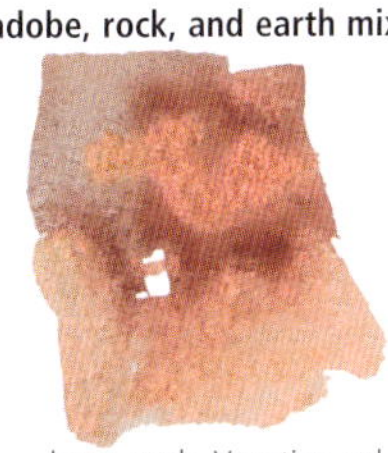

lunar earth, Venetian red, Duochrome adobe

foliage mix

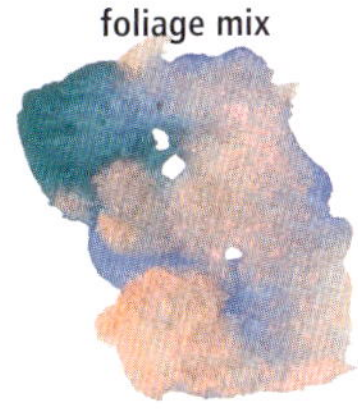

ultramarine turquoise, ultramarine blue, Duochrome adobe

How the artist can use the luminescents

Highlighting An artist can apply the luminescent colors or medium heavily, along with strongly saturated mixtures and coatings of bright paints. This approach is well suited to decorative art as well as specific subject matter; e.g., butterflies and other naturally iridescent subjects. The pigment is used to paint areas of iridescence in animals or shells or to emphasize a peculiar quality of light.

Glazing The colorless Pearlescent, Interference paints, or separate Iridescent Medium are used nicely as glazes. Thinned sufficiently, they give a nacreous sheen to any color they are glazed over. If they are glazed heavily over a dark underpainting, the iridescent colors explode (see left).

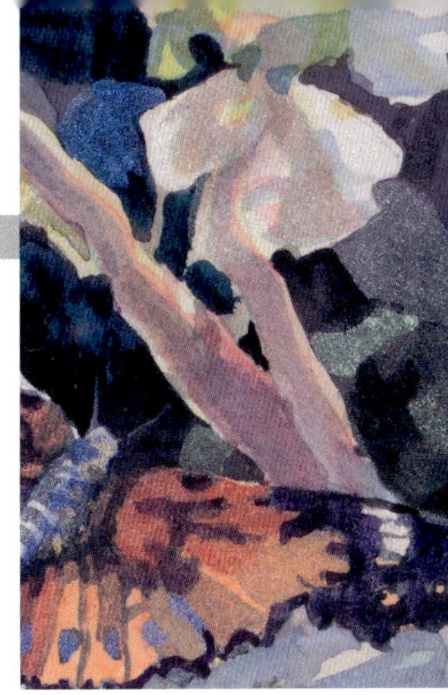

Butterfly Moment
Here, the author used nonstaining transparents, Interference, and Iridescent pigments. Turn to page 6 for the exact pigments used.

Still Pond
The author applied a mixed dark of ultramarine turquoise and napthamide maroon for the tree reflections to still damp/wet cobalt blue water. Then, when fully dry, a Duochrome Cabo blue wash was slowly pulled across the surface horizontally. An exhilarating experience!

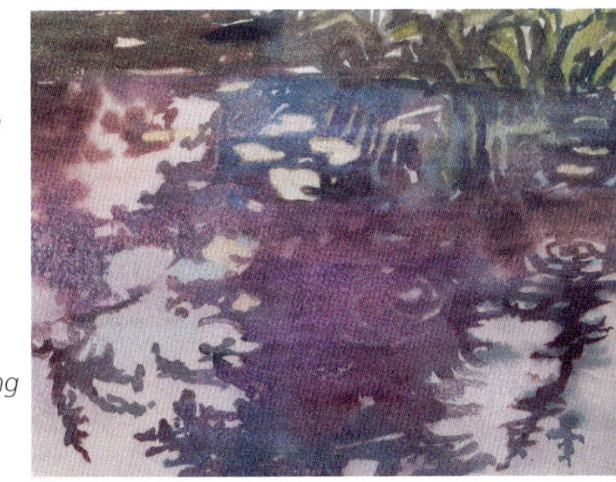

Passion
Sharon Porter selected a few of her favorite Iridescents—Iridescent goldstone, Interference red, Duochrome mauve, and mineral pigment zoisite—and treated them like any of her other pigments. As an intuitive painter, Sharon prefers to allow the spontaneity of a moment's choice guide her process.

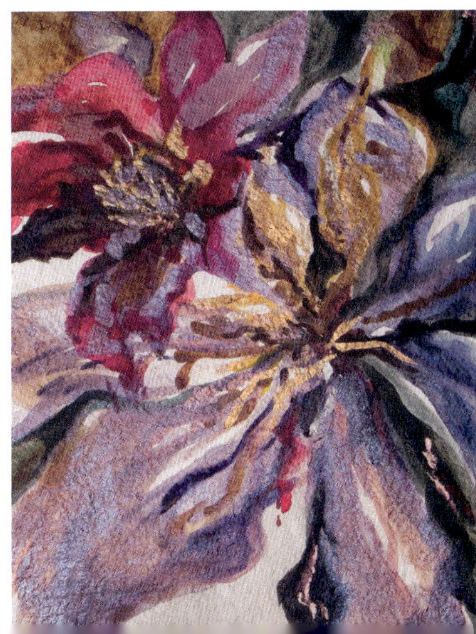

INDEX

AUTHOR CREDITS AND ACKNOWLEDGMENTS

This book is the result of many questions. And I thank those who asked and answered.
I give credit first of all to my many students and colleagues, both past and present who have asked the questions. The "whys" and "hows" have been especially instrumental in suggesting direction for my quests. And special thanks to Allen, who came to paint with me when I got tired of doing it all alone!
I credit Bruce MacEvoy who provides an amazing website (www.handprint.com) that answers and explains more about watercolor pigments than I have thought to ask. All of us who paint in watercolor owe him our gratitude.
I credit artists Hilary Page and Jim Wilcox, as well as Bruce MacEvoy who tested the pigments and provided their results and opinions for the rest of us.
I credit the editors and art staff at Quarto publishing—Kate Kirby, Liz Pasfield, Ruth Patrick, Tanya Field and Moira Clinch who encouraged me and kept me moving ahead!
And I credit special individuals:
Credits to Martha Blue and Steve Whitney who separately encouraged me to write from my experience.
Credit to Debra Kehoe, who first connected me to Quarto Publishing.
Jonathan, for his steadfast encouragement and belief.
Deanne Lemley, for providing the guidance and inspiration.
My dogs, cat, and parrots who were there with me when I wrote long into the night.
Please feel free to email me at j-hart@cybermesa.net

PUBLISHER CREDITS AND NOTES

The publisher would like to thank Daniel Smith Inc. (www.danielsmith.com), Winsor & Newton (www.winsornewton.com), and HK Holbein Inc. (www.holbeinhk.com) for supplying paint samples.

The reader should note that watercolor is an unpredictable medium. The same paint can produce varied tones if progressively diluted, which should be taken into account when referring to the featured swatches.

While every care has been taken with the printing of the watercolor paints and swatches, the four-color printing process means that the publishers cannot guarantee total accuracy in every case.

Some paints used in the book are followed by bracketed supplier information—these paints are specific to the credited suppliers. Daniel Smith has been abbreviated to DS.

Quarto would like to thank the following artists, who are acknowledged beside their work:

Garth Allen www.garthallan.co.uk
Lucy Arnold www.lucyarnold.com
Glynis Barnes-Mellish www.barnesmellish.com
Judi Betts
Jennifer Bowman www.jenniferbowman.com
Julian Bray www.kyracanejulianbray.co.uk
Allen Brown
Dana Brown www.danabrown.net
Donna Caulton www.donnacaulton.com
Moira Clinch www.londonart.co.uk
John Deyloff
Sheila Gill www.sheilagill.co.uk
Joan Gregory www.joangregory.org
Jan Hart www.janhart.com
Adrian James www.picturescape.co.uk
Peter Kelly
Judy Linnell
Kathleen Murray
Connie McCLure www.mccluresfineart.com
Nancy Meadows Taylor www.nancymeadowstaylor.com
Karen Norris
Alan Oliver www.alan-oliver.co.uk
Hilary Page www.hilarypage.com
Sharon Porter
Kim Richardson-Meyrick www.kim-richardson.co.uk
Ann Smith www.annsmithwatercolors.com
Aselka Syzdykova
Carol Tasheck
Robert Tilling
Steve Whitney
Susan Wiig
Michael Wrigglesworth www.michaelwrigglesworth.com

Quarto would also like to acknowledge the following:

a = above, b = below
p54b Brooklyn Museum/Corbis
p62a The Art Archive/Victoria and Albert Museum London/Sally Chappell
Bruce MacEvoy
p14, p52, p70 http://www.handprint.com/HP/WCL/cwheel06.pdf
p66 http://www.handprint.com/HP/WCL/vwheel.pdf

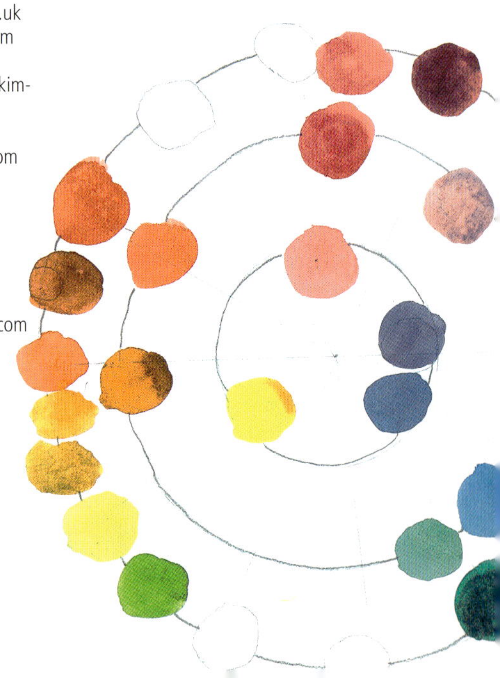